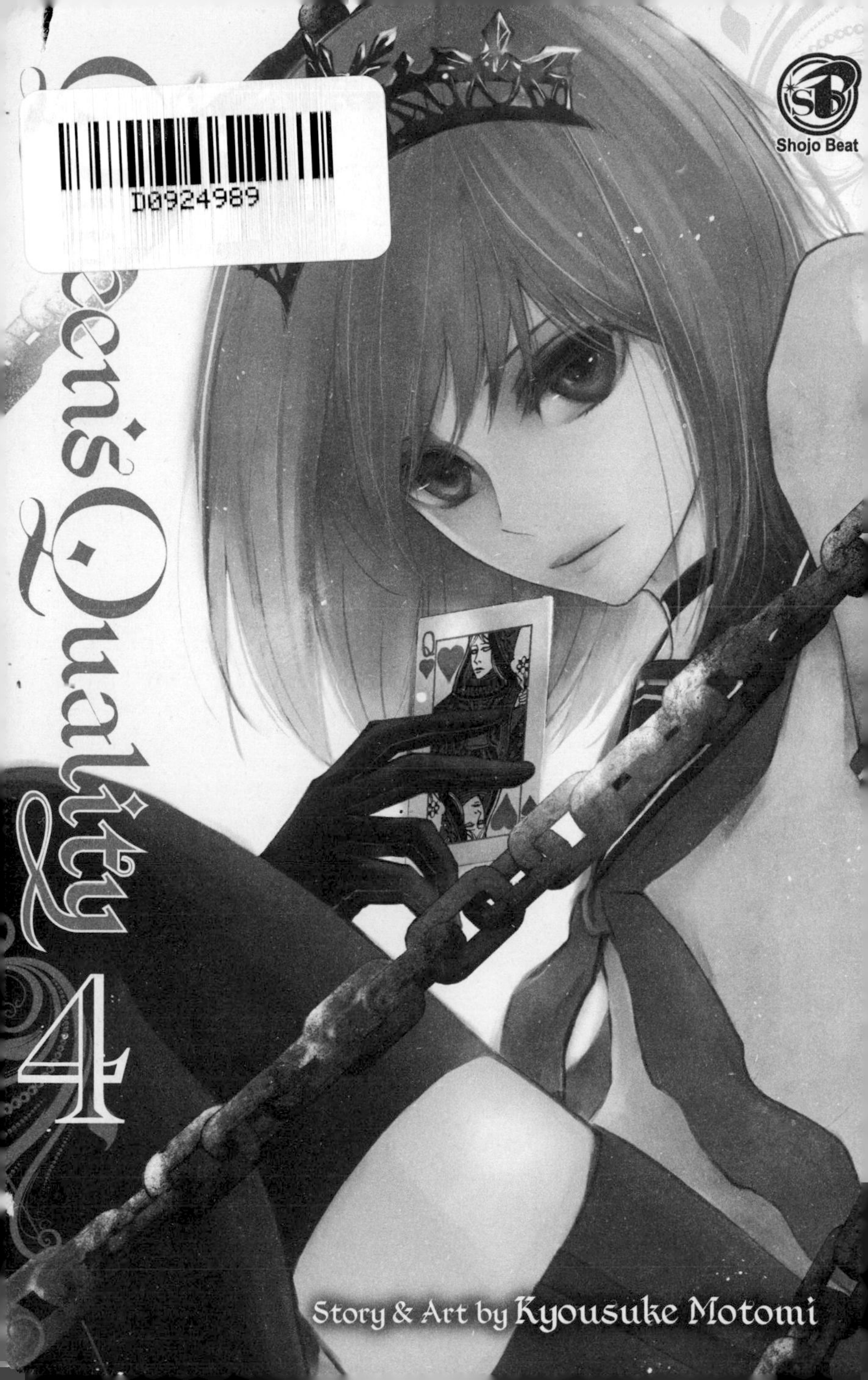
Shojo Beat
een's Quality
4
Story & Art by Kyousuke Motomi

# Queen's Quality

## CONTENTS

4

## Cast of Characters

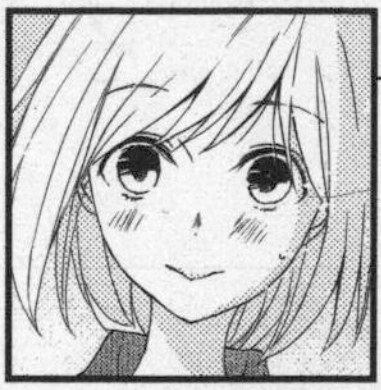

**Fumi Nishioka**

An apprentice Sweeper with the powers of a Queen, this second-year high school student dreams of finding her very own Prince Charming.

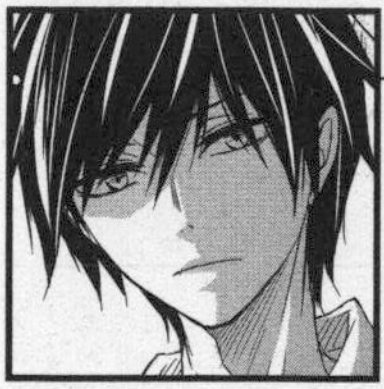

**Kyutaro Horikita**

A mind Sweeper who cleanses people's minds of dangerous impurities. He's incredibly awkward with people, but he has feelings for Fumi.

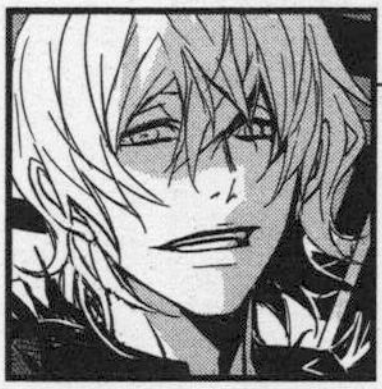

**Ataru Shikata**

A bug handler who uses bugs to manipulate people. He wants to ensure that Fumi awakens as a Black Queen.

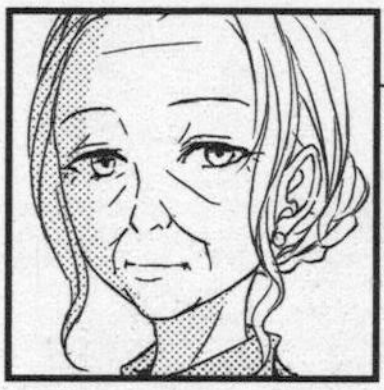

**Miyako Horikita**

The prior head of the Genbu Gate Sweepers. She can be both strict and kind, and she watches over and advises Fumi.

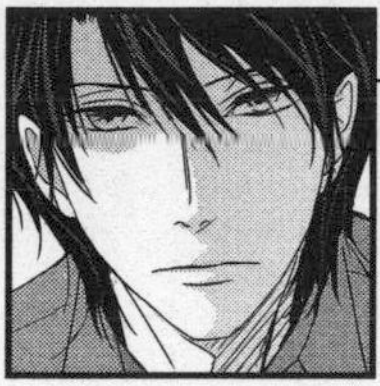

**Koichi Kitagawa**

The chairman of the school Fumi and Kyutaro attend. He's a Sweeper as well as being Kyutaro's brother-in-law.

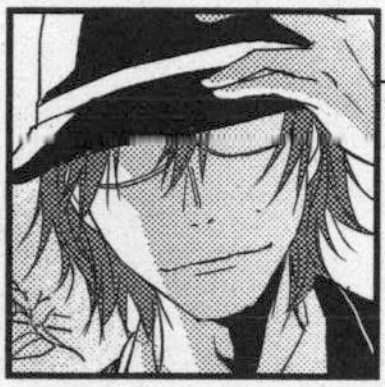

**Takaya Kitahara**

A psychiatrist who's related to the Genbu Gate Sweepers. He's an expert with suggestive therapy, and he counsels Fumi.

## Story Thus Far

The Horikitas are a family of Sweepers—people who cleanse impurities from human hearts. After seeing Fumi's potential, they take her on as an assistant and trainee. However, Fumi has the untapped, immense power of a Queen, and she's awakened both the White Queen and the Black Queen inside of her.

The awakening within Fumi causes other Sweeper groups to target her for her powers. Meanwhile, Fumi is tasked with another difficult challenge—that of killing the Black Queen within her.

# CHAPTER 16

MONTHLY BETSUCOMI SALE DATE NOTICE ON TWITTER

Hey, Teru...
Did you tell Kyutaro how I completely blanked on my speech at Kiyoshi's wedding?
You heard about that, huh? Oops.
Kyutaro seemed happy about it, though! He said he felt like you were brothers.

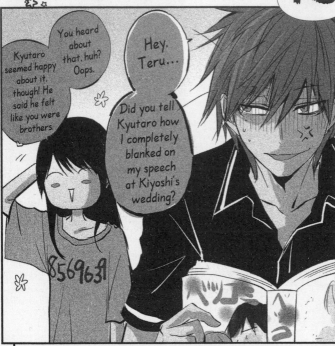

← Kurosaki and Teru are characters from my previous series *Dengeki Daisy*. I often mention them on Twitter.

**WHAT'S UP IN *QUEEN'S QUALITY* THIS MONTH?**

(1) THE IMPOSSIBLE HAPPENS AS KUROSAKI MAKES HIS FIRST *QUEEQUA* APPEARANCE.
(2) I'M TIRED OF GLASSES! I HATE THEM! (SAYS THE AUTHOR...)
(3) I THINK THE PICTURE OF FUMI LEAVING STXXXXXKS WAS THE CUTEST THIS MONTH. (FEELING GREAT!)

I EXPECTED CHAPTER 16 TO BE ENTIRELY MADE UP OF EVERYDAY THINGS, BUT QUITE A BIT HAPPENS!

I post tweets like this every month. You'll find me muttering about other silly stuff too.

@motomikyosuke

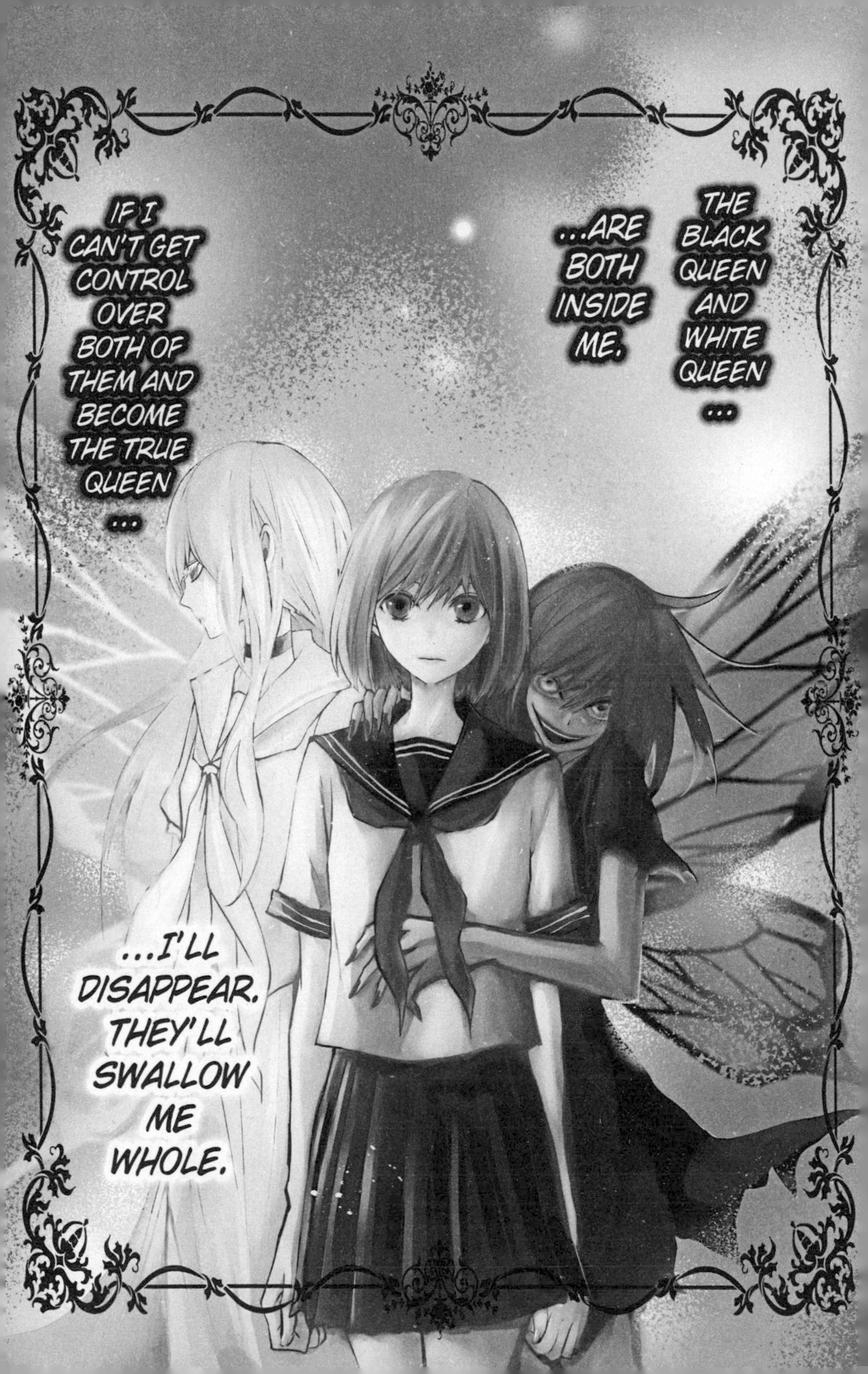
THE BLACK QUEEN AND WHITE QUEEN...
...ARE BOTH INSIDE ME.
IF I CAN'T GET CONTROL OVER BOTH OF THEM AND BECOME THE TRUE QUEEN...
...I'LL DISAPPEAR. THEY'LL SWALLOW ME WHOLE.

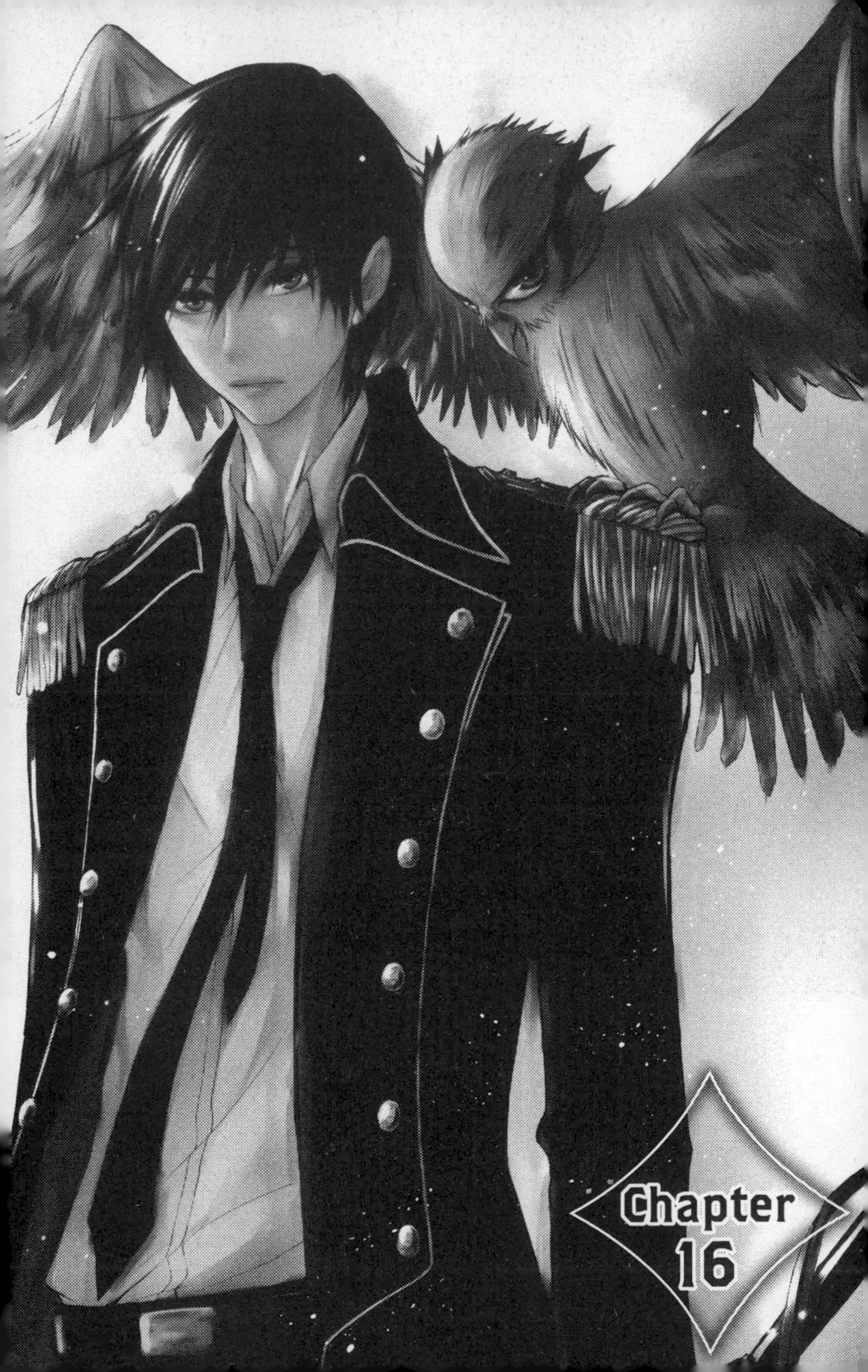
Chapter
16

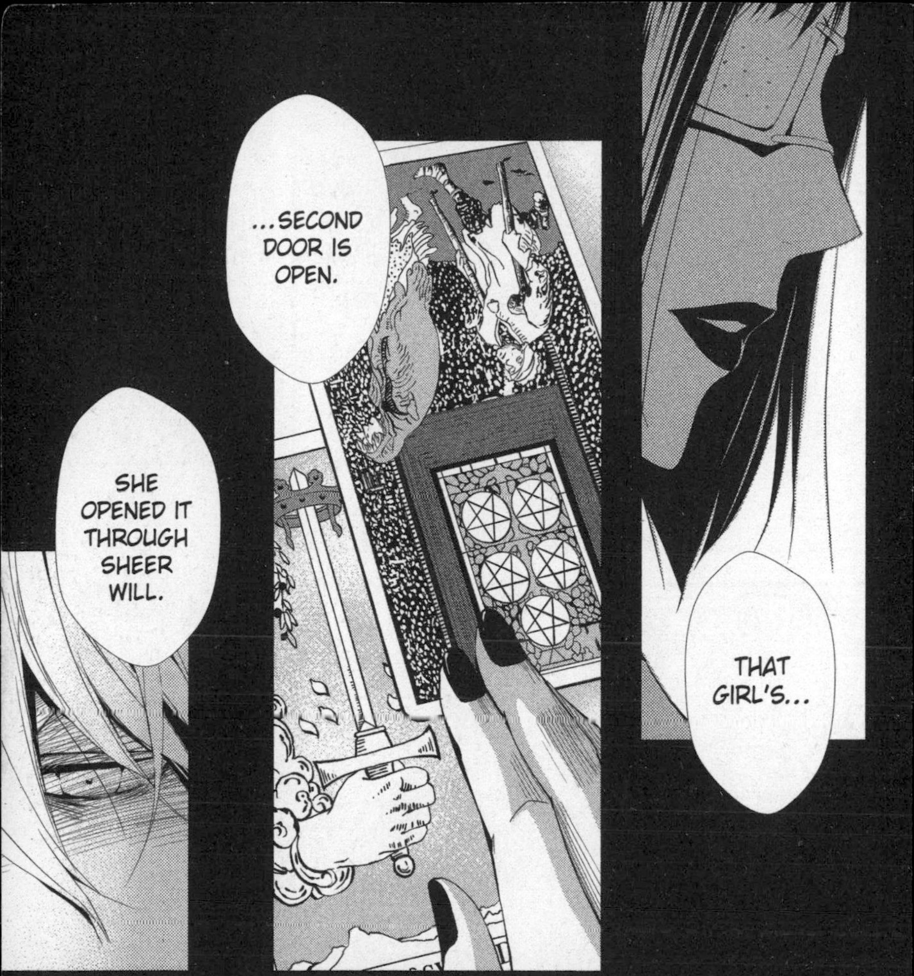
THAT GIRL'S...
...SECOND DOOR IS OPEN.
SHE OPENED IT THROUGH SHEER WILL.

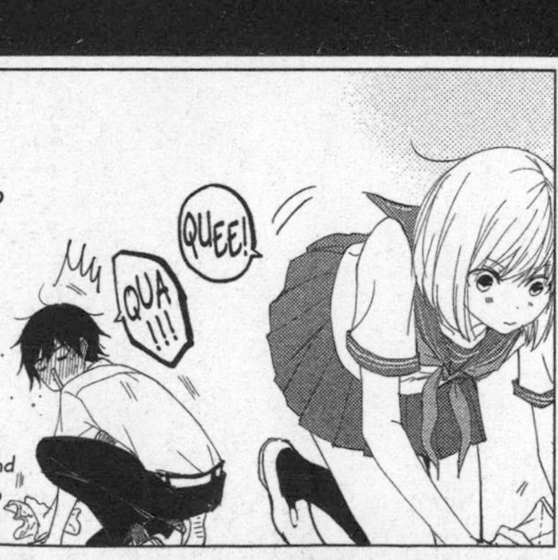
QUEE!
QUA !!!

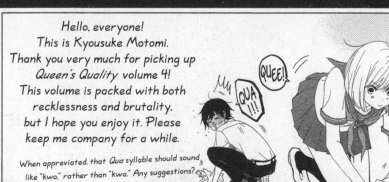

Hello, everyone!
This is Kyousuke Motomi.
Thank you very much for picking up
*Queen's Quality* volume 4!
This volume is packed with both
recklessness and brutality,
but I hope you enjoy it. Please
keep me company for a while.

When appreviated, that *Qua* syllable should sound like "kwo," rather than "kwa." Any suggestions?

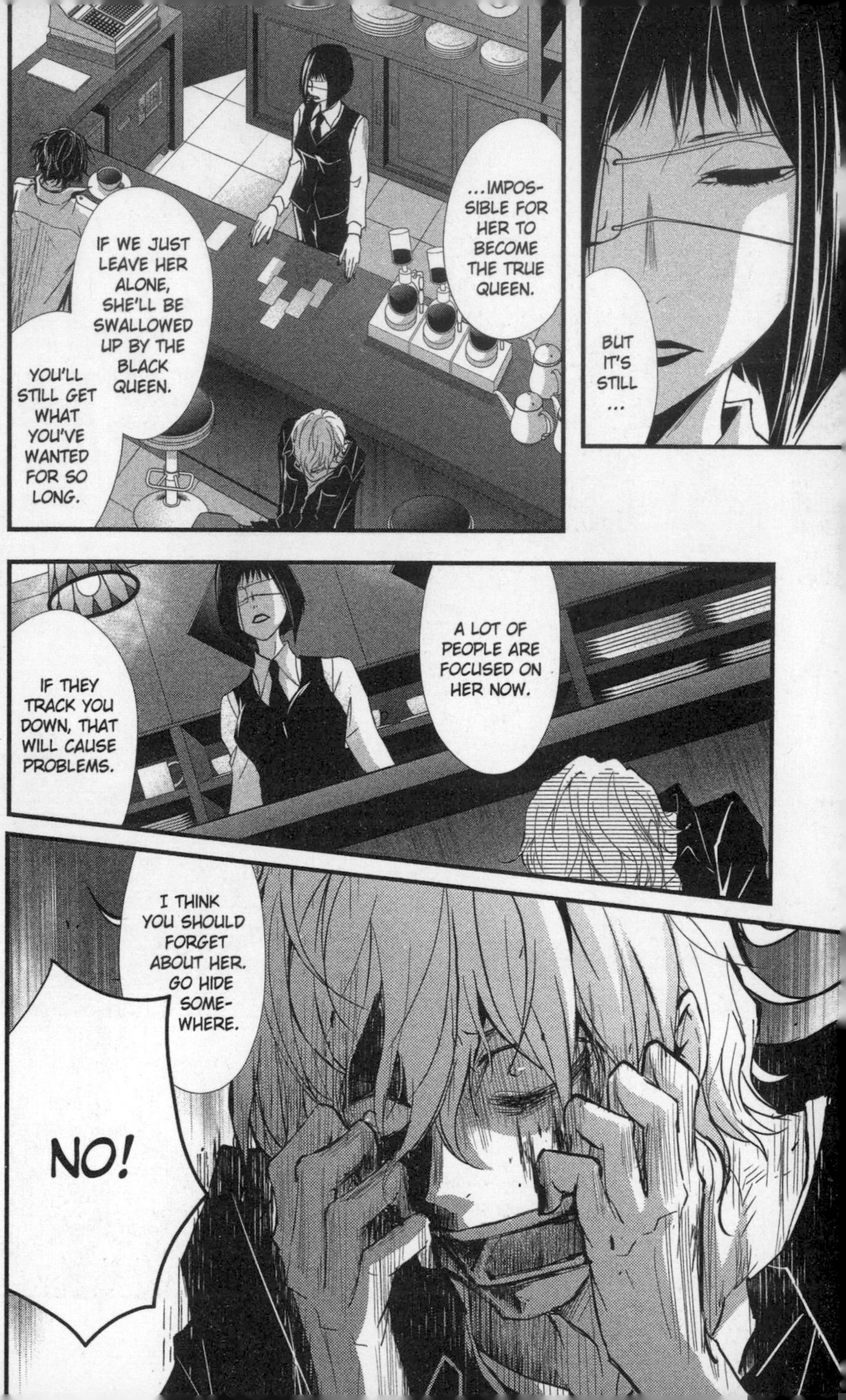
BUT IT'S STILL ...
...IMPOSSIBLE FOR HER TO BECOME THE TRUE QUEEN.
IF WE JUST LEAVE HER ALONE, SHE'LL BE SWALLOWED UP BY THE BLACK QUEEN.
YOU'LL STILL GET WHAT YOU'VE WANTED FOR SO LONG.
A LOT OF PEOPLE ARE FOCUSED ON HER NOW.
IF THEY TRACK YOU DOWN, THAT WILL CAUSE PROBLEMS.
I THINK YOU SHOULD FORGET ABOUT HER. GO HIDE SOME-WHERE.
NO!

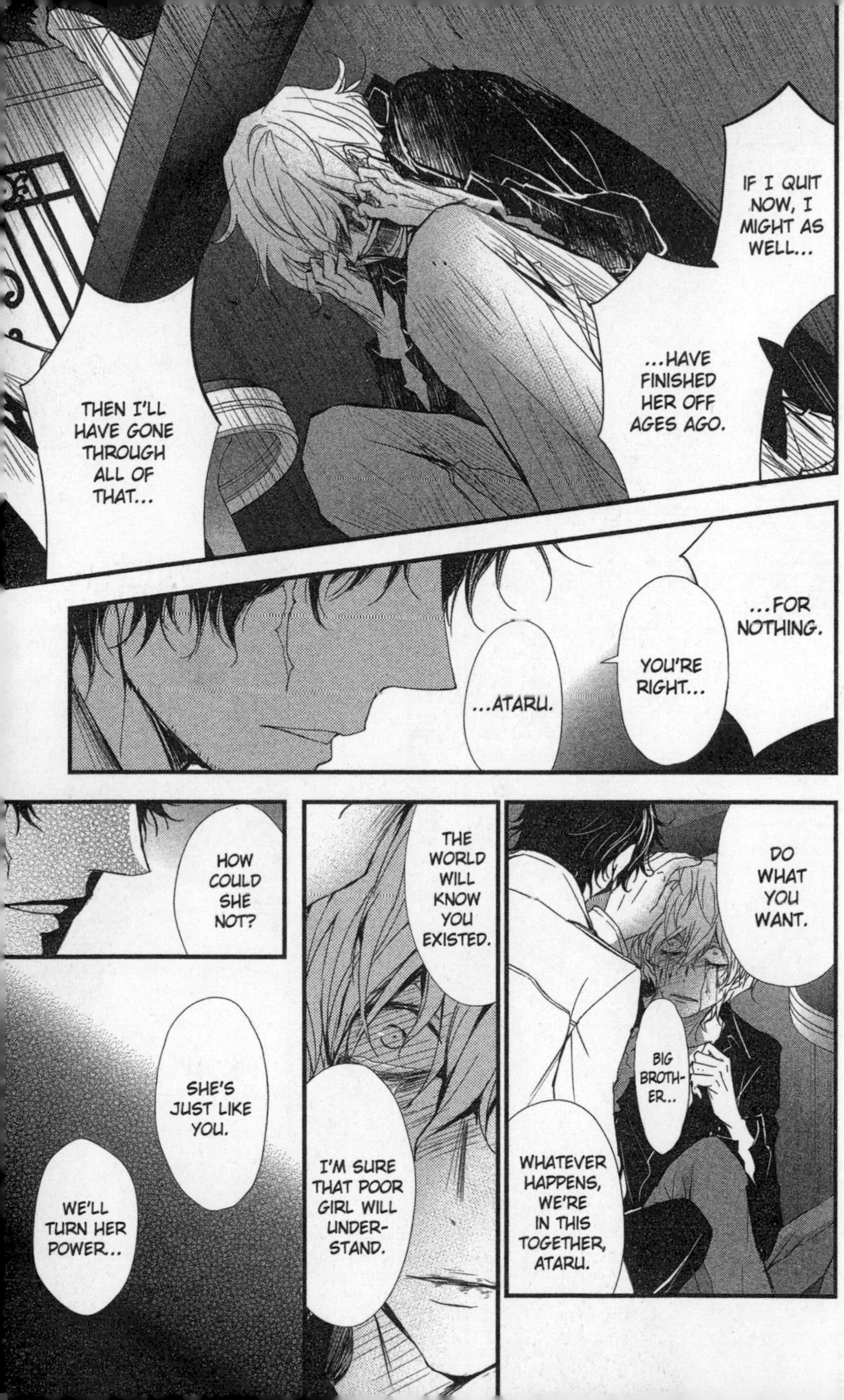
IF I QUIT NOW, I MIGHT AS WELL...
...HAVE FINISHED HER OFF AGES AGO.
THEN I'LL HAVE GONE THROUGH ALL OF THAT...
...FOR NOTHING.
YOU'RE RIGHT...
...ATARU.
DO WHAT YOU WANT.
BIG BROTH-ER...
WHATEVER HAPPENS, WE'RE IN THIS TOGETHER, ATARU.
THE WORLD WILL KNOW YOU EXISTED.
I'M SURE THAT POOR GIRL WILL UNDER-STAND.
HOW COULD SHE NOT?
SHE'S JUST LIKE YOU.
WE'LL TURN HER POWER...

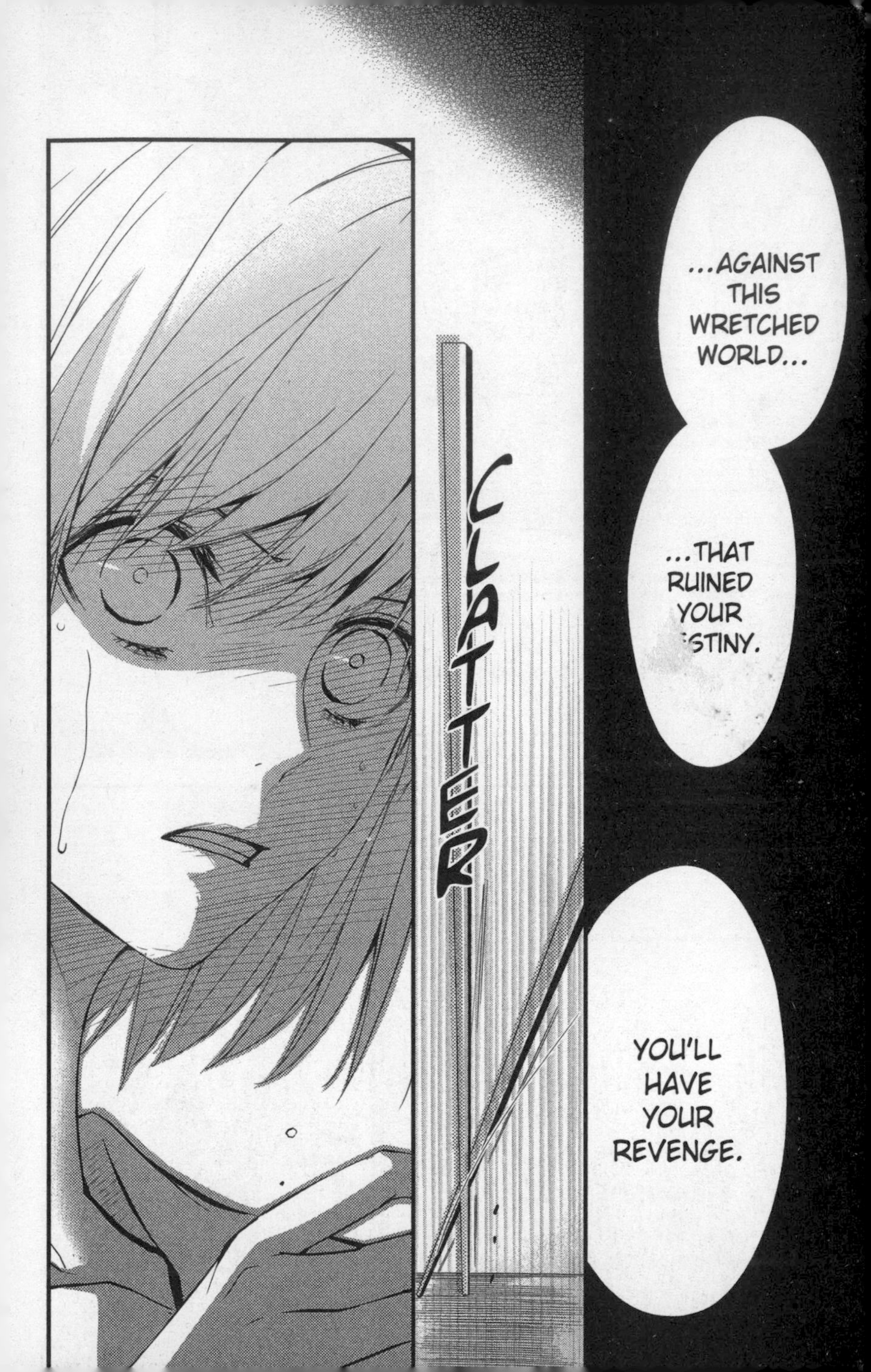
...AGAINST THIS WRETCHED WORLD...
...THAT RUINED YOUR STINY.
YOU'LL HAVE YOUR REVENGE.
CLATTER

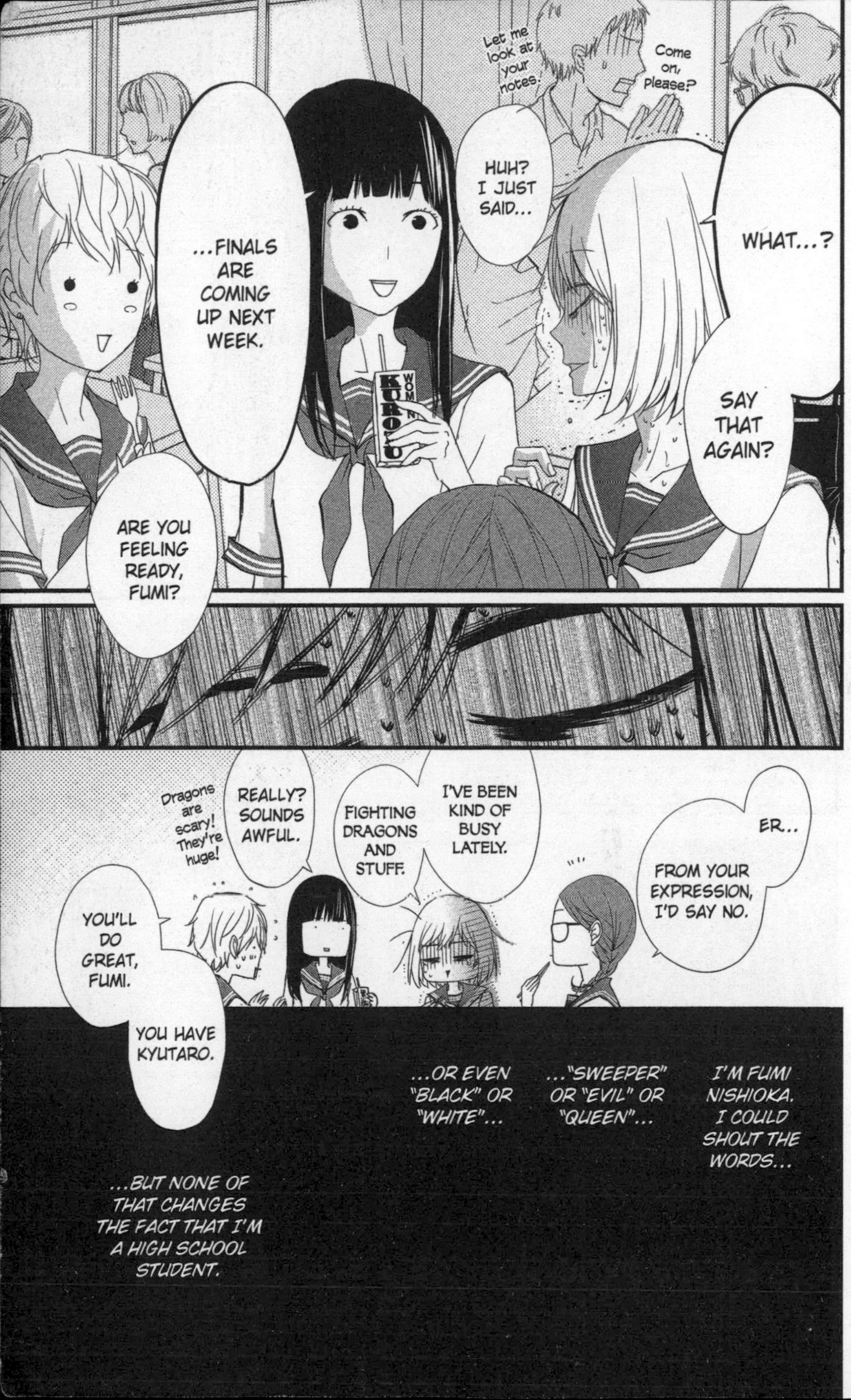
WHAT...? SAY THAT AGAIN?
Come on, please?
Let me look at your notes.
HUH? I JUST SAID...
...FINALS ARE COMING UP NEXT WEEK.
ARE YOU FEELING READY, FUMI?
ER... FROM YOUR EXPRESSION, I'D SAY NO.
I'VE BEEN KIND OF BUSY LATELY.
FIGHTING DRAGONS AND STUFF.
REALLY? SOUNDS AWFUL.
Dragons are scary! They're huge!
YOU'LL DO GREAT, FUMI.
YOU HAVE KYUTARO.
I'M FUMI NISHIOKA. I COULD SHOUT THE WORDS...
..."SWEEPER" OR "EVIL" OR "QUEEN"...
...OR EVEN "BLACK" OR "WHITE"...
...BUT NONE OF THAT CHANGES THE FACT THAT I'M A HIGH SCHOOL STUDENT.

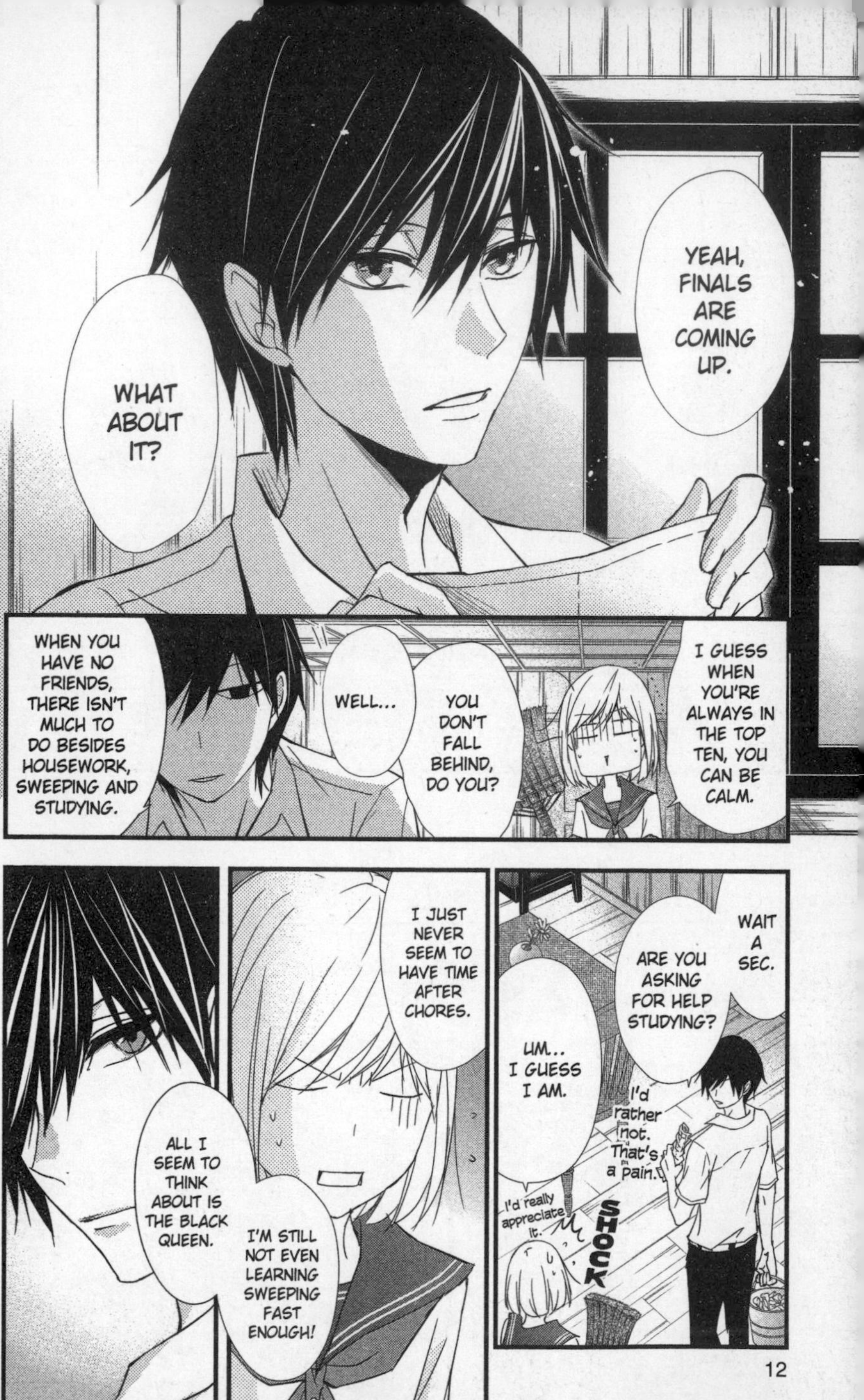
YEAH, FINALS ARE COMING UP.
WHAT ABOUT IT?
I GUESS WHEN YOU'RE ALWAYS IN THE TOP TEN, YOU CAN BE CALM.
YOU DON'T FALL BEHIND, DO YOU?
WELL...
WHEN YOU HAVE NO FRIENDS, THERE ISN'T MUCH TO DO BESIDES HOUSEWORK, SWEEPING AND STUDYING.
WAIT A SEC.
ARE YOU ASKING FOR HELP STUDYING?
UM.. I GUESS I AM.
I'd rather not. That's a pain.
SHOCK
I'd really appreciate it.
I JUST NEVER SEEM TO HAVE TIME AFTER CHORES.
I'M STILL NOT EVEN LEARNING SWEEPING FAST ENOUGH!
ALL I SEEM TO THINK ABOUT IS THE BLACK QUEEN.

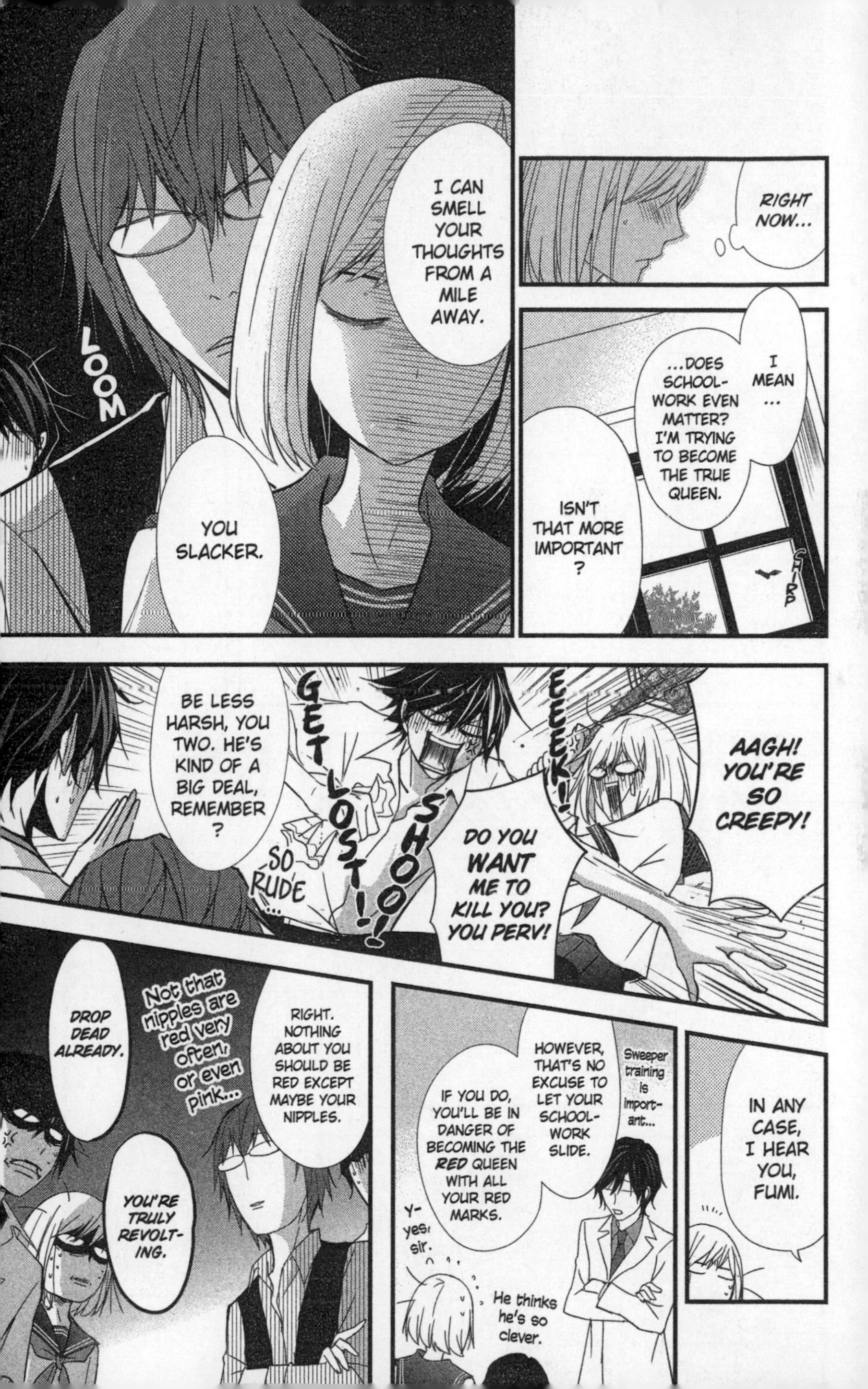
RIGHT NOW...
I MEAN ...
...DOES SCHOOL-WORK EVEN MATTER? I'M TRYING TO BECOME THE TRUE QUEEN.
ISN'T THAT MORE IMPORTANT?
CHIRP
I CAN SMELL YOUR THOUGHTS FROM A MILE AWAY.
LOOM
YOU SLACKER.
AAGH! YOU'RE SO CREEPY!
EEEEK!!
DO YOU WANT ME TO KILL YOU? YOU PERV!
SHOO!!
GET LOST!!
BE LESS HARSH, YOU TWO. HE'S KIND OF A BIG DEAL, REMEMBER?
SO RUDE...
IN ANY CASE, I HEAR YOU, FUMI.
Sweeper training is import-ant...
HOWEVER, THAT'S NO EXCUSE TO LET YOUR SCHOOL-WORK SLIDE.
IF YOU DO, YOU'LL BE IN DANGER OF BECOMING THE RED QUEEN WITH ALL YOUR RED MARKS.
Y-yes, sir.
He thinks he's so clever.
RIGHT. NOTHING ABOUT YOU SHOULD BE RED EXCEPT MAYBE YOUR NIPPLES.
Not that nipples are red very often, or even pink...
DROP DEAD ALREADY.
YOU'RE TRULY REVOLT-ING.

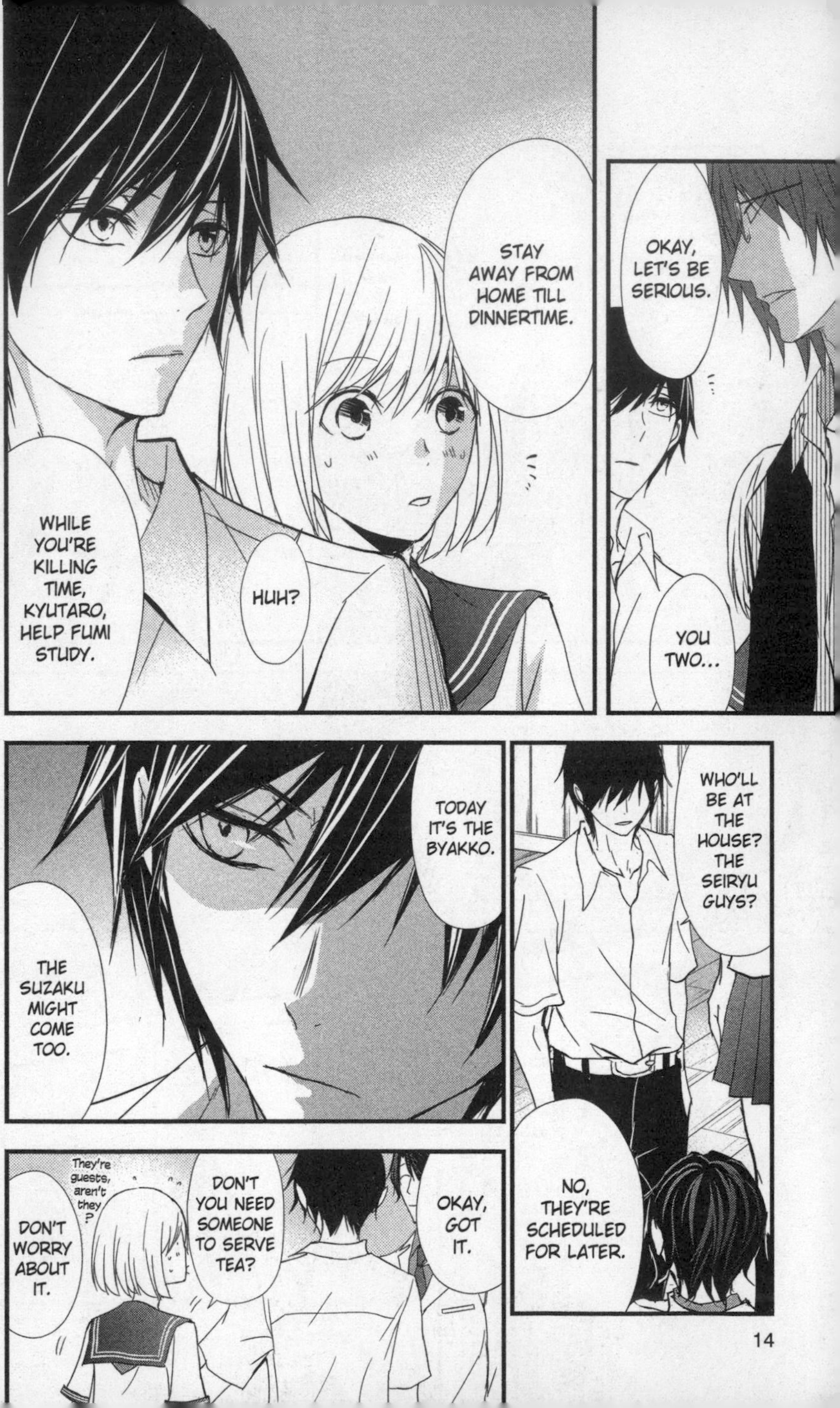
OKAY, LET'S BE SERIOUS.
YOU TWO...
STAY AWAY FROM HOME TILL DINNERTIME.
HUH?
WHILE YOU'RE KILLING TIME, KYUTARO, HELP FUMI STUDY.
WHO'LL BE AT THE HOUSE? THE SEIRYU GUYS?
NO, THEY'RE SCHEDULED FOR LATER.
TODAY IT'S THE BYAKKO.
THE SUZAKU MIGHT COME TOO.
OKAY, GOT IT.
DON'T YOU NEED SOMEONE TO SERVE TEA?
They're guests, aren't they?
DON'T WORRY ABOUT IT.

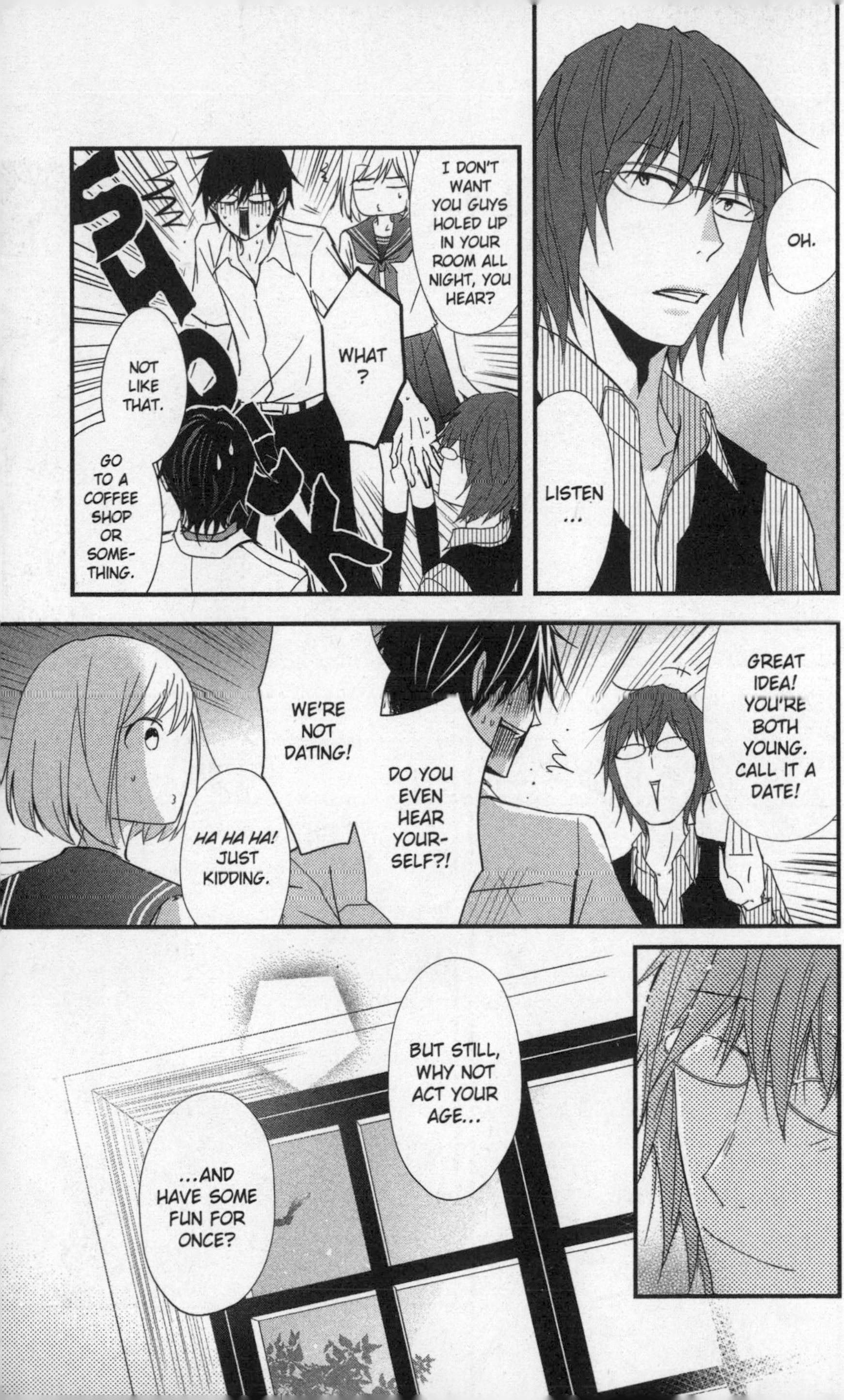
OH.
LISTEN...
I DON'T WANT YOU GUYS HOLED UP IN YOUR ROOM ALL NIGHT, YOU HEAR?
SHOCK
WHAT?
NOT LIKE THAT.
GO TO A COFFEE SHOP OR SOME-THING.
GREAT IDEA! YOU'RE BOTH YOUNG. CALL IT A DATE!
DO YOU EVEN HEAR YOUR-SELF?!
WE'RE NOT DATING!
HA HA HA! JUST KIDDING.
BUT STILL, WHY NOT ACT YOUR AGE...
...AND HAVE SOME FUN FOR ONCE?

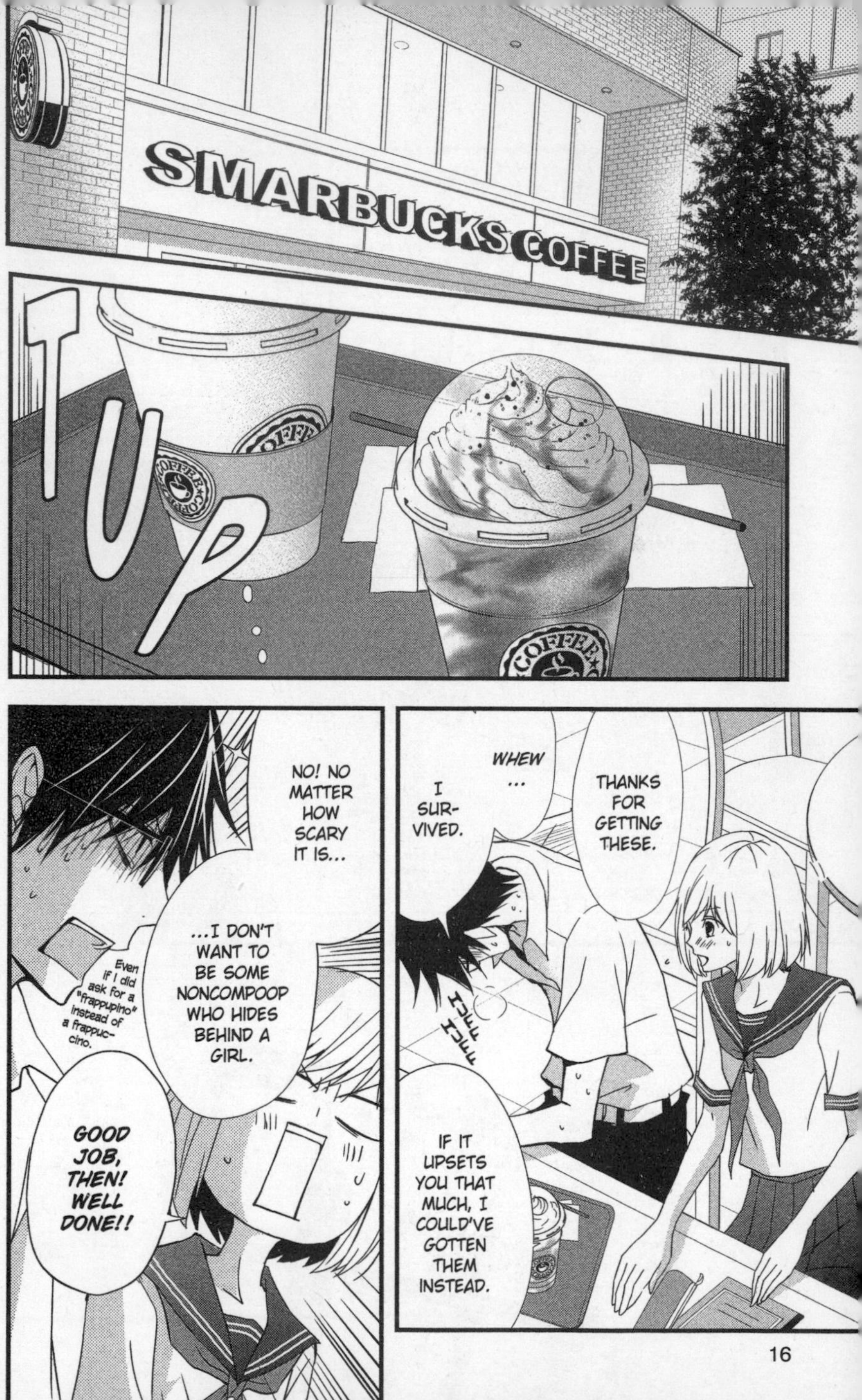
SMARBUCKS COFFEE
TUP
THANKS FOR GETTING THESE.
WHEW ...
I SURVIVED.
IF IT UPSETS YOU THAT MUCH, I COULD'VE GOTTEN THEM INSTEAD.
NO! NO MATTER HOW SCARY IT IS...
...I DON'T WANT TO BE SOME NONCOMPOOP WHO HIDES BEHIND A GIRL.
Even if I did ask for a "frappupino" instead of a frappuccino.
GOOD JOB, THEN! WELL DONE!!

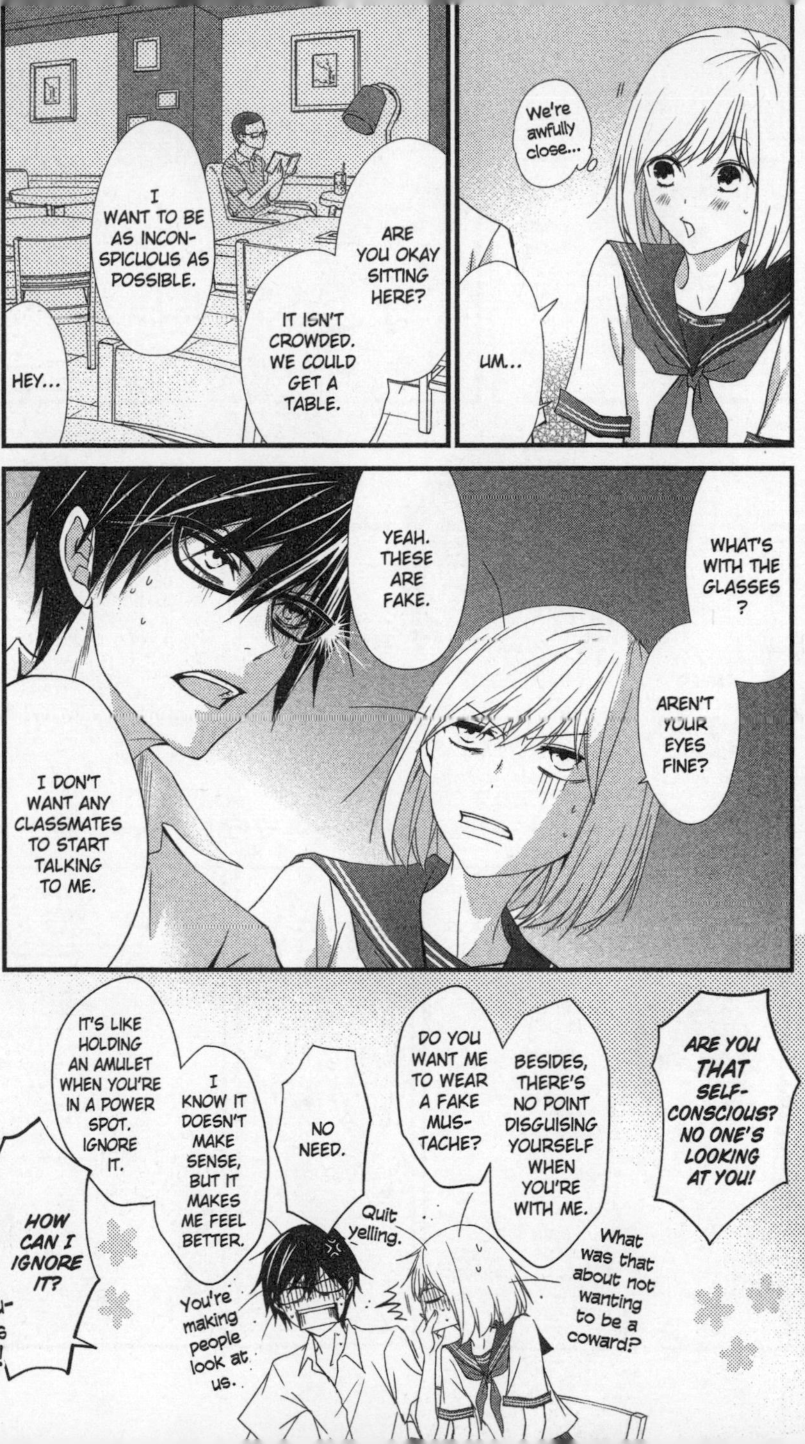
We're awfully close...
UM...
ARE YOU OKAY SITTING HERE?
IT ISN'T CROWDED. WE COULD GET A TABLE.
HEY...
I WANT TO BE AS INCONSPICUOUS AS POSSIBLE.
WHAT'S WITH THE GLASSES?
AREN'T YOUR EYES FINE?
YEAH. THESE ARE FAKE.
I DON'T WANT ANY CLASSMATES TO START TALKING TO ME.
ARE YOU THAT SELF-CONSCIOUS? NO ONE'S LOOKING AT YOU!
BESIDES, THERE'S NO POINT DISGUISING YOURSELF WHEN YOU'RE WITH ME.
DO YOU WANT ME TO WEAR A FAKE MUSTACHE?
NO NEED.
I KNOW IT DOESN'T MAKE SENSE, BUT IT MAKES ME FEEL BETTER.
IT'S LIKE HOLDING AN AMULET WHEN YOU'RE IN A POWER SPOT. IGNORE IT.
What was that about not wanting to be a coward?
Quit yelling.
You're making people look at us.
HOW CAN I IGNORE IT?
This is too ridiculous!!!

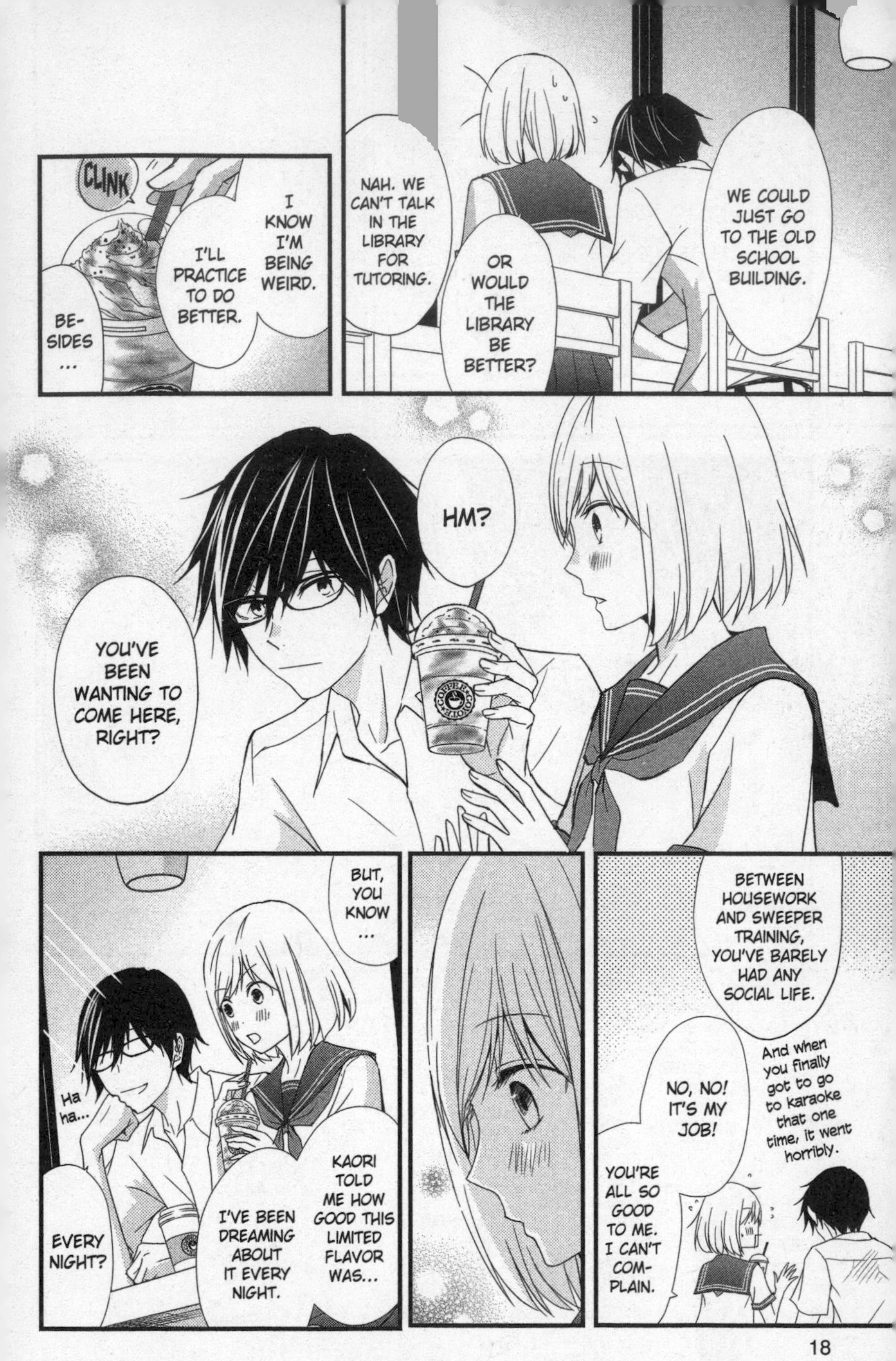
WE COULD JUST GO TO THE OLD SCHOOL BUILDING.
OR WOULD THE LIBRARY BE BETTER?
NAH. WE CAN'T TALK IN THE LIBRARY FOR TUTORING.
CLINK
I KNOW I'M BEING WEIRD.
I'LL PRACTICE TO DO BETTER.
BE-SIDES…
HM?
YOU'VE BEEN WANTING TO COME HERE, RIGHT?
BETWEEN HOUSEWORK AND SWEEPER TRAINING, YOU'VE BARELY HAD ANY SOCIAL LIFE.
And when you finally got to go to karaoke that one time, it went horribly.
NO, NO! IT'S MY JOB!
YOU'RE ALL SO GOOD TO ME. I CAN'T COM-PLAIN.
BUT, YOU KNOW…
KAORI TOLD ME HOW GOOD THIS LIMITED FLAVOR WAS…
I'VE BEEN DREAMING ABOUT IT EVERY NIGHT.
Ha ha…
EVERY NIGHT?

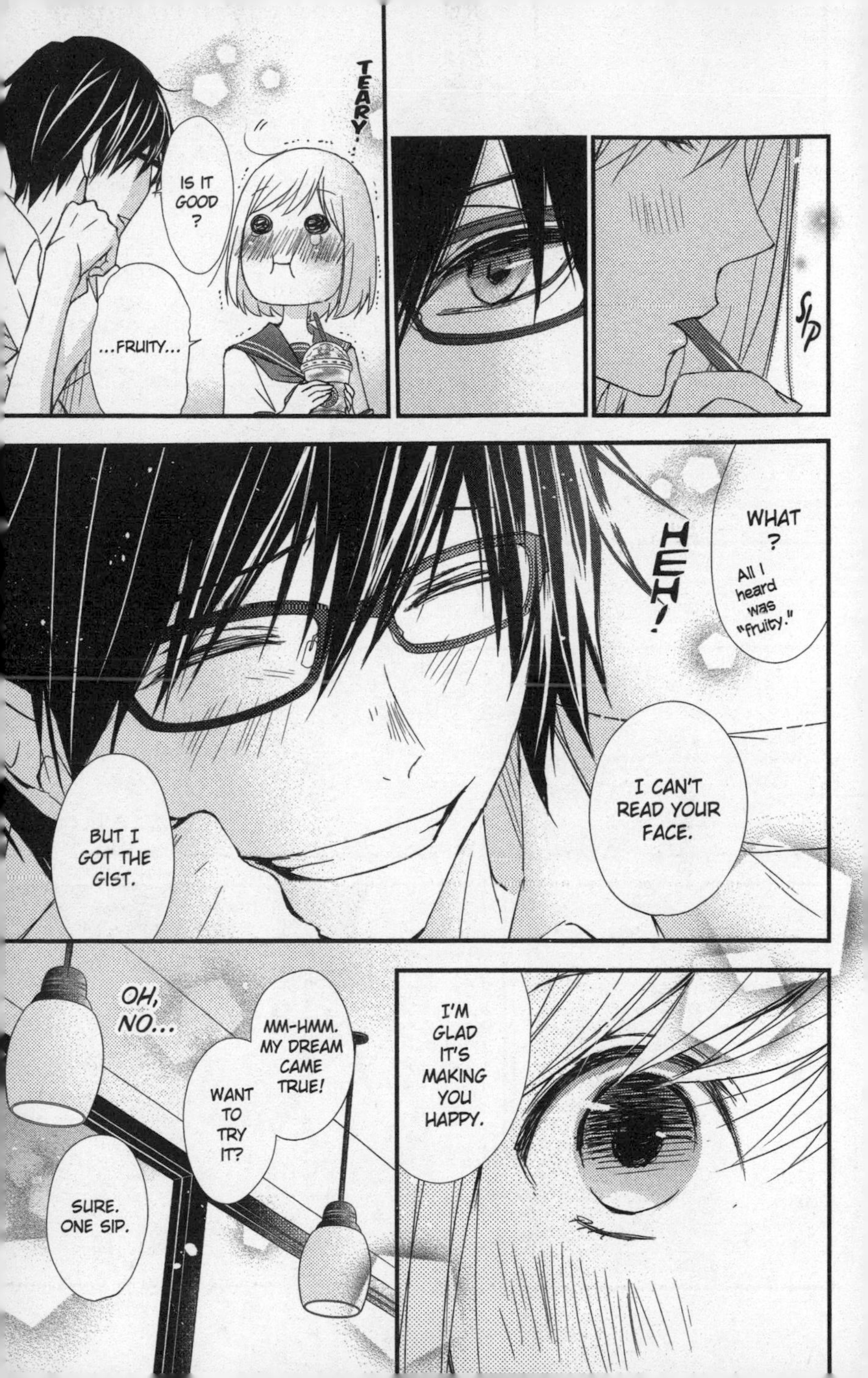
SIP
TEARY
IS IT GOOD?
...FRUITY...
WHAT? All I heard was "fruity."
HEH!
I CAN'T READ YOUR FACE.
BUT I GOT THE GIST.
I'M GLAD IT'S MAKING YOU HAPPY.
MM-HMM. MY DREAM CAME TRUE!
OH, NO...
WANT TO TRY IT?
SURE. ONE SIP.

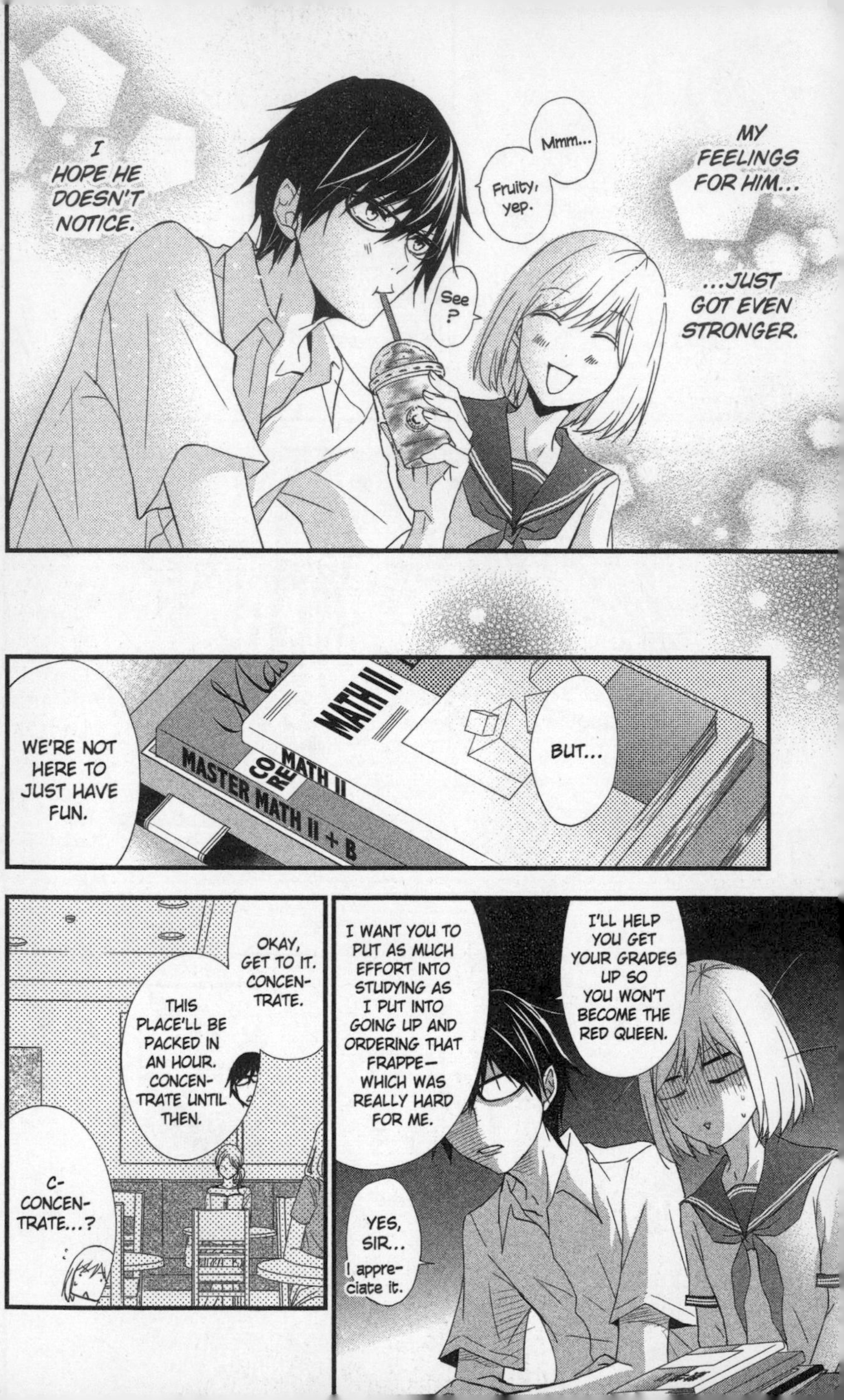
MY FEELINGS FOR HIM...
Mmm...
Fruity, yep.
...JUST GOT EVEN STRONGER.
See?
I HOPE HE DOESN'T NOTICE.
BUT...
MATH II
CORE
MATH II
MASTER MATH II + B
WE'RE NOT HERE TO JUST HAVE FUN.
I'LL HELP YOU GET YOUR GRADES UP SO YOU WON'T BECOME THE RED QUEEN.
I WANT YOU TO PUT AS MUCH EFFORT INTO STUDYING AS I PUT INTO GOING UP AND ORDERING THAT FRAPPE—WHICH WAS REALLY HARD FOR ME.
YES, SIR...
I appreciate it.
OKAY, GET TO IT. CONCENTRATE.
THIS PLACE'LL BE PACKED IN AN HOUR. CONCENTRATE UNTIL THEN.
C-CONCENTRATE...?

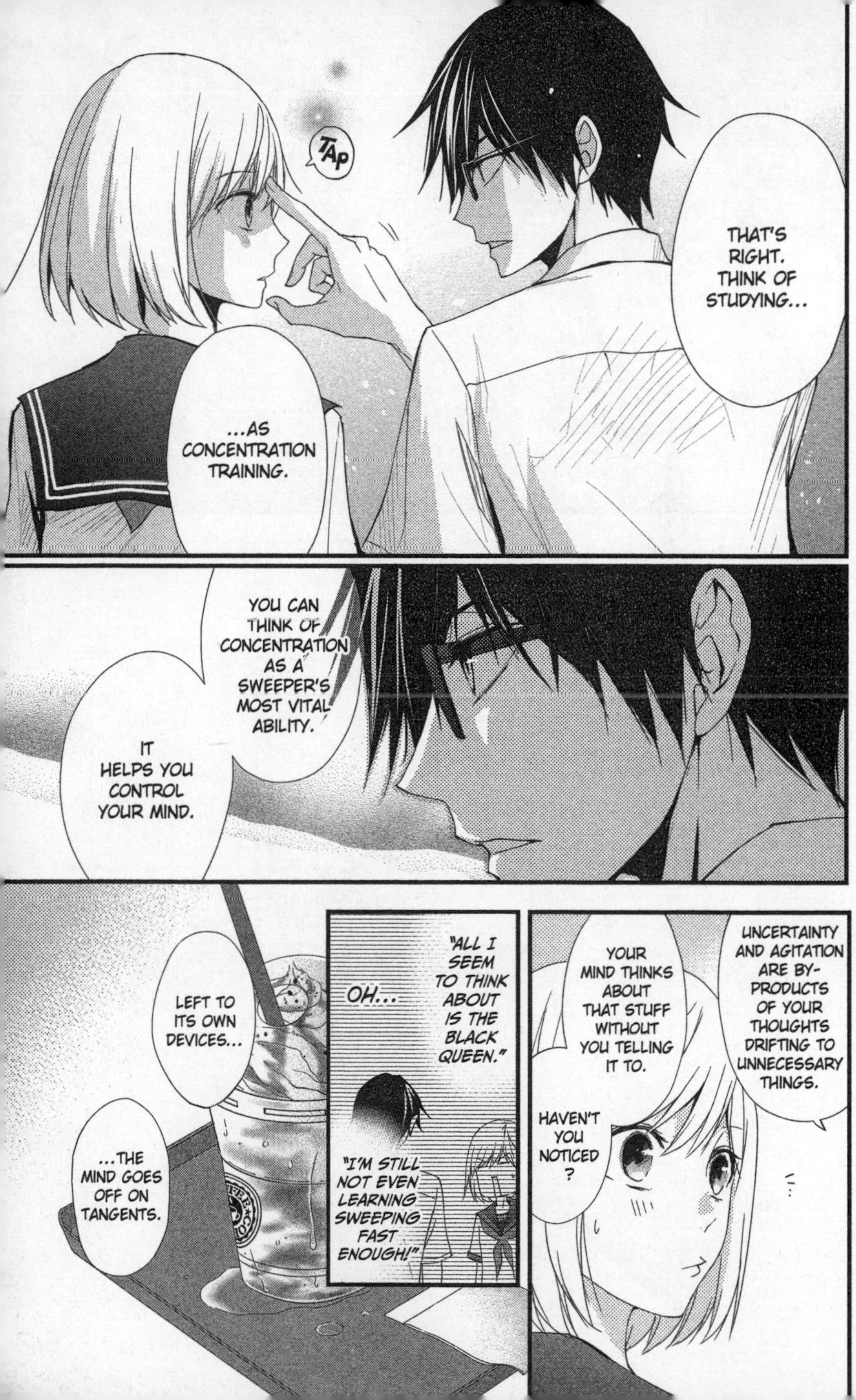
TAP
THAT'S RIGHT. THINK OF STUDYING...
...AS CONCENTRATION TRAINING.
YOU CAN THINK OF CONCENTRATION AS A SWEEPER'S MOST VITAL ABILITY.
IT HELPS YOU CONTROL YOUR MIND.
UNCERTAINTY AND AGITATION ARE BY-PRODUCTS OF YOUR THOUGHTS DRIFTING TO UNNECESSARY THINGS.
YOUR MIND THINKS ABOUT THAT STUFF WITHOUT YOU TELLING IT TO.
HAVEN'T YOU NOTICED?
"ALL I SEEM TO THINK ABOUT IS THE BLACK QUEEN."
OH...
"I'M STILL NOT EVEN LEARNING SWEEPING FAST ENOUGH!"
LEFT TO ITS OWN DEVICES...
...THE MIND GOES OFF ON TANGENTS.

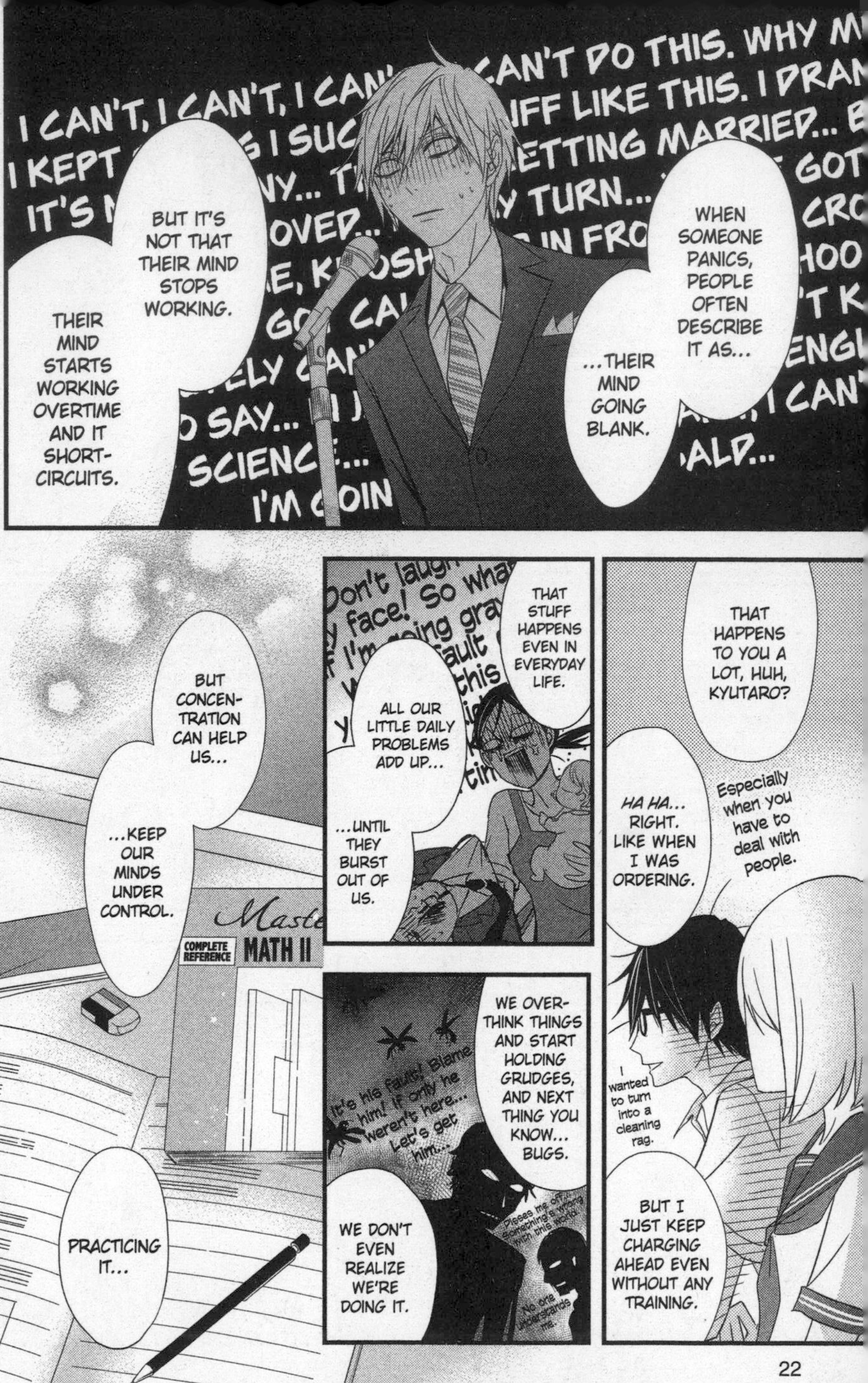
WHEN SOMEONE PANICS, PEOPLE OFTEN DESCRIBE IT AS...
...THEIR MIND GOING BLANK.
BUT IT'S NOT THAT THEIR MIND STOPS WORKING.
THEIR MIND STARTS WORKING OVERTIME AND IT SHORT-CIRCUITS.
THAT HAPPENS TO YOU A LOT, HUH, KYUTARO?
Especially when you have to deal with people.
HA HA... RIGHT. LIKE WHEN I WAS ORDERING.
I wanted to turn into a cleaning rag.
BUT I JUST KEEP CHARGING AHEAD EVEN WITHOUT ANY TRAINING.
THAT STUFF HAPPENS EVEN IN EVERYDAY LIFE.
ALL OUR LITTLE DAILY PROBLEMS ADD UP...
...UNTIL THEY BURST OUT OF US.
WE OVER-THINK THINGS AND START HOLDING GRUDGES, AND NEXT THING YOU KNOW... BUGS.
Pisses me off... Something's wrong with this world!
No one understands me.
WE DON'T EVEN REALIZE WE'RE DOING IT.
BUT CONCEN-TRATION CAN HELP US...
...KEEP OUR MINDS UNDER CONTROL.
COMPLETE REFERENCE
MATH II
PRACTICING IT...

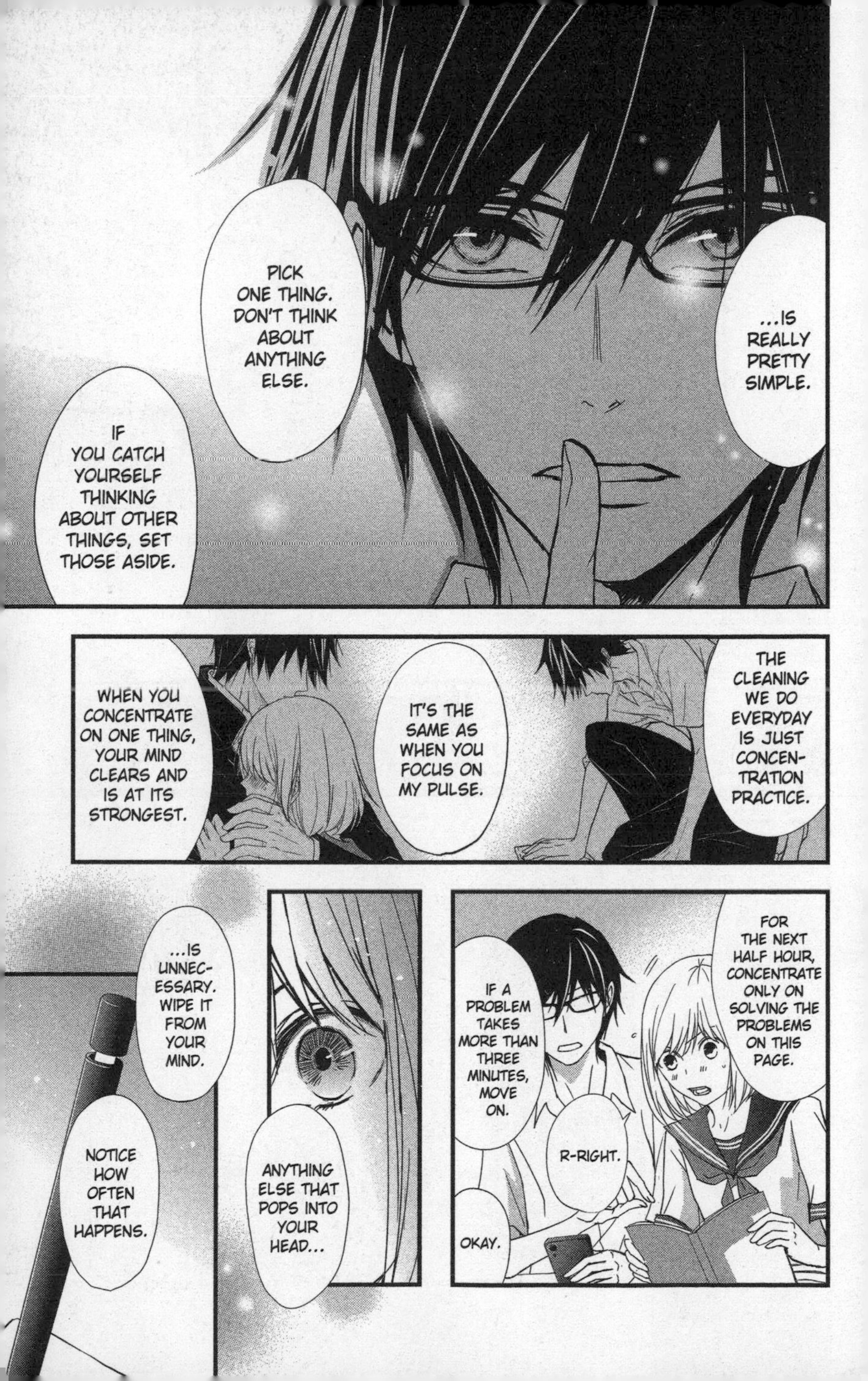
...IS REALLY PRETTY SIMPLE.
PICK ONE THING. DON'T THINK ABOUT ANYTHING ELSE.
IF YOU CATCH YOURSELF THINKING ABOUT OTHER THINGS, SET THOSE ASIDE.
THE CLEANING WE DO EVERYDAY IS JUST CONCEN-TRATION PRACTICE.
IT'S THE SAME AS WHEN YOU FOCUS ON MY PULSE.
WHEN YOU CONCENTRATE ON ONE THING, YOUR MIND CLEARS AND IS AT ITS STRONGEST.
FOR THE NEXT HALF HOUR, CONCENTRATE ONLY ON SOLVING THE PROBLEMS ON THIS PAGE.
IF A PROBLEM TAKES MORE THAN THREE MINUTES, MOVE ON.
R-RIGHT.
OKAY.
ANYTHING ELSE THAT POPS INTO YOUR HEAD...
...IS UNNEC-ESSARY. WIPE IT FROM YOUR MIND.
NOTICE HOW OFTEN THAT HAPPENS.

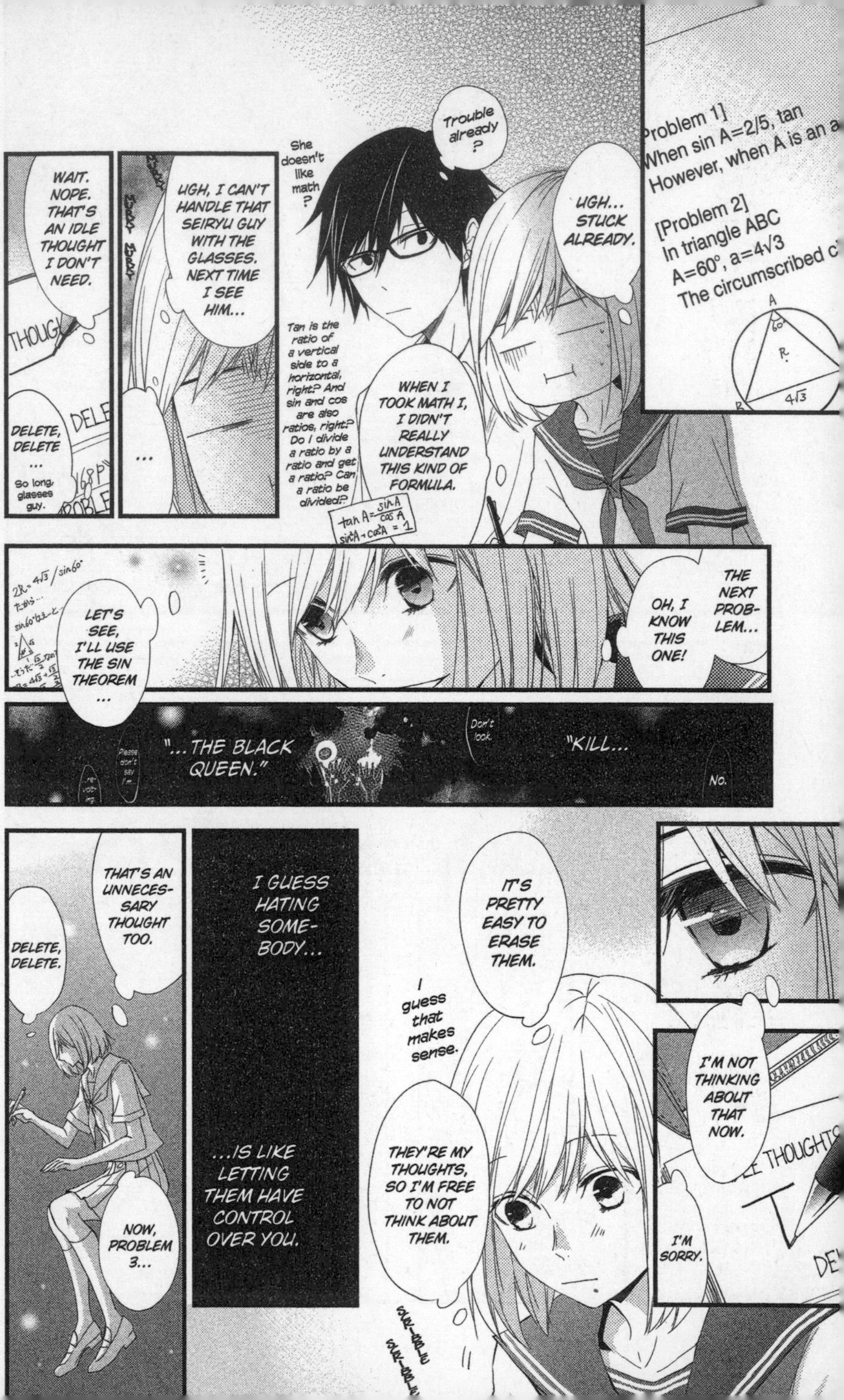
[Problem 1]
When sin A=2/5, tan
However, when A is an a
[Problem 2]
In triangle ABC
A=60°, a=4√3
The circumscribed c
UGH... STUCK ALREADY.
Trouble already?
She doesn't like math?
WHEN I TOOK MATH I, I DIDN'T REALLY UNDERSTAND THIS KIND OF FORMULA.
Tan is the ratio of a vertical side to a horizontal, right? And sin and cos are also ratios, right? Do I divide a ratio by a ratio and get a ratio? Can a ratio be divided?
tan A = sin A / cos A
sin²A + cos²A = 1
UGH, I CAN'T HANDLE THAT SEIRYU GUY WITH THE GLASSES. NEXT TIME I SEE HIM...
...
WAIT. NOPE. THAT'S AN IDLE THOUGHT I DON'T NEED.
DELETE, DELETE ...
So long, glasses guy.
THE NEXT PROBLEM...
OH, I KNOW THIS ONE!
LET'S SEE, I'LL USE THE SIN THEOREM ...
"KILL...
No.
Don't look.
"...THE BLACK QUEEN."
I'M NOT THINKING ABOUT THAT NOW.
I'M SORRY.
IT'S PRETTY EASY TO ERASE THEM.
I guess that makes sense.
THEY'RE MY THOUGHTS, SO I'M FREE TO NOT THINK ABOUT THEM.
I GUESS HATING SOMEBODY...
...IS LIKE LETTING THEM HAVE CONTROL OVER YOU.
THAT'S AN UNNECESSARY THOUGHT TOO.
DELETE, DELETE.
NOW, PROBLEM 3...

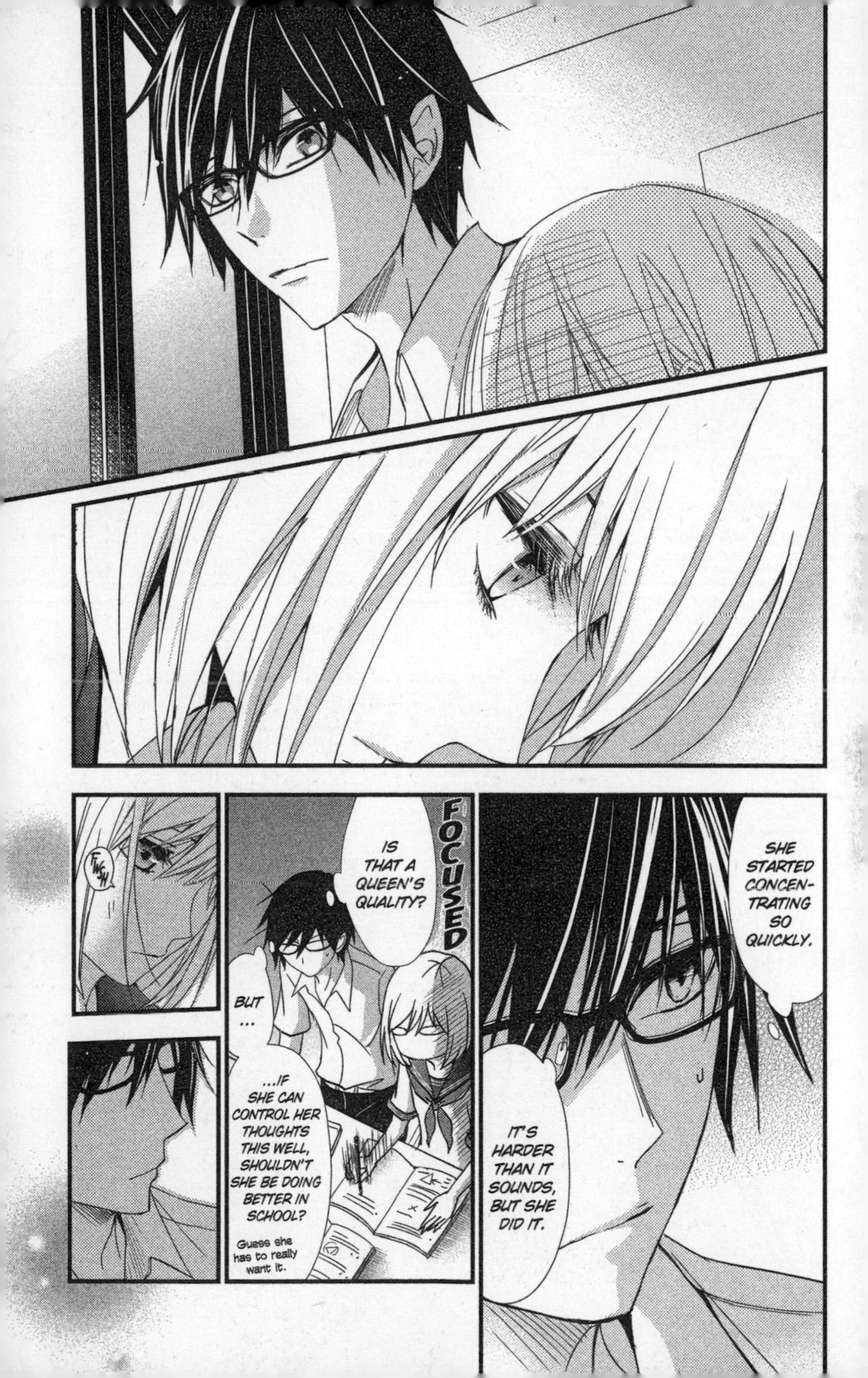
SHE STARTED CONCENTRATING SO QUICKLY.
IT'S HARDER THAN IT SOUNDS, BUT SHE DID IT.
FOCUSED
IS THAT A QUEEN'S QUALITY?
BUT ...
...IF SHE CAN CONTROL HER THOUGHTS THIS WELL, SHOULDN'T SHE BE DOING BETTER IN SCHOOL?
Guess she has to really want it.
FWSH

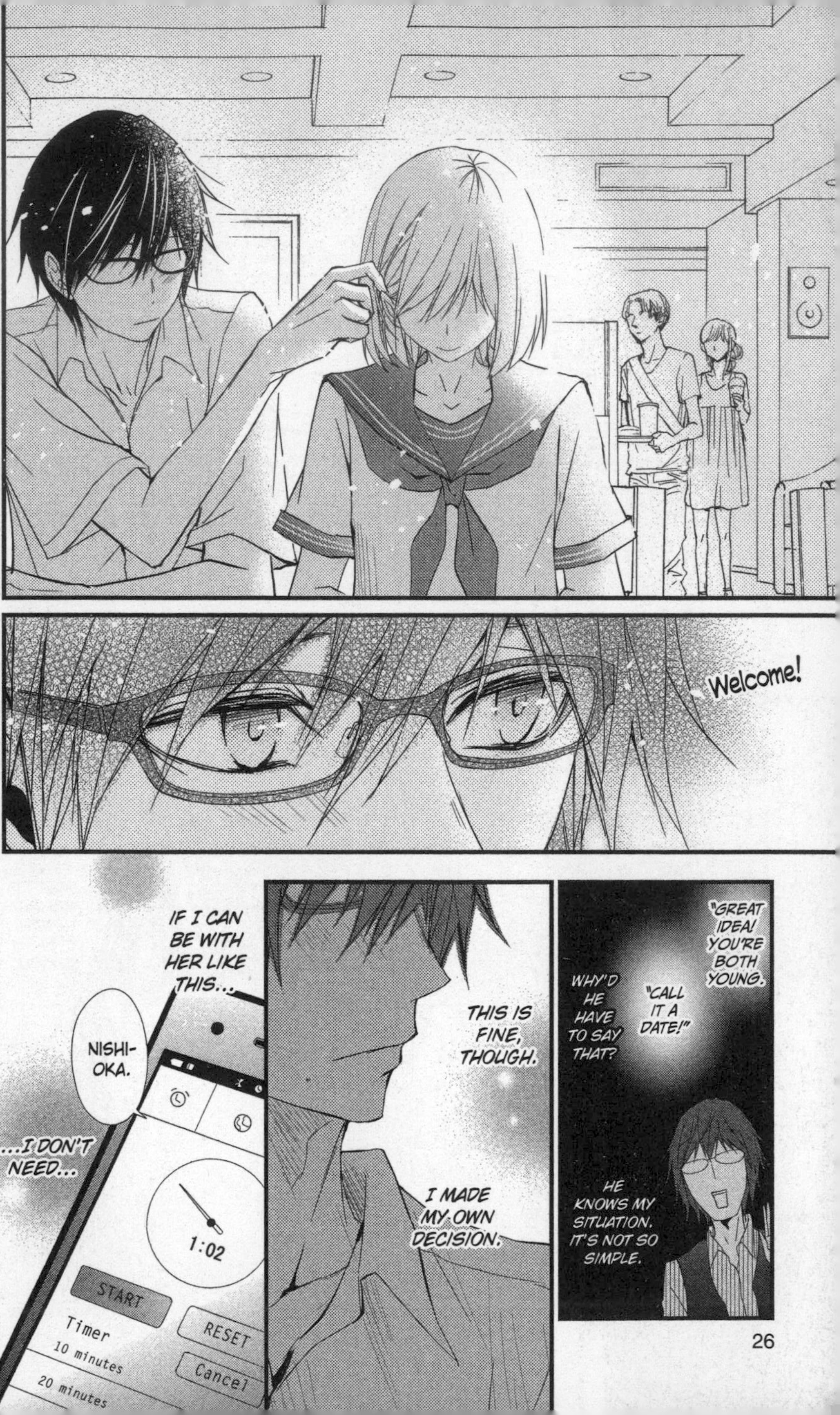
Welcome!
"GREAT IDEA! YOU'RE BOTH YOUNG.
"CALL IT A DATE!"
WHY'D HE HAVE TO SAY THAT?
HE KNOWS MY SITUATION. IT'S NOT SO SIMPLE.
THIS IS FINE, THOUGH.
I MADE MY OWN DECISION.
IF I CAN BE WITH HER LIKE THIS...
NISHI-OKA.
...I DON'T NEED...
1:02
START
RESET
Timer
10 minutes
Cancel
20 minutes

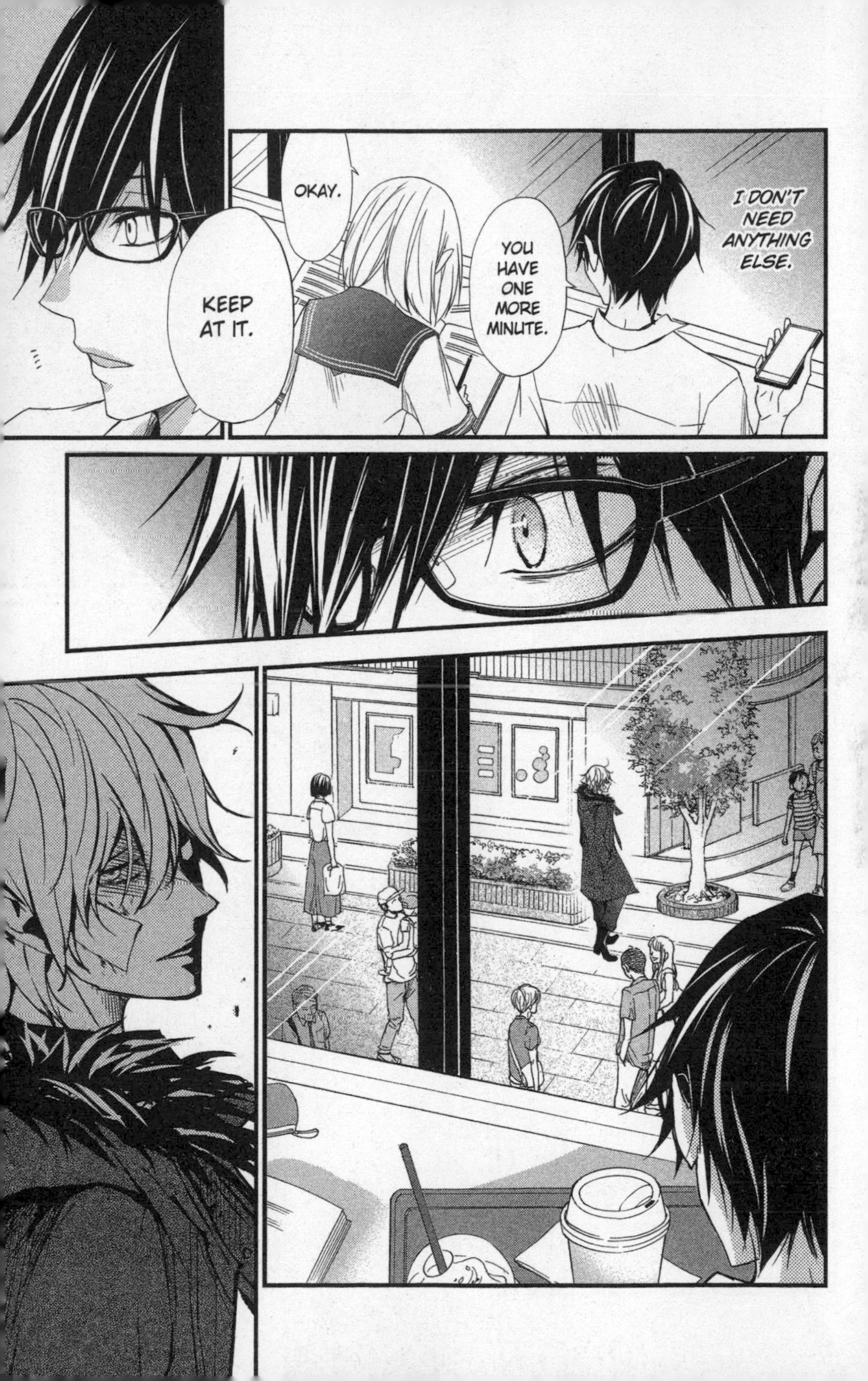
I DON'T NEED ANYTHING ELSE.
YOU HAVE ONE MORE MINUTE.
OKAY.
KEEP AT IT.

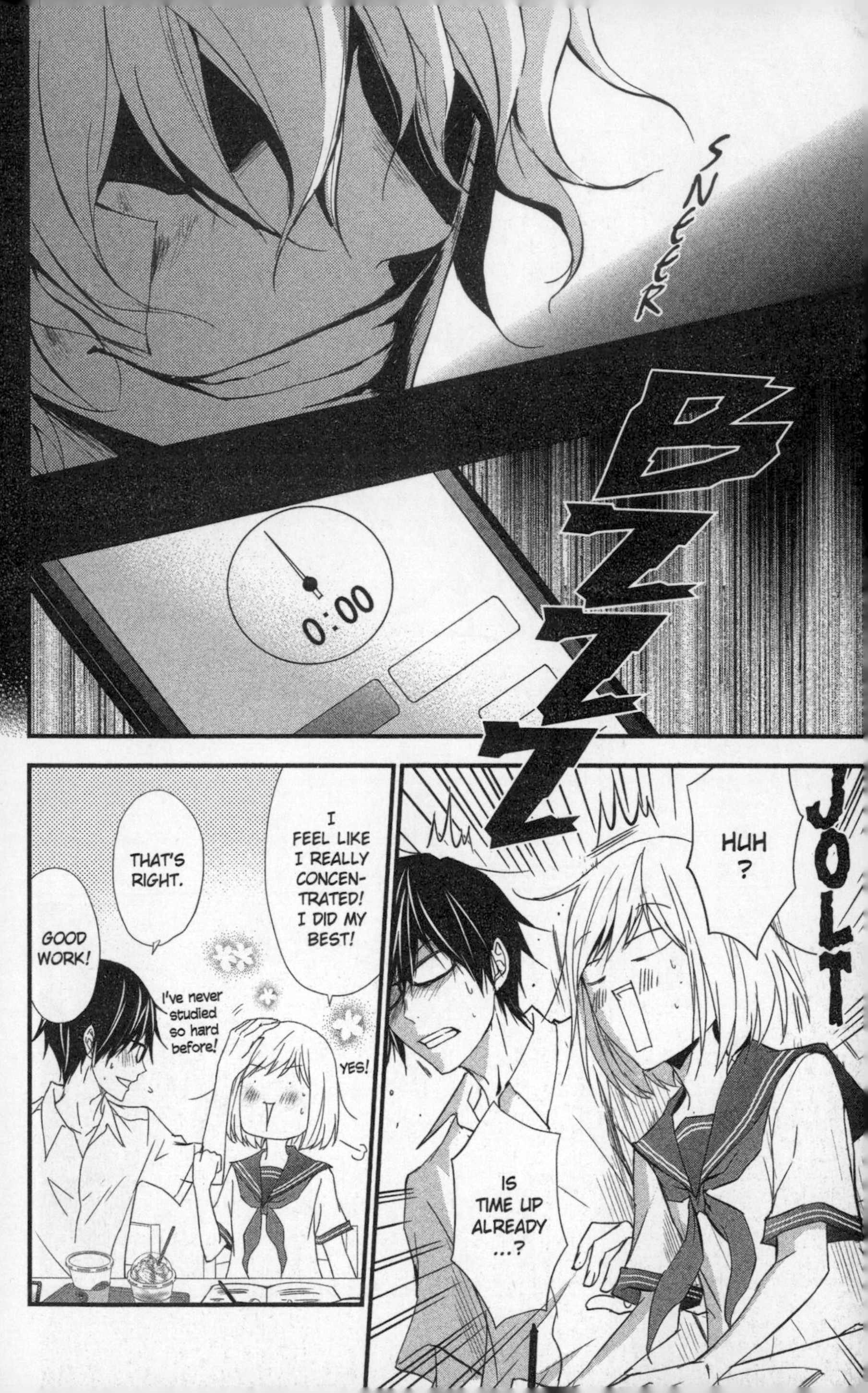
SNEER
0:00
BZZZZ
JOLT
HUH?
IS TIME UP ALREADY...?
I FEEL LIKE I REALLY CONCEN-TRATED! I DID MY BEST!
YES!
THAT'S RIGHT.
I've never studied so hard before!
GOOD WORK!

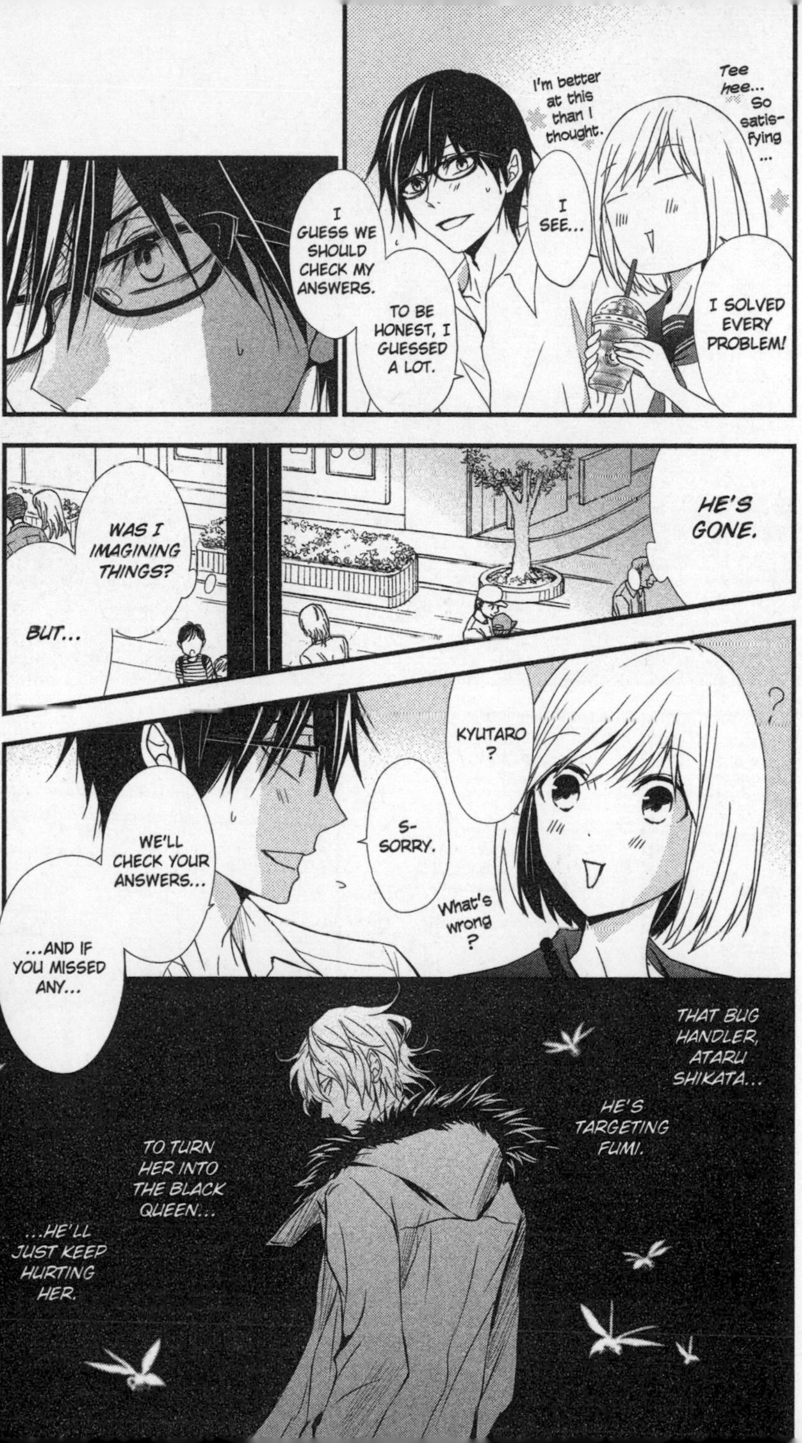
Tee hee... So satisfying...
I'm better at this than I thought.
I SOLVED EVERY PROBLEM!
I SEE...
I GUESS WE SHOULD CHECK MY ANSWERS.
TO BE HONEST, I GUESSED A LOT.
HE'S GONE.
WAS I IMAGINING THINGS?
BUT...
KYUTARO?
?
S-SORRY.
What's wrong?
WE'LL CHECK YOUR ANSWERS...
...AND IF YOU MISSED ANY...
THAT BUG HANDLER, ATARU SHIKATA...
HE'S TARGETING FUMI.
TO TURN HER INTO THE BLACK QUEEN...
...HE'LL JUST KEEP HURTING HER.

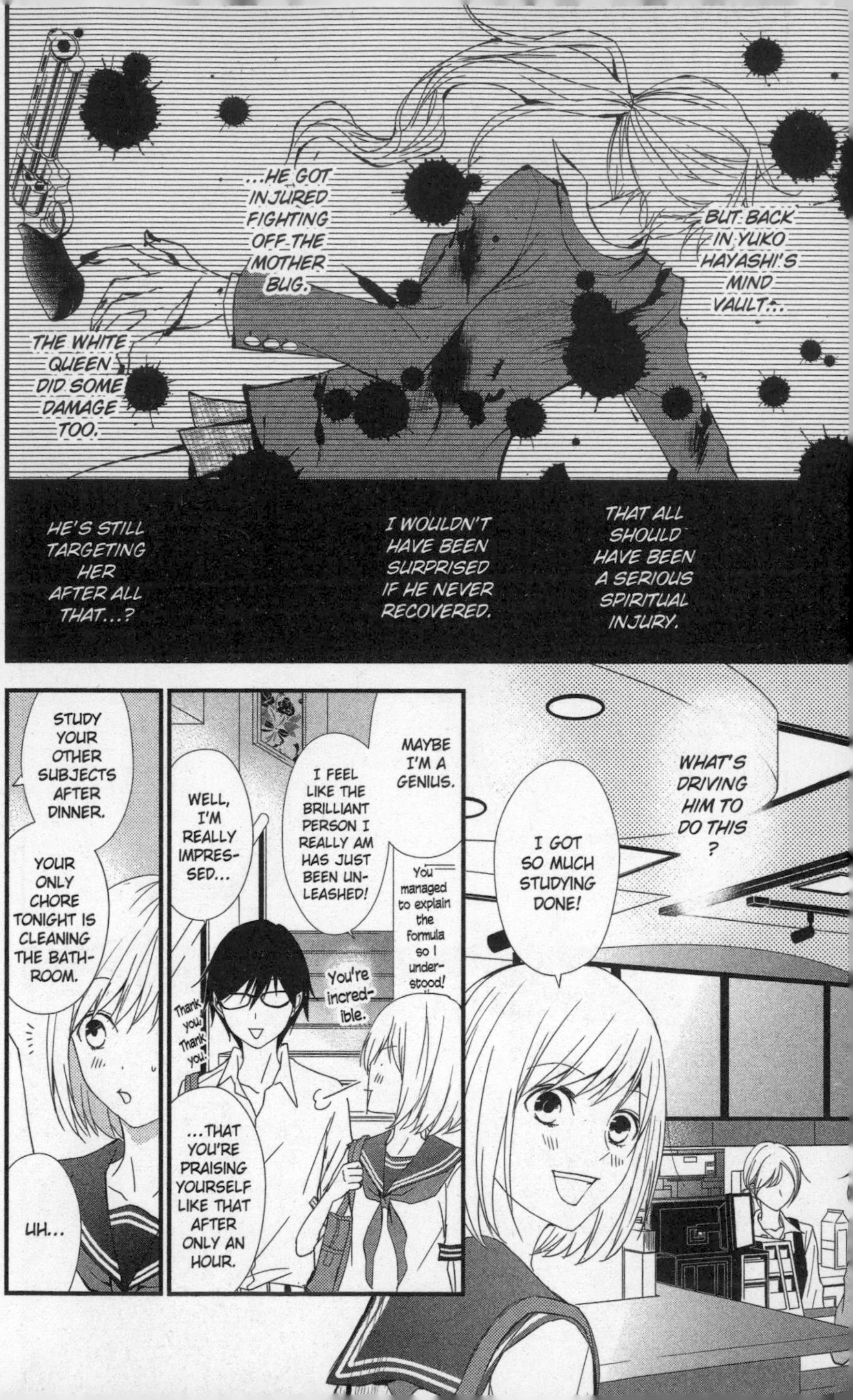
BUT BACK IN YUKO HAYASHI'S MIND VAULT...
...HE GOT INJURED FIGHTING OFF THE MOTHER BUG.
THE WHITE QUEEN DID SOME DAMAGE TOO.
THAT ALL SHOULD HAVE BEEN A SERIOUS SPIRITUAL INJURY.
I WOULDN'T HAVE BEEN SURPRISED IF HE NEVER RECOVERED.
HE'S STILL TARGETING HER AFTER ALL THAT...?
WHAT'S DRIVING HIM TO DO THIS?
I GOT SO MUCH STUDYING DONE!
MAYBE I'M A GENIUS.
I FEEL LIKE THE BRILLIANT PERSON I REALLY AM HAS JUST BEEN UNLEASHED!
You managed to explain the formula so I understood!
You're incredible.
WELL, I'M REALLY IMPRESSED...
Thank you. Thank you!
...THAT YOU'RE PRAISING YOURSELF LIKE THAT AFTER ONLY AN HOUR.
STUDY YOUR OTHER SUBJECTS AFTER DINNER.
YOUR ONLY CHORE TONIGHT IS CLEANING THE BATHROOM.
UH...

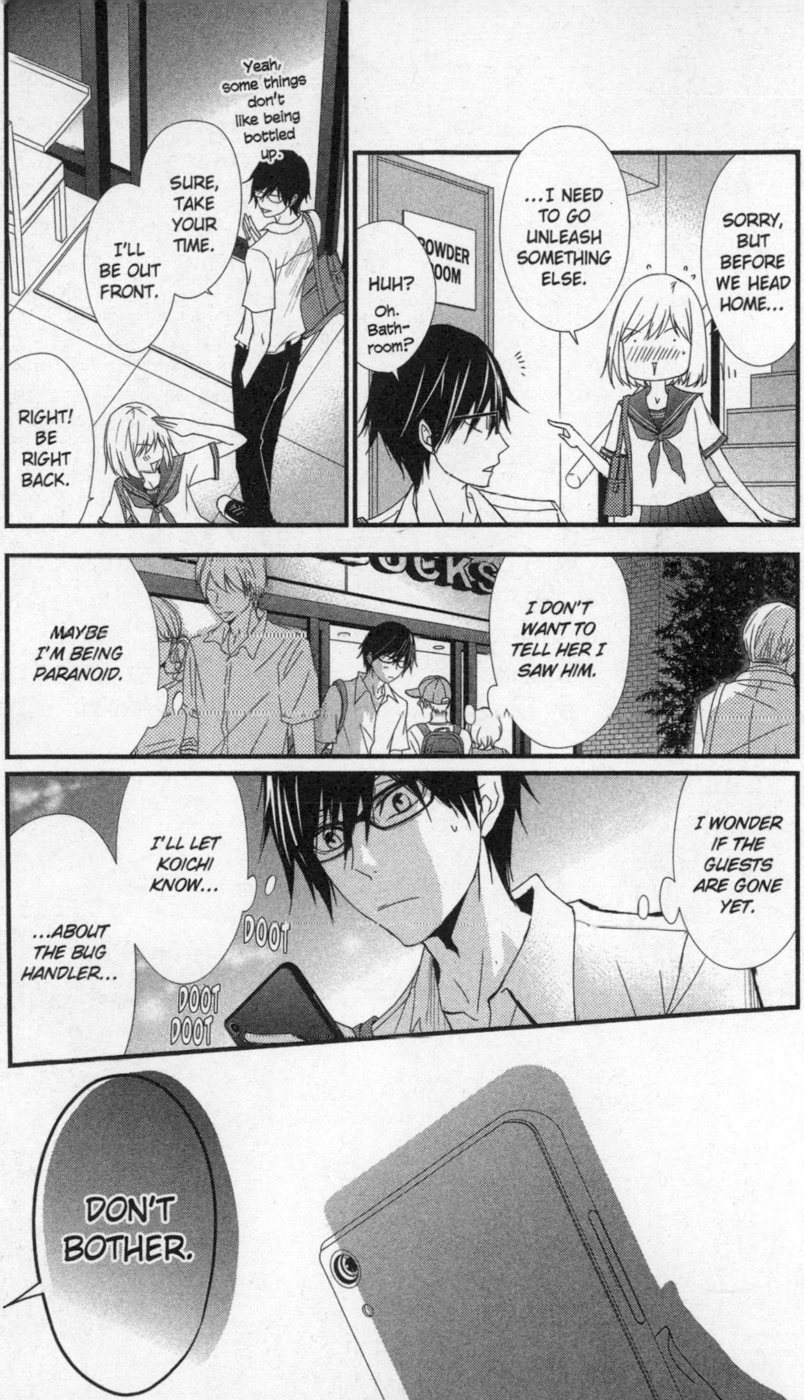
SORRY, BUT BEFORE WE HEAD HOME...
...I NEED TO GO UNLEASH SOMETHING ELSE.
POWDER OOM
HUH? Oh. Bathroom?
SURE, TAKE YOUR TIME. I'LL BE OUT FRONT.
Yeah, some things don't like being bottled up.
RIGHT! BE RIGHT BACK.
I DON'T WANT TO TELL HER I SAW HIM.
MAYBE I'M BEING PARANOID.
I WONDER IF THE GUESTS ARE GONE YET.
DOOT
DOOT DOOT
I'LL LET KOICHI KNOW...
...ABOUT THE BUG HANDLER...
DON'T BOTHER.

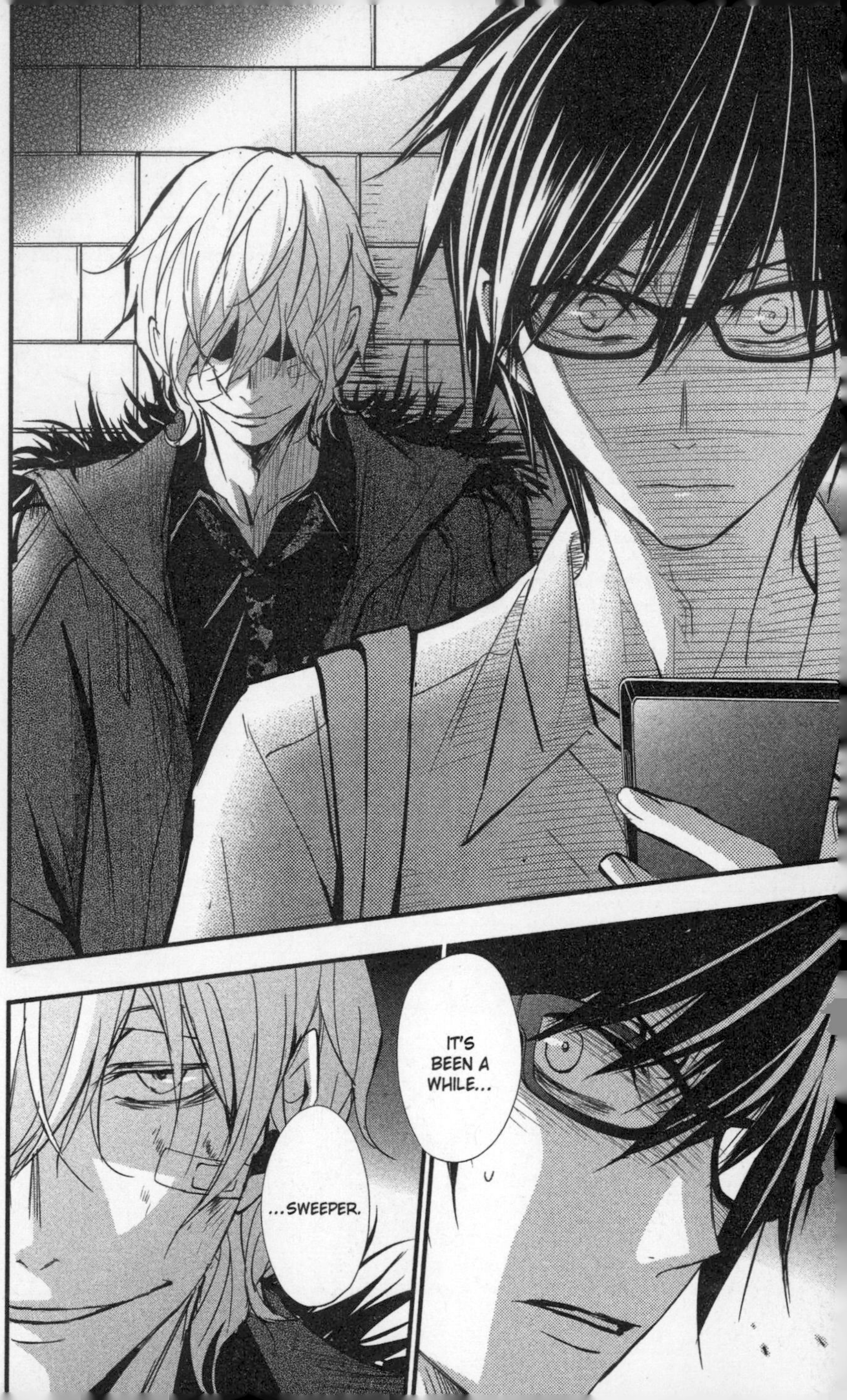
IT'S BEEN A WHILE...
...SWEEPER.

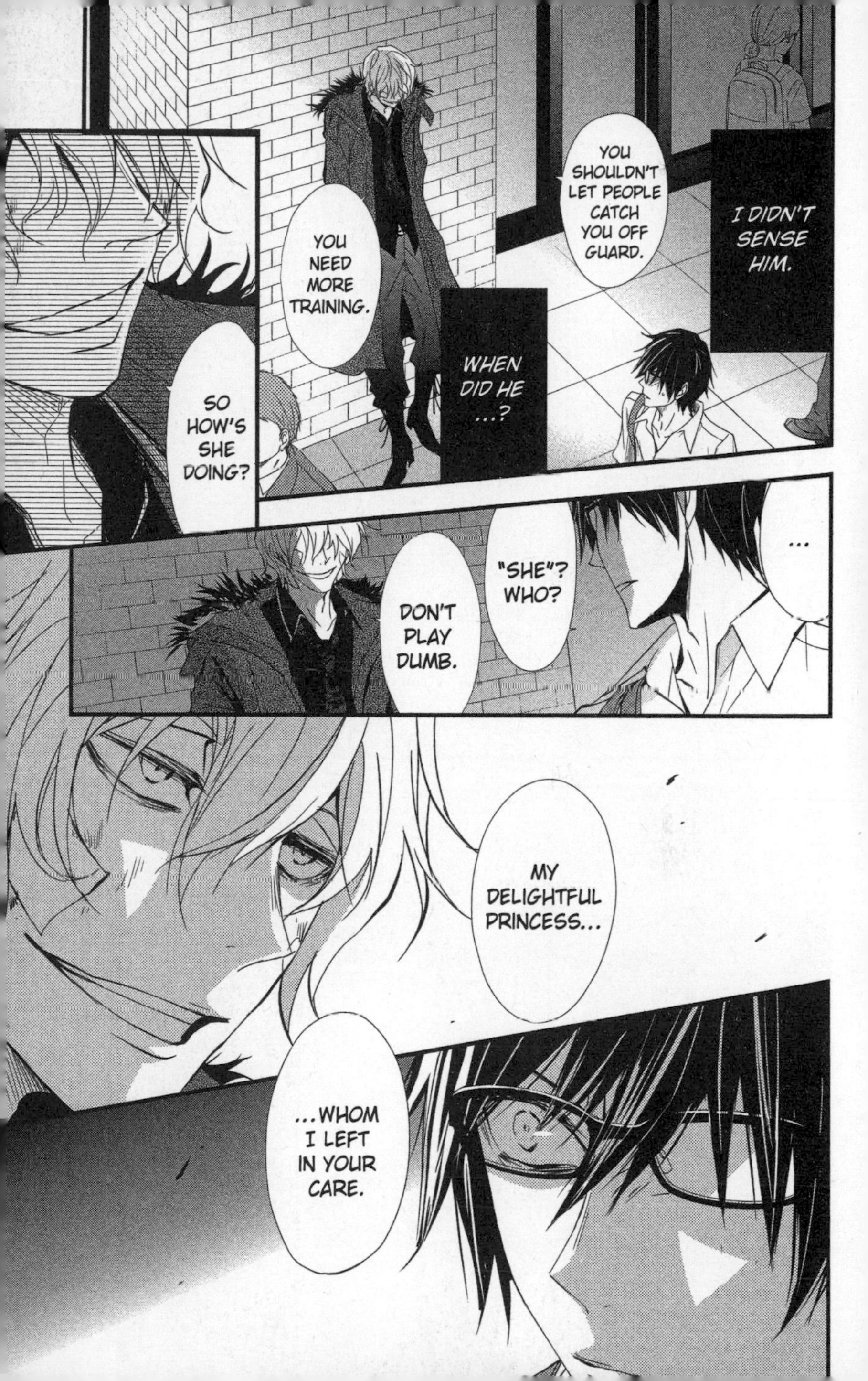
I DIDN'T SENSE HIM.
YOU SHOULDN'T LET PEOPLE CATCH YOU OFF GUARD.
WHEN DID HE ...?
YOU NEED MORE TRAINING.
SO HOW'S SHE DOING?
...
"SHE"? WHO?
DON'T PLAY DUMB.
MY DELIGHTFUL PRINCESS...
...WHOM I LEFT IN YOUR CARE.

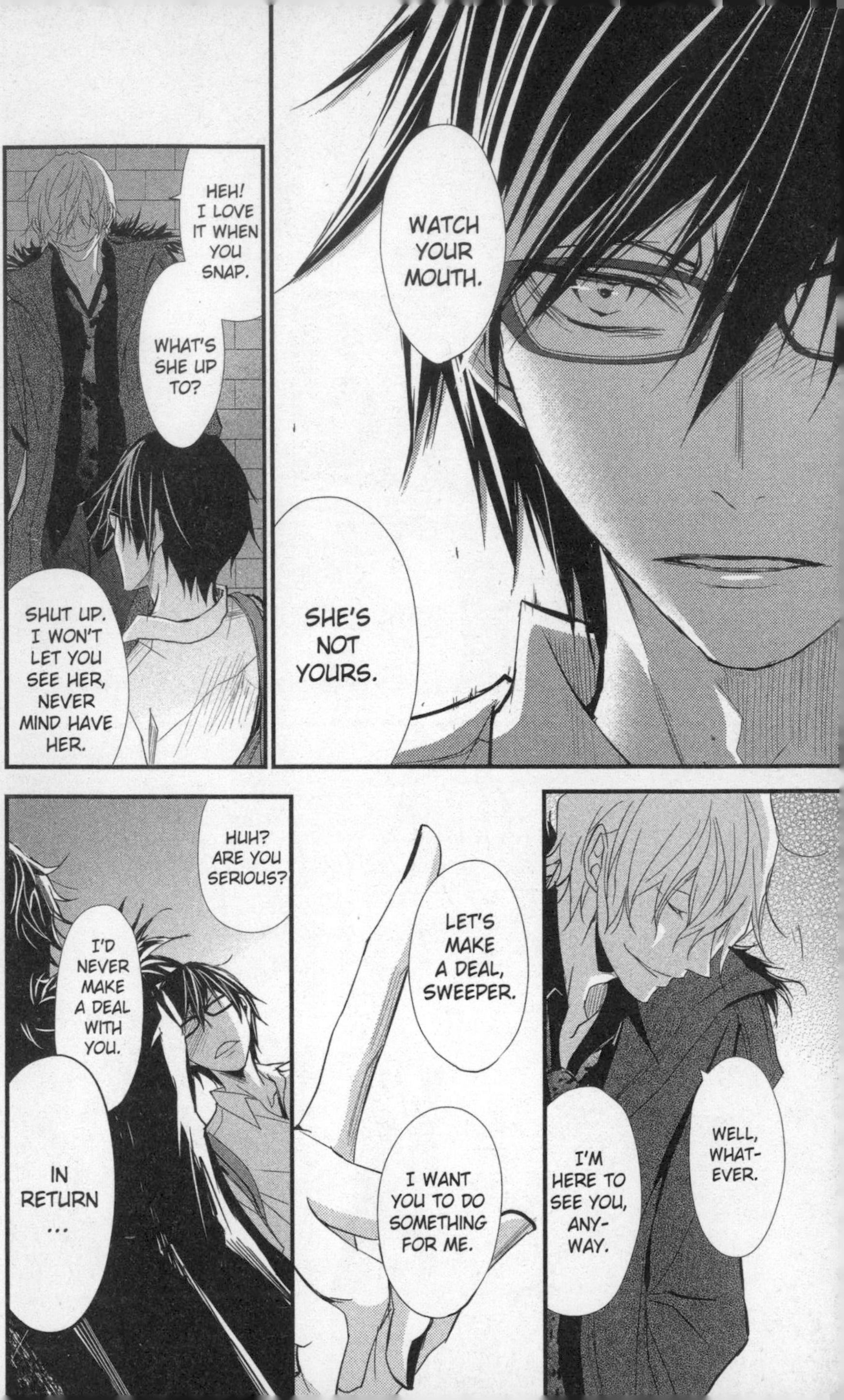
WATCH YOUR MOUTH.
SHE'S NOT YOURS.
HEH! I LOVE IT WHEN YOU SNAP.
WHAT'S SHE UP TO?
SHUT UP. I WON'T LET YOU SEE HER, NEVER MIND HAVE HER.
WELL, WHATEVER.
I'M HERE TO SEE YOU, ANYWAY.
LET'S MAKE A DEAL, SWEEPER.
I WANT YOU TO DO SOMETHING FOR ME.
HUH? ARE YOU SERIOUS?
I'D NEVER MAKE A DEAL WITH YOU.
IN RETURN...

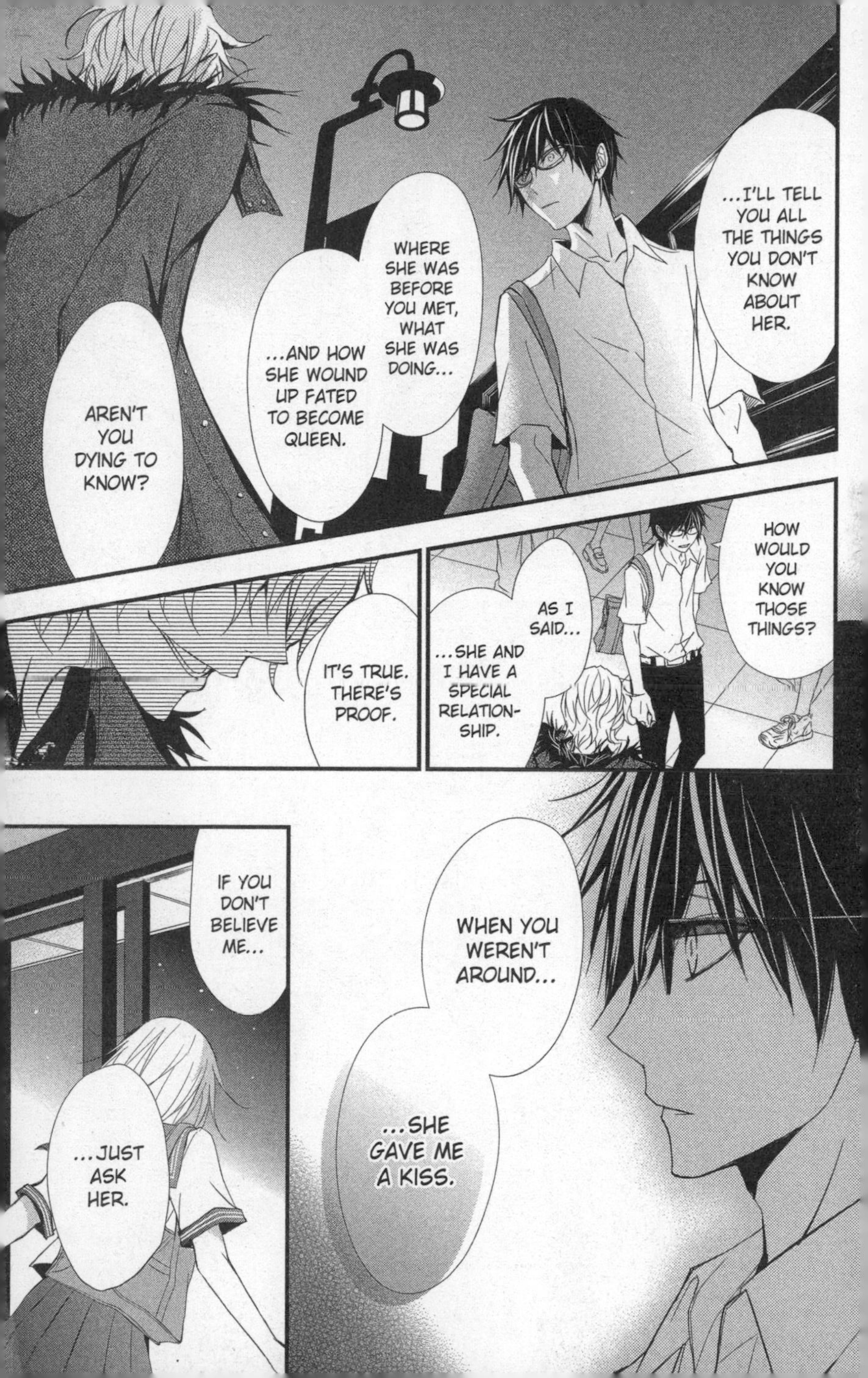
...I'LL TELL YOU ALL THE THINGS YOU DON'T KNOW ABOUT HER.
WHERE SHE WAS BEFORE YOU MET, WHAT SHE WAS DOING...
...AND HOW SHE WOUND UP FATED TO BECOME QUEEN.
AREN'T YOU DYING TO KNOW?
HOW WOULD YOU KNOW THOSE THINGS?
AS I SAID...
...SHE AND I HAVE A SPECIAL RELATION-SHIP.
IT'S TRUE. THERE'S PROOF.
WHEN YOU WEREN'T AROUND...
...SHE GAVE ME A KISS.
IF YOU DON'T BELIEVE ME...
...JUST ASK HER.

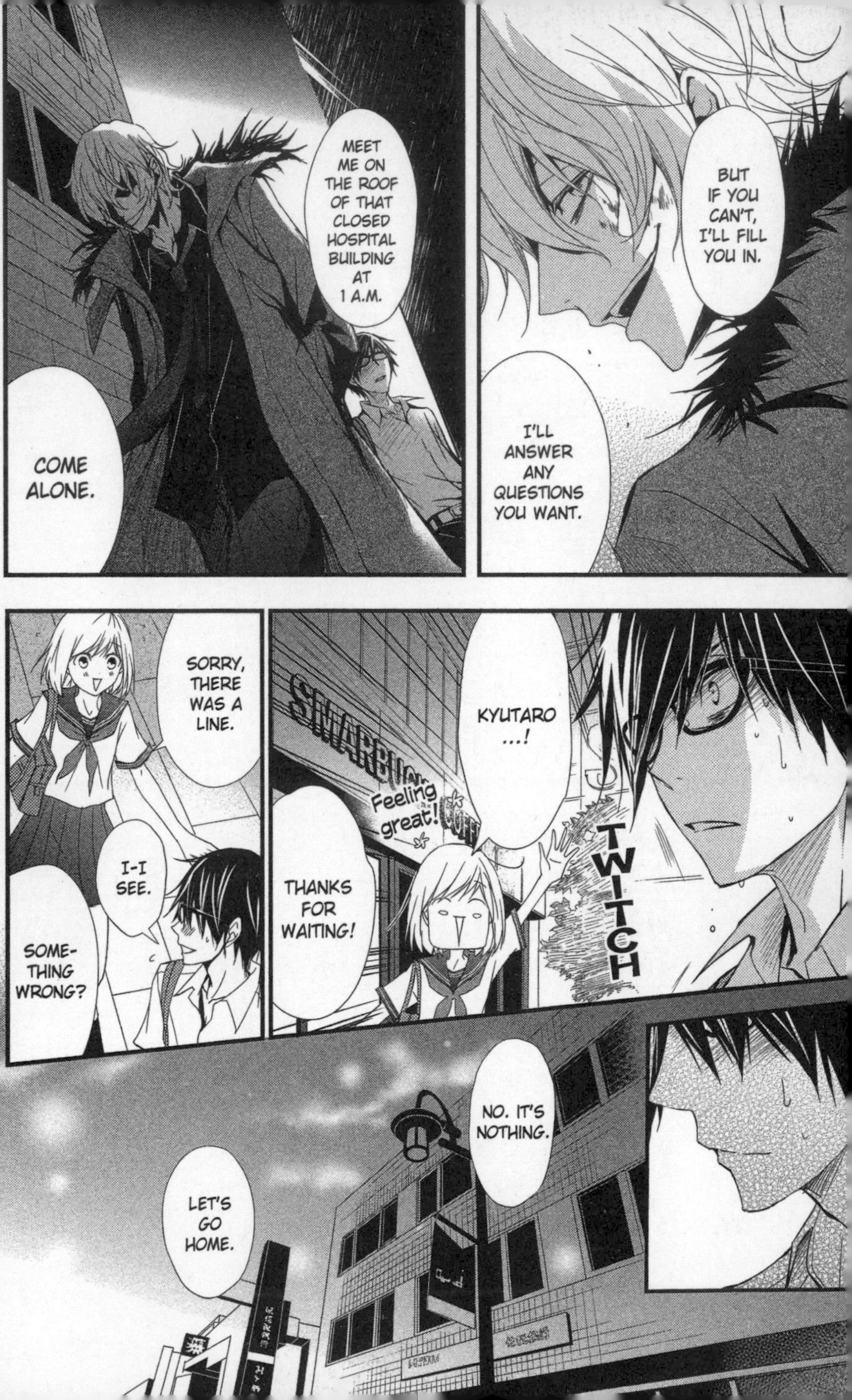
BUT IF YOU CAN'T, I'LL FILL YOU IN.
I'LL ANSWER ANY QUESTIONS YOU WANT.
MEET ME ON THE ROOF OF THAT CLOSED HOSPITAL BUILDING AT 1 A.M.
COME ALONE.
TWITCH
KYUTARO ...!
Feeling great!
THANKS FOR WAITING!
SORRY, THERE WAS A LINE.
I-I SEE.
SOME-THING WRONG?
NO. IT'S NOTHING.
LET'S GO HOME.

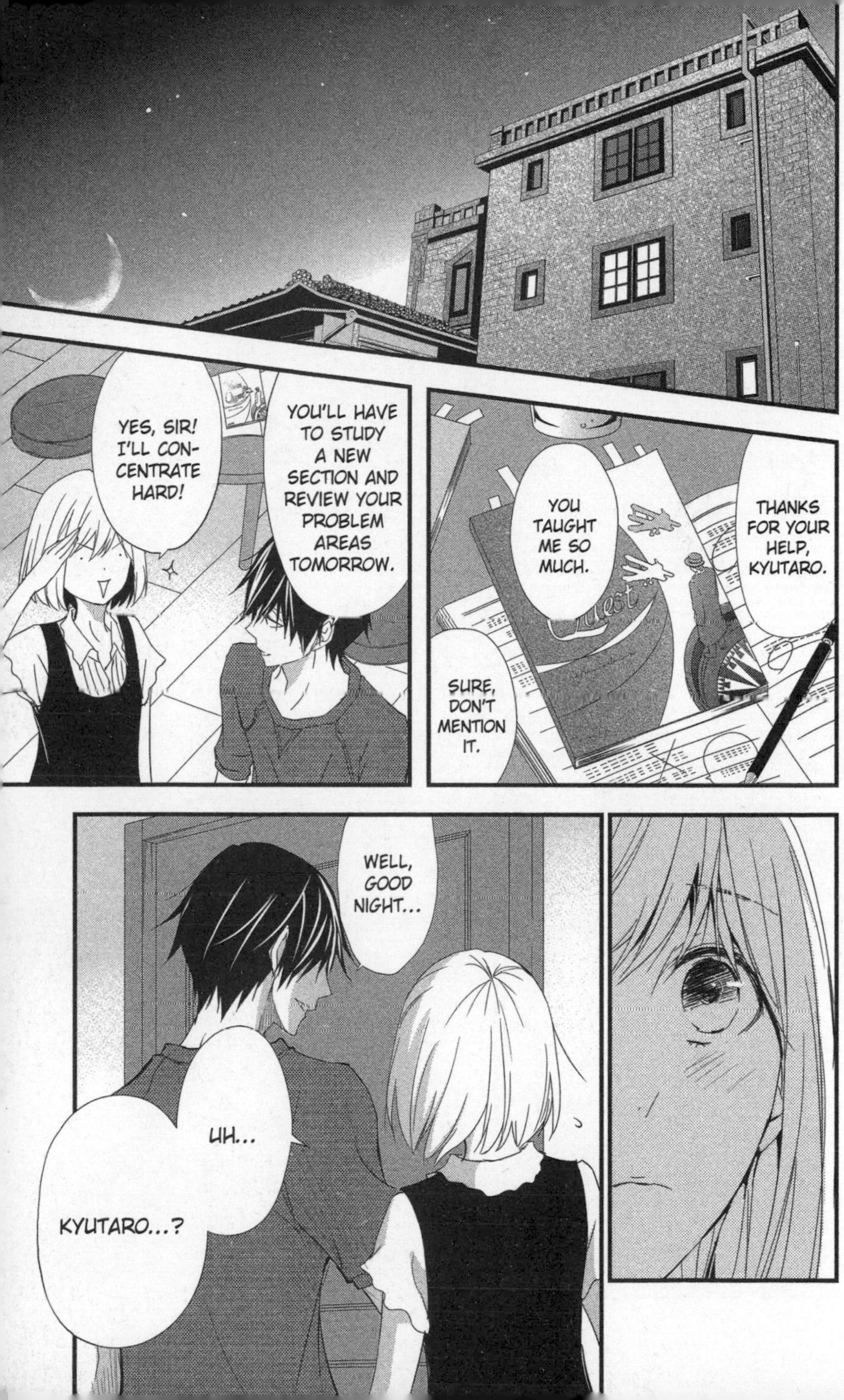
THANKS FOR YOUR HELP, KYUTARO.
YOU TAUGHT ME SO MUCH.
SURE, DON'T MENTION IT.
YOU'LL HAVE TO STUDY A NEW SECTION AND REVIEW YOUR PROBLEM AREAS TOMORROW.
YES, SIR! I'LL CON-CENTRATE HARD!
WELL, GOOD NIGHT...
UH...
KYUTARO...?

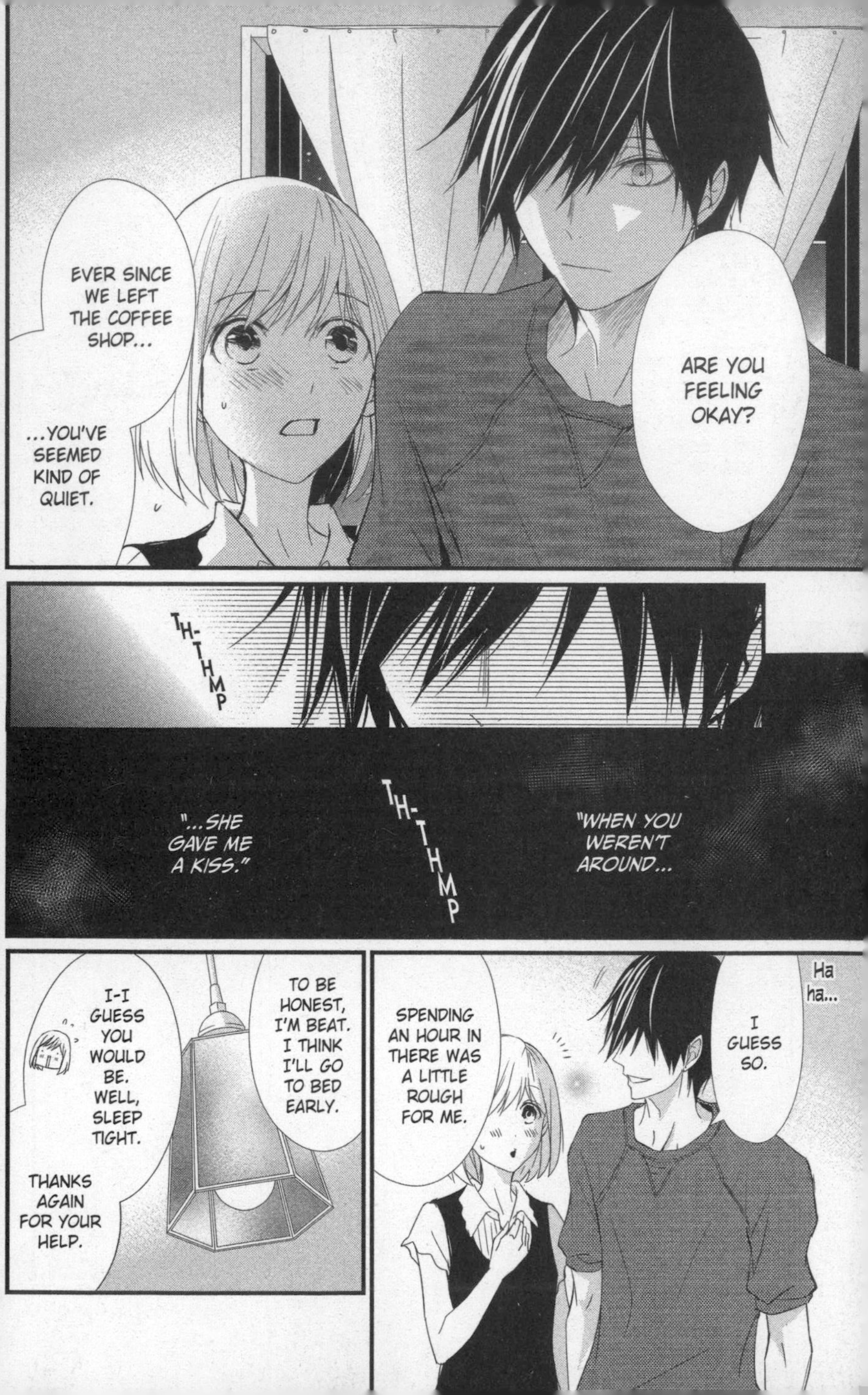
ARE YOU FEELING OKAY?
EVER SINCE WE LEFT THE COFFEE SHOP...
...YOU'VE SEEMED KIND OF QUIET.
TH-THMP
"WHEN YOU WEREN'T AROUND...
TH-THMP
"...SHE GAVE ME A KISS."
Ha ha...
I GUESS SO.
SPENDING AN HOUR IN THERE WAS A LITTLE ROUGH FOR ME.
TO BE HONEST, I'M BEAT. I THINK I'LL GO TO BED EARLY.
I-I GUESS YOU WOULD BE. WELL, SLEEP TIGHT.
THANKS AGAIN FOR YOUR HELP.

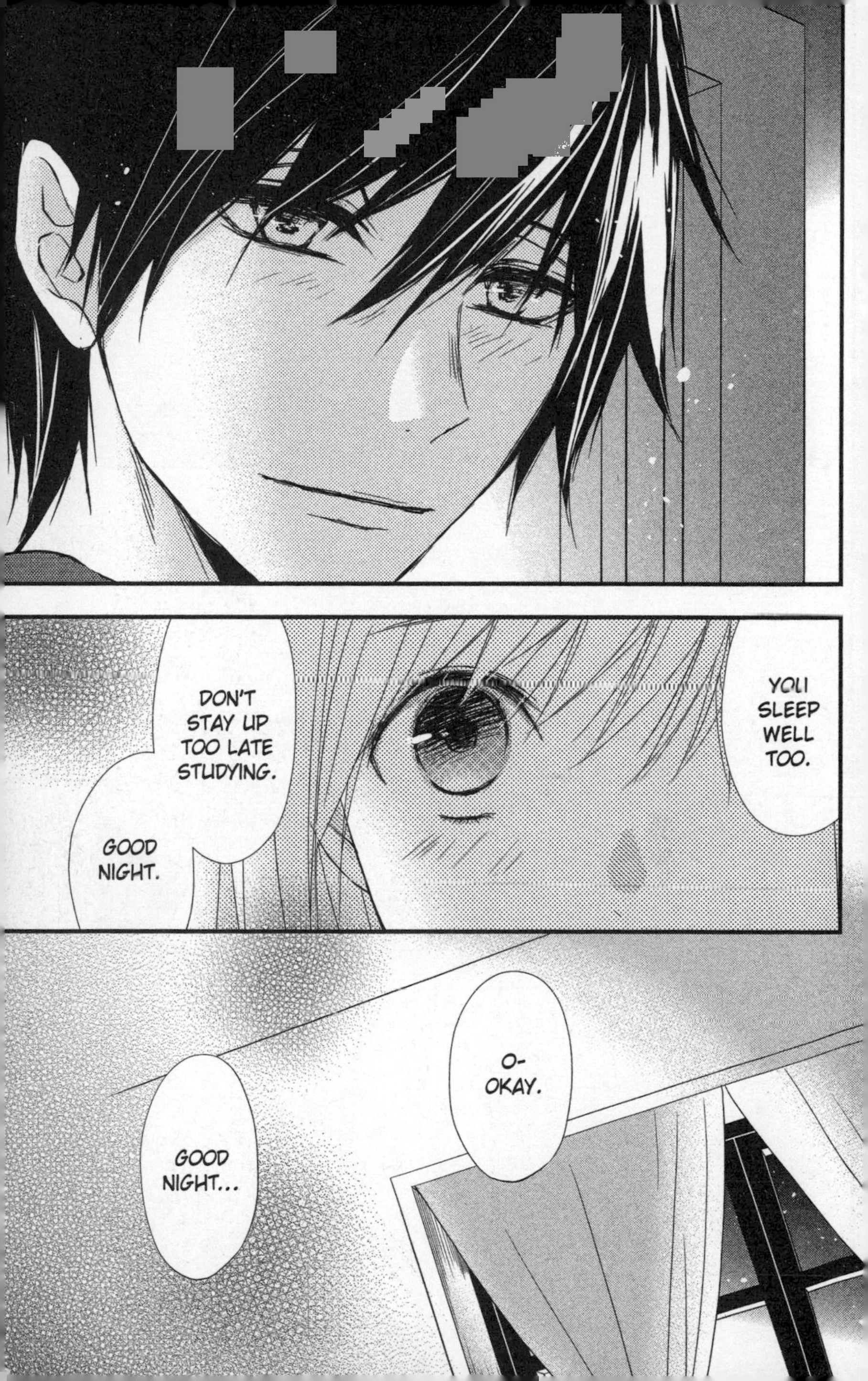
YOU SLEEP WELL TOO.
DON'T STAY UP TOO LATE STUDYING.
GOOD NIGHT.
O-OKAY.
GOOD NIGHT...

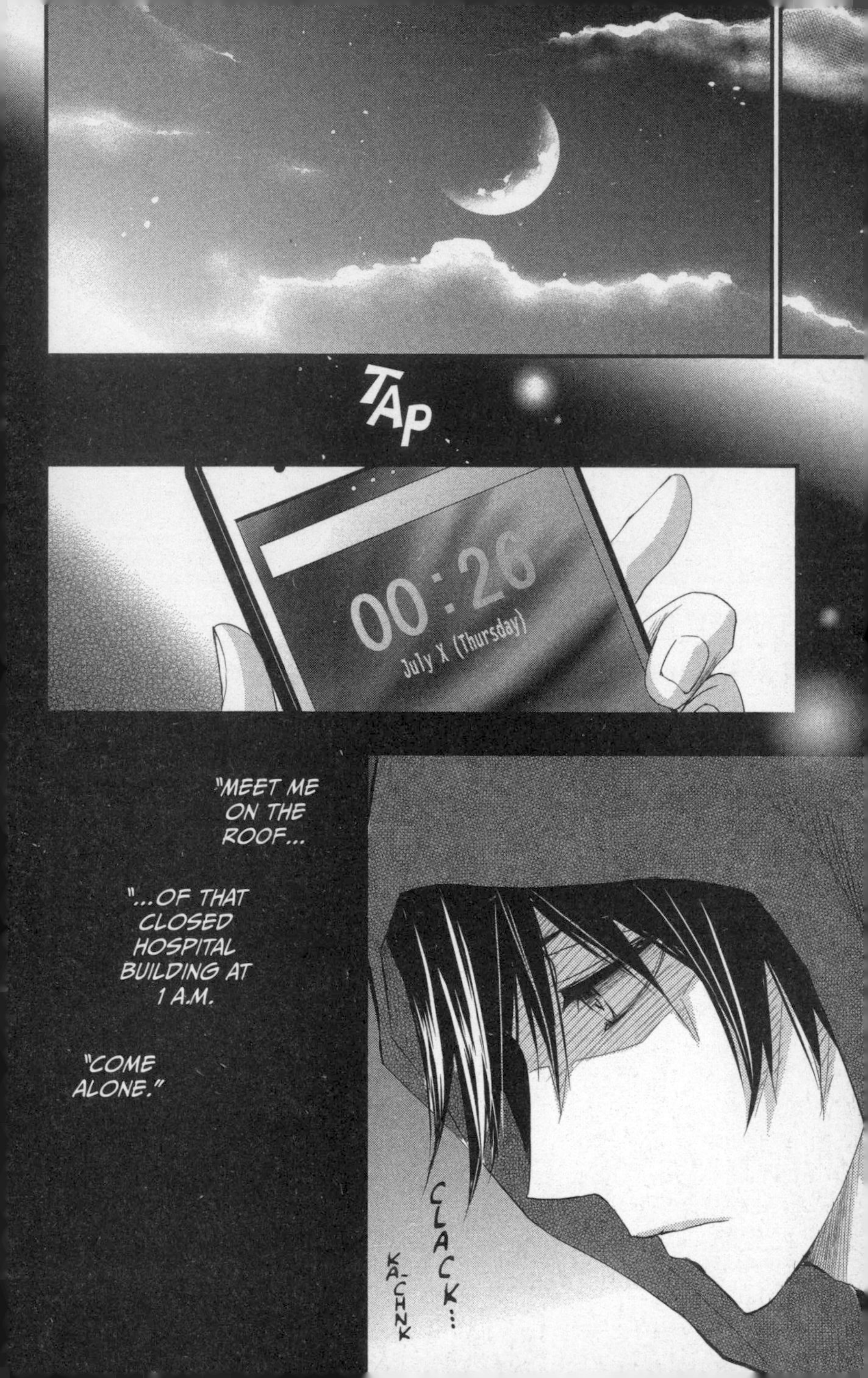
TAP
00:26
July X (Thursday)
"MEET ME ON THE ROOF...
"...OF THAT CLOSED HOSPITAL BUILDING AT 1 A.M.
"COME ALONE."
CLACK...
KA-CHNK

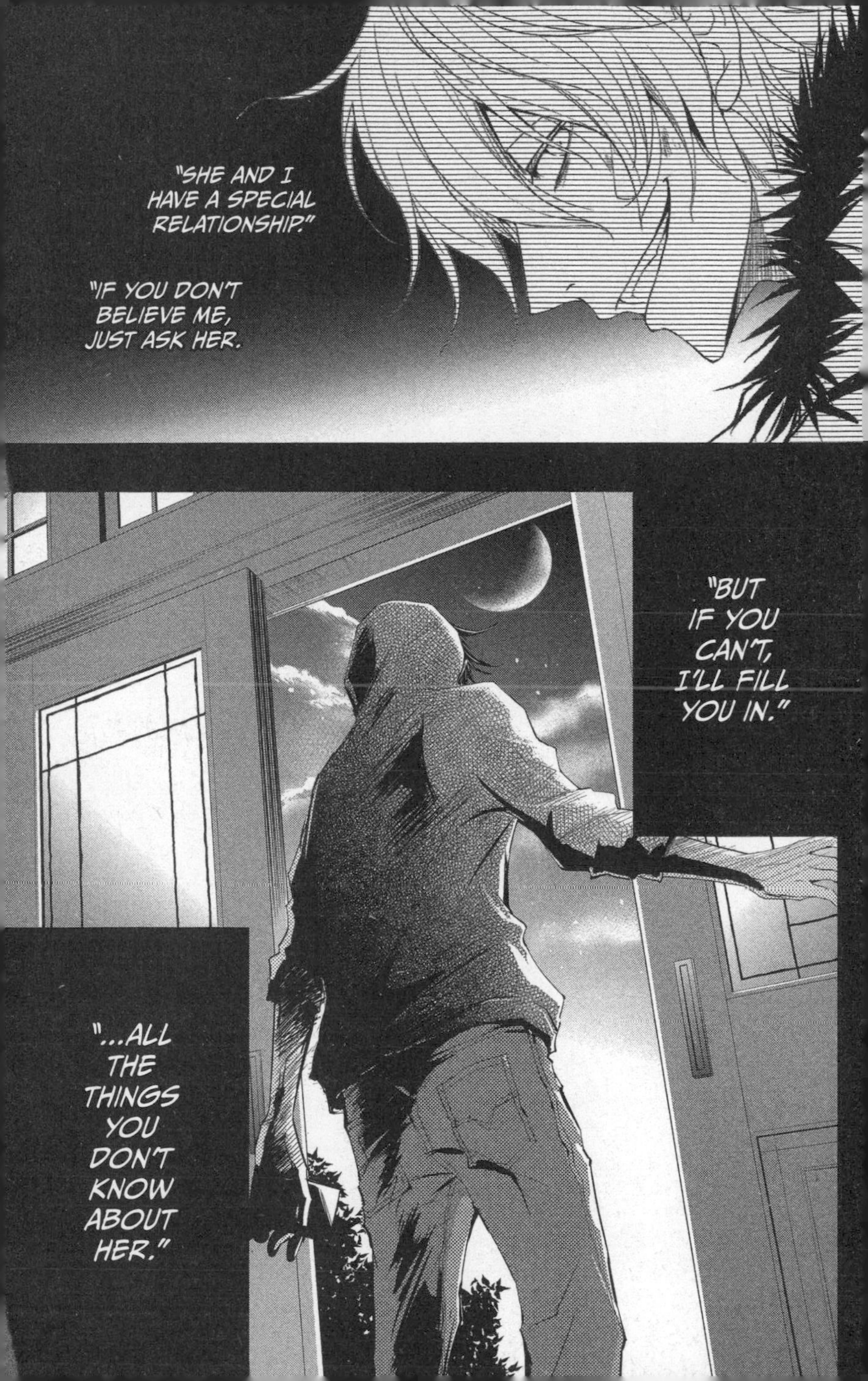
"SHE AND I HAVE A SPECIAL RELATIONSHIP."
"IF YOU DON'T BELIEVE ME, JUST ASK HER.
"BUT IF YOU CAN'T, I'LL FILL YOU IN."
"...ALL THE THINGS YOU DON'T KNOW ABOUT HER."

MONTHLY BETSUCOMI SALE DATE NOTICE ON TWITTER

# CHAPTER 17

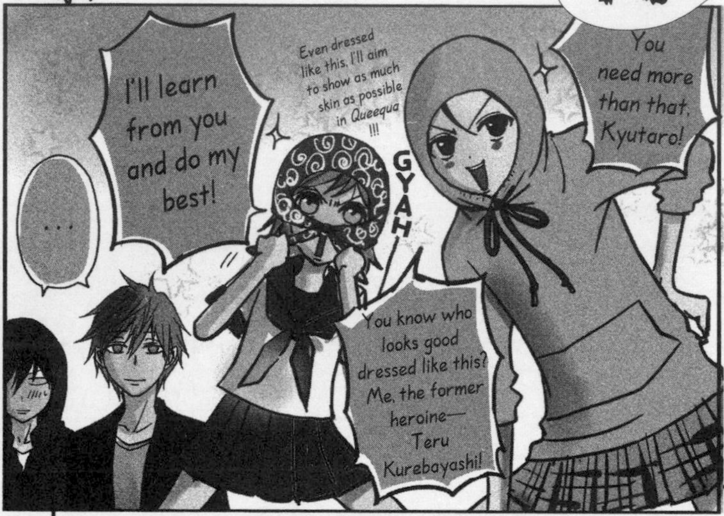
You need more than that, Kyutaro!
Even dressed like this, I'll aim to show as much skin as possible in Queequa!!!
GYAH
I'll learn from you and do my best!
...
You know who looks good dressed like this? Me, the former heroine—Teru Kurebayashi!

**WHAT'S UP IN *QUEEN'S QUALITY* THIS MONTH?**

(1) FUMI, THAT BANDANA LOOKS GOOD ON YOU.
(2) WHY, KYUTARO! YOU LOOK GOOD IN THAT PARKA TOO. MAYBE YOU SHOULD ALWAYS WEAR IT. I'M SAYING THAT BECAUSE IT'S EASIER FOR ME, THOUGH—IT MEANS I DON'T HAVE TO DRAW YOUR HEAD AND NECK.
(3) YOU'RE SUCH A MASOCHIST, KYUTARO. DID YOU KNOW THAT?

WE EVEN HAVE A CHAINSAW IN CHAPTER 17!

I enjoy your comments on Twitter, but I love receiving letters too.

Your words are treasures that invigorate me. Thank you for them.

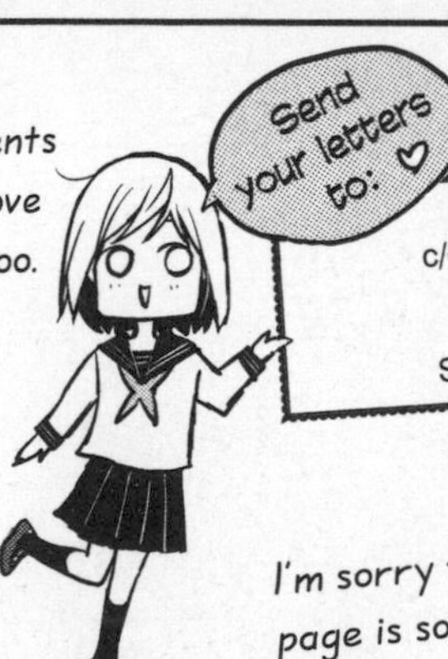
Send your letters to: ♡

Kyousuke Motomi
c/o Queen's Quality Editor
VIZ Media
P.O. Box 77010
San Francisco, CA 94107

I'm sorry that this page is so silly...

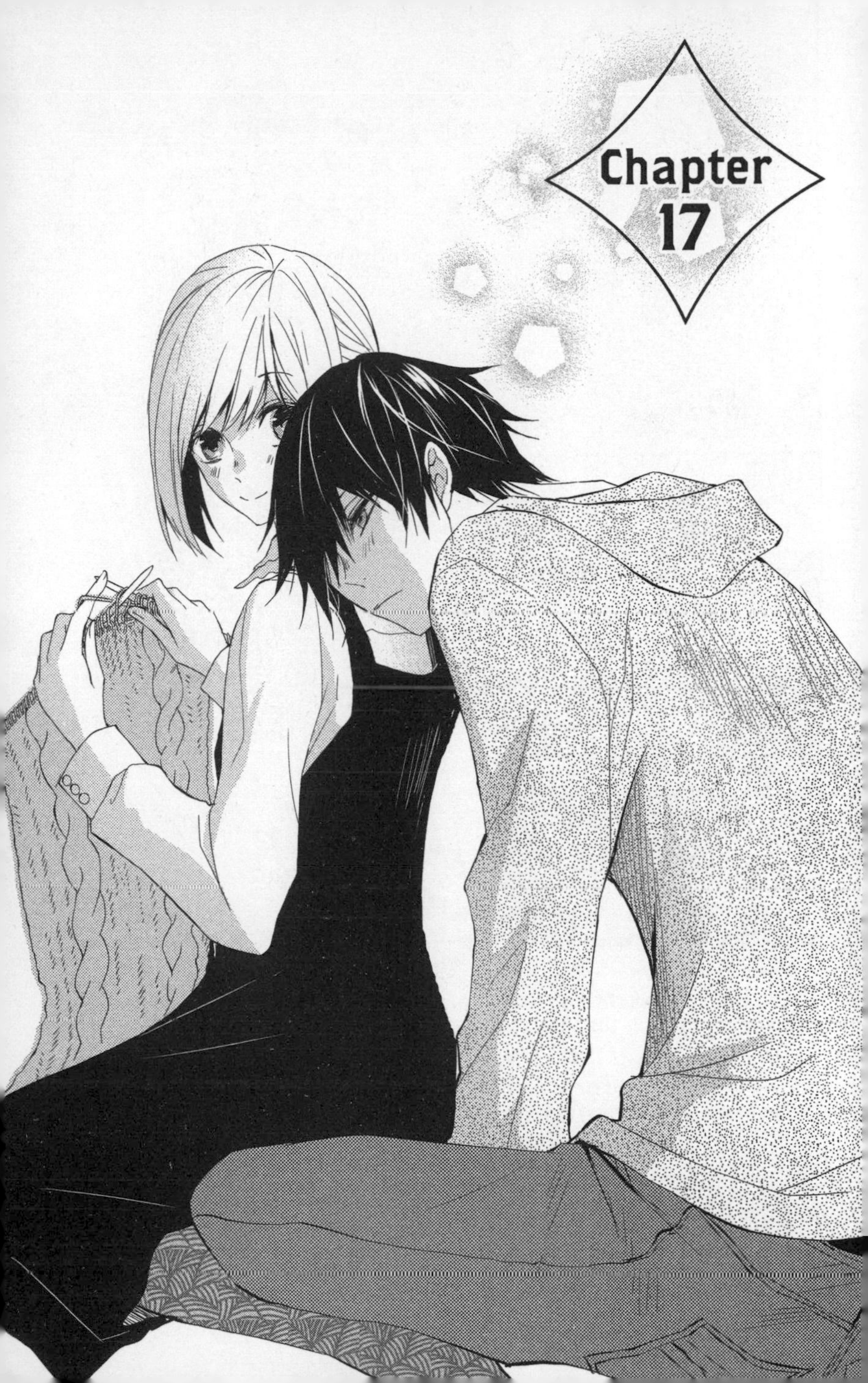
Chapter
17

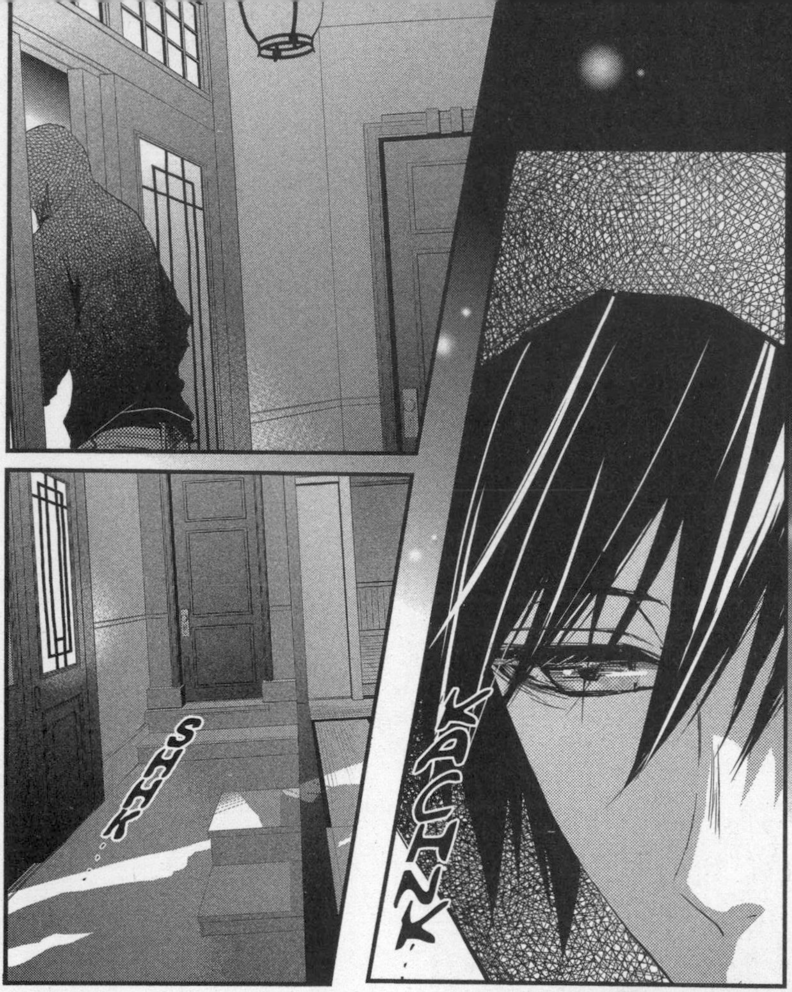
KACHUNK...
SHHK

I have yet to try that frappuccino at StXXXXXks. It looks so delicious, and I really want to taste it, but what's the right way to go about it? Do you eat that fluffy stuff on top? Stir it in? When do you stir it in? Can I take off the lid? Do I leave it and paddle the straw through the hole like an oar?

Yes, I do tend to overthink things. I'm a noncompoop too.

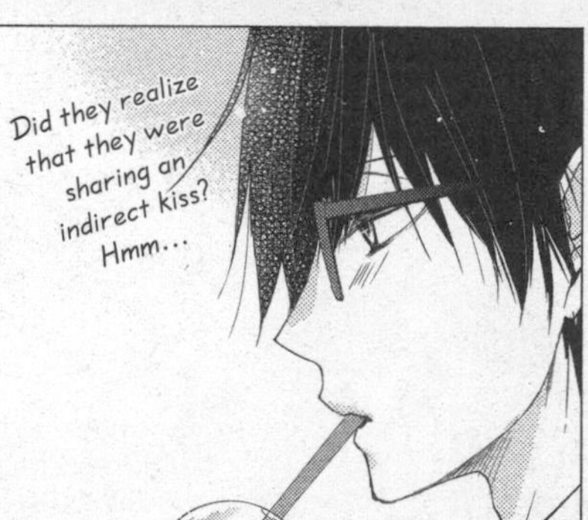
Did they realize that they were sharing an indirect kiss? Hmm...

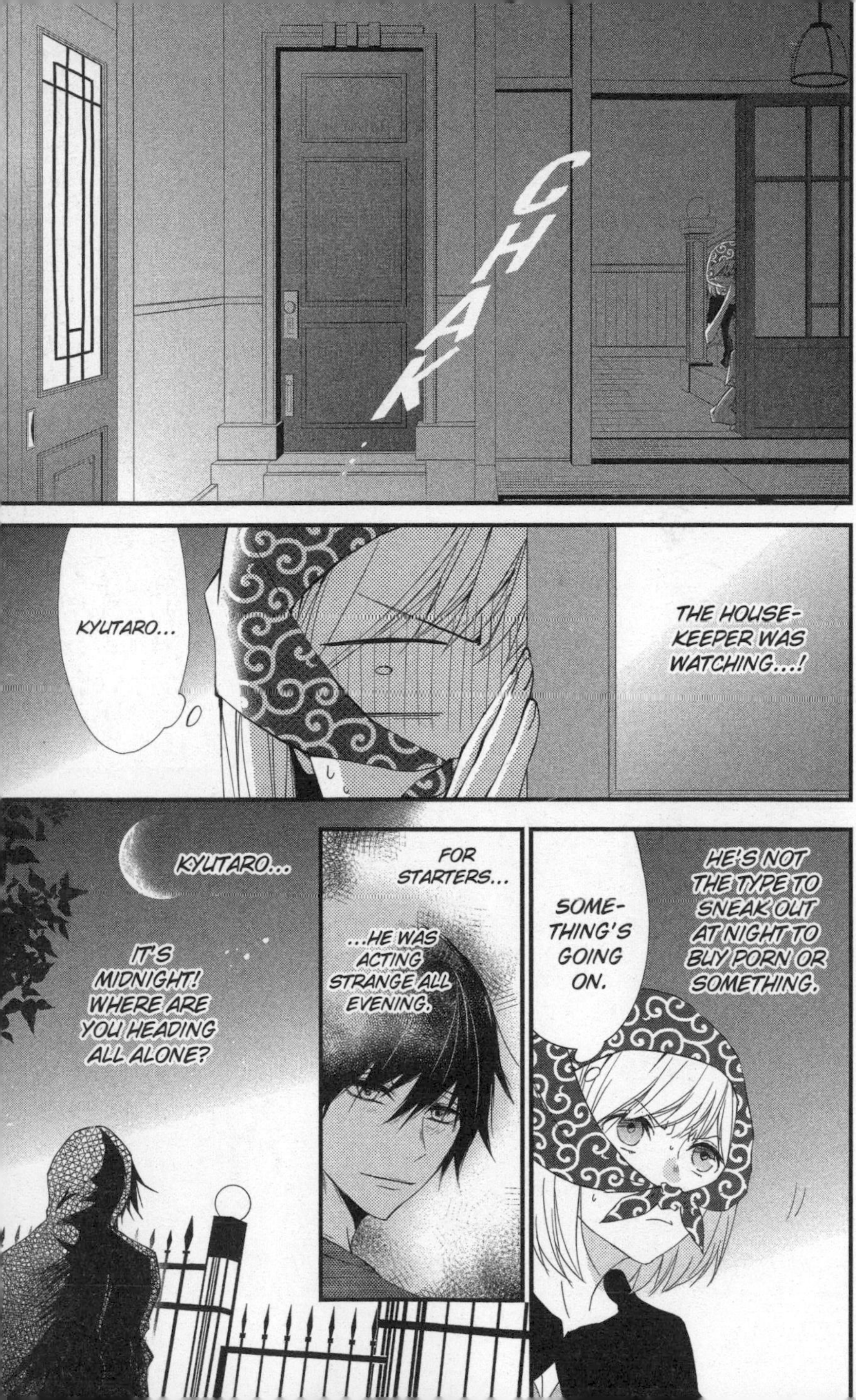
CHAK
THE HOUSE-KEEPER WAS WATCHING...!
KYUTARO...
HE'S NOT THE TYPE TO SNEAK OUT AT NIGHT TO BUY PORN OR SOMETHING.
SOME-THING'S GOING ON.
FOR STARTERS...
...HE WAS ACTING STRANGE ALL EVENING.
KYUTARO...
IT'S MIDNIGHT! WHERE ARE YOU HEADING ALL ALONE?

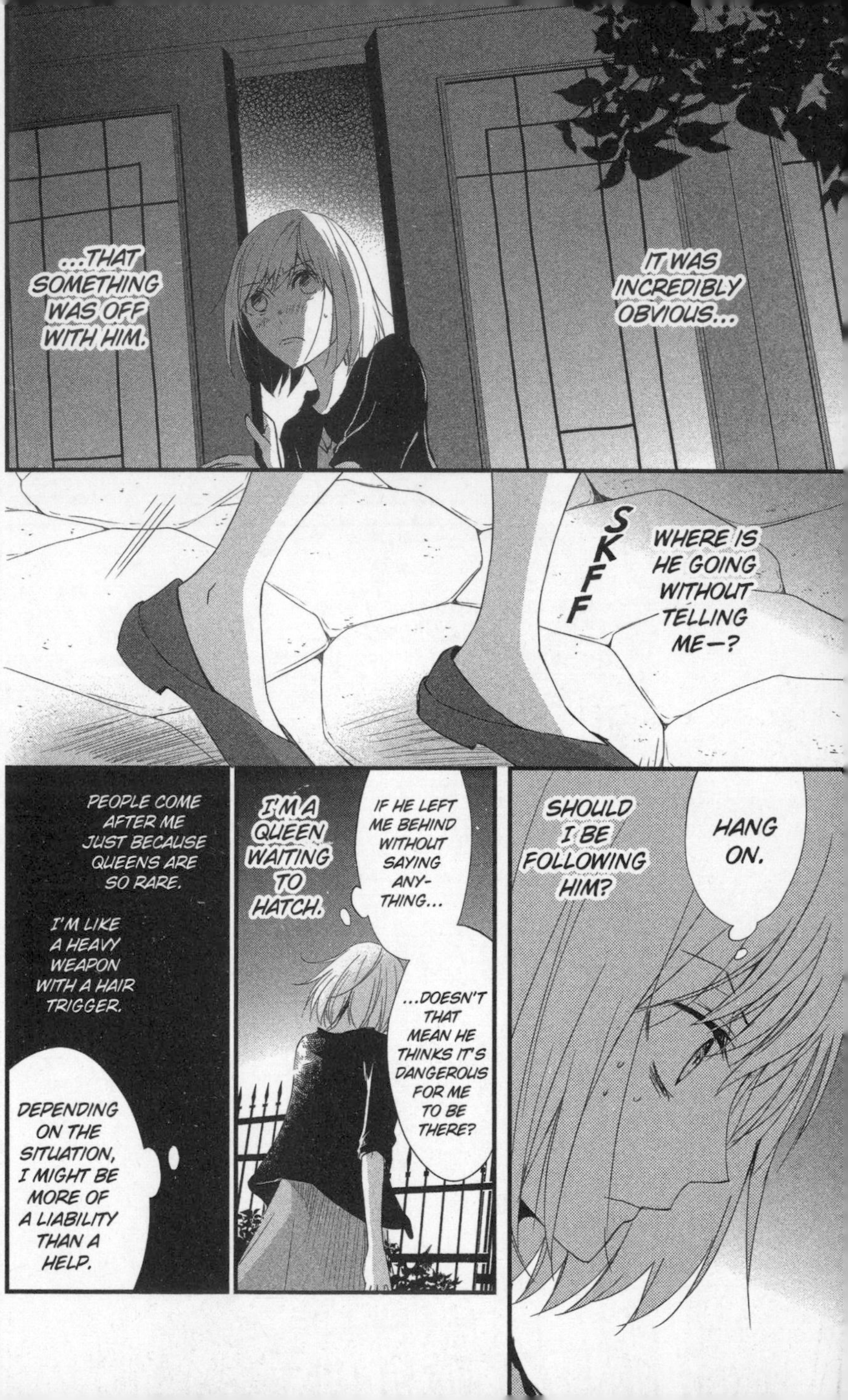
IT WAS INCREDIBLY OBVIOUS...
...THAT SOMETHING WAS OFF WITH HIM.
SKFF
WHERE IS HE GOING WITHOUT TELLING ME—?
HANG ON.
SHOULD I BE FOLLOWING HIM?
IF HE LEFT ME BEHIND WITHOUT SAYING ANY-THING...
...DOESN'T THAT MEAN HE THINKS IT'S DANGEROUS FOR ME TO BE THERE?
I'M A QUEEN WAITING TO HATCH.
PEOPLE COME AFTER ME JUST BECAUSE QUEENS ARE SO RARE.
I'M LIKE A HEAVY WEAPON WITH A HAIR TRIGGER.
DEPENDING ON THE SITUATION, I MIGHT BE MORE OF A LIABILITY THAN A HELP.

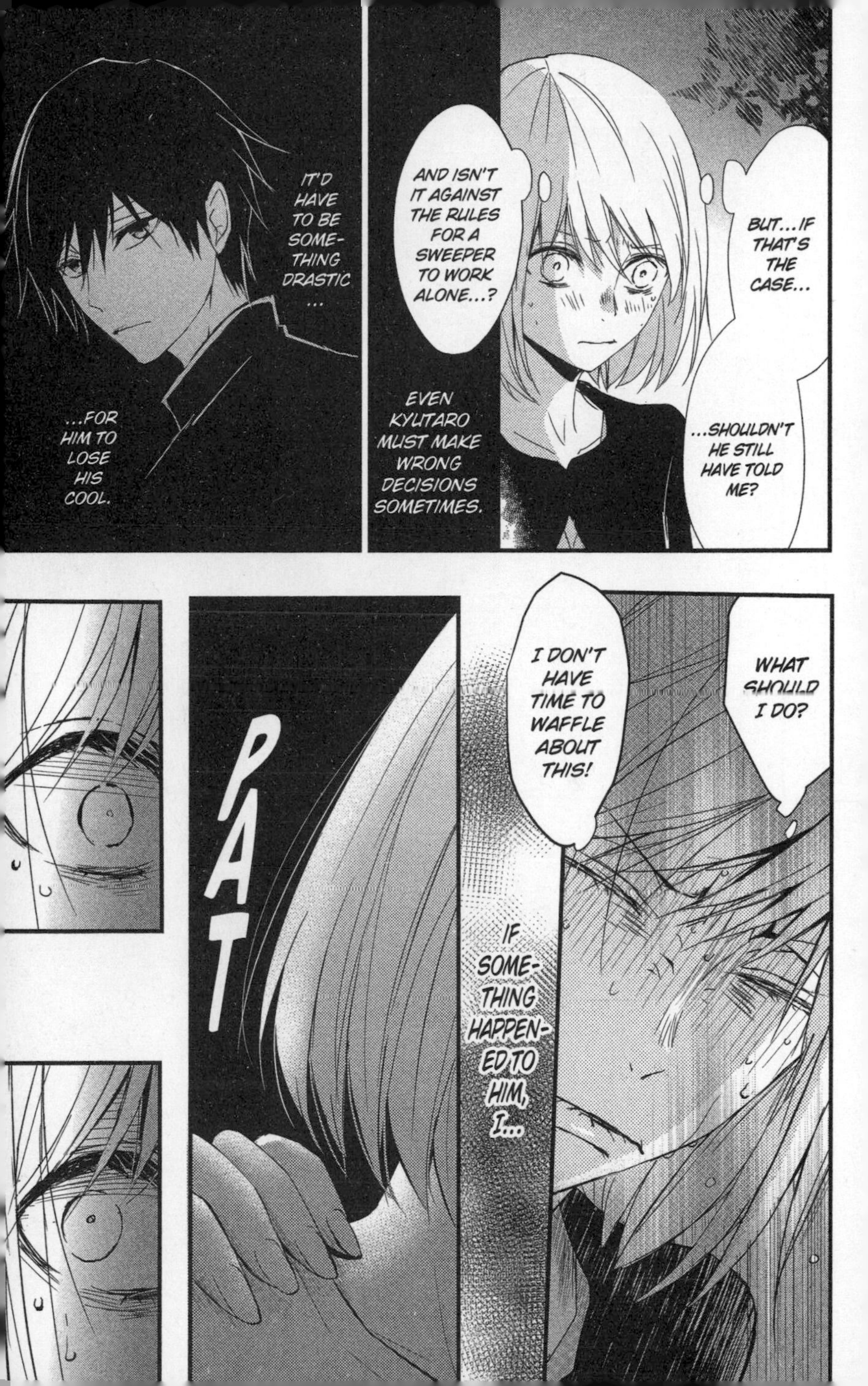
BUT... IF THAT'S THE CASE...
...SHOULDN'T HE STILL HAVE TOLD ME?
AND ISN'T IT AGAINST THE RULES FOR A SWEEPER TO WORK ALONE...?
EVEN KYUTARO MUST MAKE WRONG DECISIONS SOMETIMES.
IT'D HAVE TO BE SOMETHING DRASTIC...
...FOR HIM TO LOSE HIS COOL.
WHAT SHOULD I DO?
I DON'T HAVE TIME TO WAFFLE ABOUT THIS!
IF SOMETHING HAPPENED TO HIM, I...
PAT

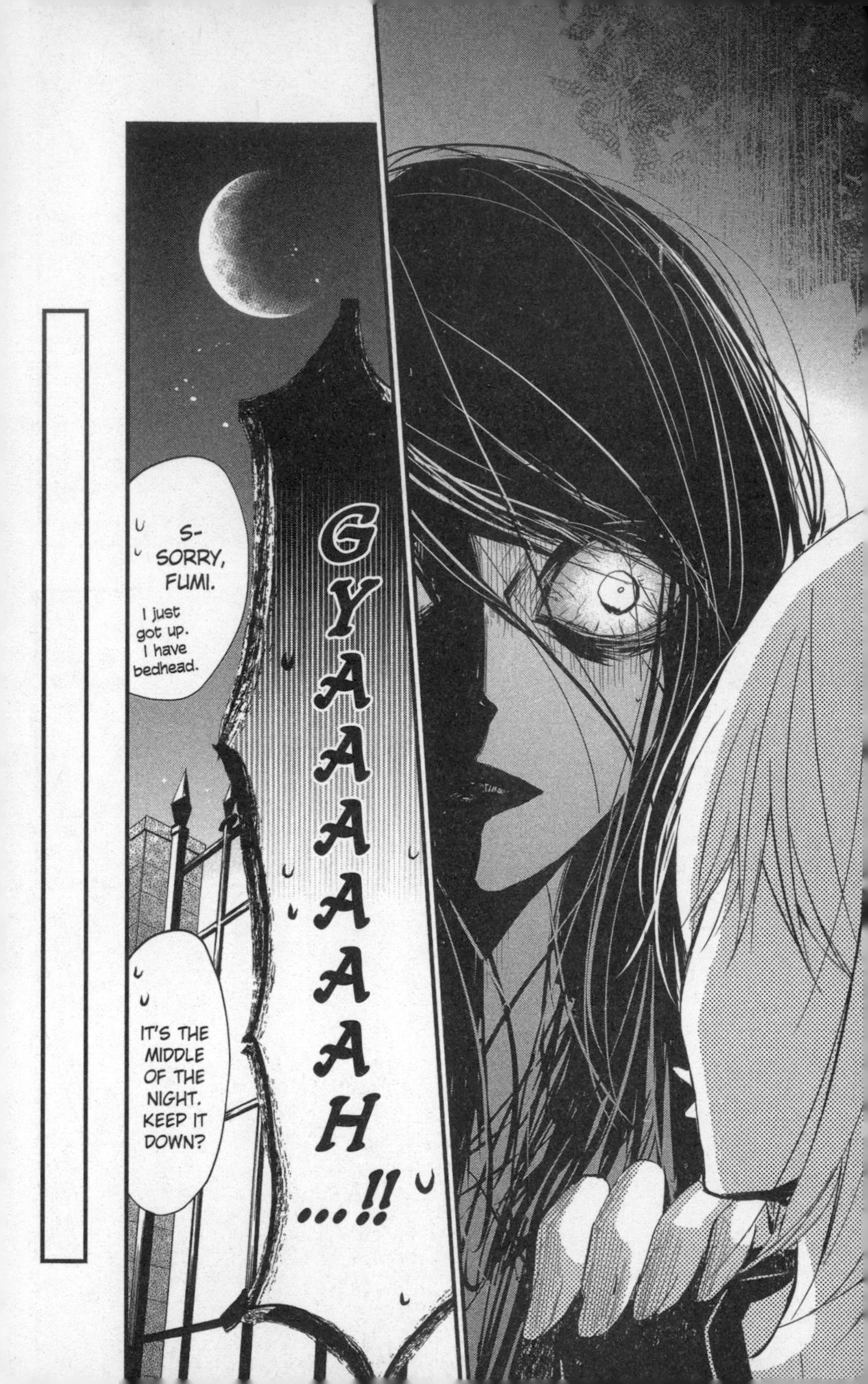
GYAAAAAAH...!!
S-SORRY, FUMI.
I just got up. I have bedhead.
IT'S THE MIDDLE OF THE NIGHT. KEEP IT DOWN?

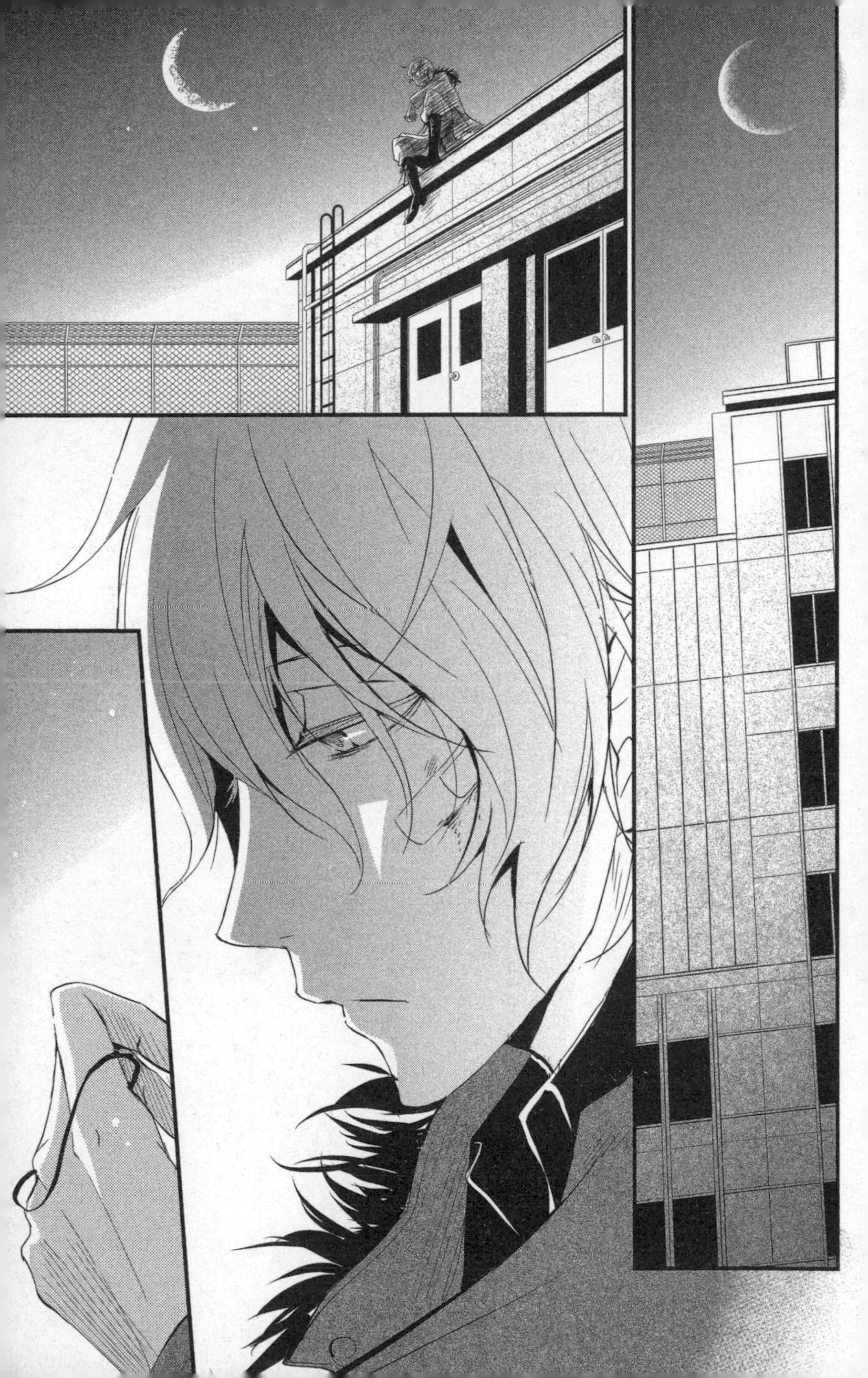

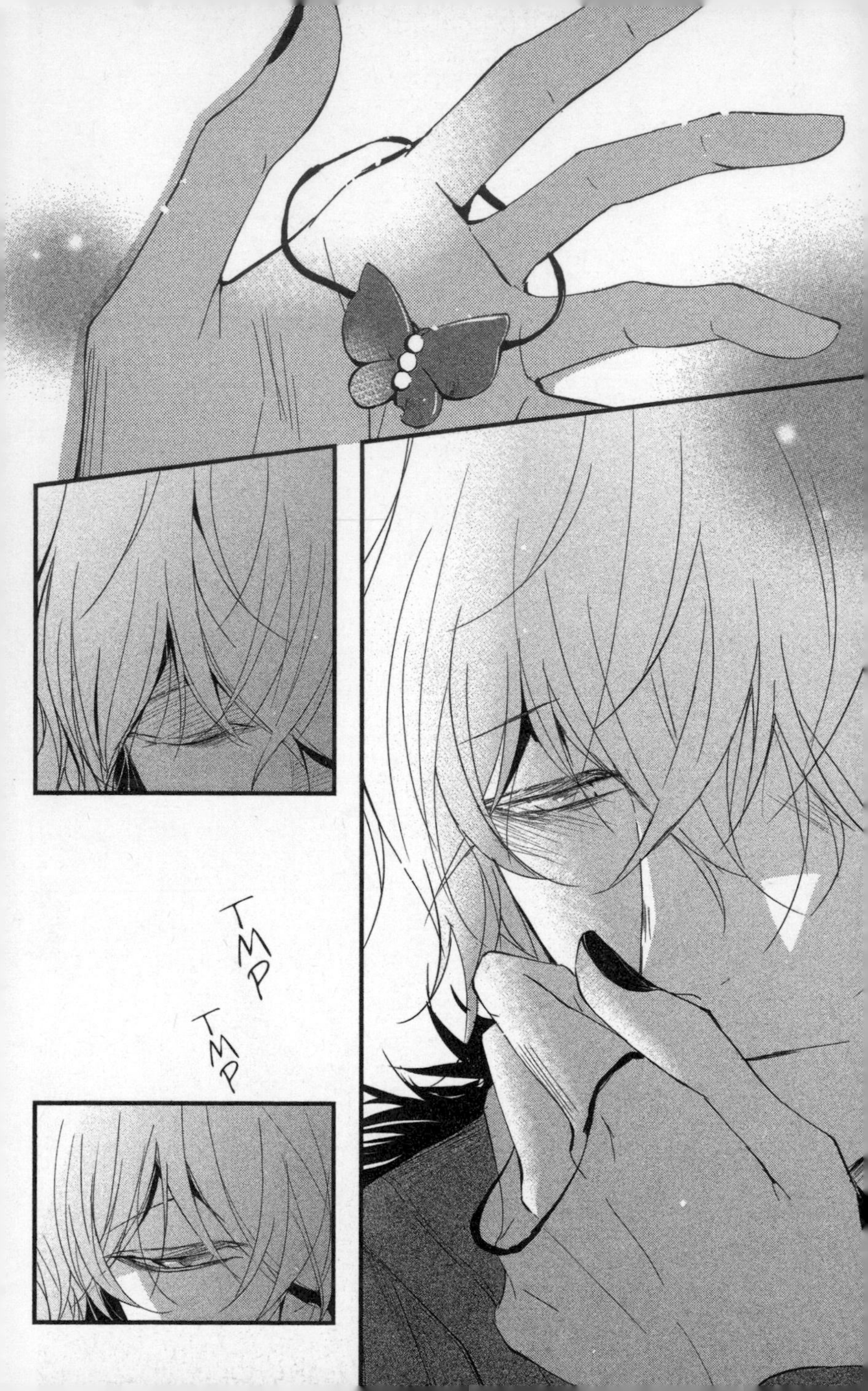
TMP
TMP

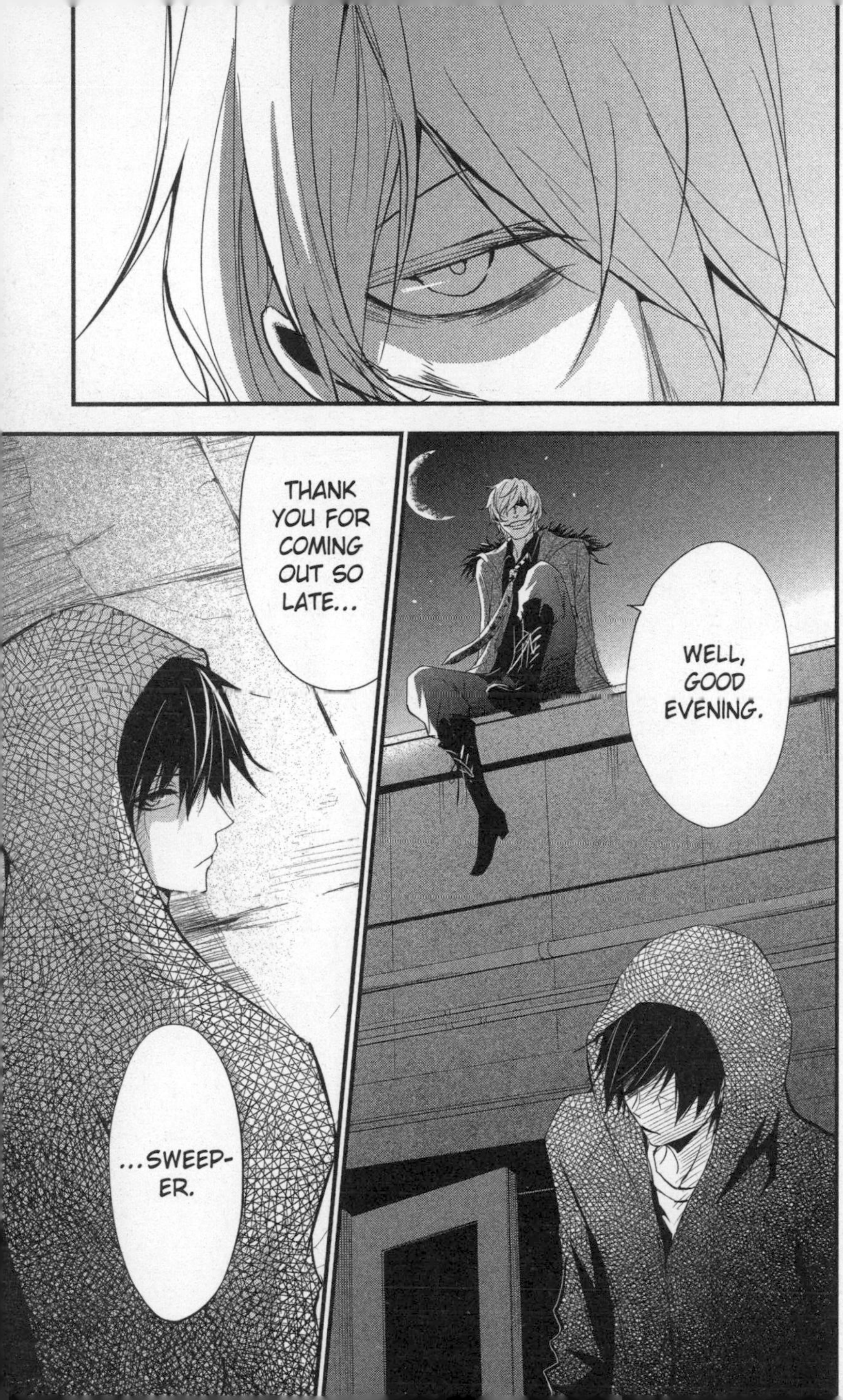
WELL, GOOD EVENING.
THANK YOU FOR COMING OUT SO LATE...
...SWEEPER.

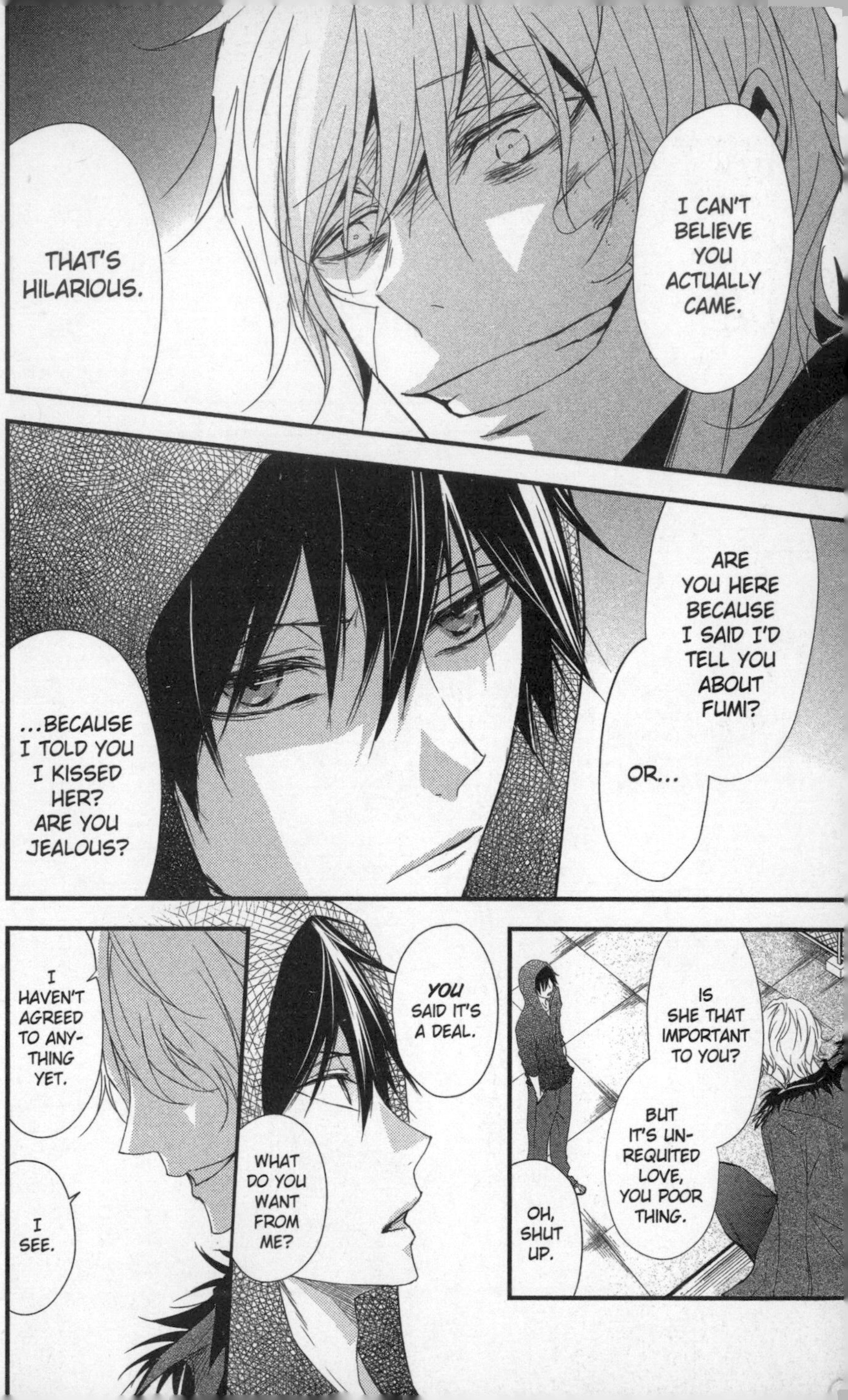
I CAN'T BELIEVE YOU ACTUALLY CAME.
THAT'S HILARIOUS.
ARE YOU HERE BECAUSE I SAID I'D TELL YOU ABOUT FUMI?
OR...
...BECAUSE I TOLD YOU I KISSED HER? ARE YOU JEALOUS?
IS SHE THAT IMPORTANT TO YOU?
BUT IT'S UN-REQUITED LOVE, YOU POOR THING.
OH, SHUT UP.
*YOU* SAID IT'S A DEAL.
WHAT DO YOU WANT FROM ME?
I HAVEN'T AGREED TO ANY-THING YET.
I SEE.

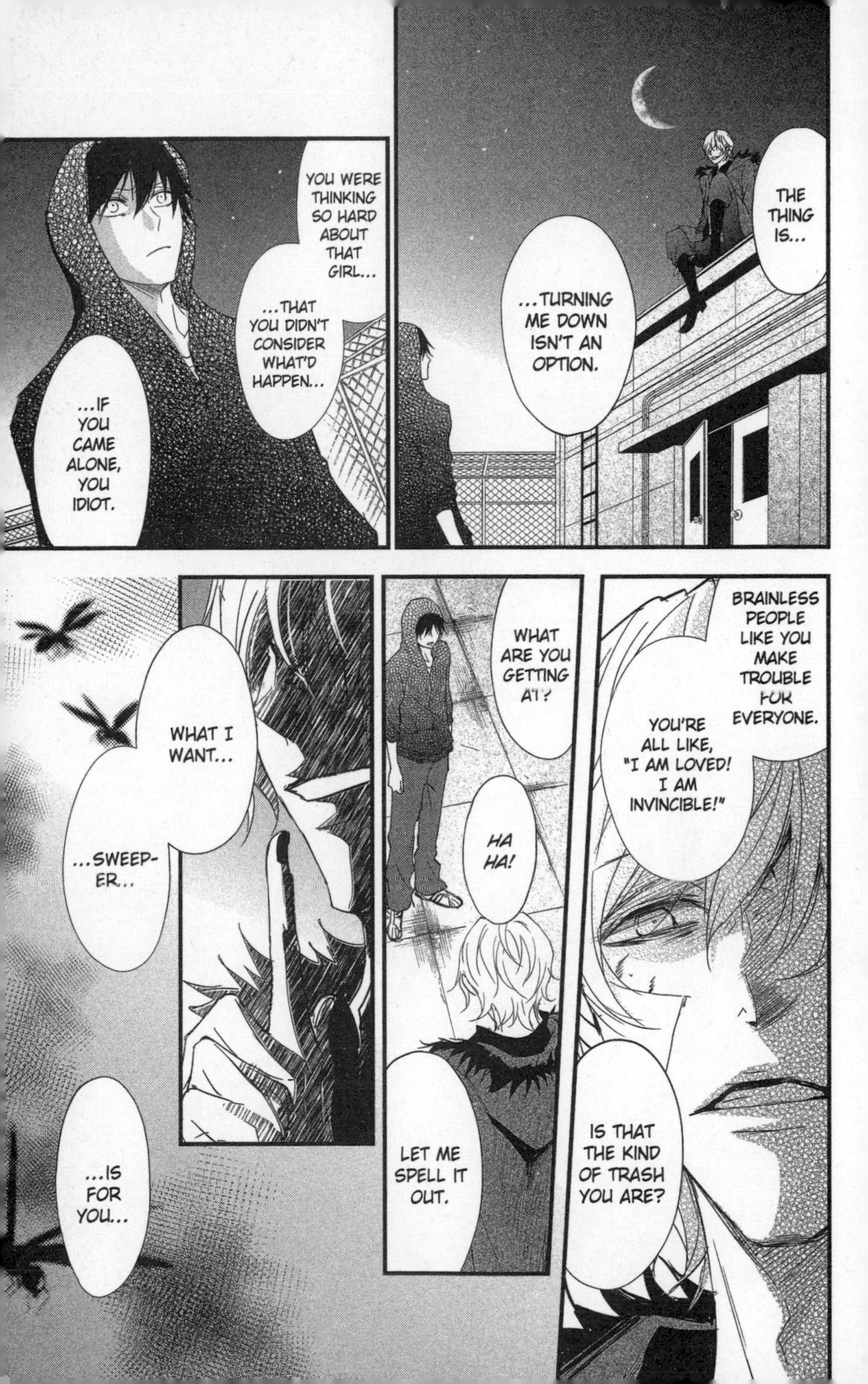
THE THING IS...
...TURNING ME DOWN ISN'T AN OPTION.
YOU WERE THINKING SO HARD ABOUT THAT GIRL...
...THAT YOU DIDN'T CONSIDER WHAT'D HAPPEN...
...IF YOU CAME ALONE, YOU IDIOT.
BRAINLESS PEOPLE LIKE YOU MAKE TROUBLE FOR EVERYONE.
YOU'RE ALL LIKE, "I AM LOVED! I AM INVINCIBLE!"
IS THAT THE KIND OF TRASH YOU ARE?
WHAT ARE YOU GETTING AT?
HA HA!
LET ME SPELL IT OUT.
WHAT I WANT...
...SWEEPER...
...IS FOR YOU...

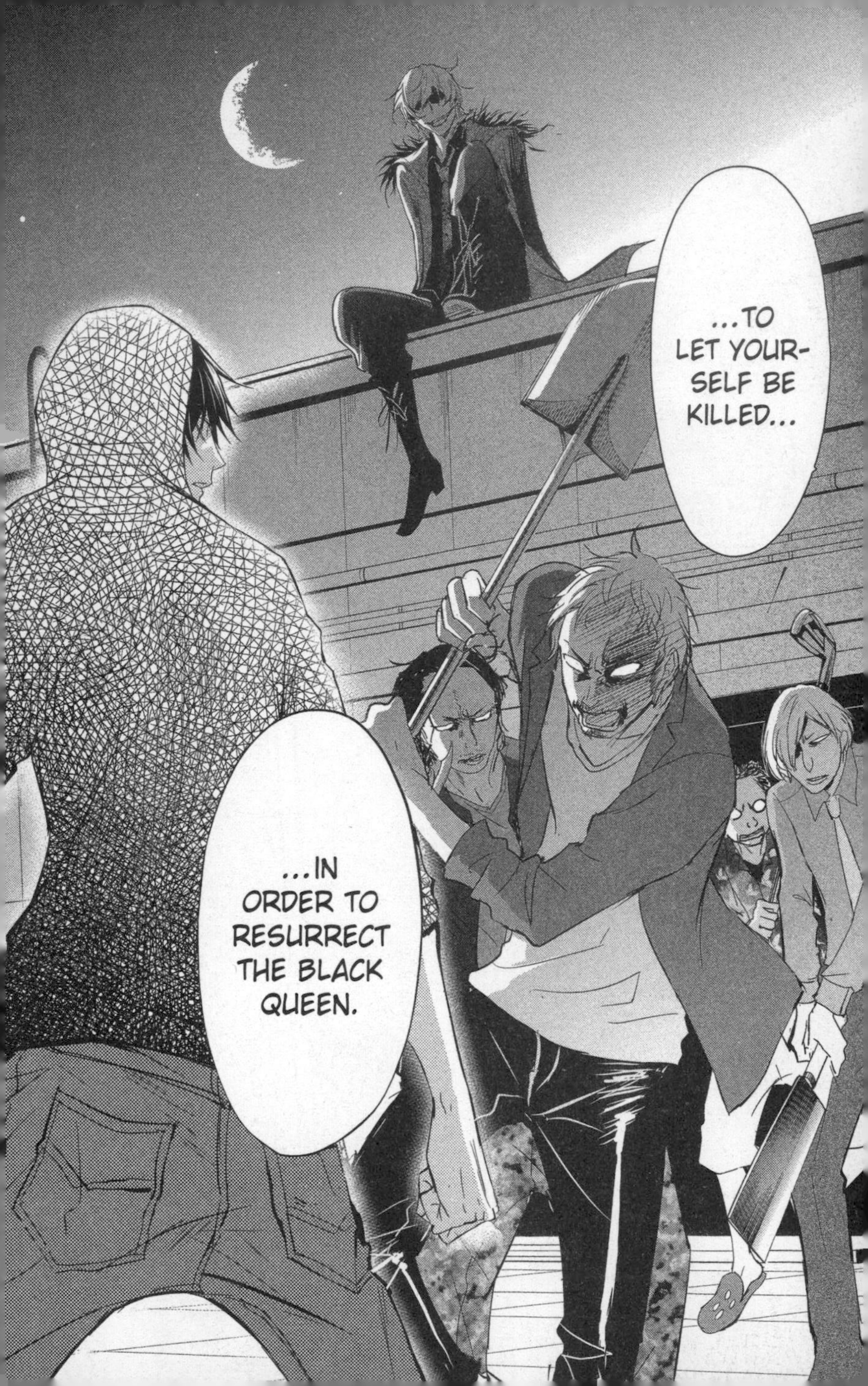
...TO LET YOUR-SELF BE KILLED...
...IN ORDER TO RESURRECT THE BLACK QUEEN.

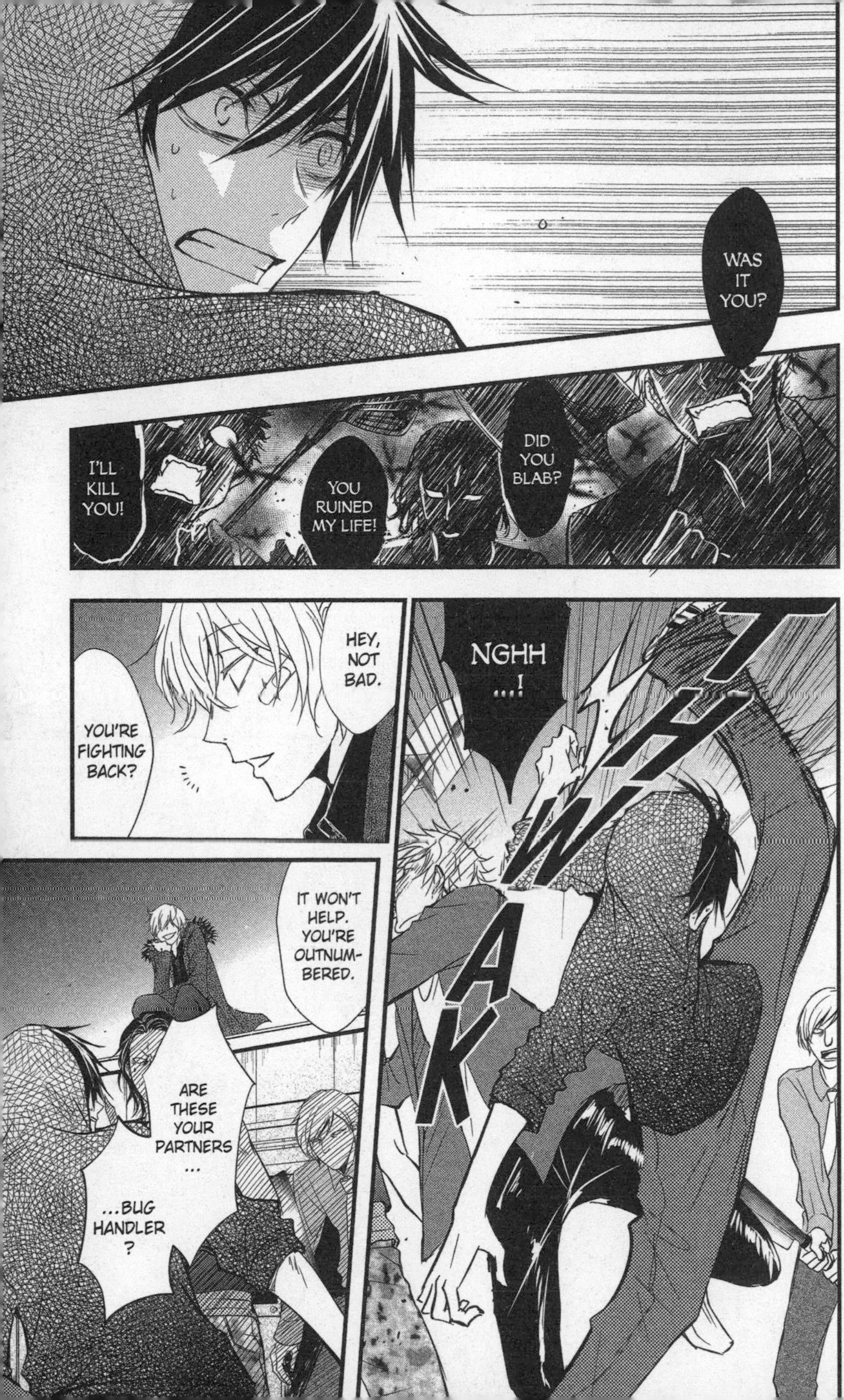
WAS IT YOU?
DID YOU BLAB?
YOU RUINED MY LIFE!
I'LL KILL YOU!
NGHH ...!
WHAK
HEY, NOT BAD.
YOU'RE FIGHTING BACK?
IT WON'T HELP. YOU'RE OUTNUM-BERED.
ARE THESE YOUR PARTNERS ...
...BUG HANDLER ?

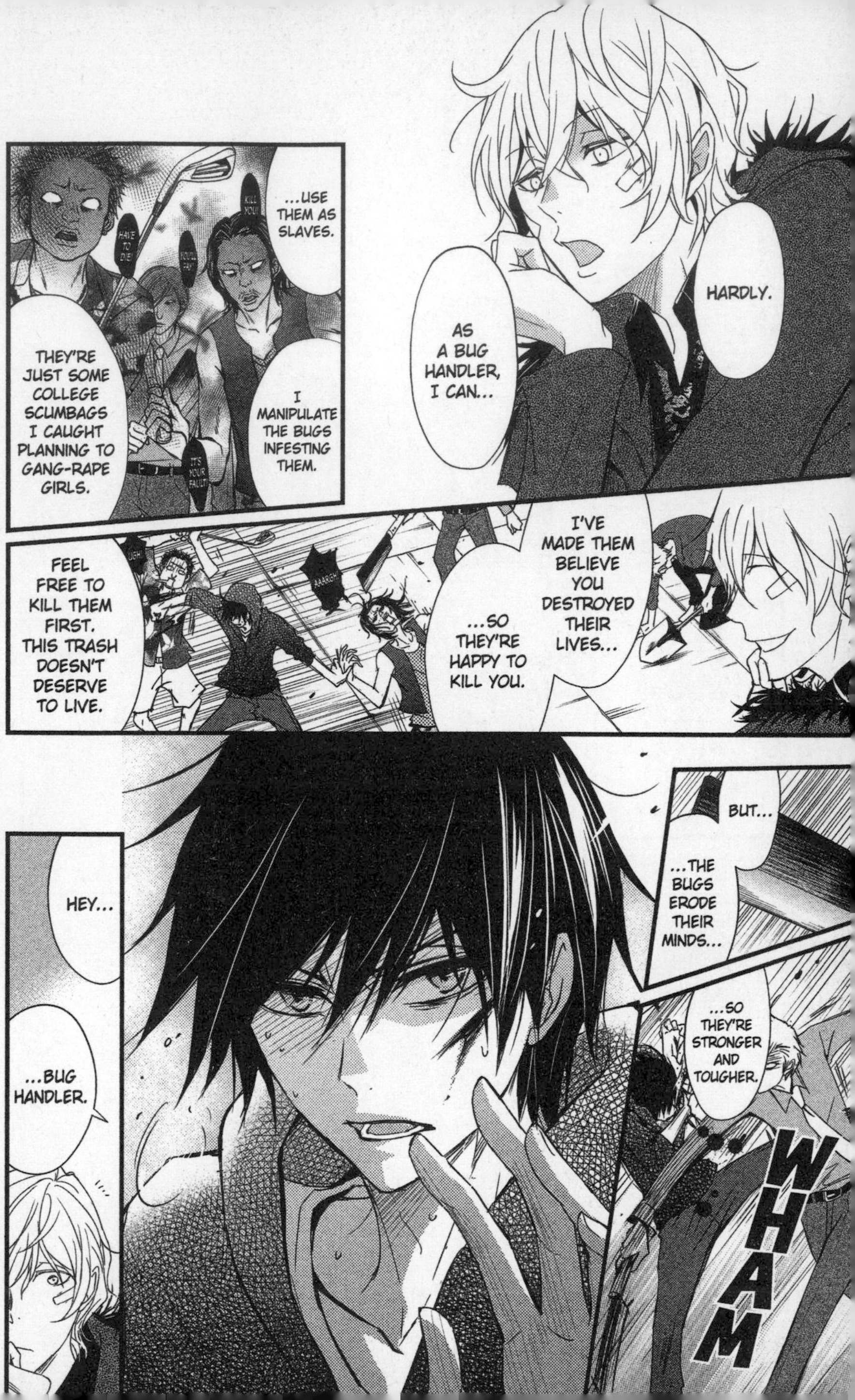

HARDLY.
AS A BUG HANDLER, I CAN...
...USE THEM AS SLAVES.
KILL YOU!
HAVE TO DIE!
YOU'LL PAY!
I MANIPULATE THE BUGS INFESTING THEM.
THEY'RE JUST SOME COLLEGE SCUMBAGS I CAUGHT PLANNING TO GANG-RAPE GIRLS.
IT'S YOUR FAULT!
I'VE MADE THEM BELIEVE YOU DESTROYED THEIR LIVES...
...SO THEY'RE HAPPY TO KILL YOU.
AAARGH!
UGH!
FEEL FREE TO KILL THEM FIRST. THIS TRASH DOESN'T DESERVE TO LIVE.
BUT...
...THE BUGS ERODE THEIR MINDS...
...SO THEY'RE STRONGER AND TOUGHER.
WHAM
HEY...
...BUG HANDLER.

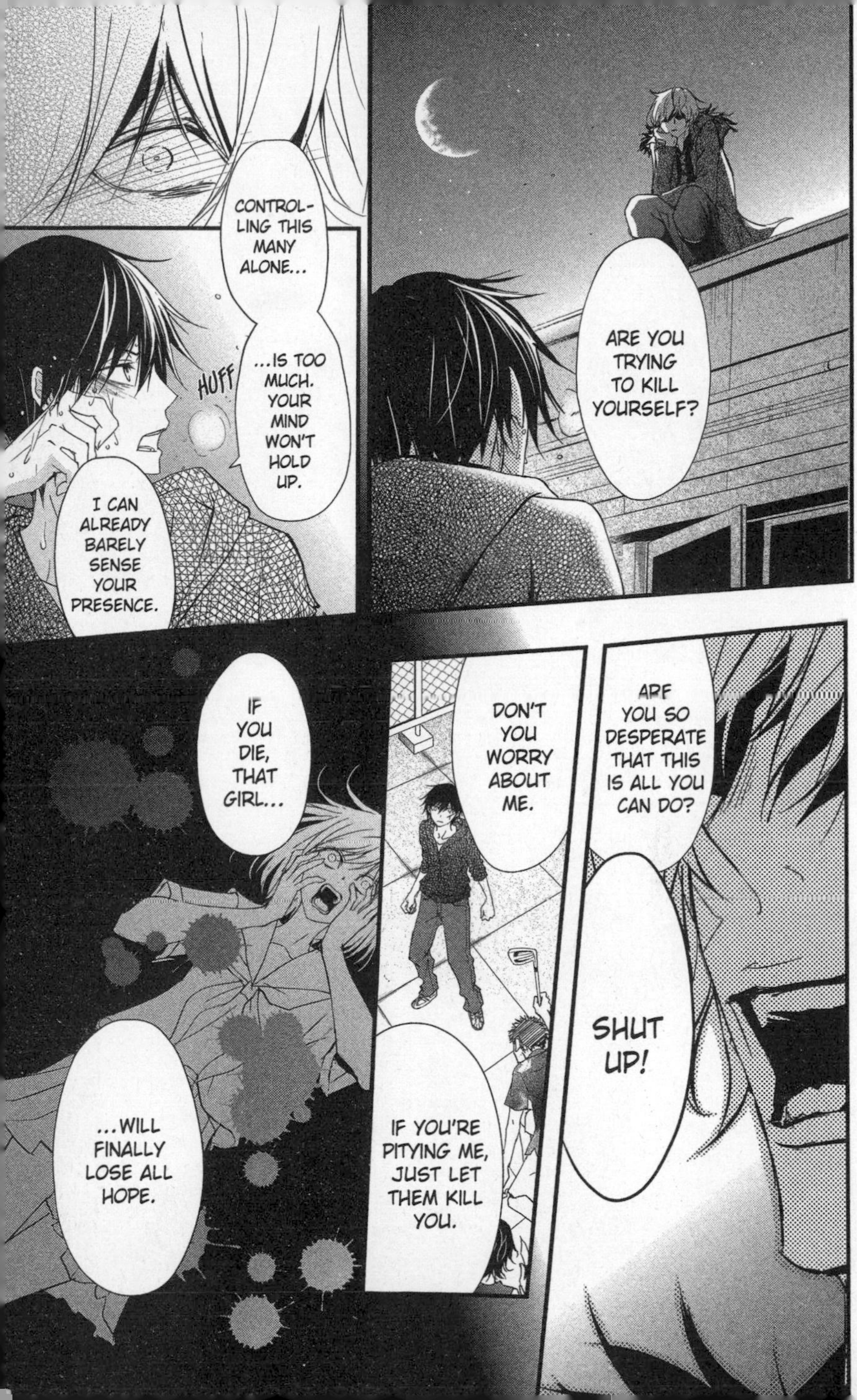
ARE YOU TRYING TO KILL YOURSELF?
CONTROL-LING THIS MANY ALONE...
...IS TOO MUCH. YOUR MIND WON'T HOLD UP.
HUFF
I CAN ALREADY BARELY SENSE YOUR PRESENCE.
ARE YOU SO DESPERATE THAT THIS IS ALL YOU CAN DO?
SHUT UP!
DON'T YOU WORRY ABOUT ME.
IF YOU'RE PITYING ME, JUST LET THEM KILL YOU.
IF YOU DIE, THAT GIRL...
...WILL FINALLY LOSE ALL HOPE.

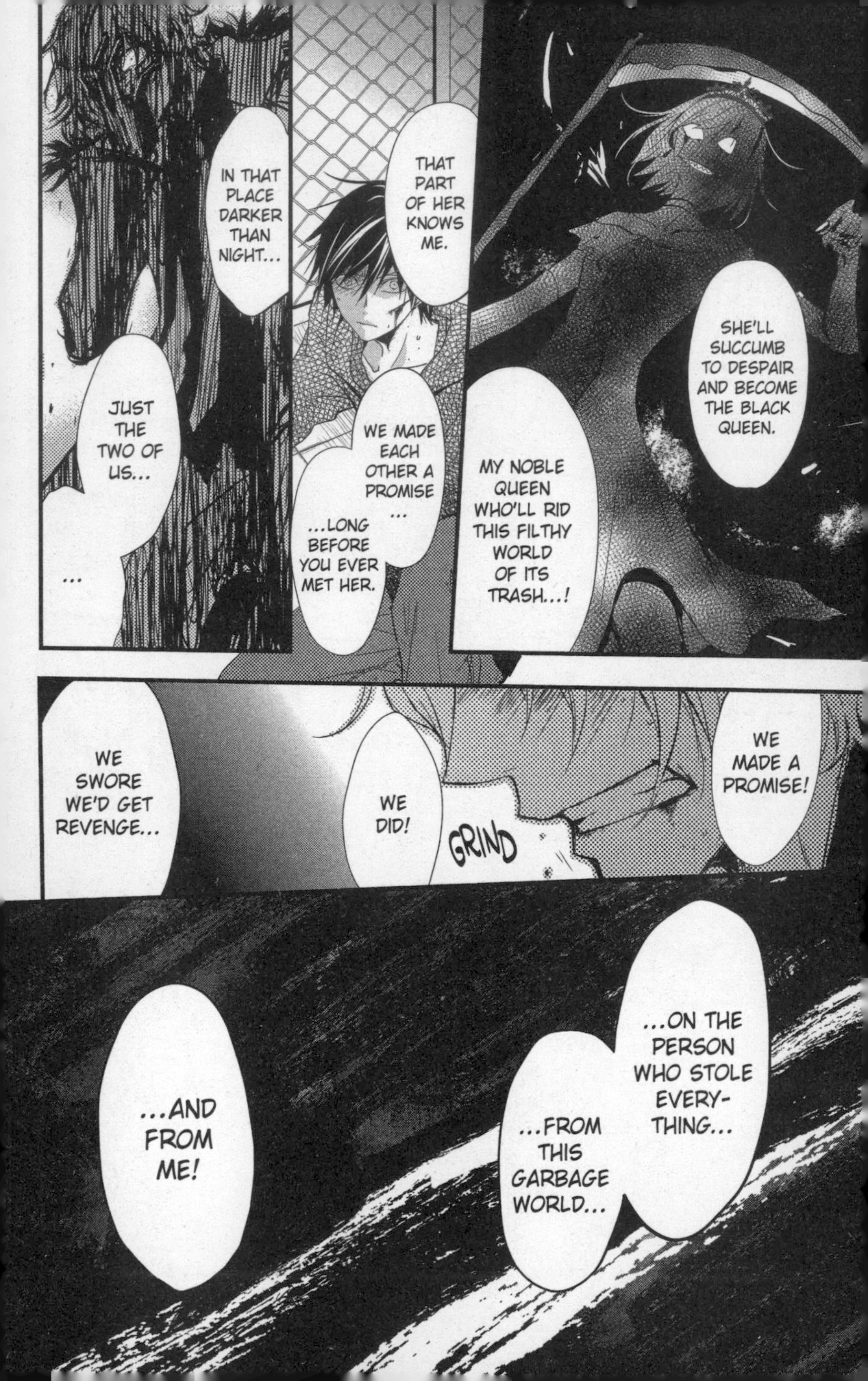
SHE'LL SUCCUMB TO DESPAIR AND BECOME THE BLACK QUEEN.
MY NOBLE QUEEN WHO'LL RID THIS FILTHY WORLD OF ITS TRASH...!
THAT PART OF HER KNOWS ME.
WE MADE EACH OTHER A PROMISE ...
...LONG BEFORE YOU EVER MET HER.
IN THAT PLACE DARKER THAN NIGHT...
JUST THE TWO OF US...
...
WE MADE A PROMISE!
WE DID!
GRIND
WE SWORE WE'D GET REVENGE...
...ON THE PERSON WHO STOLE EVERY-THING...
...FROM THIS GARBAGE WORLD...
...AND FROM ME!

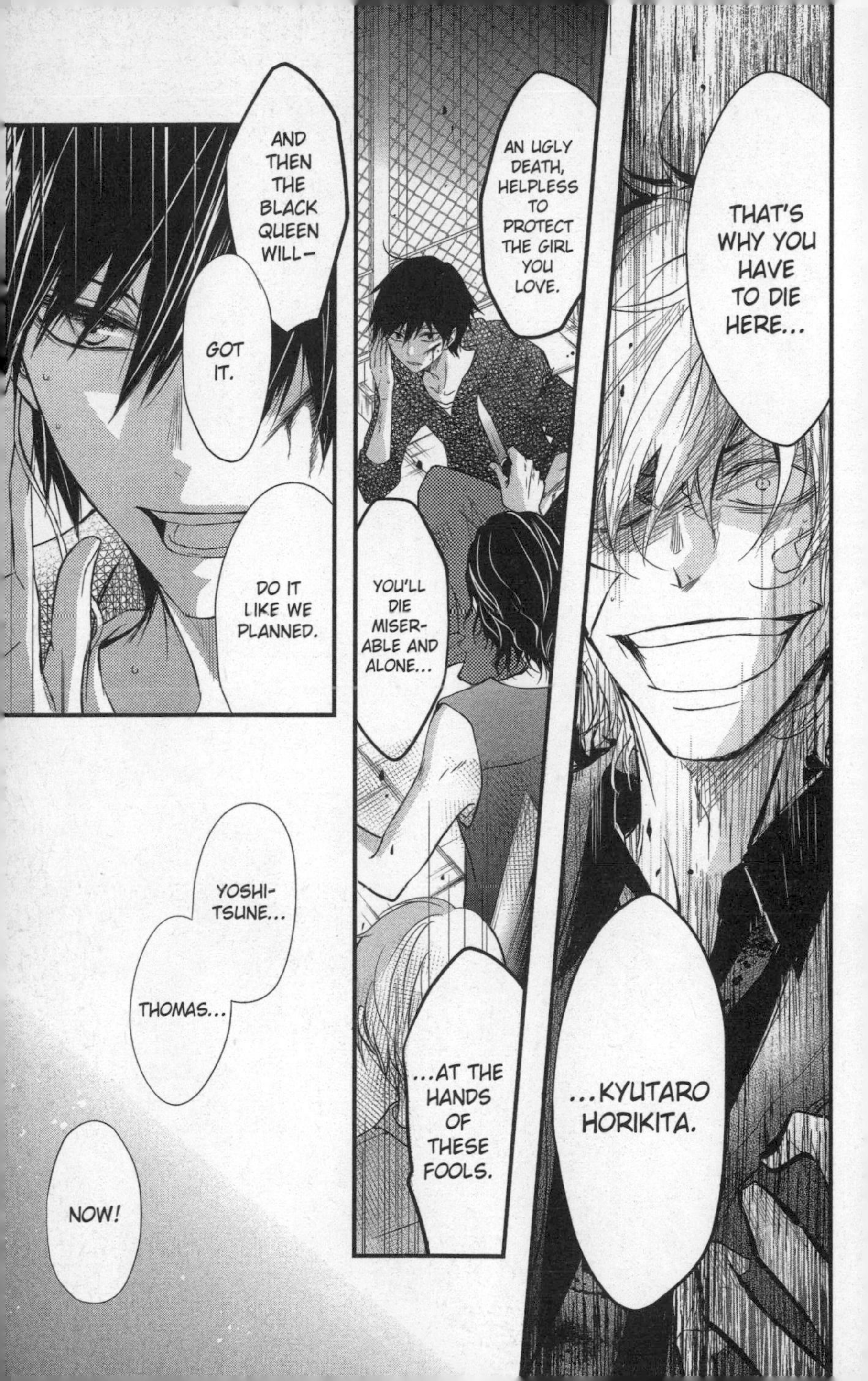
THAT'S WHY YOU HAVE TO DIE HERE...
...KYUTARO HORIKITA.
AN UGLY DEATH, HELPLESS TO PROTECT THE GIRL YOU LOVE.
YOU'LL DIE MISER-ABLE AND ALONE...
...AT THE HANDS OF THESE FOOLS.
AND THEN THE BLACK QUEEN WILL–
GOT IT.
DO IT LIKE WE PLANNED.
YOSHI-TSUNE...
THOMAS...
NOW!

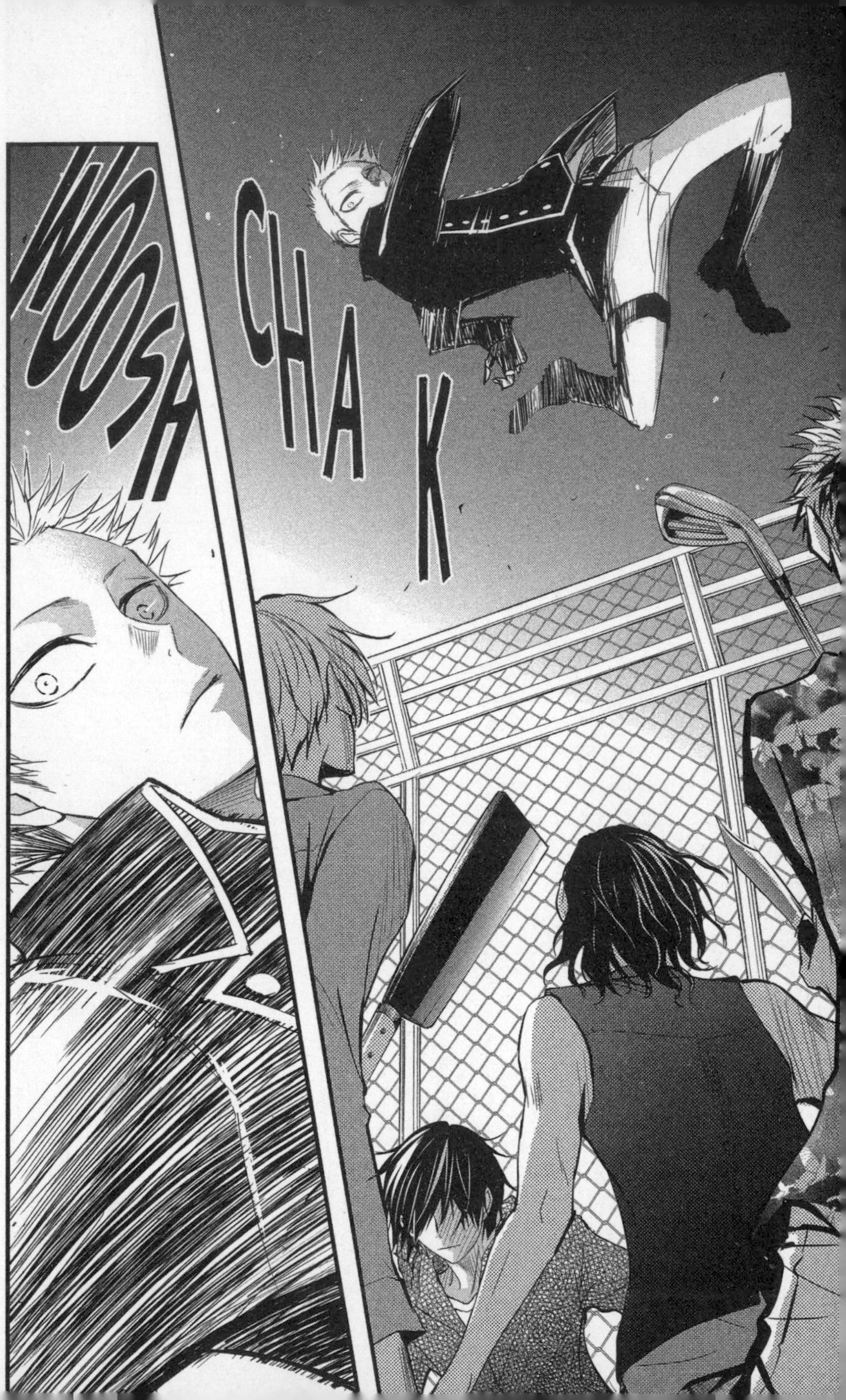
CHAK
WOOSH

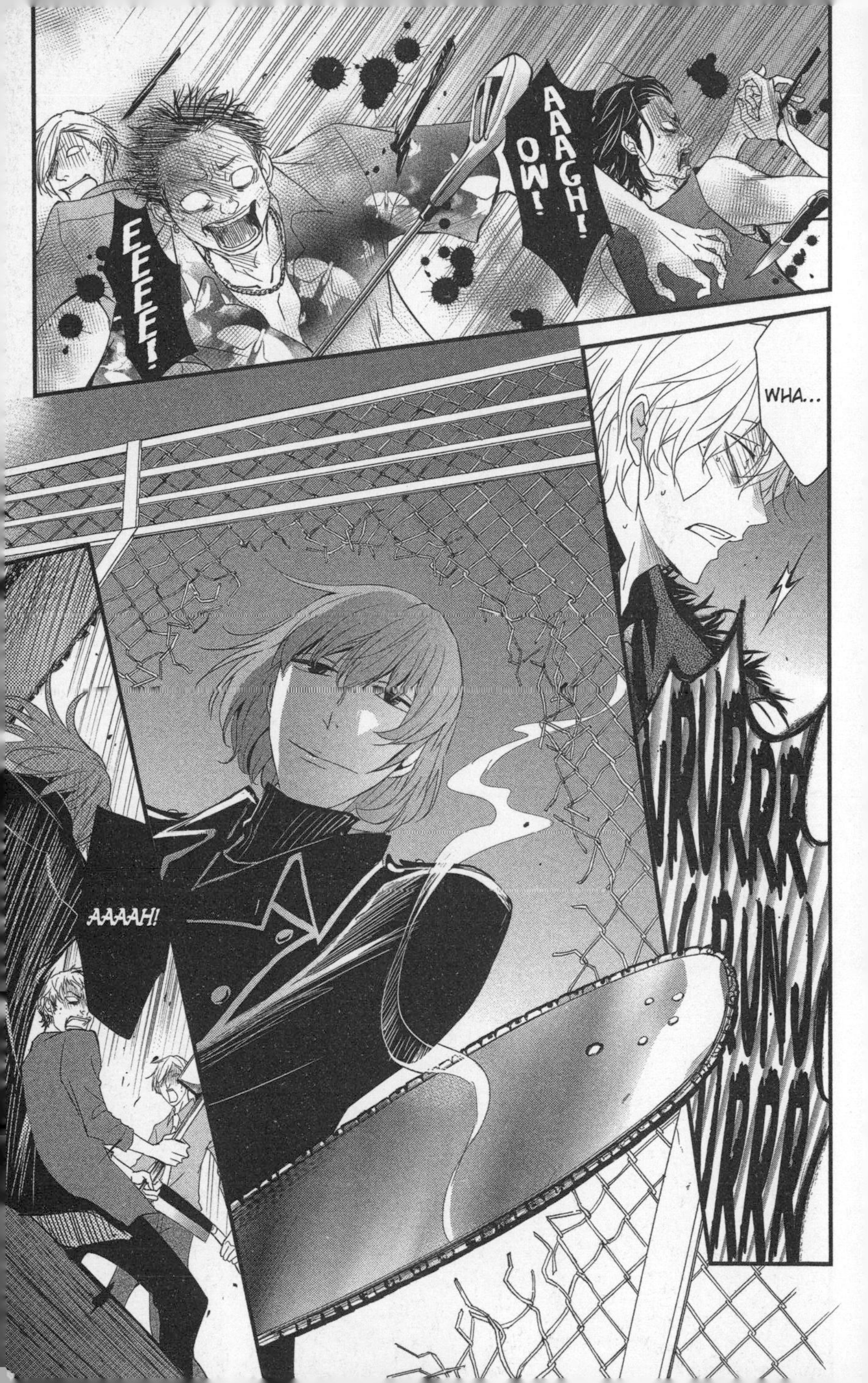
AAAGH! OW!
EEEEEE!
WHA...
VRURRR
VRRRR
AAAAH!

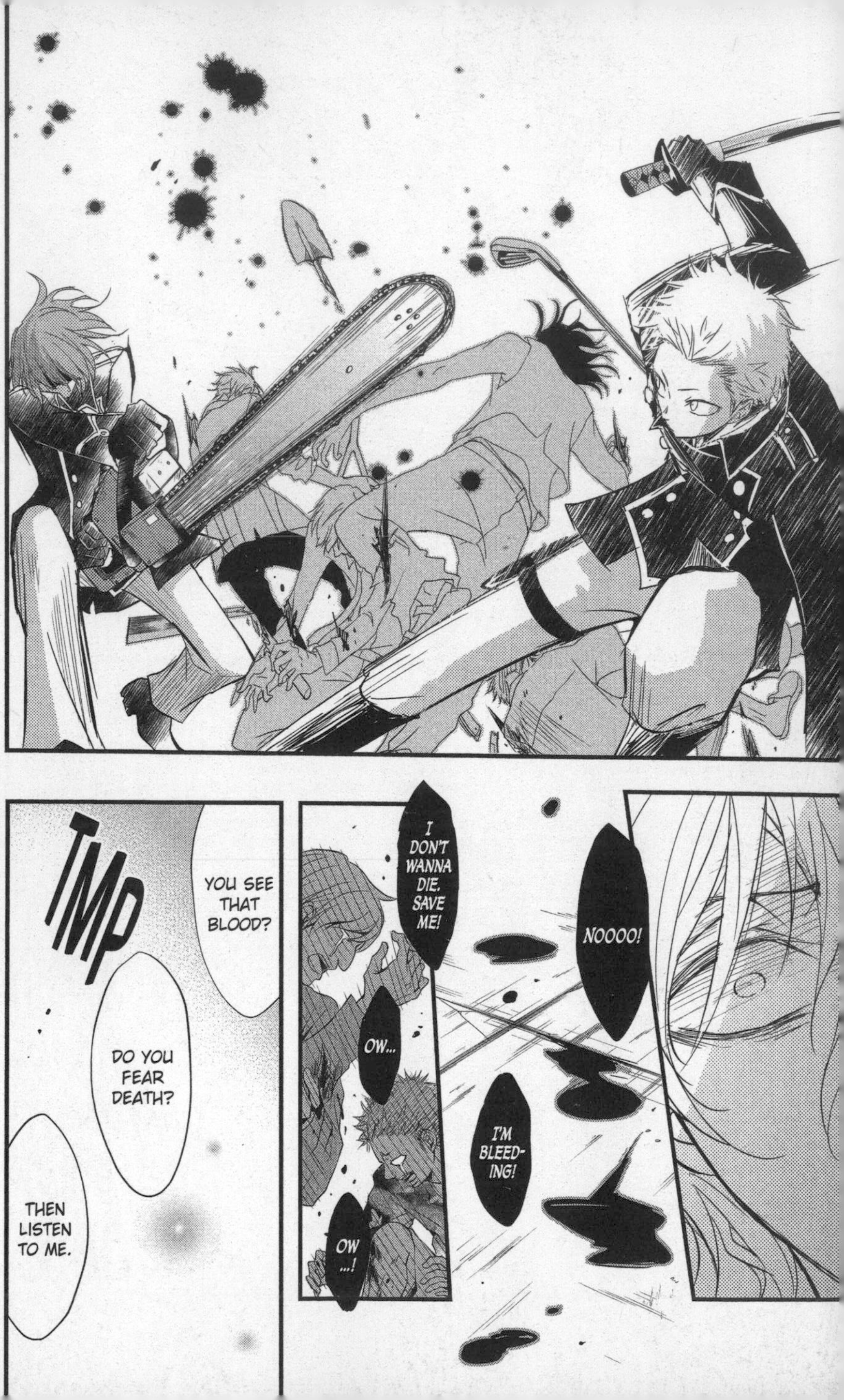
NOOOO!
I DON'T WANNA DIE. SAVE ME!
I'M BLEED-ING!
OW...
OW ...!
TMP
YOU SEE THAT BLOOD?
DO YOU FEAR DEATH?
THEN LISTEN TO ME.

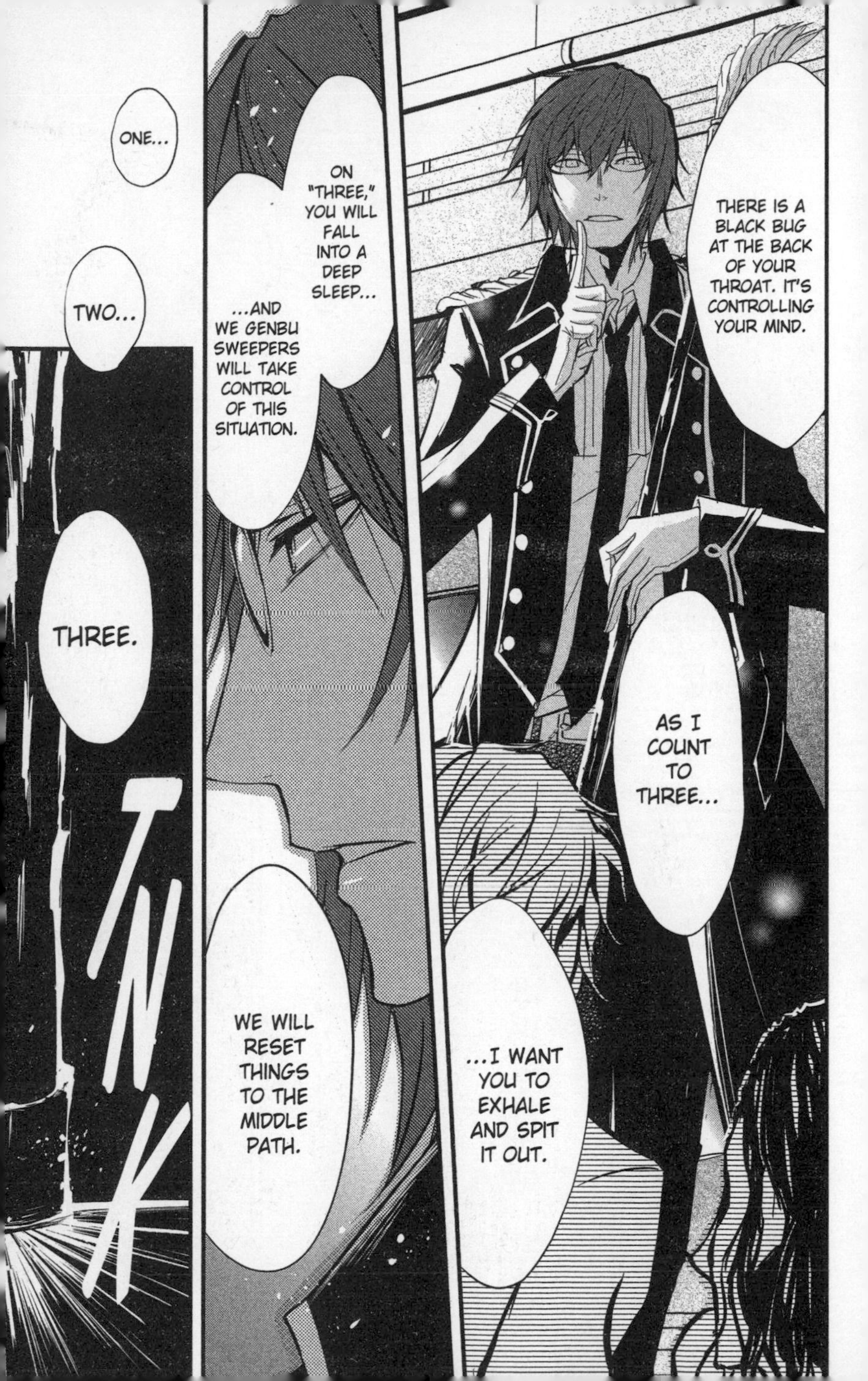
THERE IS A BLACK BUG AT THE BACK OF YOUR THROAT. IT'S CONTROLLING YOUR MIND.
AS I COUNT TO THREE...
...I WANT YOU TO EXHALE AND SPIT IT OUT.
ON "THREE," YOU WILL FALL INTO A DEEP SLEEP...
...AND WE GENBU SWEEPERS WILL TAKE CONTROL OF THIS SITUATION.
WE WILL RESET THINGS TO THE MIDDLE PATH.
ONE...
TWO...
THREE.
TINK

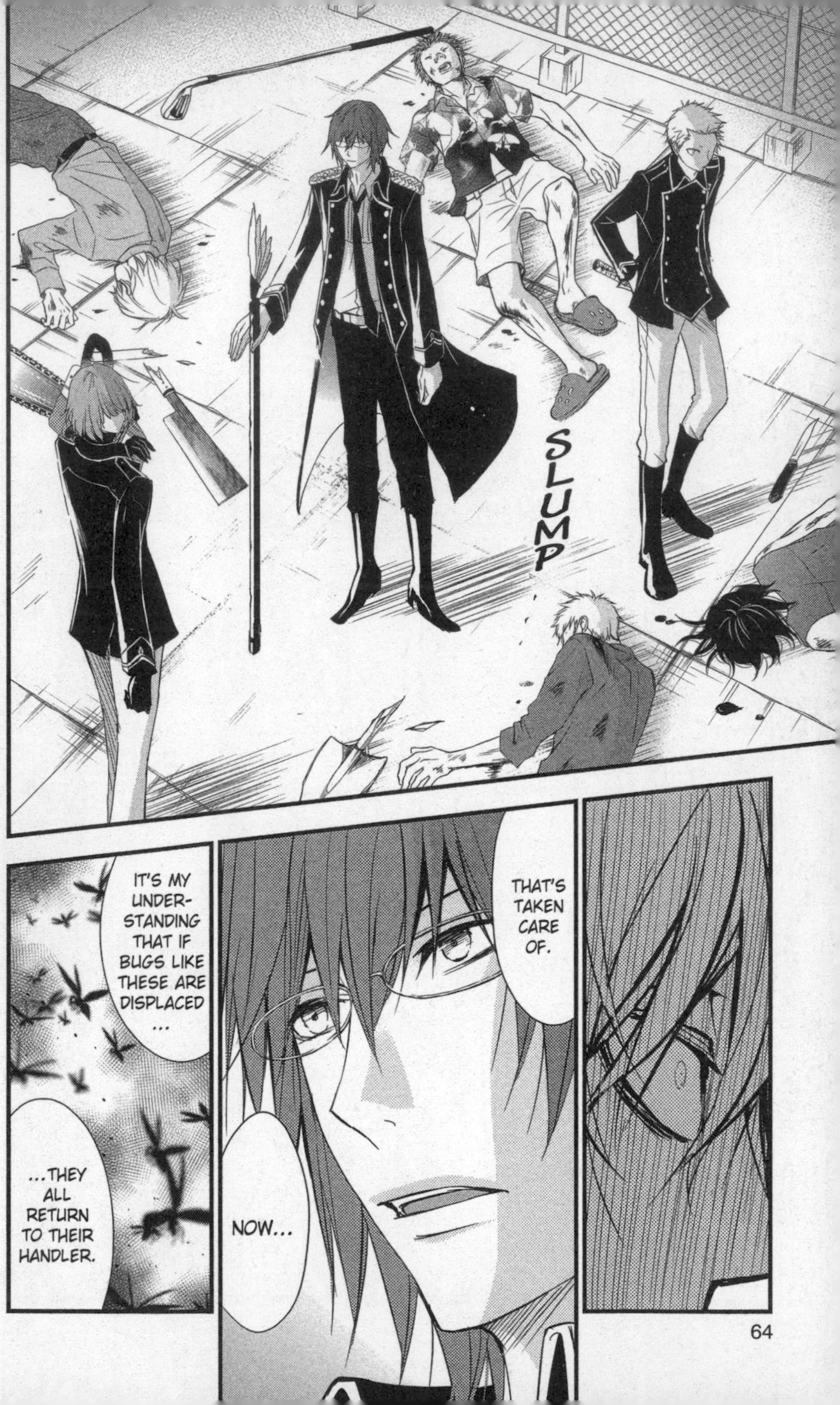
SLUMP
THAT'S TAKEN CARE OF.
NOW...
IT'S MY UNDER-STANDING THAT IF BUGS LIKE THESE ARE DISPLACED ...
...THEY ALL RETURN TO THEIR HANDLER.

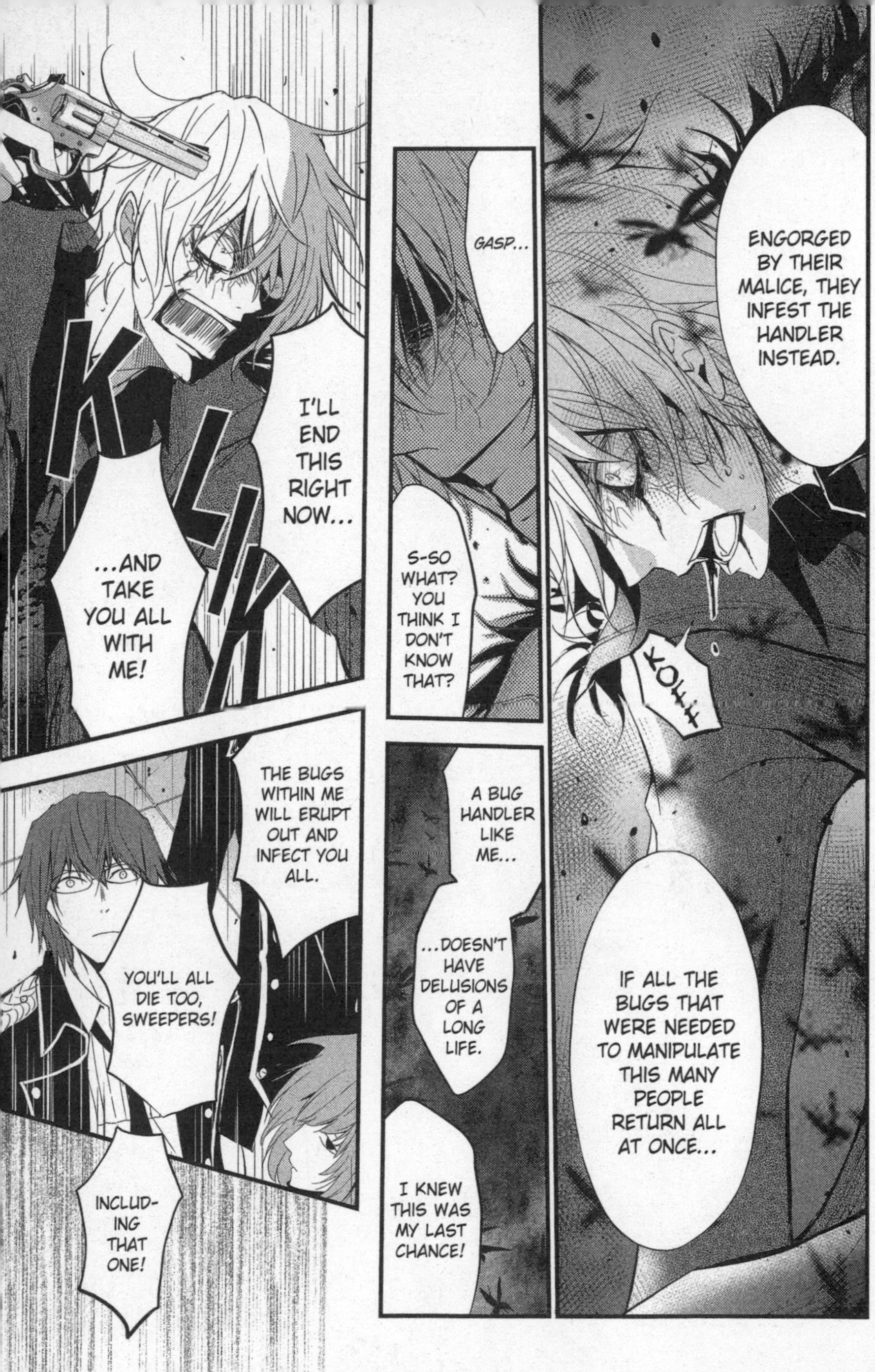
ENGORGED BY THEIR MALICE, THEY INFEST THE HANDLER INSTEAD.
KOFF
IF ALL THE BUGS THAT WERE NEEDED TO MANIPULATE THIS MANY PEOPLE RETURN ALL AT ONCE...
GASP...
S-SO WHAT? YOU THINK I DON'T KNOW THAT?
I'LL END THIS RIGHT NOW...
...AND TAKE YOU ALL WITH ME!
KLIK
A BUG HANDLER LIKE ME...
...DOESN'T HAVE DELUSIONS OF A LONG LIFE.
I KNEW THIS WAS MY LAST CHANCE!
THE BUGS WITHIN ME WILL ERUPT OUT AND INFECT YOU ALL.
YOU'LL ALL DIE TOO, SWEEPERS!
INCLUD-ING THAT ONE!

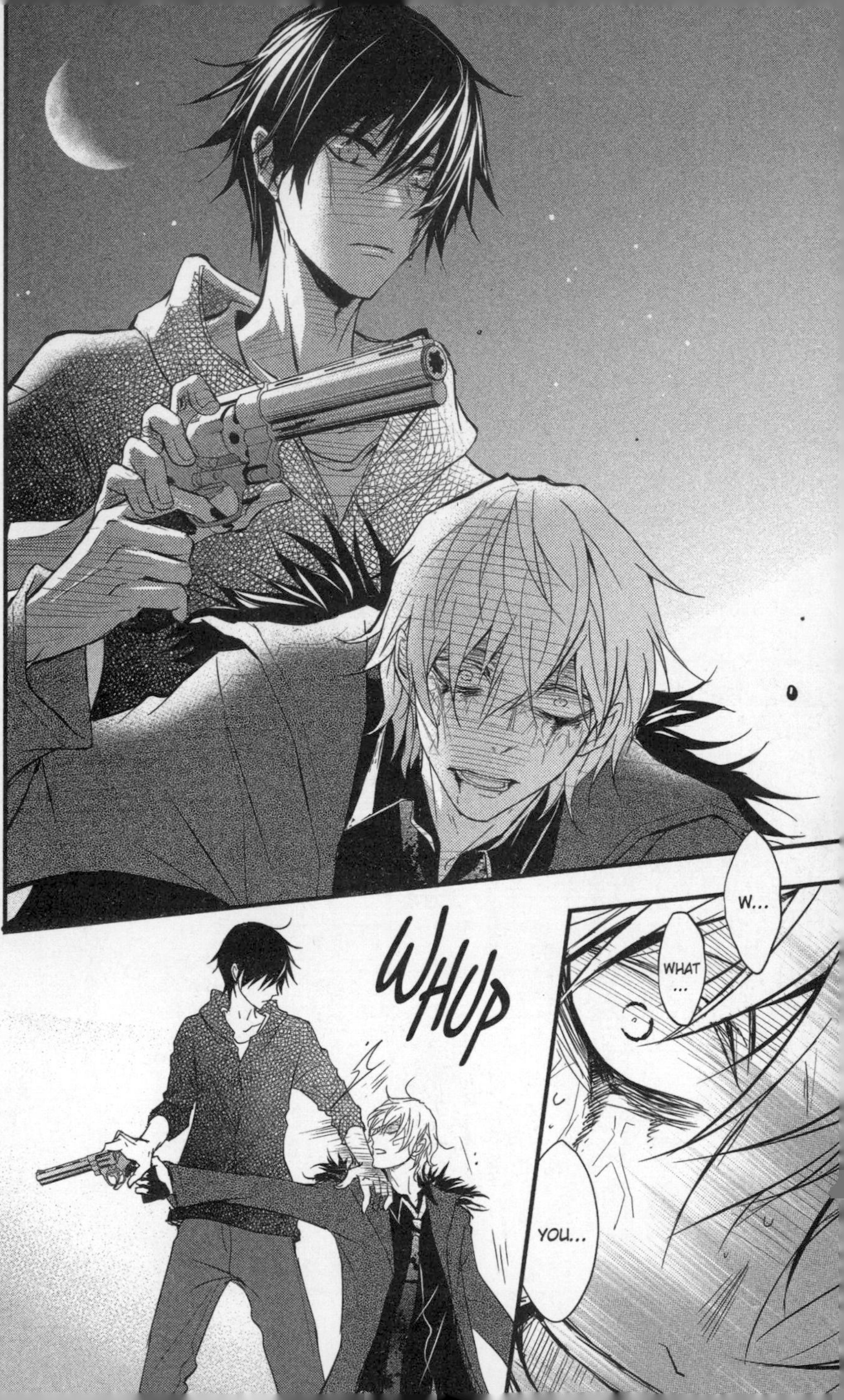
W...
WHAT ...
YOU...
WHUP

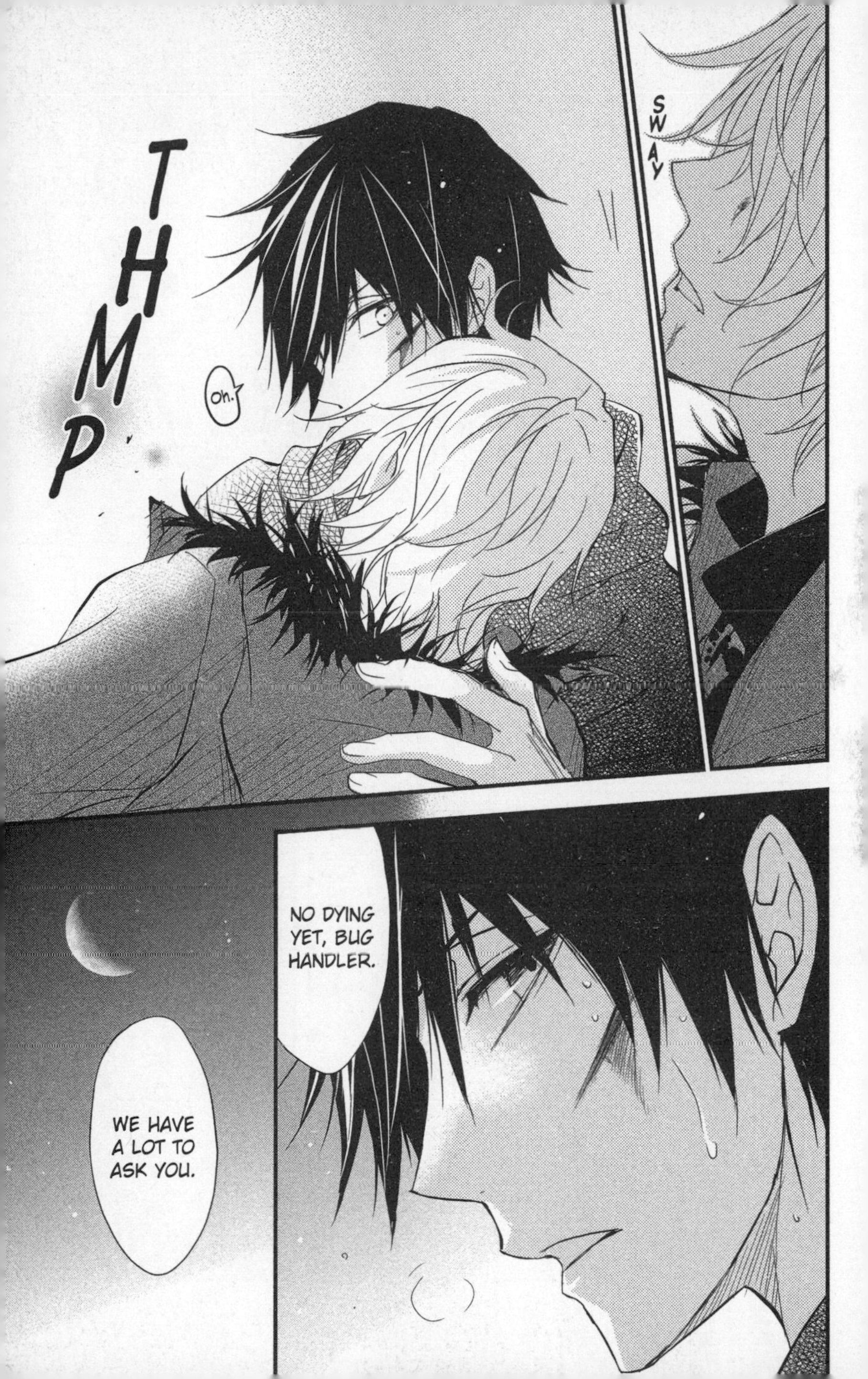
SWAY
THMP
Oh.
NO DYING YET, BUG HANDLER.
WE HAVE A LOT TO ASK YOU.

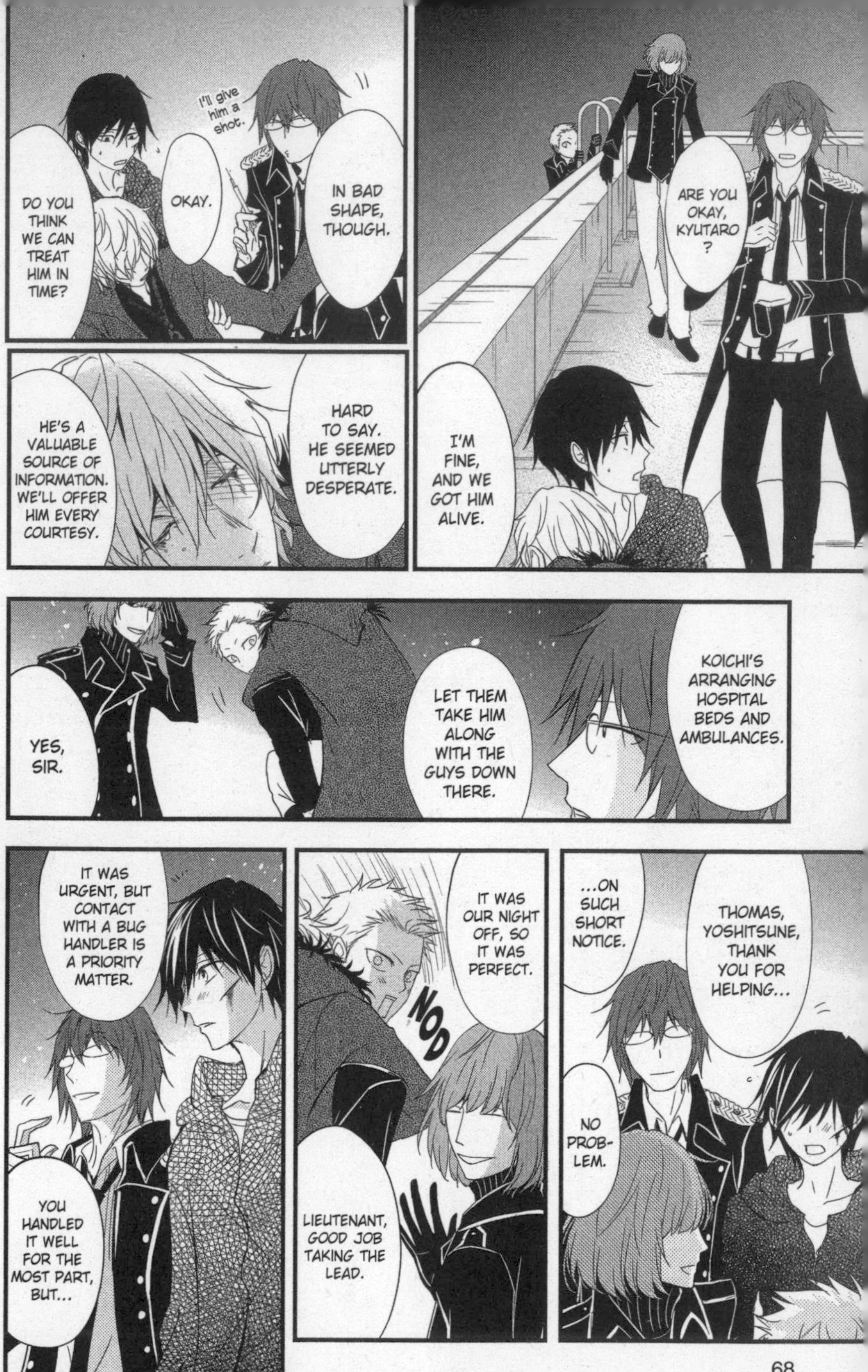
ARE YOU OKAY, KYUTARO?
I'M FINE, AND WE GOT HIM ALIVE.
IN BAD SHAPE, THOUGH.
I'll give him a shot.
OKAY.
DO YOU THINK WE CAN TREAT HIM IN TIME?
HARD TO SAY. HE SEEMED UTTERLY DESPERATE.
HE'S A VALUABLE SOURCE OF INFORMATION. WE'LL OFFER HIM EVERY COURTESY.
KOICHI'S ARRANGING HOSPITAL BEDS AND AMBULANCES.
LET THEM TAKE HIM ALONG WITH THE GUYS DOWN THERE.
YES, SIR.
THOMAS, YOSHITSUNE, THANK YOU FOR HELPING...
...ON SUCH SHORT NOTICE.
NO PROB-LEM.
IT WAS OUR NIGHT OFF, SO IT WAS PERFECT.
NOD
LIEUTENANT, GOOD JOB TAKING THE LEAD.
IT WAS URGENT, BUT CONTACT WITH A BUG HANDLER IS A PRIORITY MATTER.
YOU HANDLED IT WELL FOR THE MOST PART, BUT...

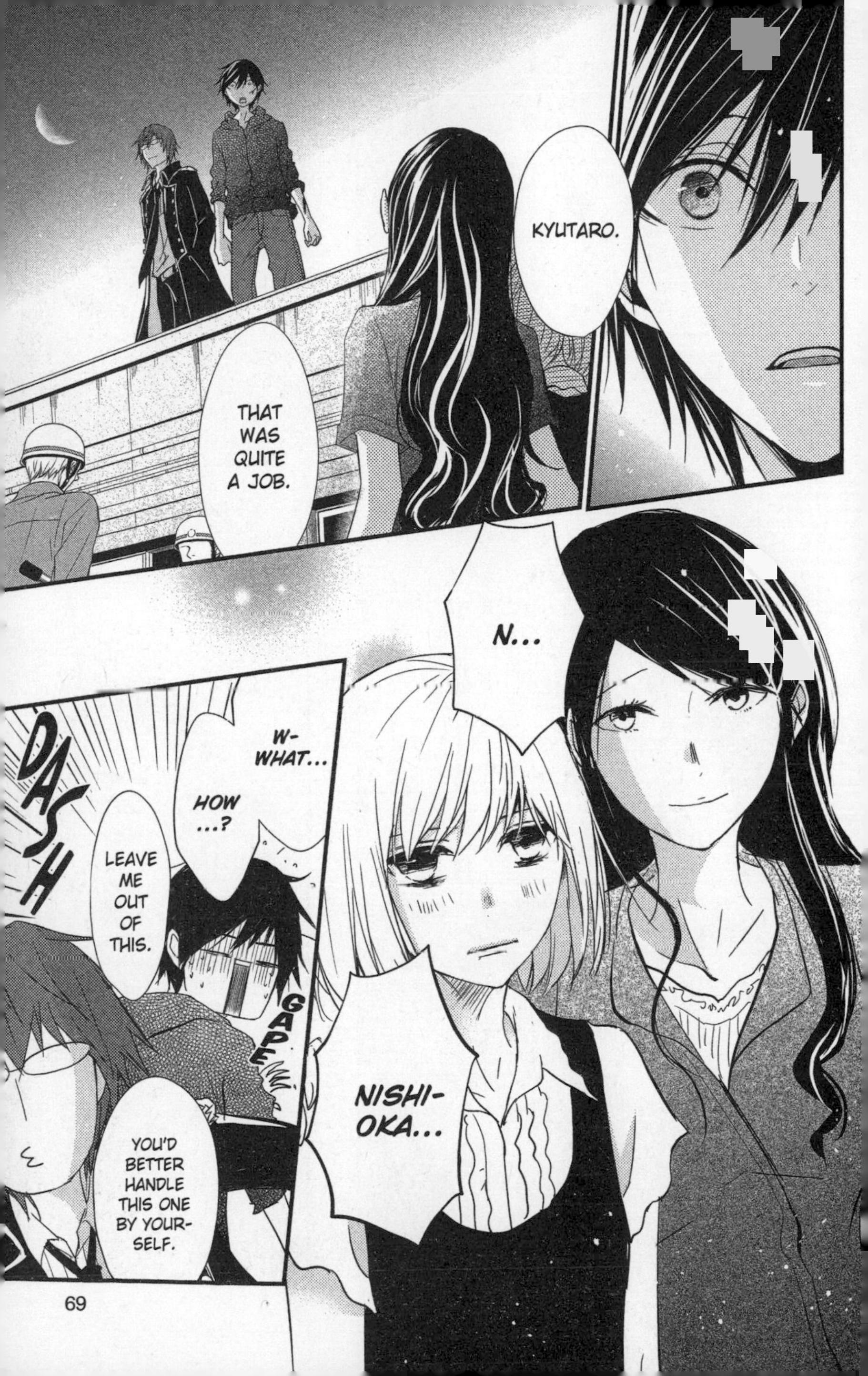
KYUTARO.
THAT WAS QUITE A JOB.
N...
NISHI-OKA...
W-WHAT...
HOW ...?
DASH
LEAVE ME OUT OF THIS.
GAPE
YOU'D BETTER HANDLE THIS ONE BY YOUR-SELF.

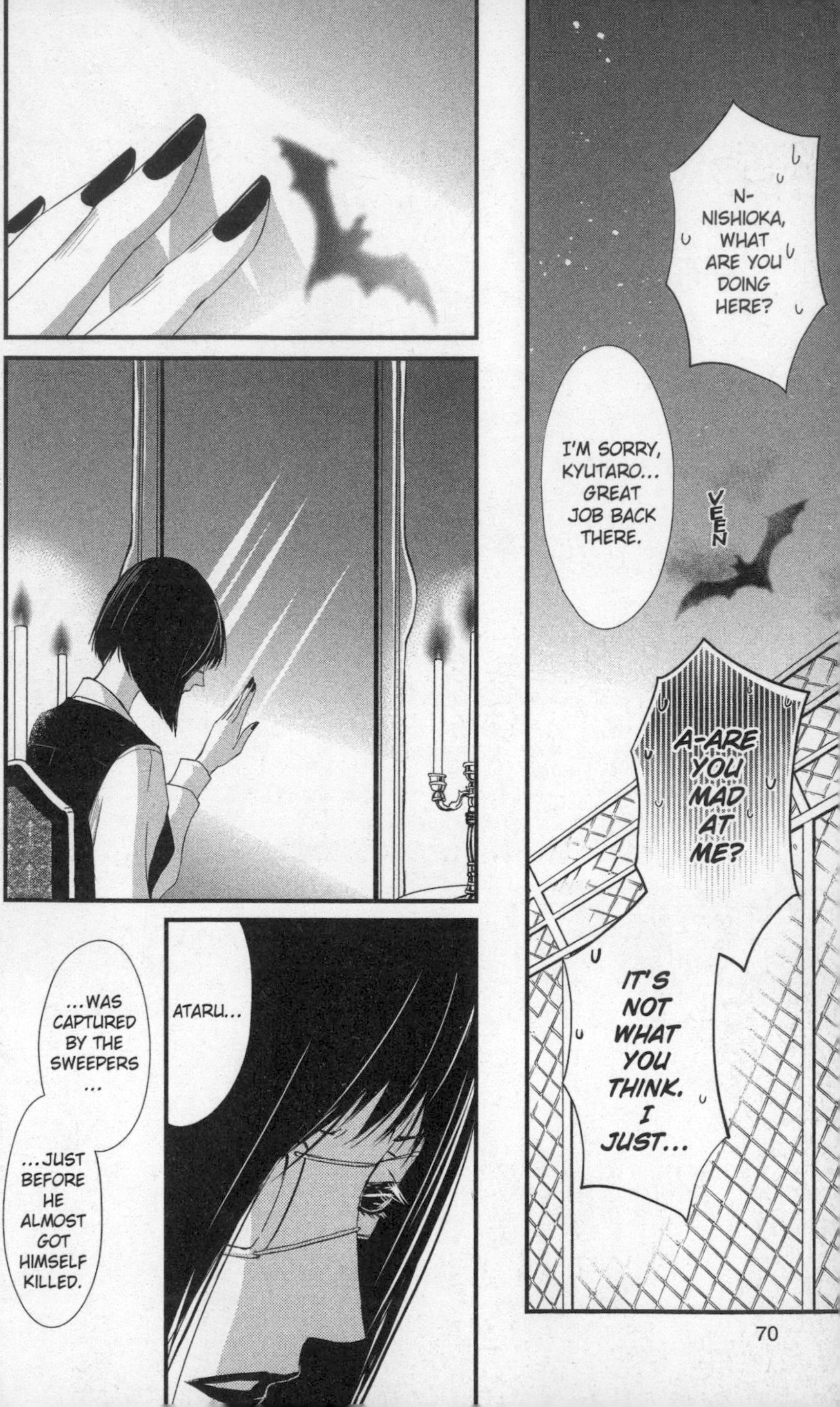
N-NISHIOKA, WHAT ARE YOU DOING HERE?
I'M SORRY, KYUTARO... GREAT JOB BACK THERE.
VEEN
A-ARE YOU MAD AT ME?
IT'S NOT WHAT YOU THINK. I JUST...
ATARU...
...WAS CAPTURED BY THE SWEEPERS...
...JUST BEFORE HE ALMOST GOT HIMSELF KILLED.

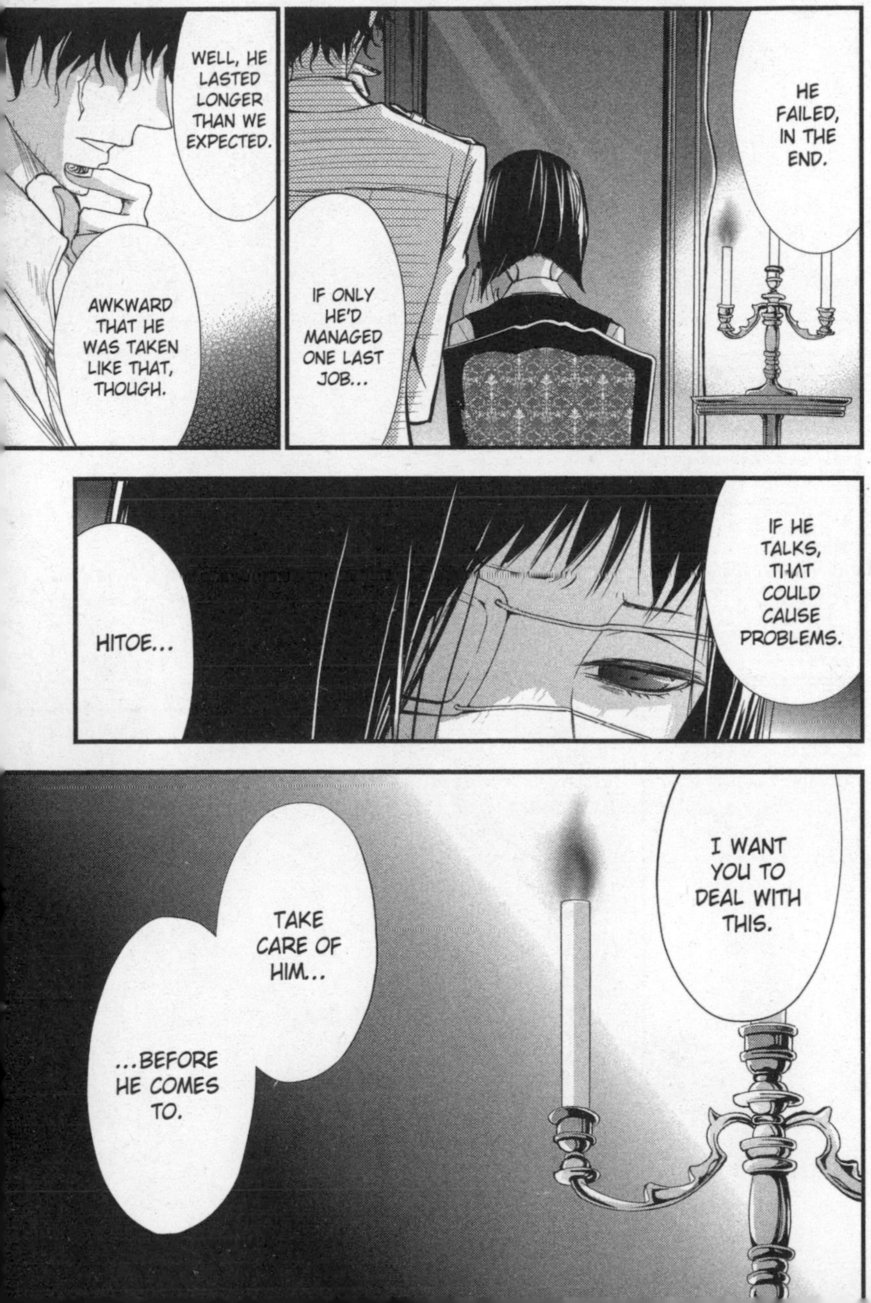
HE FAILED, IN THE END.
IF ONLY HE'D MANAGED ONE LAST JOB...
WELL, HE LASTED LONGER THAN WE EXPECTED.
AWKWARD THAT HE WAS TAKEN LIKE THAT, THOUGH.
IF HE TALKS, THAT COULD CAUSE PROBLEMS.
HITOE...
I WANT YOU TO DEAL WITH THIS.
TAKE CARE OF HIM...
...BEFORE HE COMES TO.

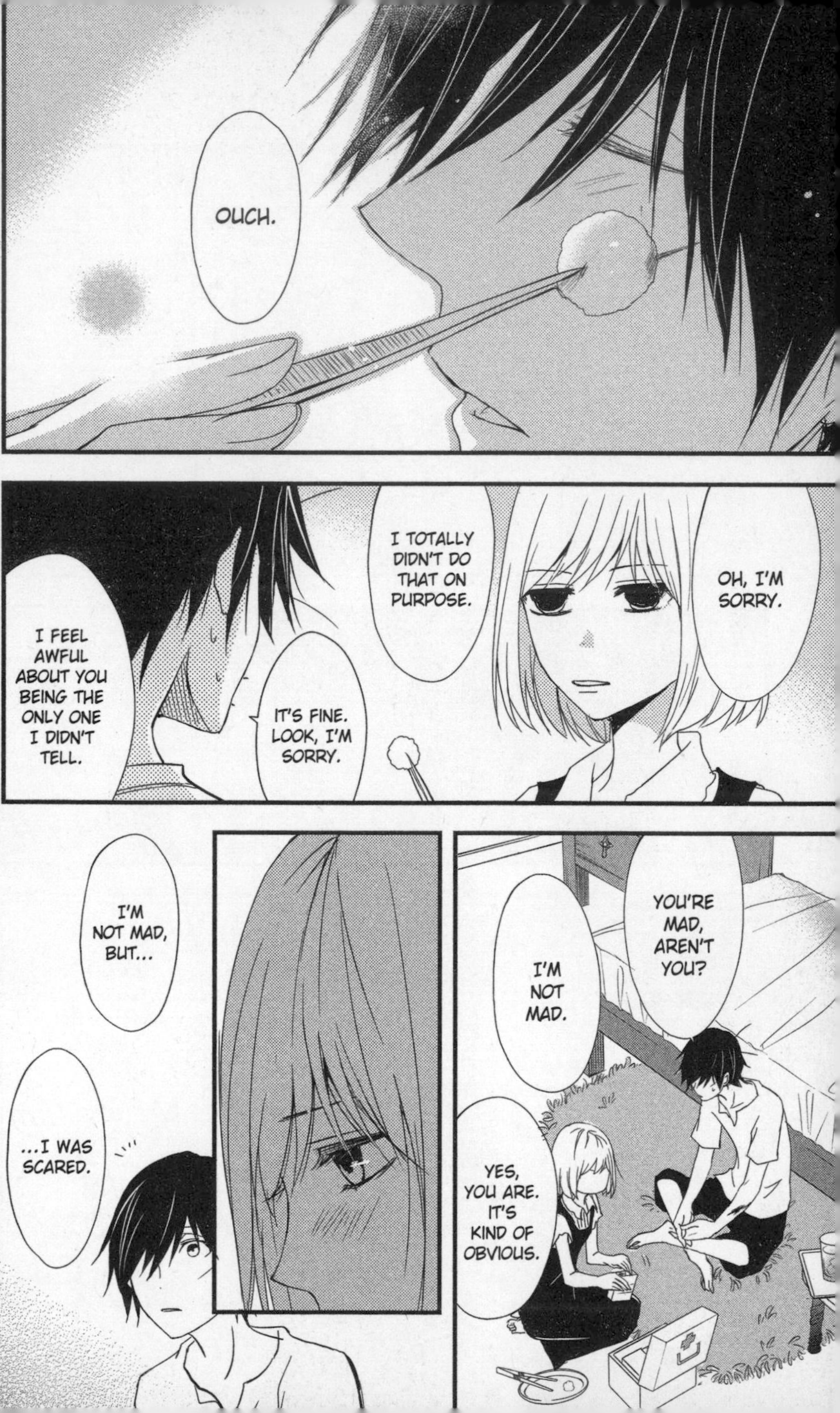
OUCH.
OH, I'M SORRY.
I TOTALLY DIDN'T DO THAT ON PURPOSE.
IT'S FINE. LOOK, I'M SORRY.
I FEEL AWFUL ABOUT YOU BEING THE ONLY ONE I DIDN'T TELL.
YOU'RE MAD, AREN'T YOU?
I'M NOT MAD.
YES, YOU ARE. IT'S KIND OF OBVIOUS.
I'M NOT MAD, BUT...
...I WAS SCARED.

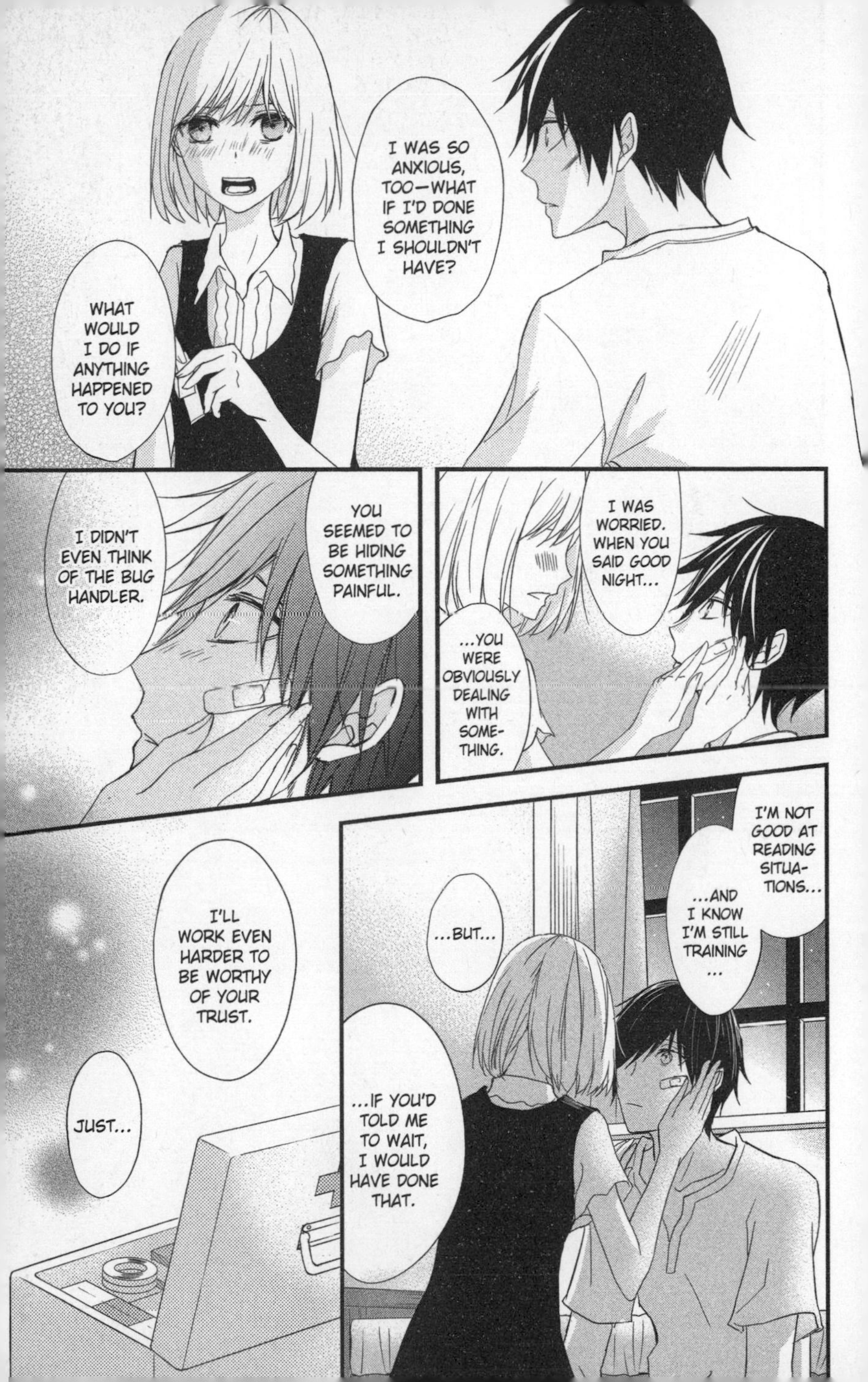
I WAS SO ANXIOUS, TOO—WHAT IF I'D DONE SOMETHING I SHOULDN'T HAVE?
WHAT WOULD I DO IF ANYTHING HAPPENED TO YOU?
I WAS WORRIED. WHEN YOU SAID GOOD NIGHT...
...YOU WERE OBVIOUSLY DEALING WITH SOME-THING.
YOU SEEMED TO BE HIDING SOMETHING PAINFUL.
I DIDN'T EVEN THINK OF THE BUG HANDLER.
I'M NOT GOOD AT READING SITUA-TIONS...
...AND I KNOW I'M STILL TRAINING...
...BUT...
...IF YOU'D TOLD ME TO WAIT, I WOULD HAVE DONE THAT.
I'LL WORK EVEN HARDER TO BE WORTHY OF YOUR TRUST.
JUST...

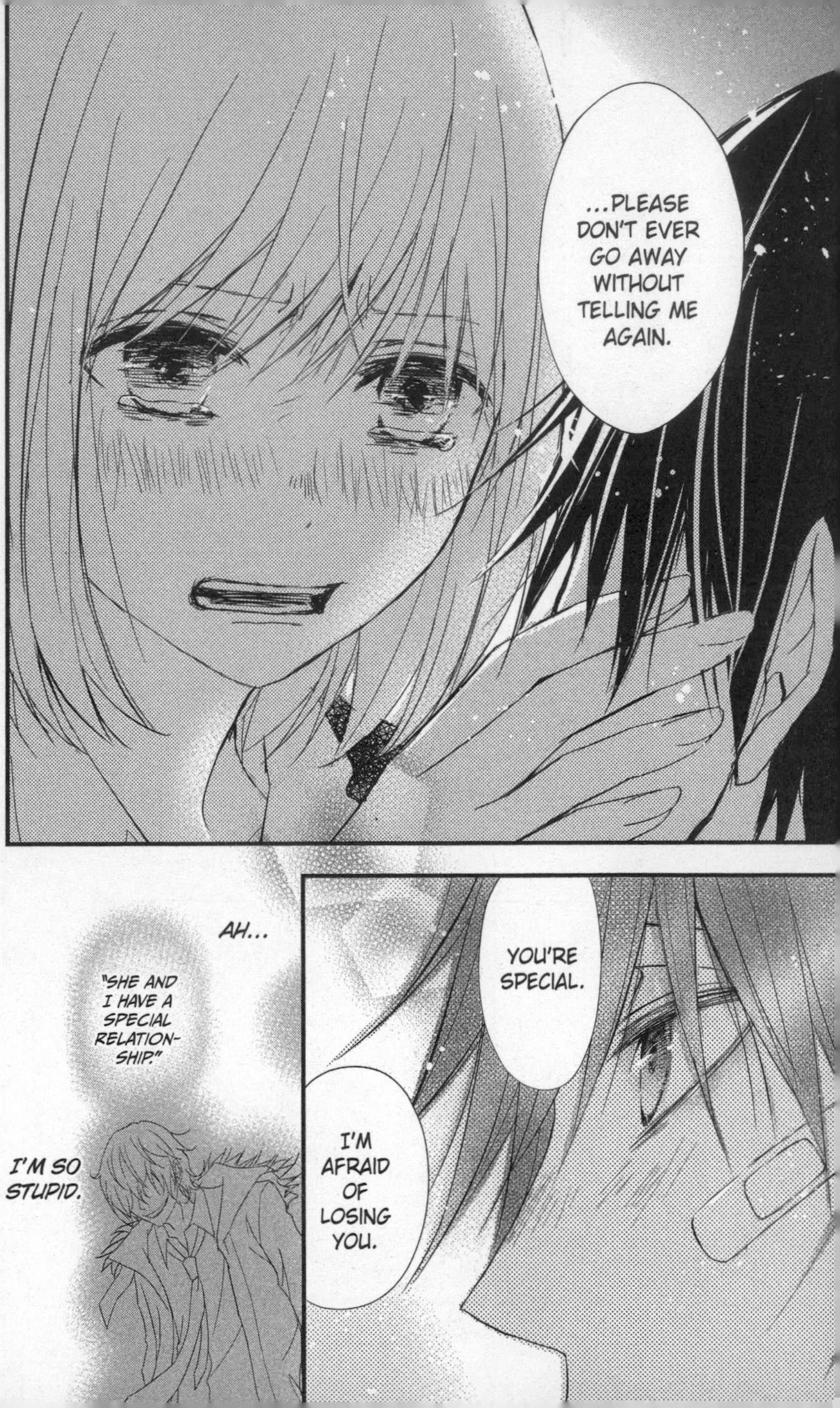
...PLEASE DON'T EVER GO AWAY WITHOUT TELLING ME AGAIN.
YOU'RE SPECIAL.
I'M AFRAID OF LOSING YOU.
AH...
"SHE AND I HAVE A SPECIAL RELATIONSHIP."
I'M SO STUPID.

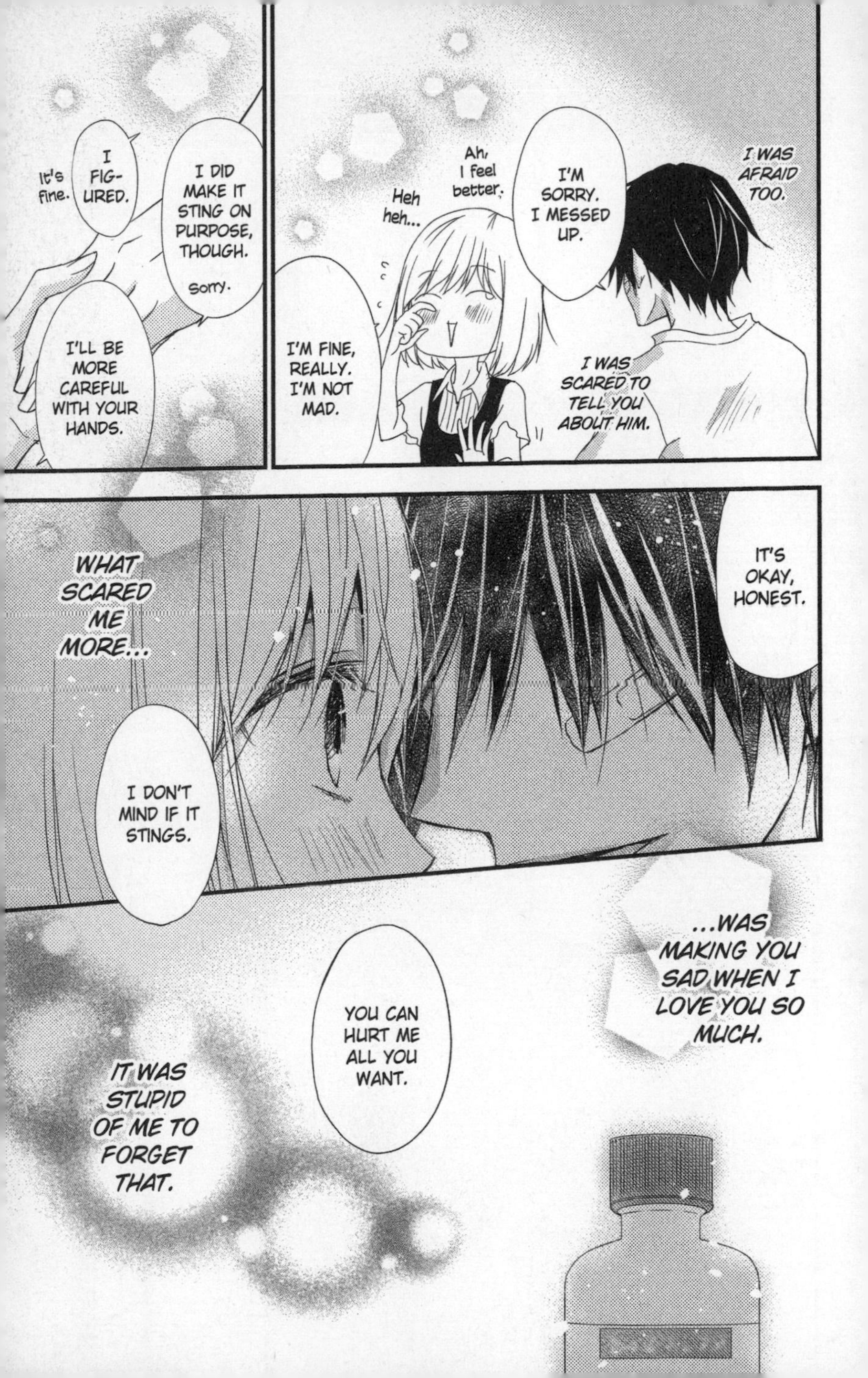
I WAS AFRAID TOO.
I'M SORRY. I MESSED UP.
Ah, I feel better.
Heh heh...
I WAS SCARED TO TELL YOU ABOUT HIM.
I'M FINE, REALLY. I'M NOT MAD.
I DID MAKE IT STING ON PURPOSE, THOUGH.
Sorry.
I FIG-URED.
It's fine.
I'LL BE MORE CAREFUL WITH YOUR HANDS.
IT'S OKAY, HONEST.
WHAT SCARED ME MORE...
I DON'T MIND IF IT STINGS.
...WAS MAKING YOU SAD WHEN I LOVE YOU SO MUCH.
YOU CAN HURT ME ALL YOU WANT.
IT WAS STUPID OF ME TO FORGET THAT.

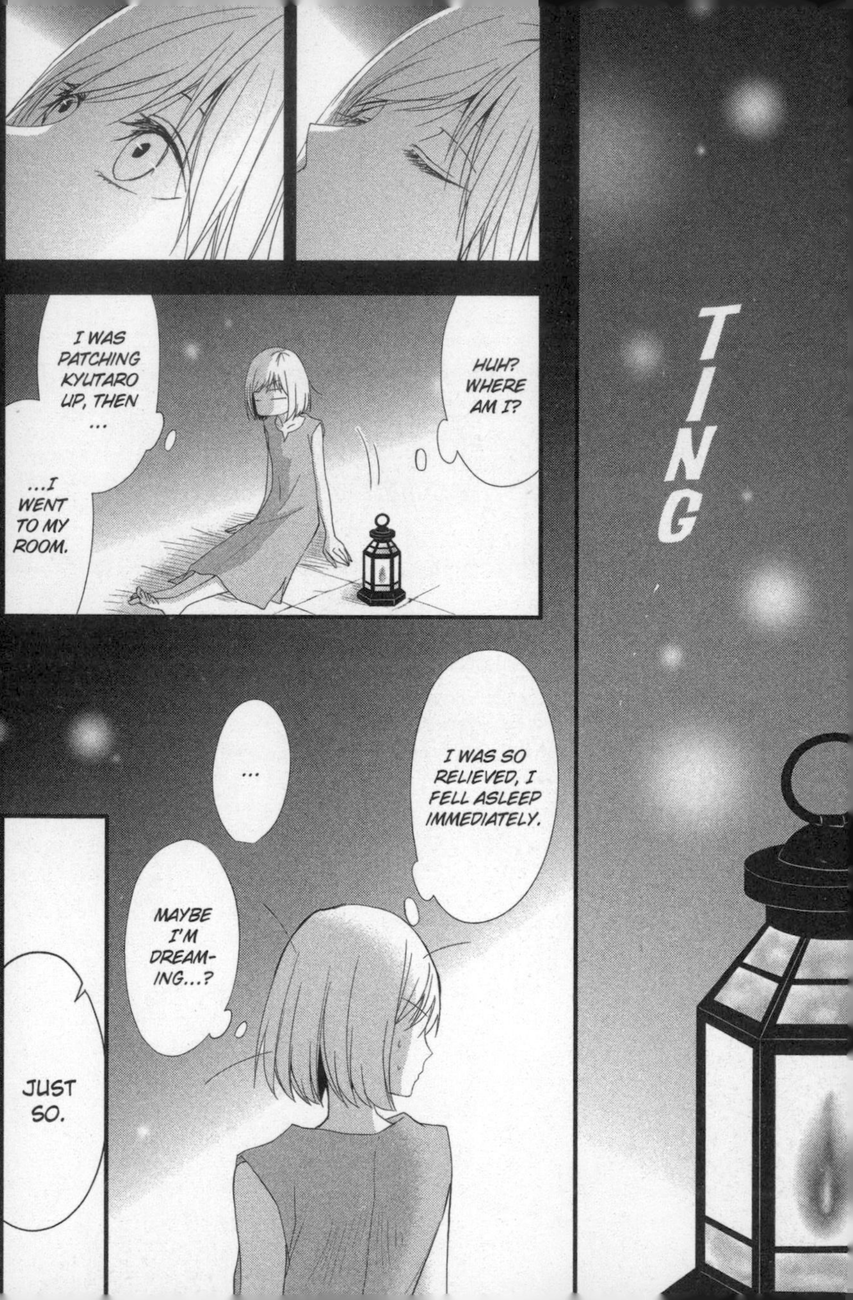
TING
HUH? WHERE AM I?
I WAS PATCHING KYUTARO UP, THEN ...
...I WENT TO MY ROOM.
I WAS SO RELIEVED, I FELL ASLEEP IMMEDIATELY.
...
MAYBE I'M DREAMING...?
JUST SO.

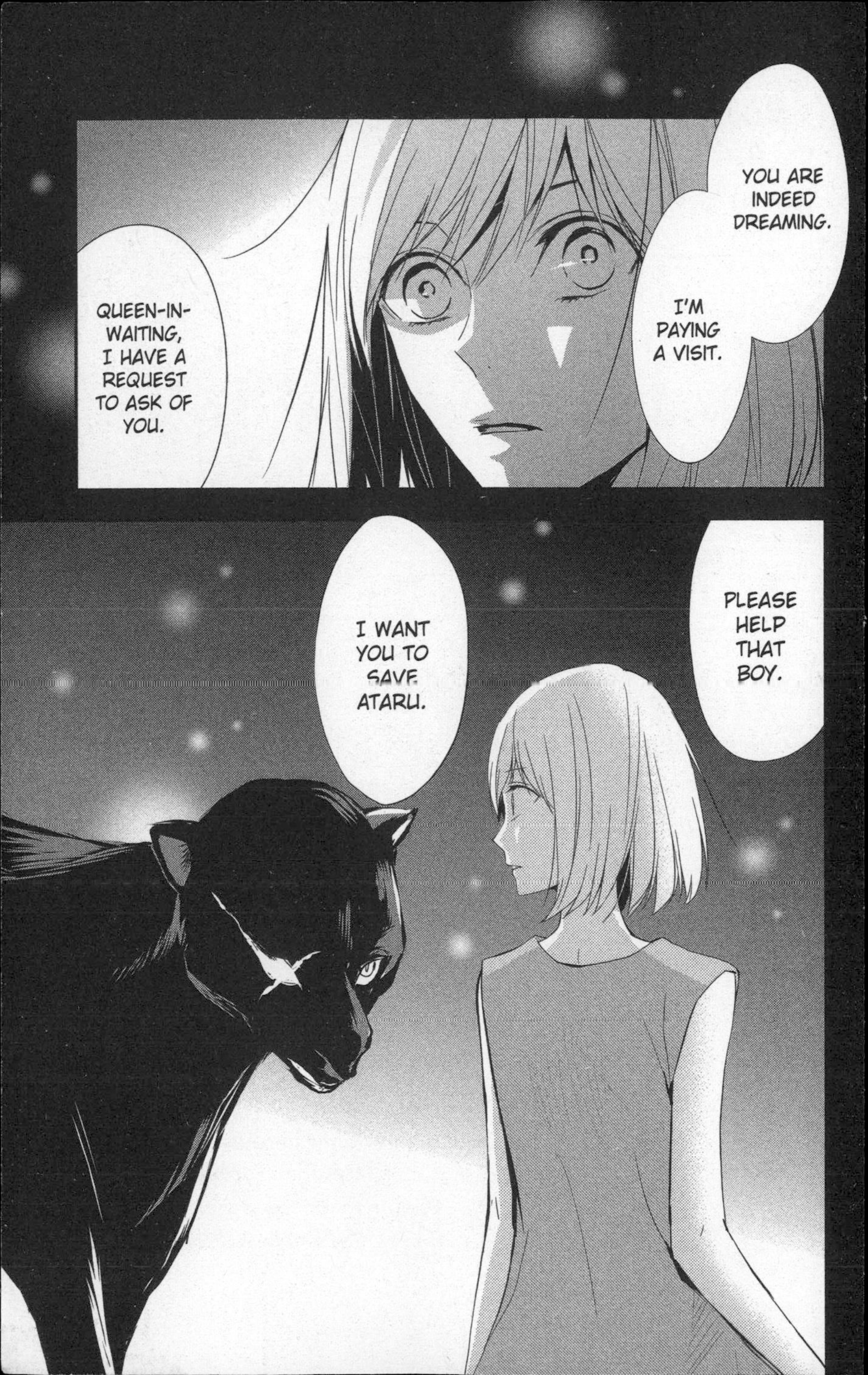
YOU ARE INDEED DREAMING.
I'M PAYING A VISIT.
QUEEN-IN-WAITING, I HAVE A REQUEST TO ASK OF YOU.
PLEASE HELP THAT BOY.
I WANT YOU TO SAVE ATARU.

MONTHLY BETSUCOMI SALE DATE NOTICE ON TWITTER

CHAPTER 18

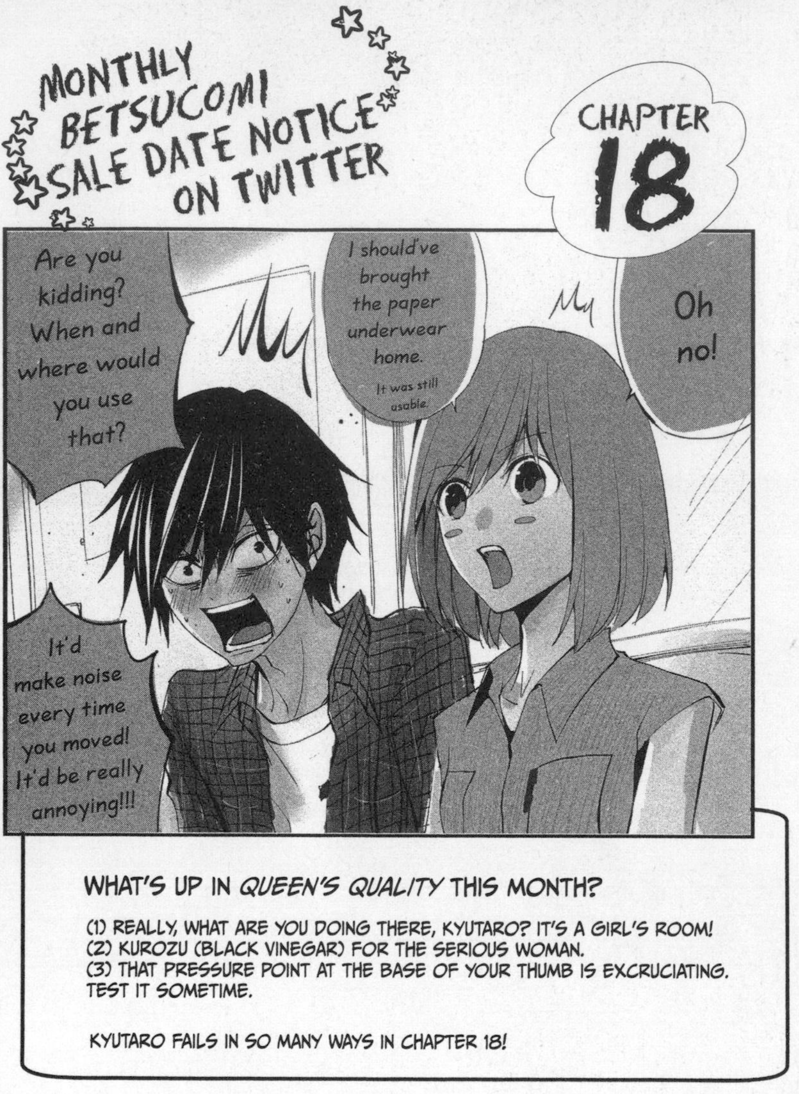
Oh no!
I should've brought the paper underwear home.
It was still usable.
Are you kidding? When and where would you use that?
It'd make noise every time you moved! It'd be really annoying!!!

**WHAT'S UP IN *QUEEN'S QUALITY* THIS MONTH?**

(1) REALLY, WHAT ARE YOU DOING THERE, KYUTARO? IT'S A GIRL'S ROOM!
(2) KUROZU (BLACK VINEGAR) FOR THE SERIOUS WOMAN.
(3) THAT PRESSURE POINT AT THE BASE OF YOUR THUMB IS EXCRUCIATING. TEST IT SOMETIME.

KYUTARO FAILS IN SO MANY WAYS IN CHAPTER 18!

*This author would like to wear those paper panties someday. I haven't gotten aesthetic or massage treatments very often. I want to get massaged until I cry "Uncle!" (Super masochistic)*

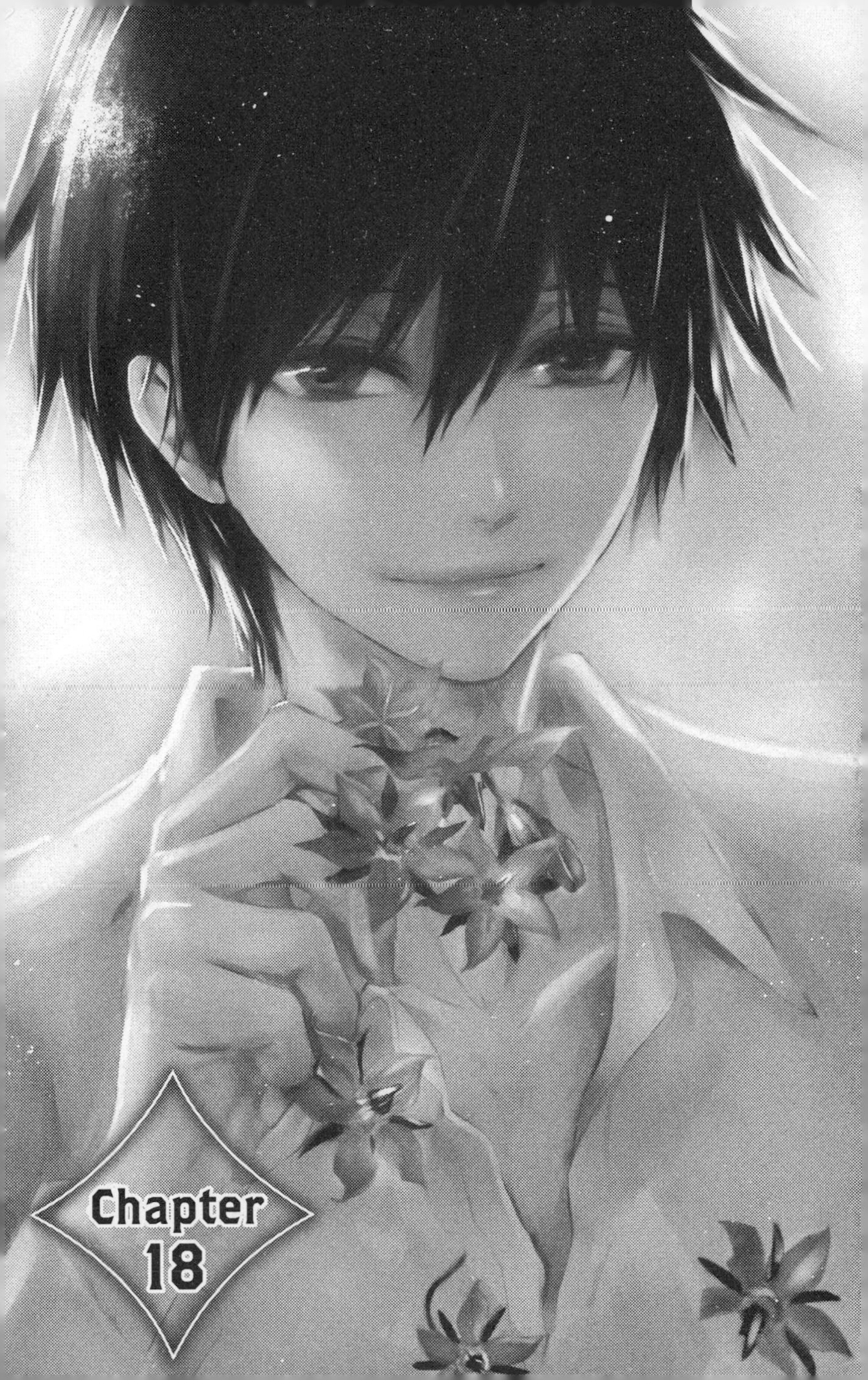
Chapter
18

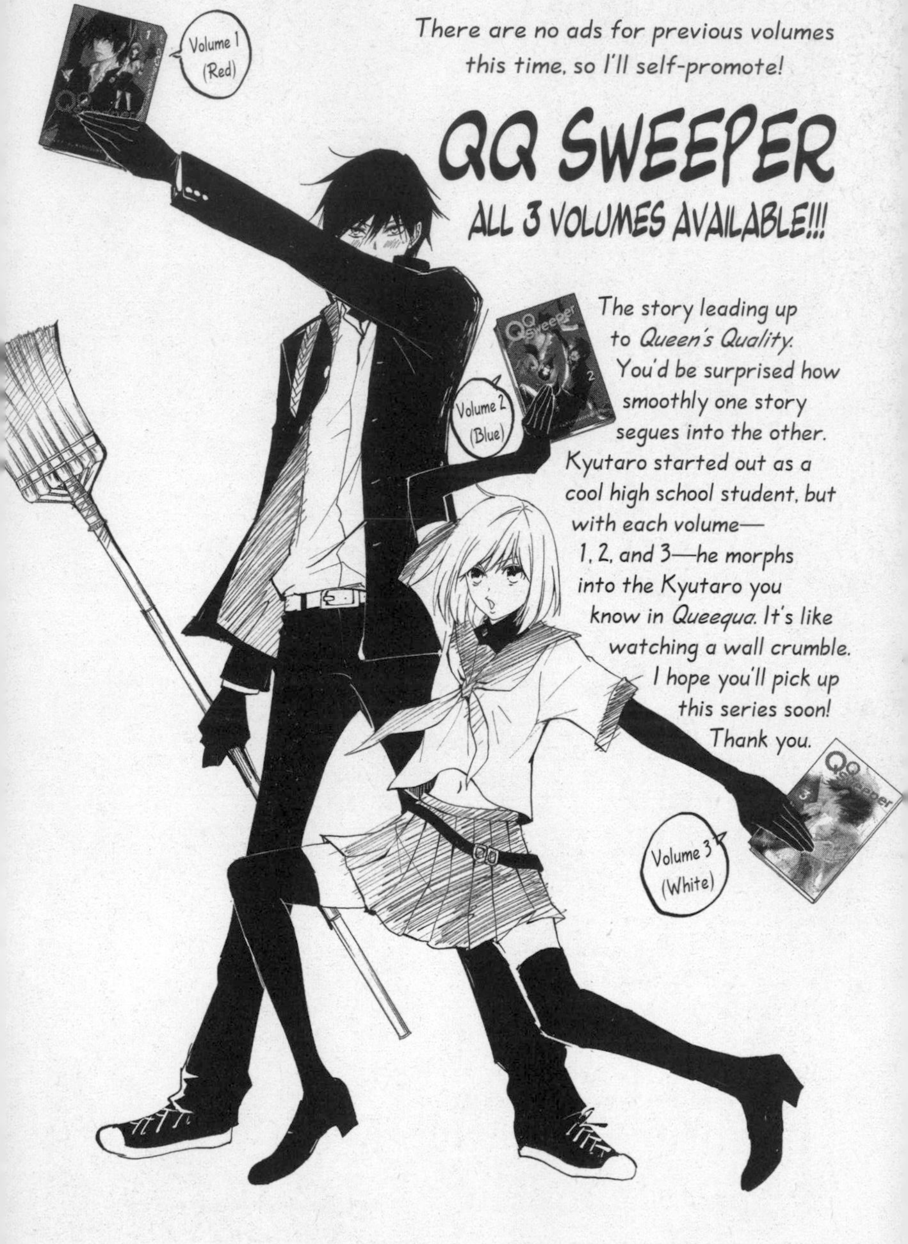
There are no ads for previous volumes this time, so I'll self-promote!
Volume 1 (Red)
QQ SWEEPER
ALL 3 VOLUMES AVAILABLE!!!
Volume 2 (Blue)
The story leading up to Queen's Quality. You'd be surprised how smoothly one story segues into the other. Kyutaro started out as a cool high school student, but with each volume—1, 2, and 3—he morphs into the Kyutaro you know in Queequa. It's like watching a wall crumble. I hope you'll pick up this series soon! Thank you.
Volume 3 (White)

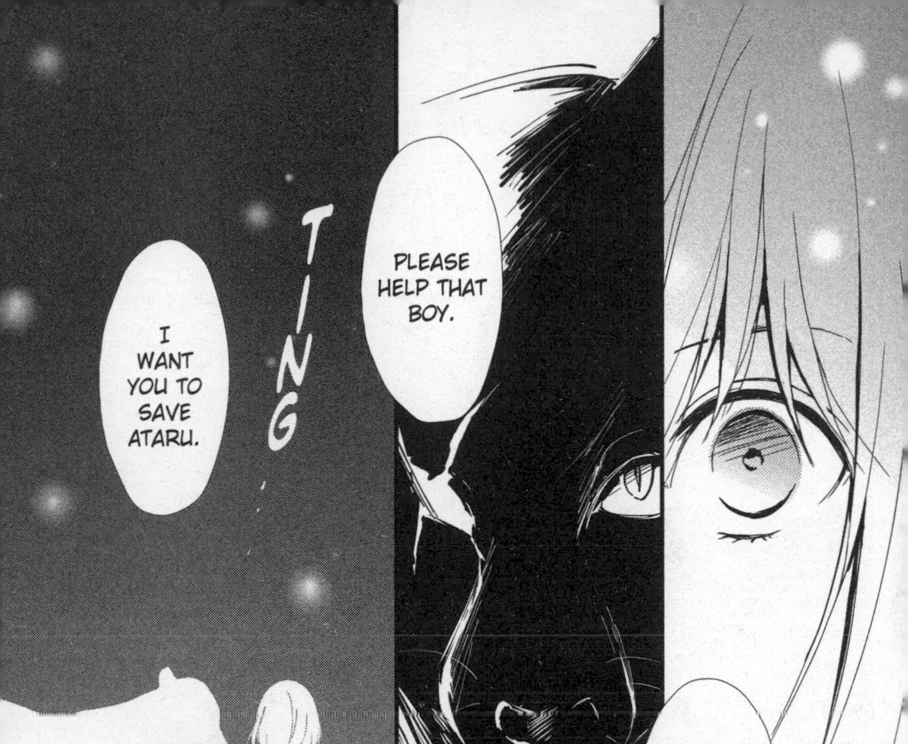
QUEEN-IN-WAITING...
PLEASE HELP THAT BOY.
I WANT YOU TO SAVE ATARU.
TING

New Characters in Chapter 17 (although they did make a brief appearance in volume 3)
The one with the bushy pageboy hairstyle is Thomas. The one with the spiky hair is Yoshitsune. Their funny names may give you a hint as to where they work, but that's something I'd like to introduce in the story someday. Many of the Genbu sweepers hold down other jobs too. They're all weird.

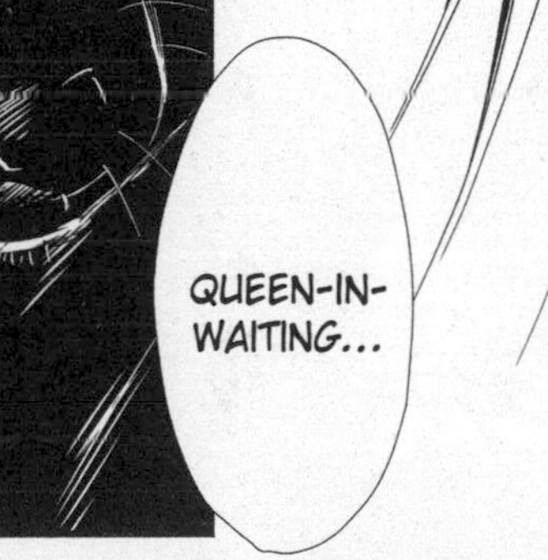
This is all meant to be happening in the summertime, so the clothes the Genbu wear look awfully hot.

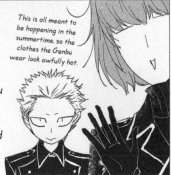

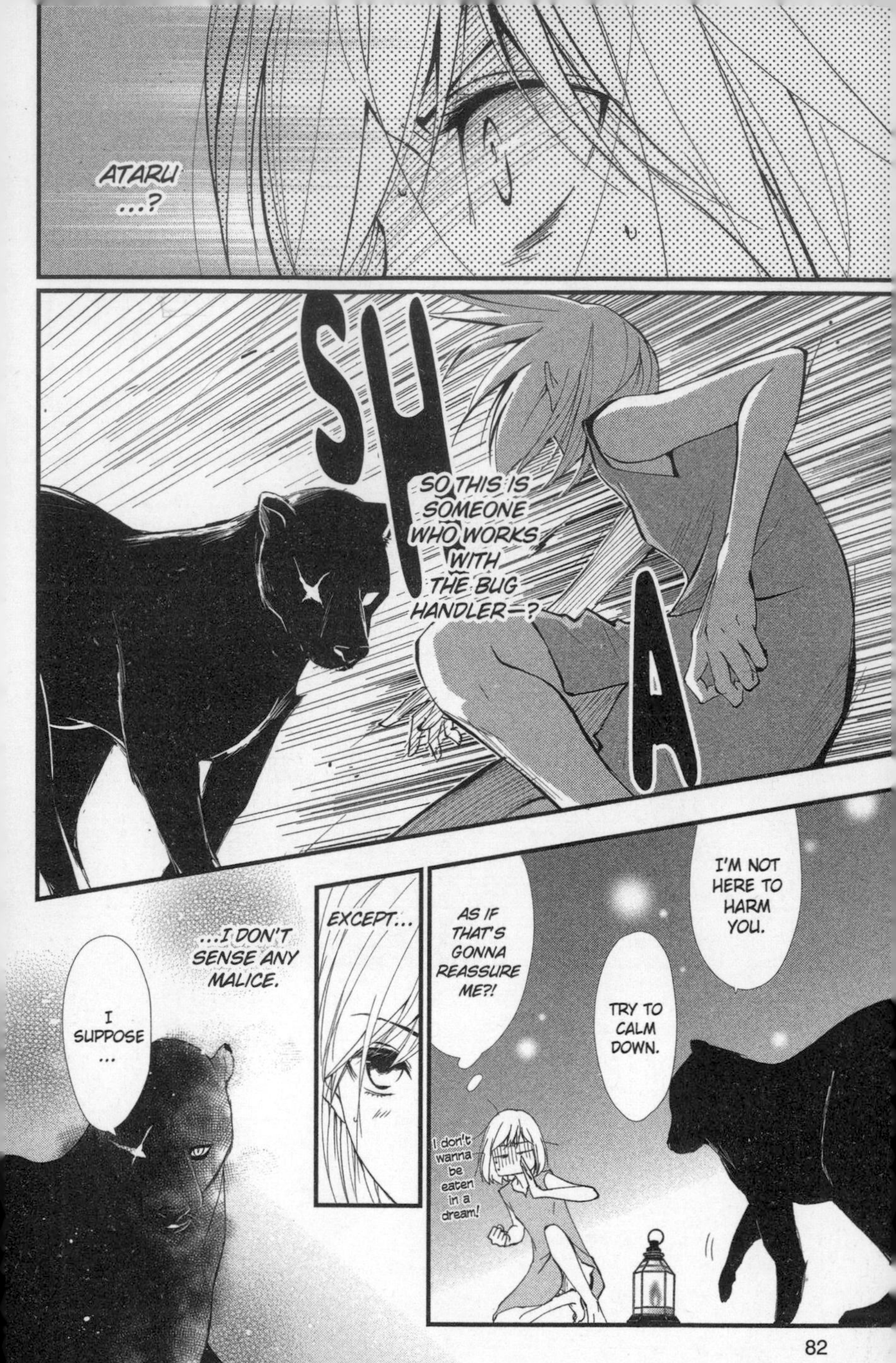
ATARU ...?
SHA
SO THIS IS SOMEONE WHO WORKS WITH THE BUG HANDLER—?
I'M NOT HERE TO HARM YOU.
TRY TO CALM DOWN.
AS IF THAT'S GONNA REASSURE ME?!
I don't wanna be eaten in a dream!
EXCEPT...
...I DON'T SENSE ANY MALICE.
I SUPPOSE ...

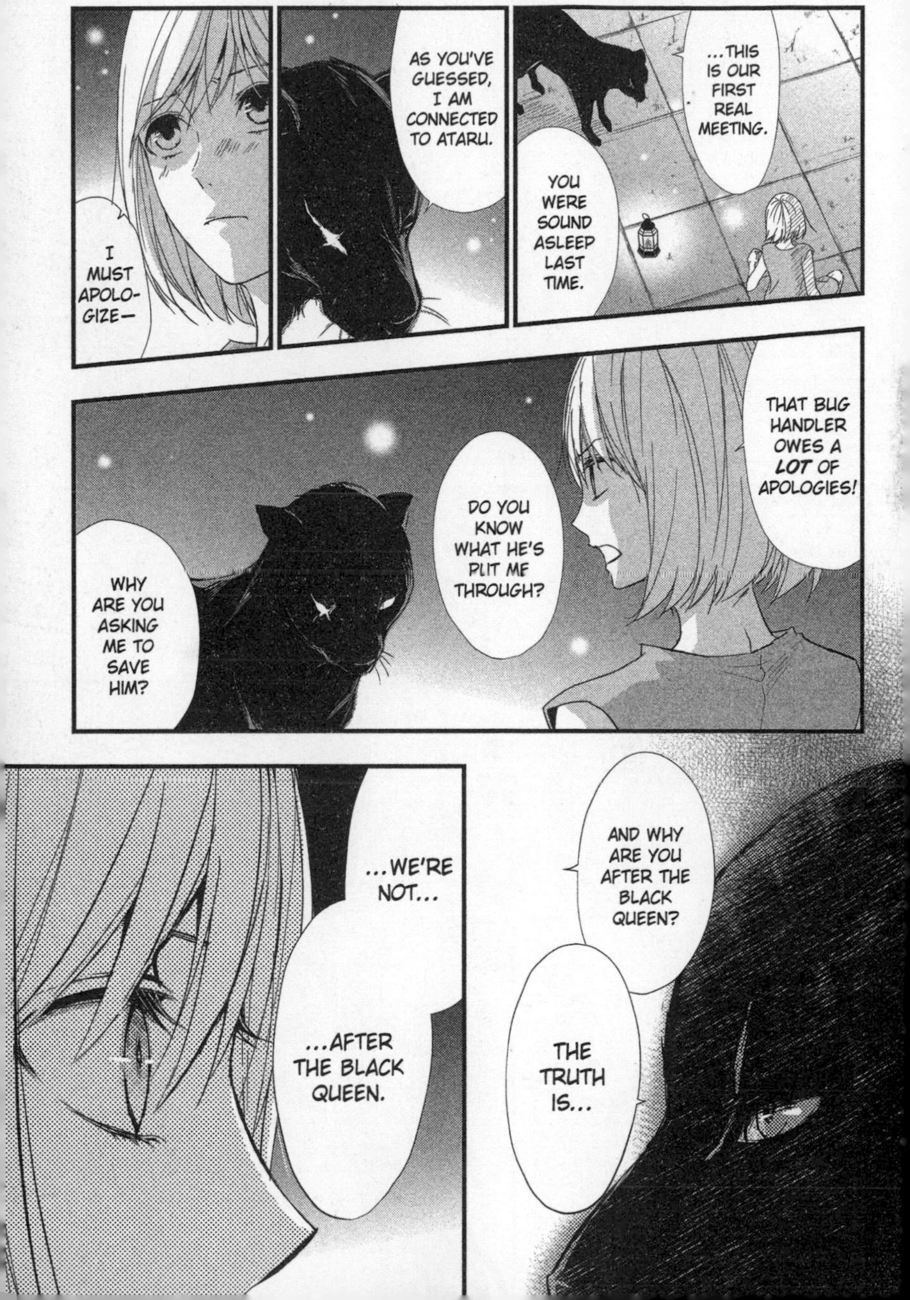
...THIS IS OUR FIRST REAL MEETING.
YOU WERE SOUND ASLEEP LAST TIME.
AS YOU'VE GUESSED, I AM CONNECTED TO ATARU.
I MUST APOLOGIZE—
THAT BUG HANDLER OWES A LOT OF APOLOGIES!
DO YOU KNOW WHAT HE'S PUT ME THROUGH?
WHY ARE YOU ASKING ME TO SAVE HIM?
AND WHY ARE YOU AFTER THE BLACK QUEEN?
THE TRUTH IS...
...WE'RE NOT...
...AFTER THE BLACK QUEEN.

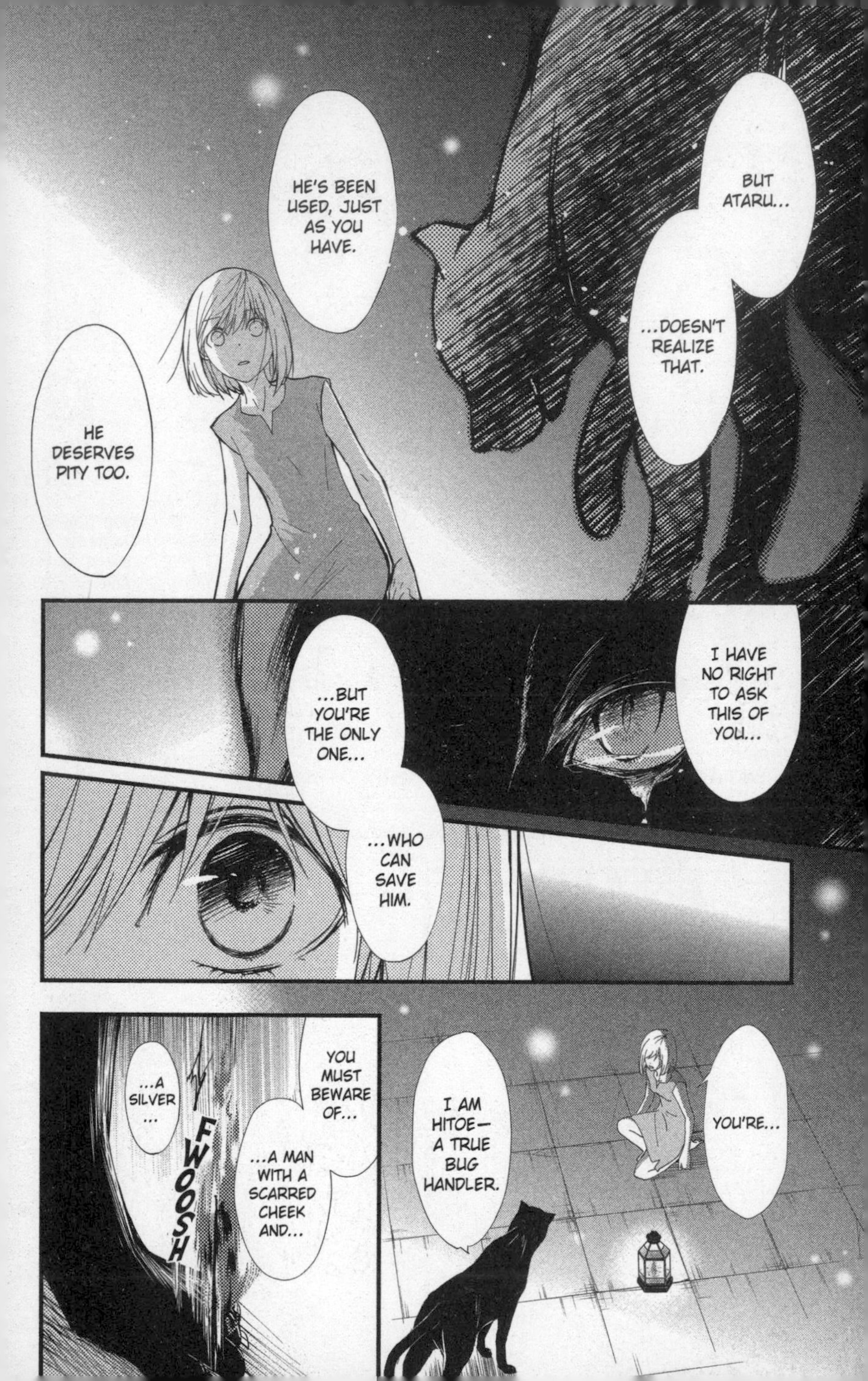
BUT ATARU...
...DOESN'T REALIZE THAT.
HE'S BEEN USED, JUST AS YOU HAVE.
HE DESERVES PITY TOO.
I HAVE NO RIGHT TO ASK THIS OF YOU...
...BUT YOU'RE THE ONLY ONE...
...WHO CAN SAVE HIM.
YOU'RE...
I AM HITOE— A TRUE BUG HANDLER.
YOU MUST BEWARE OF...
...A MAN WITH A SCARRED CHEEK AND...
...A SILVER ...
FWOOSH

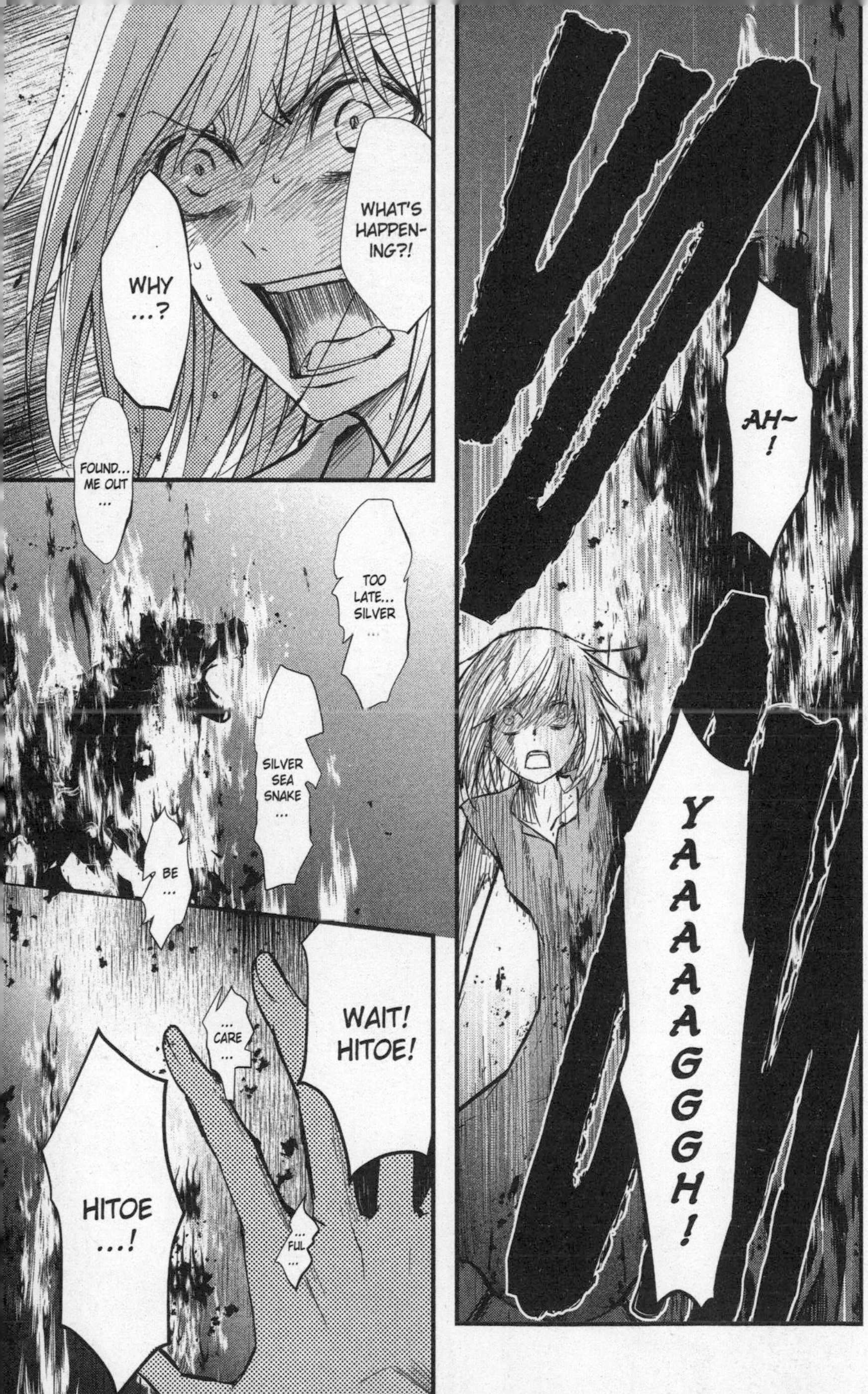
AH~!
YAAAAAAGGGH!
WHAT'S HAPPEN-ING?!
WHY ...?
FOUND... ME OUT ...
TOO LATE... SILVER ...
SILVER SEA SNAKE ...
BE ...
WAIT! HITOE!
... CARE ...
HITOE ...!
... FUL ...

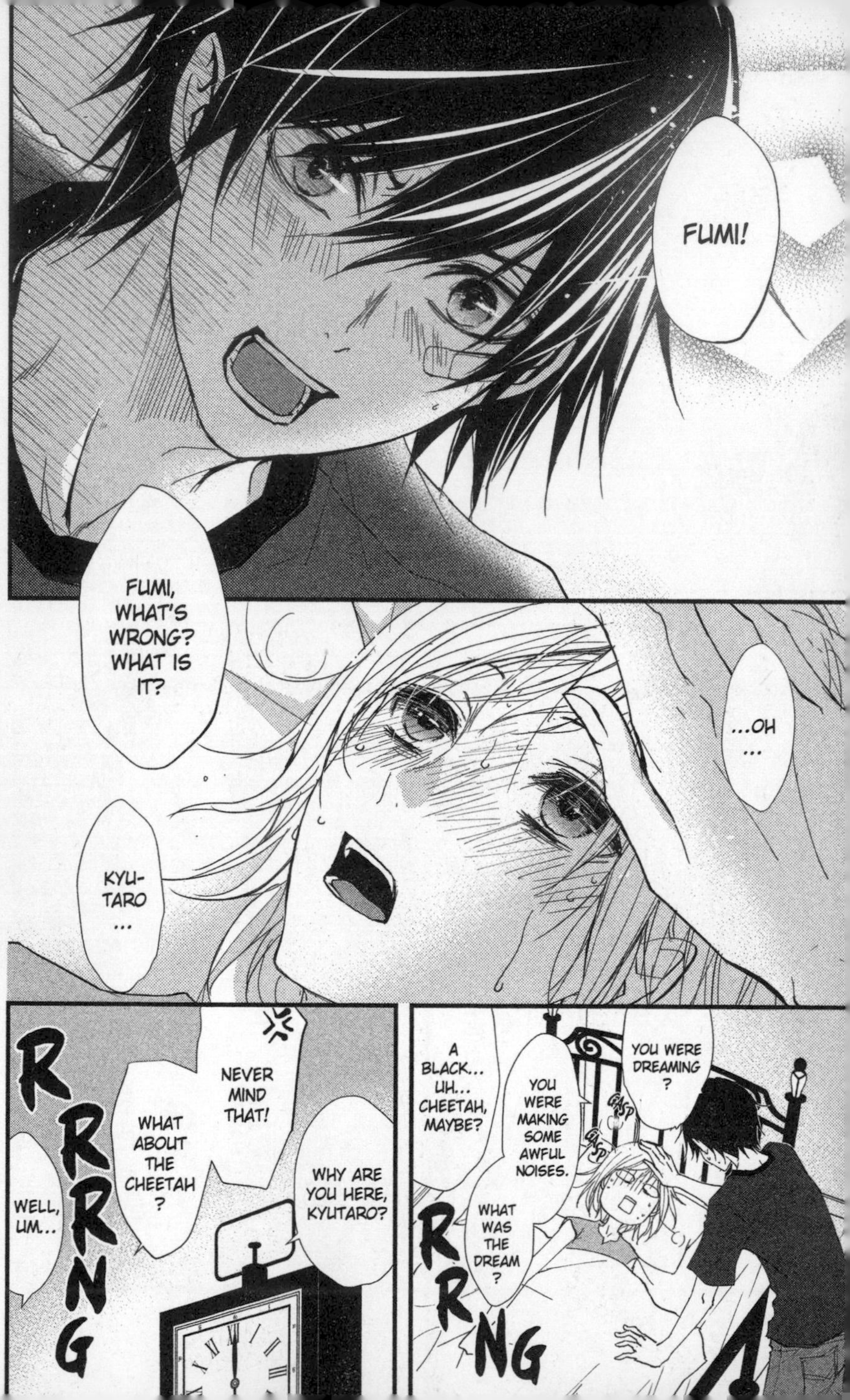
FUMI!
FUMI, WHAT'S WRONG? WHAT IS IT?
...OH ...
KYU-TARO ...
YOU WERE DREAMING ?
YOU WERE MAKING SOME AWFUL NOISES.
GASP
GASP
WHAT WAS THE DREAM ?
A BLACK... UH... CHEETAH, MAYBE?
RRRNG
WHY ARE YOU HERE, KYUTARO?
NEVER MIND THAT!
WHAT ABOUT THE CHEETAH ?
WELL, UM...
RRRRNG

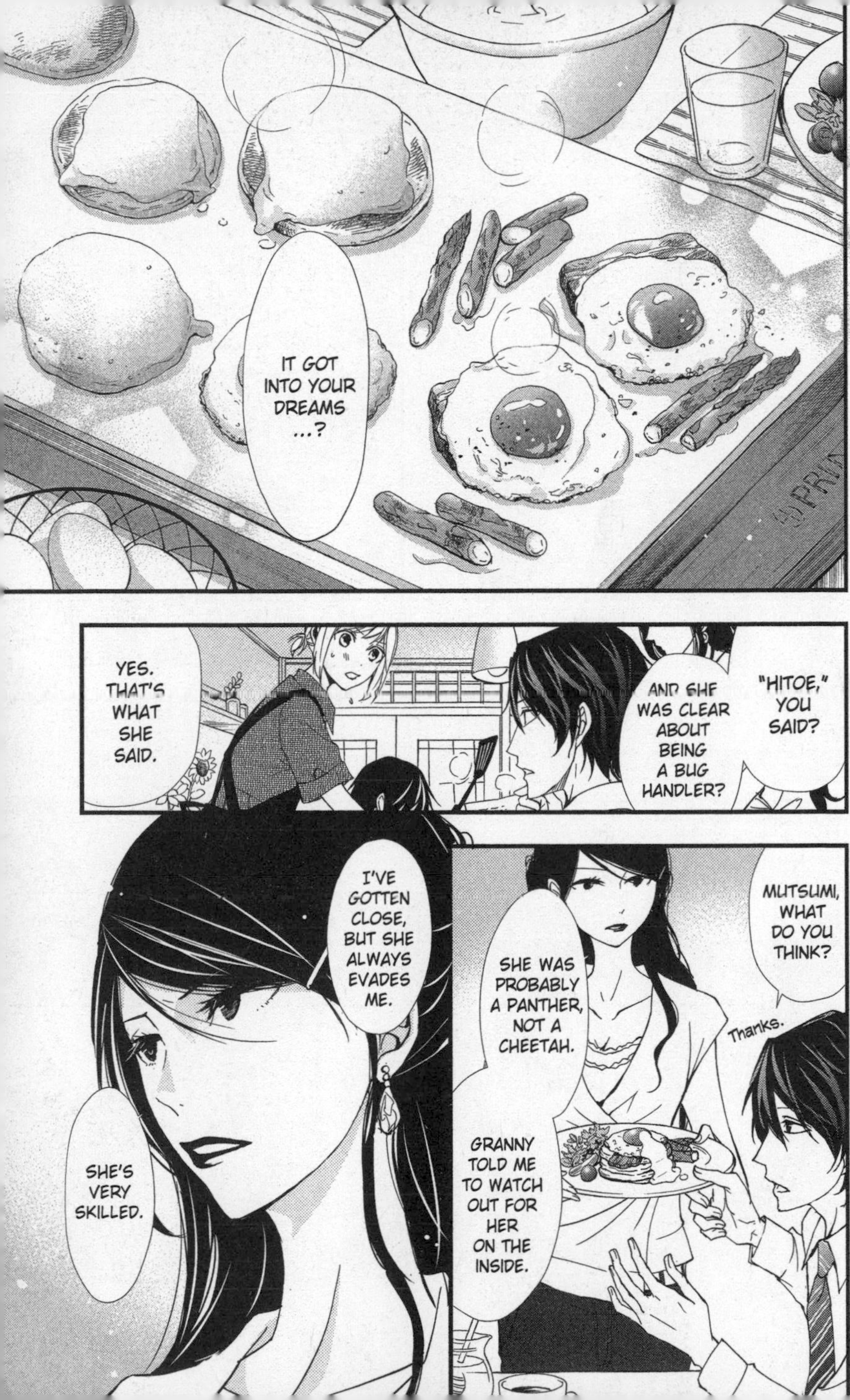
IT GOT INTO YOUR DREAMS ...?
"HITOE," YOU SAID?
AND SHE WAS CLEAR ABOUT BEING A BUG HANDLER?
YES. THAT'S WHAT SHE SAID.
MUTSUMI, WHAT DO YOU THINK?
Thanks.
SHE WAS PROBABLY A PANTHER, NOT A CHEETAH.
GRANNY TOLD ME TO WATCH OUT FOR HER ON THE INSIDE.
I'VE GOTTEN CLOSE, BUT SHE ALWAYS EVADES ME.
SHE'S VERY SKILLED.

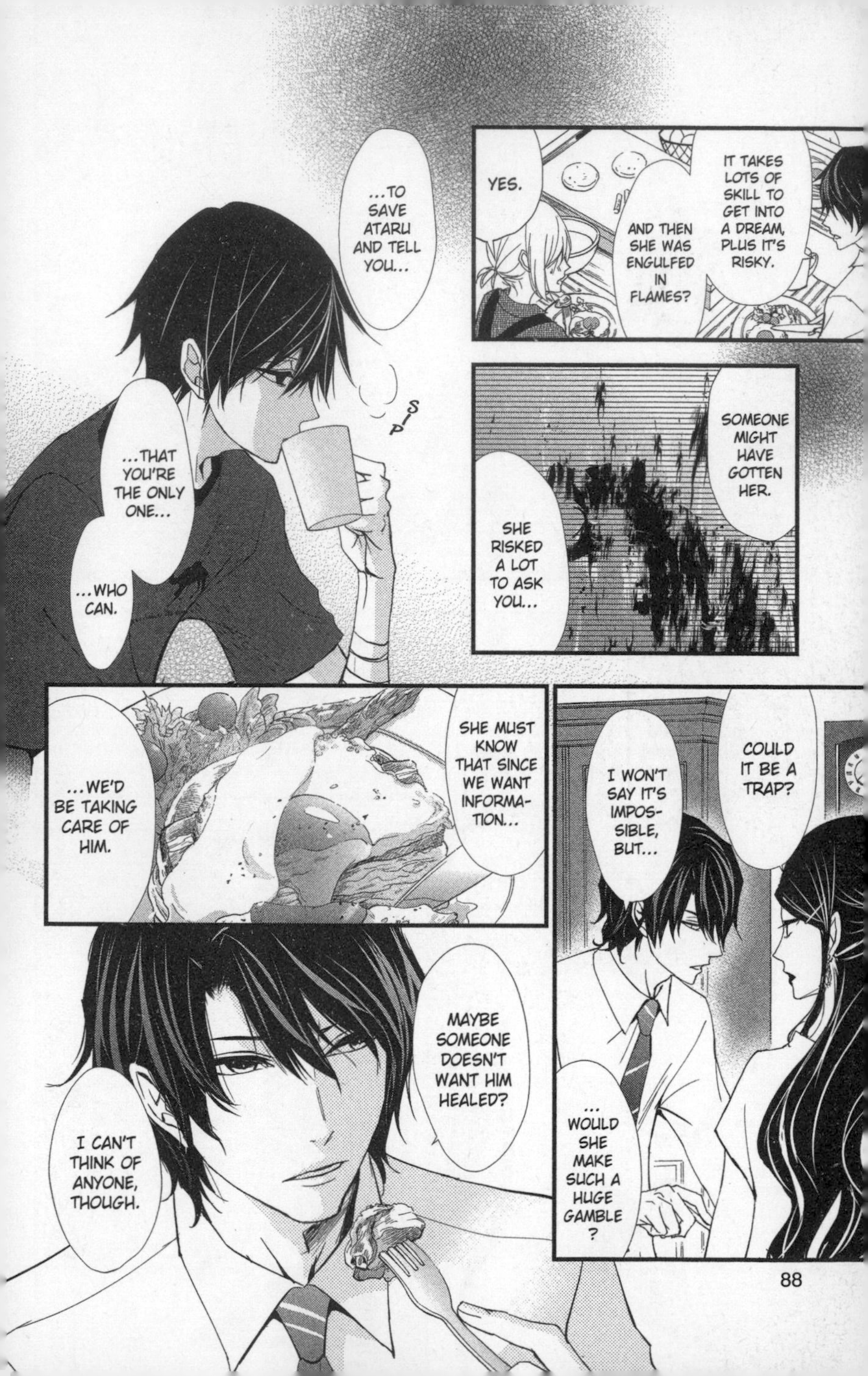
IT TAKES LOTS OF SKILL TO GET INTO A DREAM, PLUS IT'S RISKY.
AND THEN SHE WAS ENGULFED IN FLAMES?
YES.
SOMEONE MIGHT HAVE GOTTEN HER.
SHE RISKED A LOT TO ASK YOU...
...TO SAVE ATARU AND TELL YOU...
SIP
...THAT YOU'RE THE ONLY ONE...
...WHO CAN.
COULD IT BE A TRAP?
I WON'T SAY IT'S IMPOSSIBLE, BUT...
...WOULD SHE MAKE SUCH A HUGE GAMBLE?
SHE MUST KNOW THAT SINCE WE WANT INFORMATION...
...WE'D BE TAKING CARE OF HIM.
MAYBE SOMEONE DOESN'T WANT HIM HEALED?
I CAN'T THINK OF ANYONE, THOUGH.

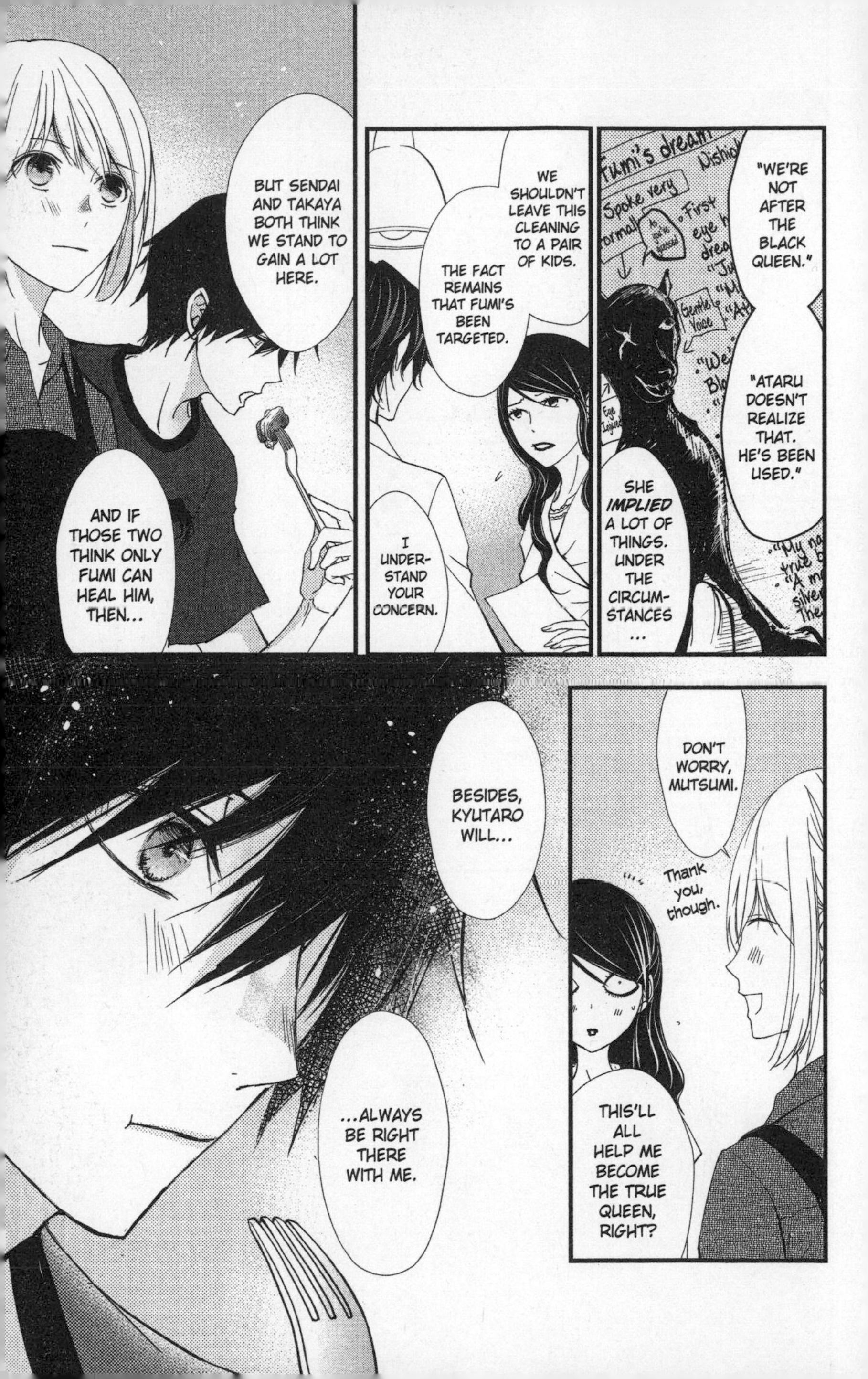
Fumi's dream
Spoke very formally
Gentle Voice
Eye Injured
"WE'RE NOT AFTER THE BLACK QUEEN."
"ATARU DOESN'T REALIZE THAT. HE'S BEEN USED."
SHE *IMPLIED* A LOT OF THINGS. UNDER THE CIRCUMSTANCES...
WE SHOULDN'T LEAVE THIS CLEANING TO A PAIR OF KIDS.
THE FACT REMAINS THAT FUMI'S BEEN TARGETED.
I UNDERSTAND YOUR CONCERN.
BUT SENDAI AND TAKAYA BOTH THINK WE STAND TO GAIN A LOT HERE.
AND IF THOSE TWO THINK ONLY FUMI CAN HEAL HIM, THEN...
DON'T WORRY, MUTSUMI.
Thank you, though.
...
THIS'LL ALL HELP ME BECOME THE TRUE QUEEN, RIGHT?
BESIDES, KYUTARO WILL...
...ALWAYS BE RIGHT THERE WITH ME.

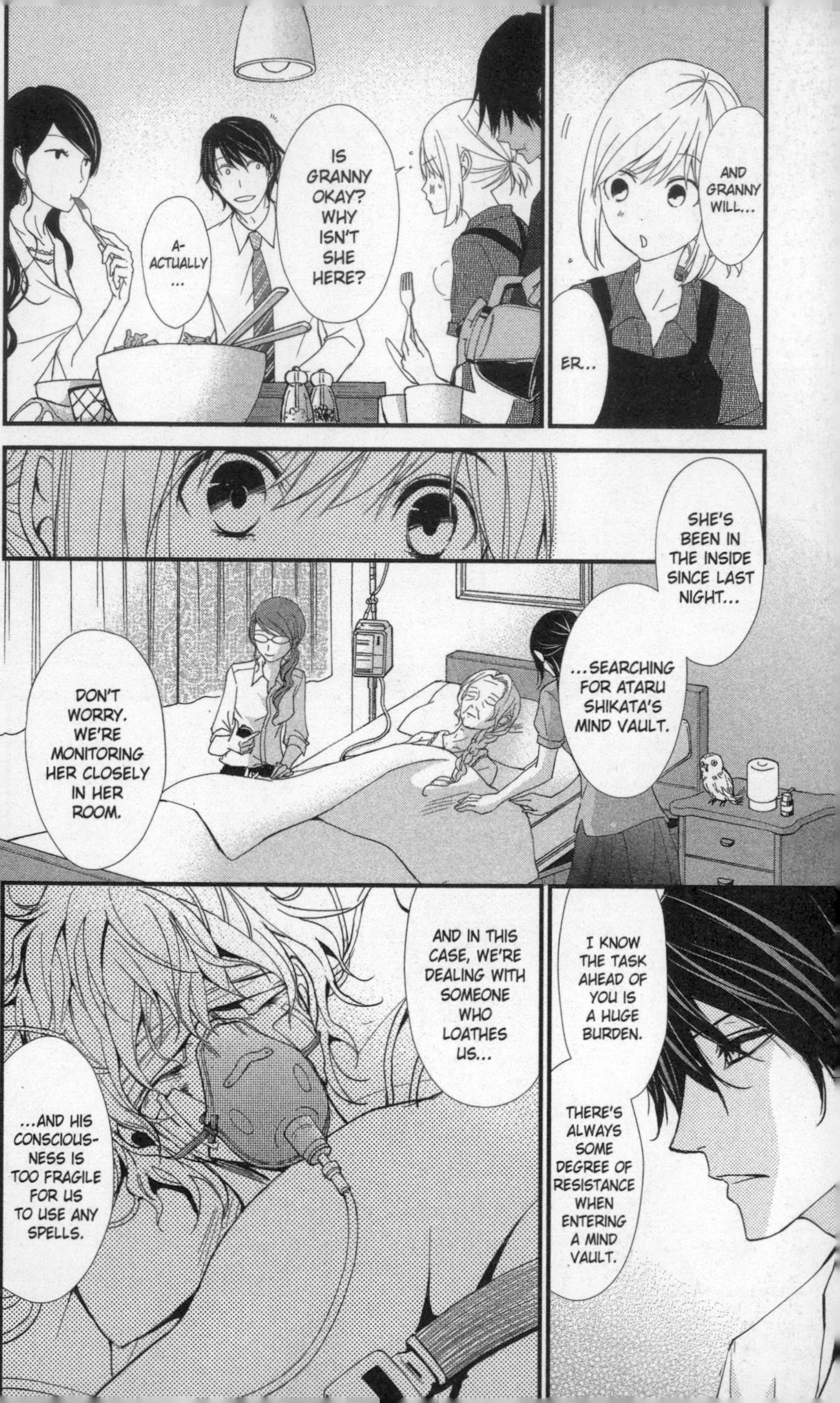
AND GRANNY WILL...
ER...
IS GRANNY OKAY? WHY ISN'T SHE HERE?
A-ACTUALLY...
SHE'S BEEN IN THE INSIDE SINCE LAST NIGHT...
...SEARCHING FOR ATARU SHIKATA'S MIND VAULT.
DON'T WORRY. WE'RE MONITORING HER CLOSELY IN HER ROOM.
I KNOW THE TASK AHEAD OF YOU IS A HUGE BURDEN.
THERE'S ALWAYS SOME DEGREE OF RESISTANCE WHEN ENTERING A MIND VAULT.
AND IN THIS CASE, WE'RE DEALING WITH SOMEONE WHO LOATHES US...
...AND HIS CONSCIOUS-NESS IS TOO FRAGILE FOR US TO USE ANY SPELLS.

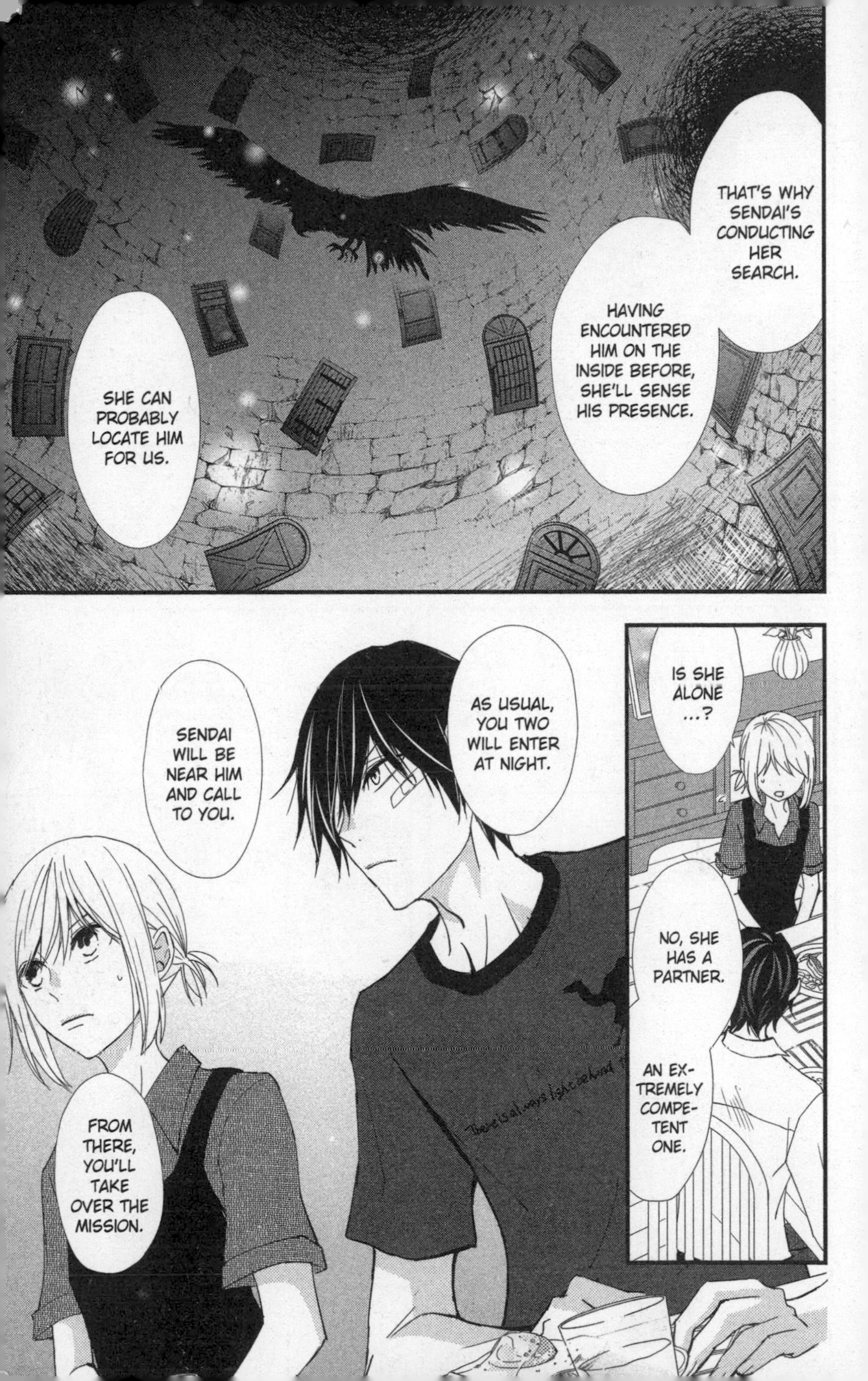
THAT'S WHY SENDAI'S CONDUCTING HER SEARCH.
HAVING ENCOUNTERED HIM ON THE INSIDE BEFORE, SHE'LL SENSE HIS PRESENCE.
SHE CAN PROBABLY LOCATE HIM FOR US.
IS SHE ALONE ...?
NO, SHE HAS A PARTNER.
AN EX-TREMELY COMPE-TENT ONE.
AS USUAL, YOU TWO WILL ENTER AT NIGHT.
SENDAI WILL BE NEAR HIM AND CALL TO YOU.
FROM THERE, YOU'LL TAKE OVER THE MISSION.

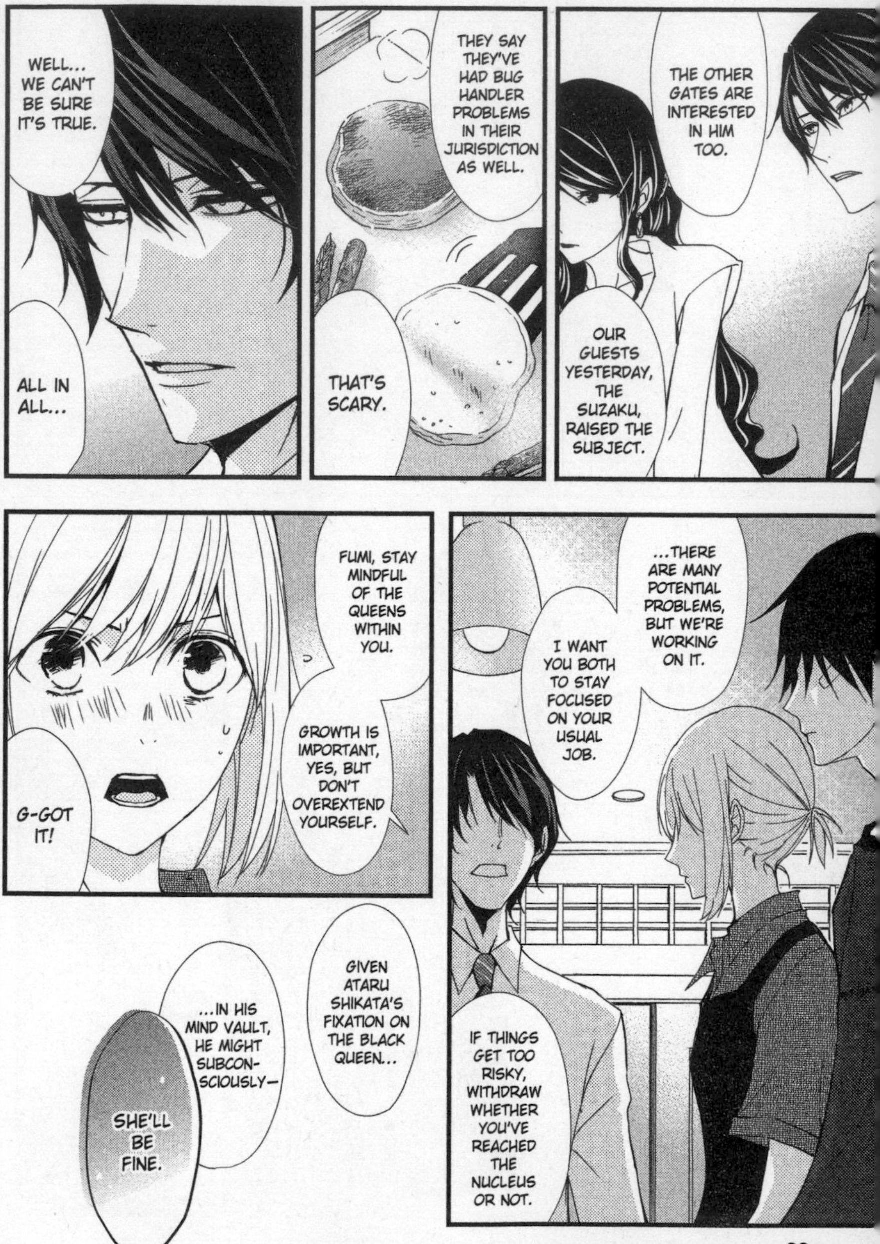
THE OTHER GATES ARE INTERESTED IN HIM TOO.
OUR GUESTS YESTERDAY, THE SUZAKU, RAISED THE SUBJECT.
THEY SAY THEY'VE HAD BUG HANDLER PROBLEMS IN THEIR JURISDICTION AS WELL.
THAT'S SCARY.
WELL... WE CAN'T BE SURE IT'S TRUE.
ALL IN ALL...
...THERE ARE MANY POTENTIAL PROBLEMS, BUT WE'RE WORKING ON IT.
I WANT YOU BOTH TO STAY FOCUSED ON YOUR USUAL JOB.
IF THINGS GET TOO RISKY, WITHDRAW WHETHER YOU'VE REACHED THE NUCLEUS OR NOT.
FUMI, STAY MINDFUL OF THE QUEENS WITHIN YOU.
GROWTH IS IMPORTANT, YES, BUT DON'T OVEREXTEND YOURSELF.
G-GOT IT!
GIVEN ATARU SHIKATA'S FIXATION ON THE BLACK QUEEN...
...IN HIS MIND VAULT, HE MIGHT SUBCON-SCIOUSLY—
SHE'LL BE FINE.

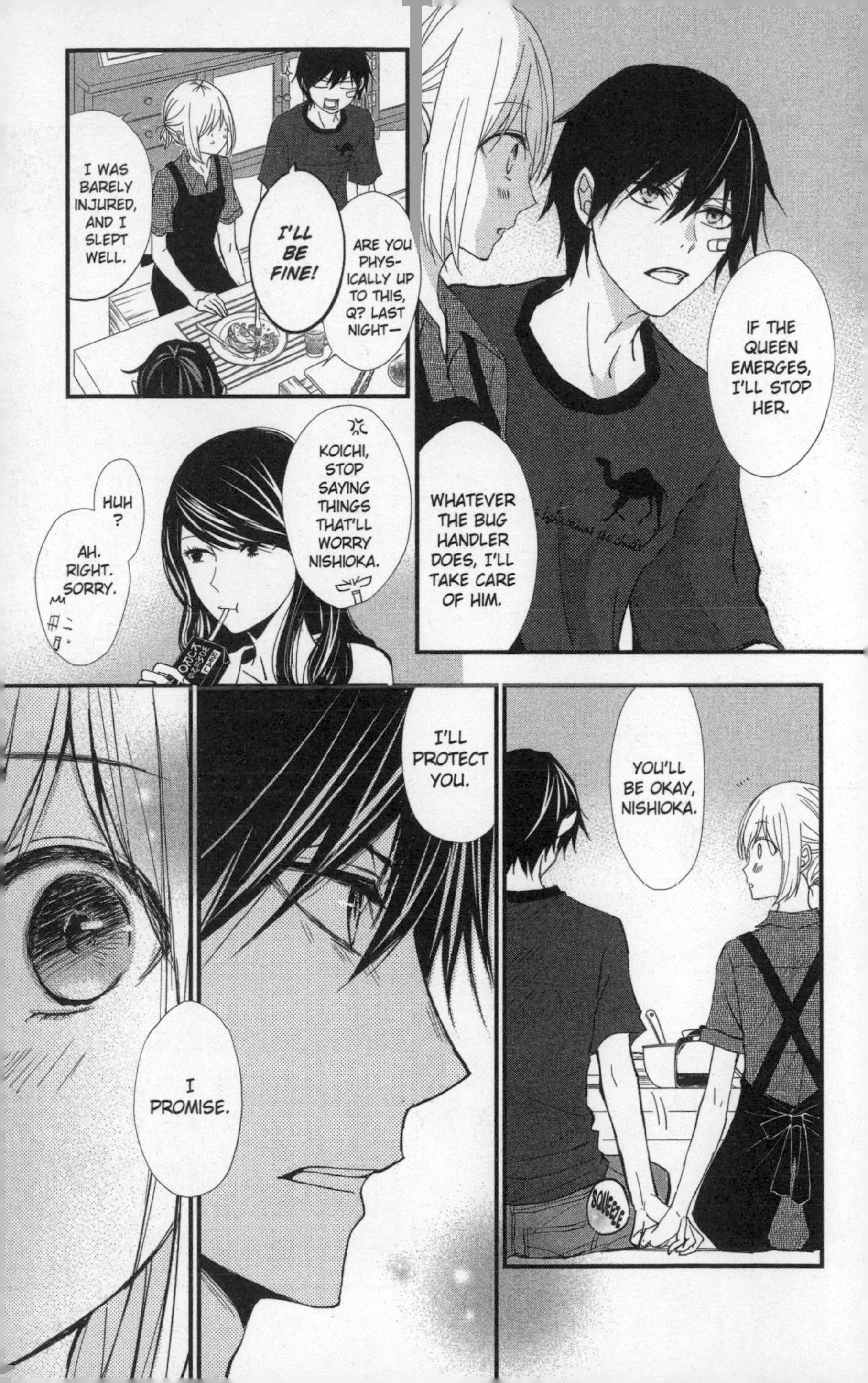
IF THE QUEEN EMERGES, I'LL STOP HER.
WHATEVER THE BUG HANDLER DOES, I'LL TAKE CARE OF HIM.
ARE YOU PHYS-ICALLY UP TO THIS, Q? LAST NIGHT—
I'LL BE FINE!
I WAS BARELY INJURED, AND I SLEPT WELL.
KOICHI, STOP SAYING THINGS THAT'LL WORRY NISHIOKA.
HUH?
AH. RIGHT. SORRY.
YOU'LL BE OKAY, NISHIOKA.
SQUEEZE
I'LL PROTECT YOU.
I PROMISE.

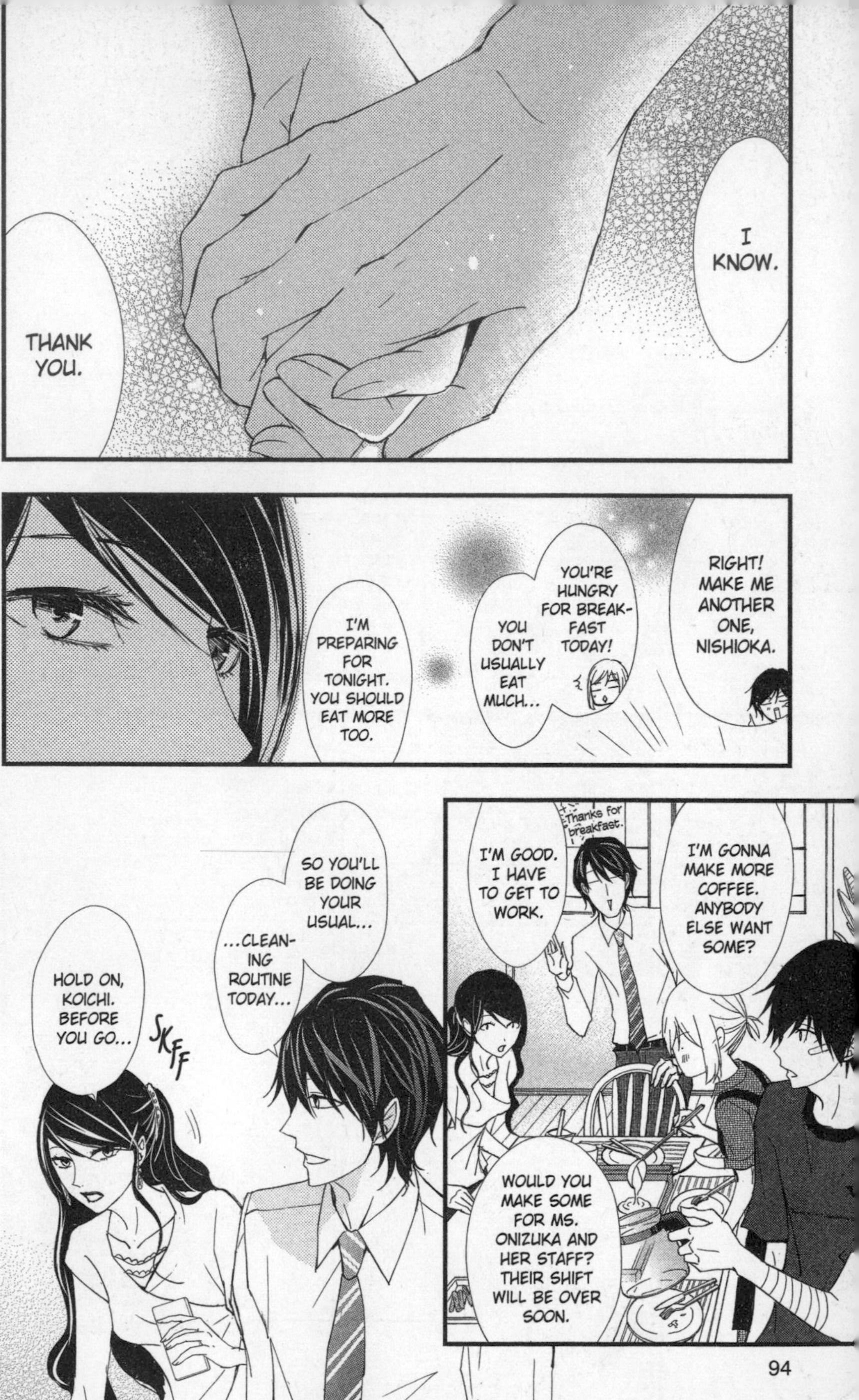
I KNOW.
THANK YOU.
RIGHT! MAKE ME ANOTHER ONE, NISHIOKA.
YOU'RE HUNGRY FOR BREAK-FAST TODAY!
YOU DON'T USUALLY EAT MUCH...
I'M PREPARING FOR TONIGHT. YOU SHOULD EAT MORE TOO.
I'M GONNA MAKE MORE COFFEE. ANYBODY ELSE WANT SOME?
Thanks for breakfast.
I'M GOOD. I HAVE TO GET TO WORK.
WOULD YOU MAKE SOME FOR MS. ONIZUKA AND HER STAFF? THEIR SHIFT WILL BE OVER SOON.
SO YOU'LL BE DOING YOUR USUAL...
...CLEAN-ING ROUTINE TODAY...
SKFF
HOLD ON, KOICHI. BEFORE YOU GO...

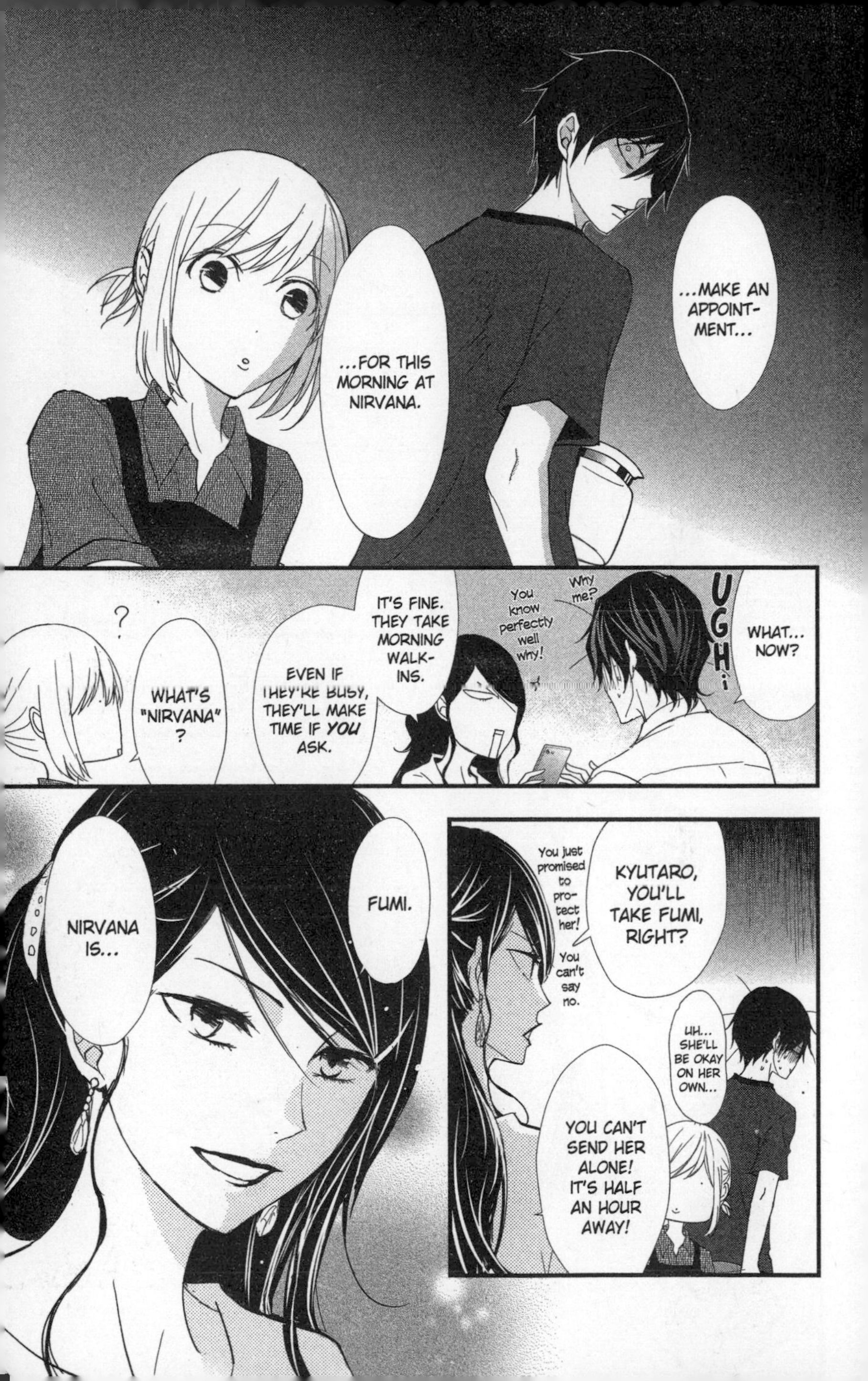
...MAKE AN APPOINTMENT...
...FOR THIS MORNING AT NIRVANA.
WHAT... NOW?
UGH!
Why me?
You know perfectly well why!
IT'S FINE. THEY TAKE MORNING WALK-INS.
EVEN IF THEY'RE BUSY, THEY'LL MAKE TIME IF *YOU* ASK.
?
WHAT'S "NIRVANA"?
KYUTARO, YOU'LL TAKE FUMI, RIGHT?
You just promised to protect her!
You can't say no.
UH... SHE'LL BE OKAY ON HER OWN...
YOU CAN'T SEND HER ALONE! IT'S HALF AN HOUR AWAY!
FUMI.
NIRVANA IS...

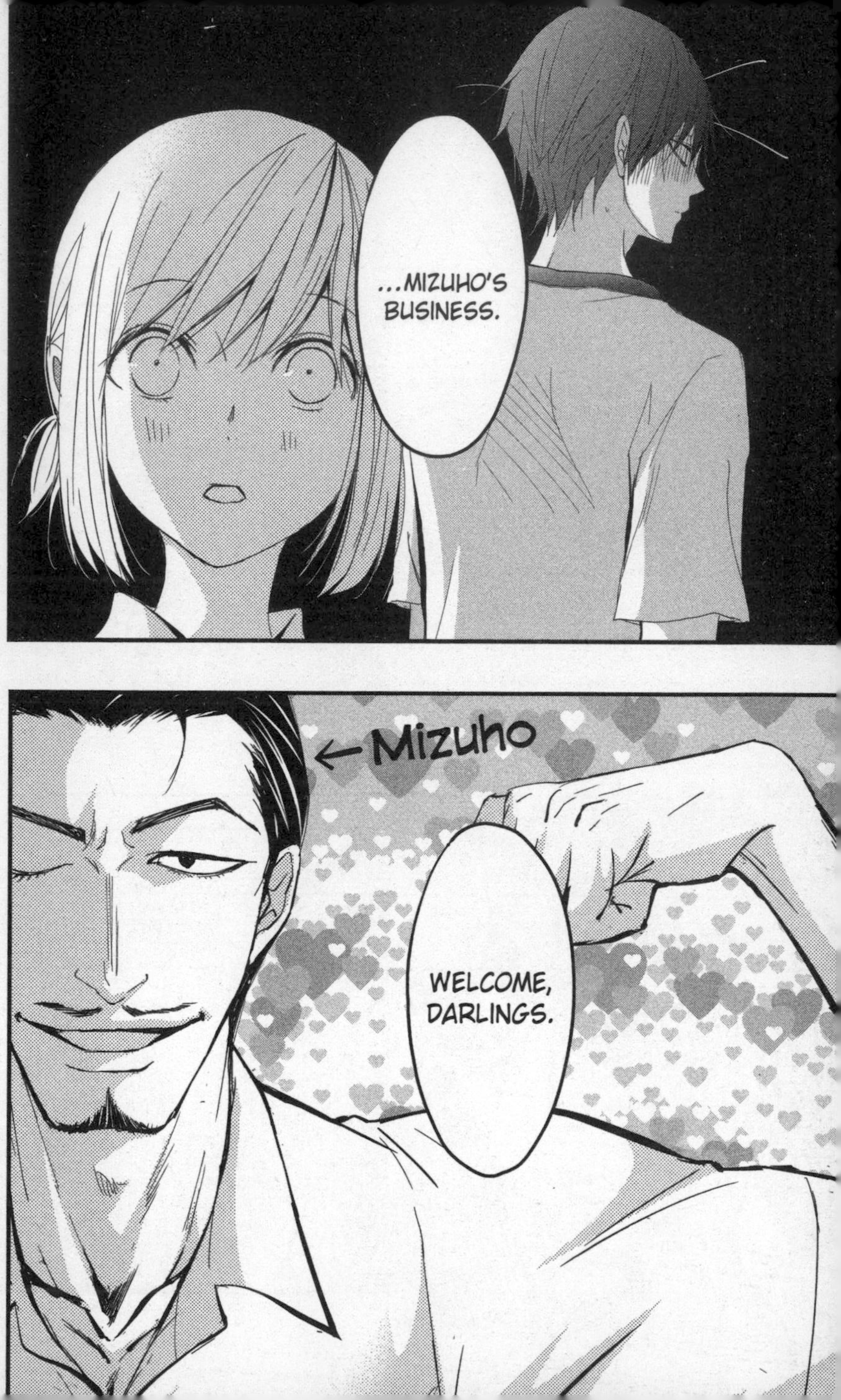
...MIZUHO'S BUSINESS.
←Mizuho
WELCOME, DARLINGS.

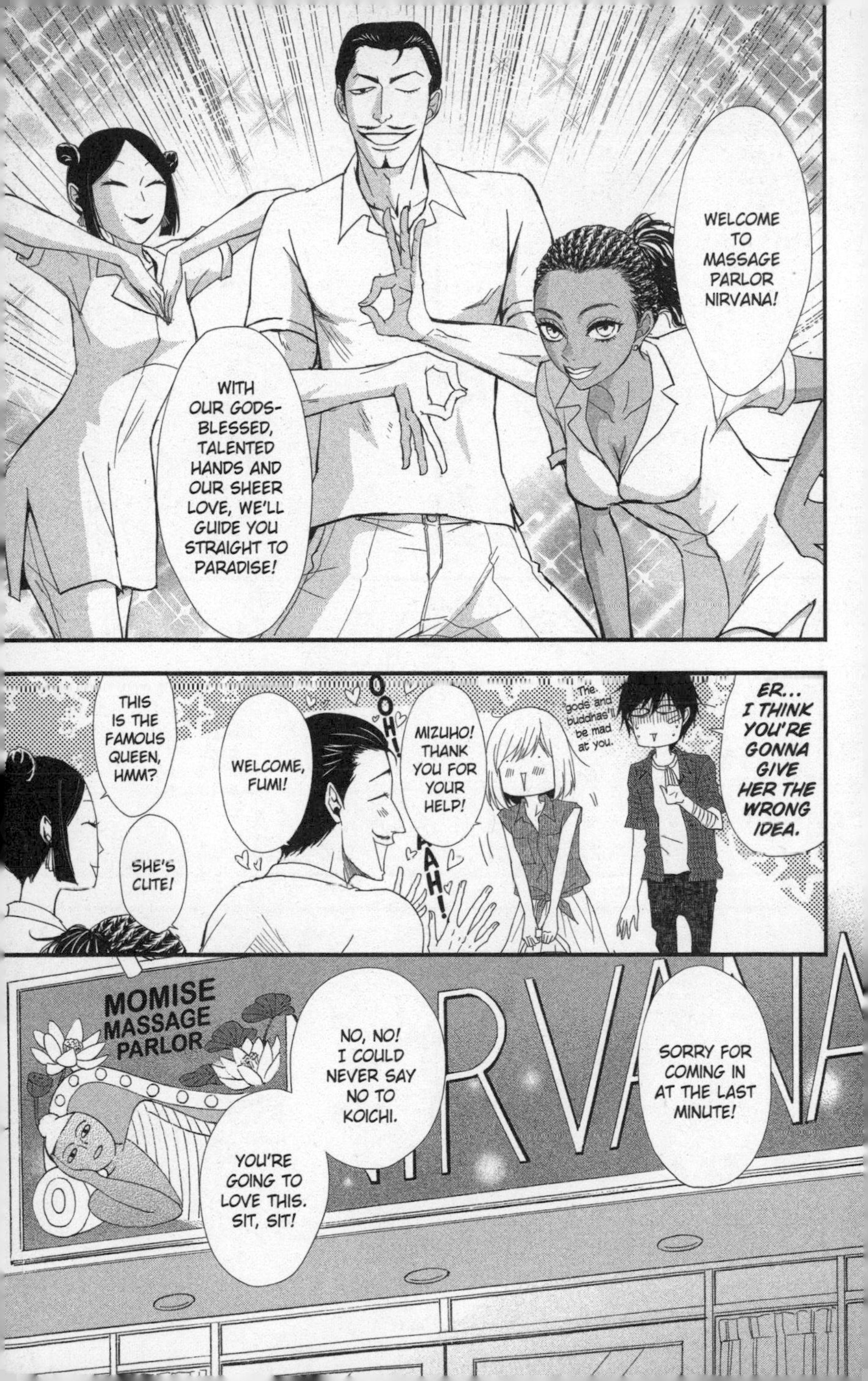
WELCOME TO MASSAGE PARLOR NIRVANA!
WITH OUR GODS-BLESSED, TALENTED HANDS AND OUR SHEER LOVE, WE'LL GUIDE YOU STRAIGHT TO PARADISE!
ER... I THINK YOU'RE GONNA GIVE HER THE WRONG IDEA.
The gods and buddhas'll be mad at you.
MIZUHO! THANK YOU FOR YOUR HELP!
OOH!
AAH!
WELCOME, FUMI!
THIS IS THE FAMOUS QUEEN, HMM?
SHE'S CUTE!
SORRY FOR COMING IN AT THE LAST MINUTE!
NO, NO! I COULD NEVER SAY NO TO KOICHI.
MOMISE MASSAGE PARLOR
YOU'RE GOING TO LOVE THIS. SIT, SIT!

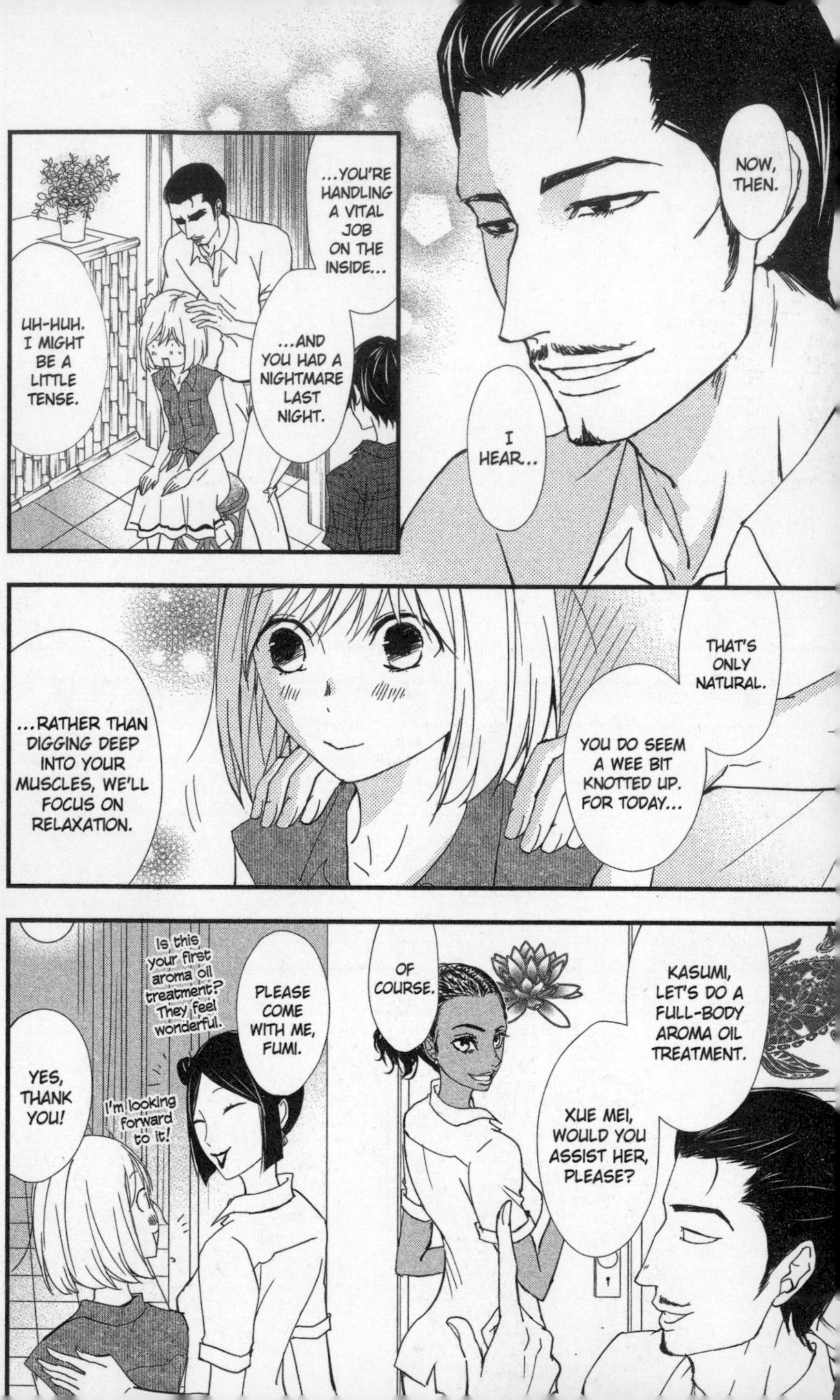
NOW, THEN.
I HEAR...
...YOU'RE HANDLING A VITAL JOB ON THE INSIDE...
...AND YOU HAD A NIGHTMARE LAST NIGHT.
UH-HUH. I MIGHT BE A LITTLE TENSE.
THAT'S ONLY NATURAL.
YOU DO SEEM A WEE BIT KNOTTED UP. FOR TODAY...
...RATHER THAN DIGGING DEEP INTO YOUR MUSCLES, WE'LL FOCUS ON RELAXATION.
KASUMI, LET'S DO A FULL-BODY AROMA OIL TREATMENT.
XUE MEI, WOULD YOU ASSIST HER, PLEASE?
OF COURSE.
PLEASE COME WITH ME, FUMI.
Is this your first aroma oil treatment? They feel wonderful.
YES, THANK YOU!
I'm looking forward to it!

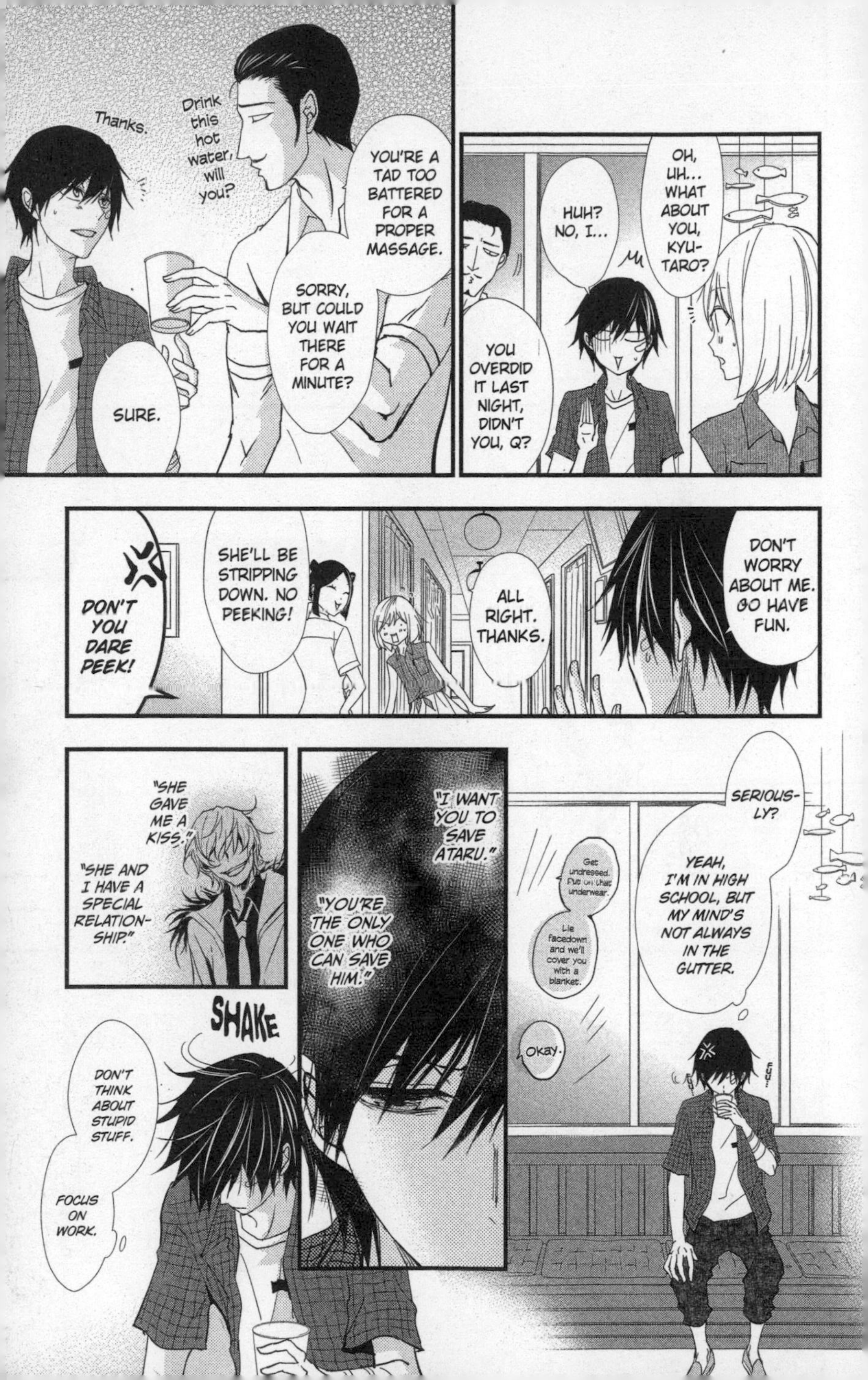
OH, UH... WHAT ABOUT YOU, KYU-TARO?
HUH? NO, I...
YOU OVERDID IT LAST NIGHT, DIDN'T YOU, Q?
YOU'RE A TAD TOO BATTERED FOR A PROPER MASSAGE.
Drink this hot water, will you?
Thanks.
SORRY, BUT COULD YOU WAIT THERE FOR A MINUTE?
SURE.
DON'T WORRY ABOUT ME. GO HAVE FUN.
ALL RIGHT. THANKS.
SHE'LL BE STRIPPING DOWN. NO PEEKING!
DON'T YOU DARE PEEK!
SERIOUS-LY?
YEAH, I'M IN HIGH SCHOOL, BUT MY MIND'S NOT ALWAYS IN THE GUTTER.
Get undressed. Put on that underwear.
Lie facedown and we'll cover you with a blanket.
Okay.
FUU...
"I WANT YOU TO SAVE ATARU."
"YOU'RE THE ONLY ONE WHO CAN SAVE HIM."
"SHE GAVE ME A KISS."
"SHE AND I HAVE A SPECIAL RELATIONSHIP."
SHAKE
DON'T THINK ABOUT STUPID STUFF.
FOCUS ON WORK.

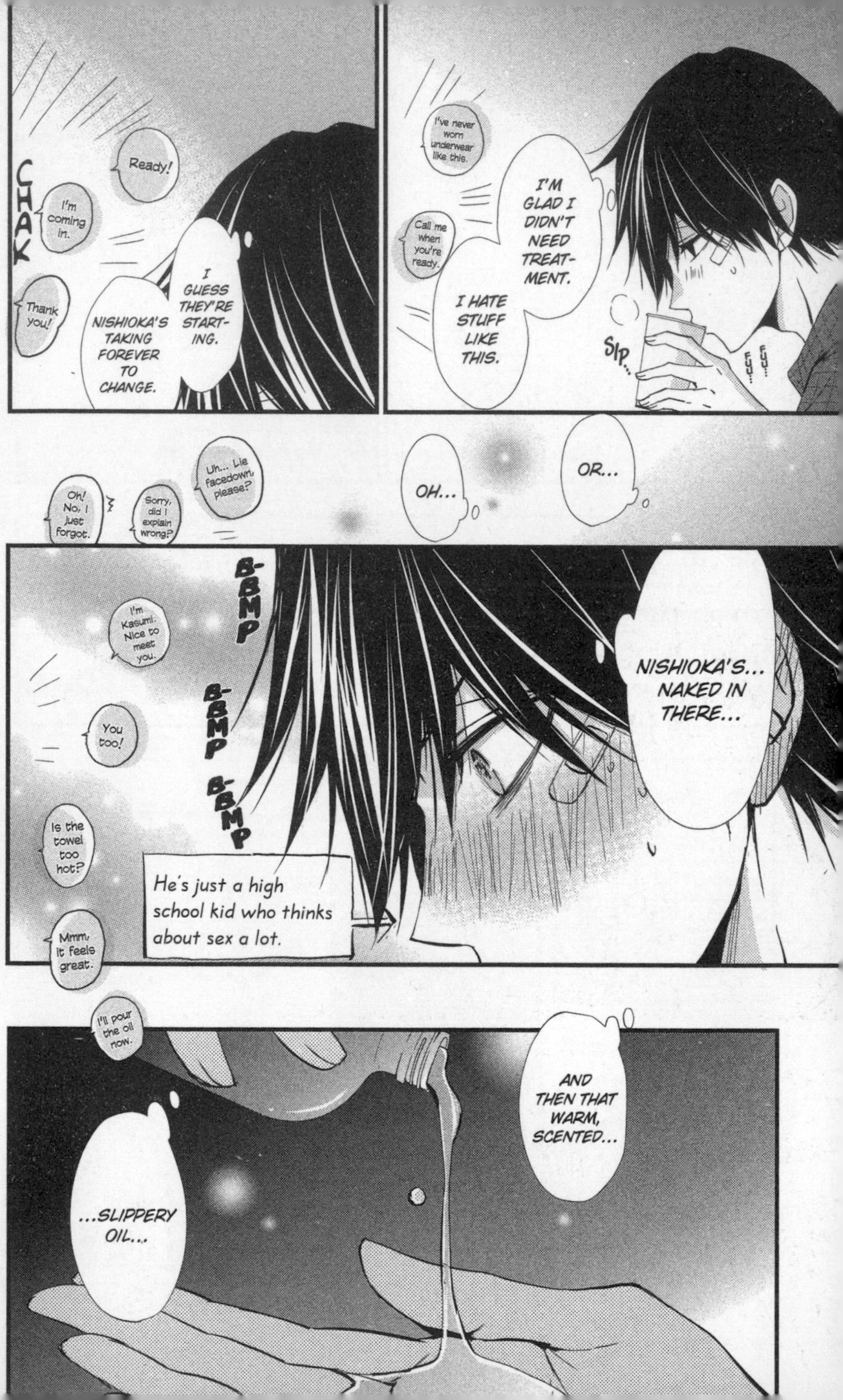
I've never worn underwear like this.
I'M GLAD I DIDN'T NEED TREATMENT.
Call me when you're ready.
I HATE STUFF LIKE THIS.
SIP...
FUU...
FUU...
Ready!
I GUESS THEY'RE STARTING.
CHAK
I'm coming in.
NISHIOKA'S TAKING FOREVER TO CHANGE.
Thank you!
OR...
OH...
Uh... Lie facedown, please?
Sorry, did I explain wrong?
Oh! No, I just forgot.
NISHIOKA'S... NAKED IN THERE...
B-BMP
B-BMP
B-BMP
I'm Kasumi. Nice to meet you.
You too!
Is the towel too hot?
He's just a high school kid who thinks about sex a lot.
Mmm, it feels great.
AND THEN THAT WARM, SCENTED...
I'll pour the oil now.
...SLIPPERY OIL...

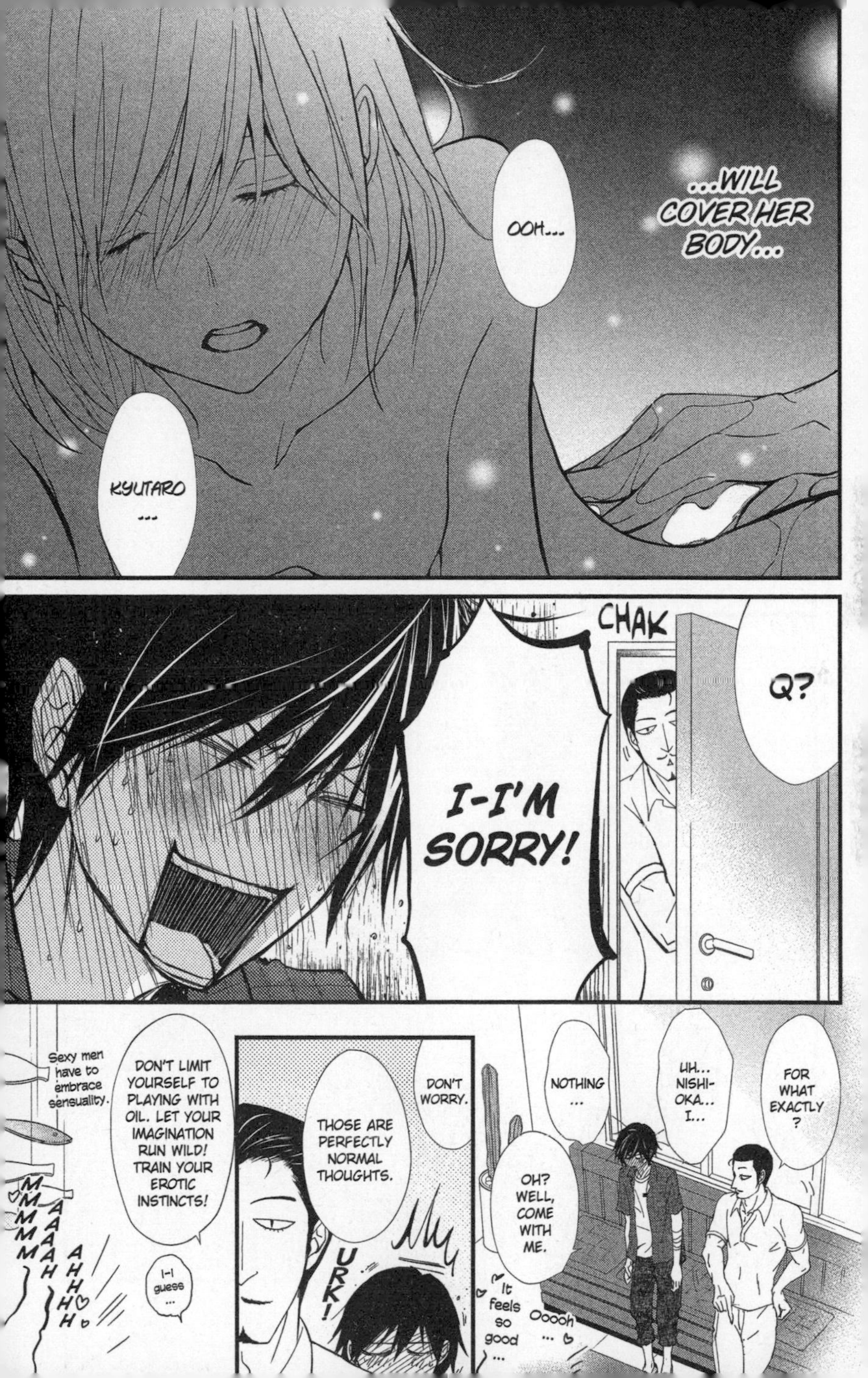
...WILL COVER HER BODY...
OOH...
KYUTARO ...
Q?
CHAK
I-I'M SORRY!
FOR WHAT EXACTLY?
UH... NISHIOKA... I...
NOTHING ...
OH? WELL, COME WITH ME.
It feels so good ...
Ooooh ...
DON'T WORRY.
THOSE ARE PERFECTLY NORMAL THOUGHTS.
URK!
DON'T LIMIT YOURSELF TO PLAYING WITH OIL. LET YOUR IMAGINATION RUN WILD! TRAIN YOUR EROTIC INSTINCTS!
I-I guess ...
Sexy men have to embrace sensuality.
MMMMMM
AAAAAH
AHHHHH

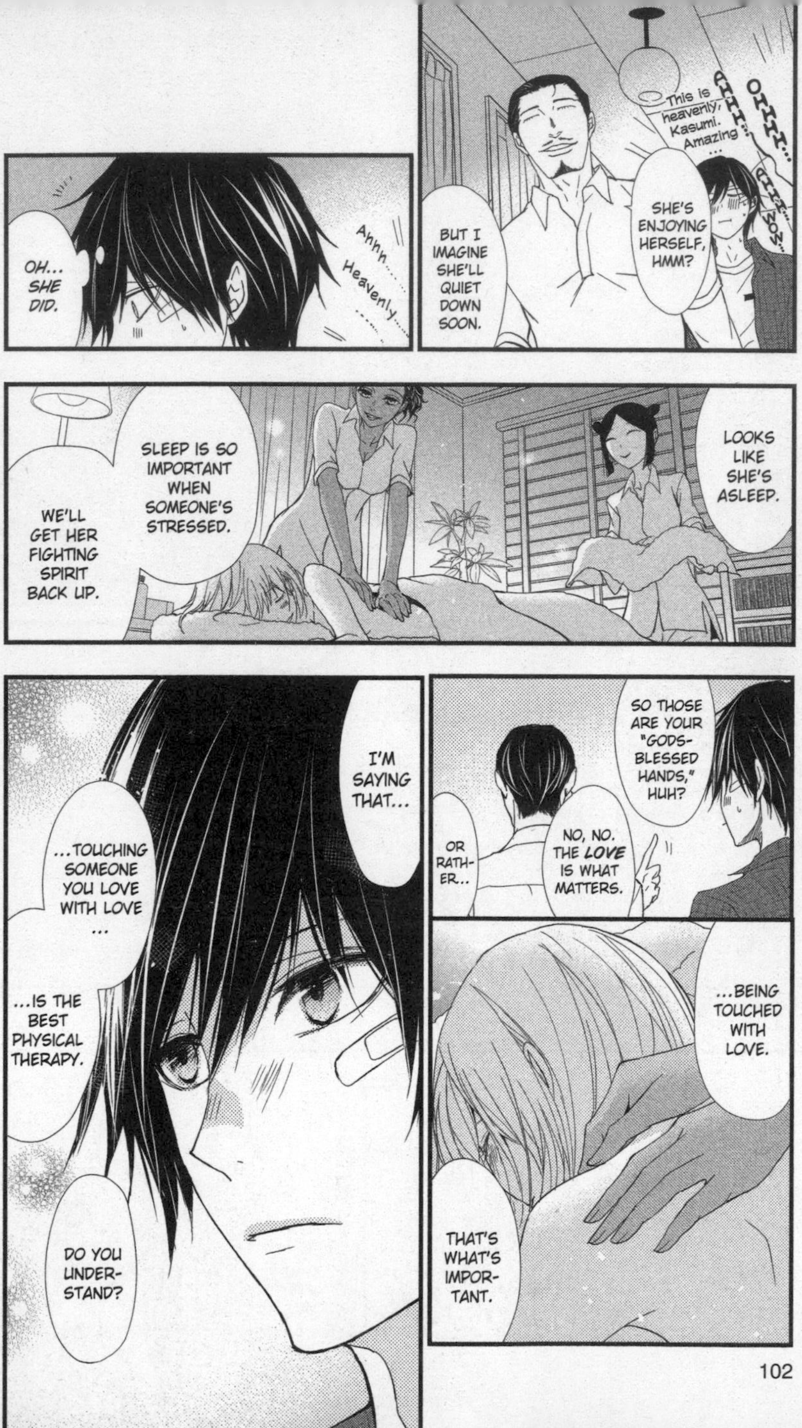
OHHHH...
AHHHH...
This is heavenly, Kasumi. Amazing...
AHHH... WOW...
SHE'S ENJOYING HERSELF, HMM?
BUT I IMAGINE SHE'LL QUIET DOWN SOON.
Annn... Heavenly......
OH... SHE DID.
LOOKS LIKE SHE'S ASLEEP.
SLEEP IS SO IMPORTANT WHEN SOMEONE'S STRESSED.
WE'LL GET HER FIGHTING SPIRIT BACK UP.
SO THOSE ARE YOUR "GODS-BLESSED HANDS," HUH?
NO, NO. THE *LOVE* IS WHAT MATTERS.
OR RATH-ER...
I'M SAYING THAT...
...TOUCHING SOMEONE YOU LOVE WITH LOVE...
...IS THE BEST PHYSICAL THERAPY.
DO YOU UNDER-STAND?
...BEING TOUCHED WITH LOVE.
THAT'S WHAT'S IMPOR-TANT.

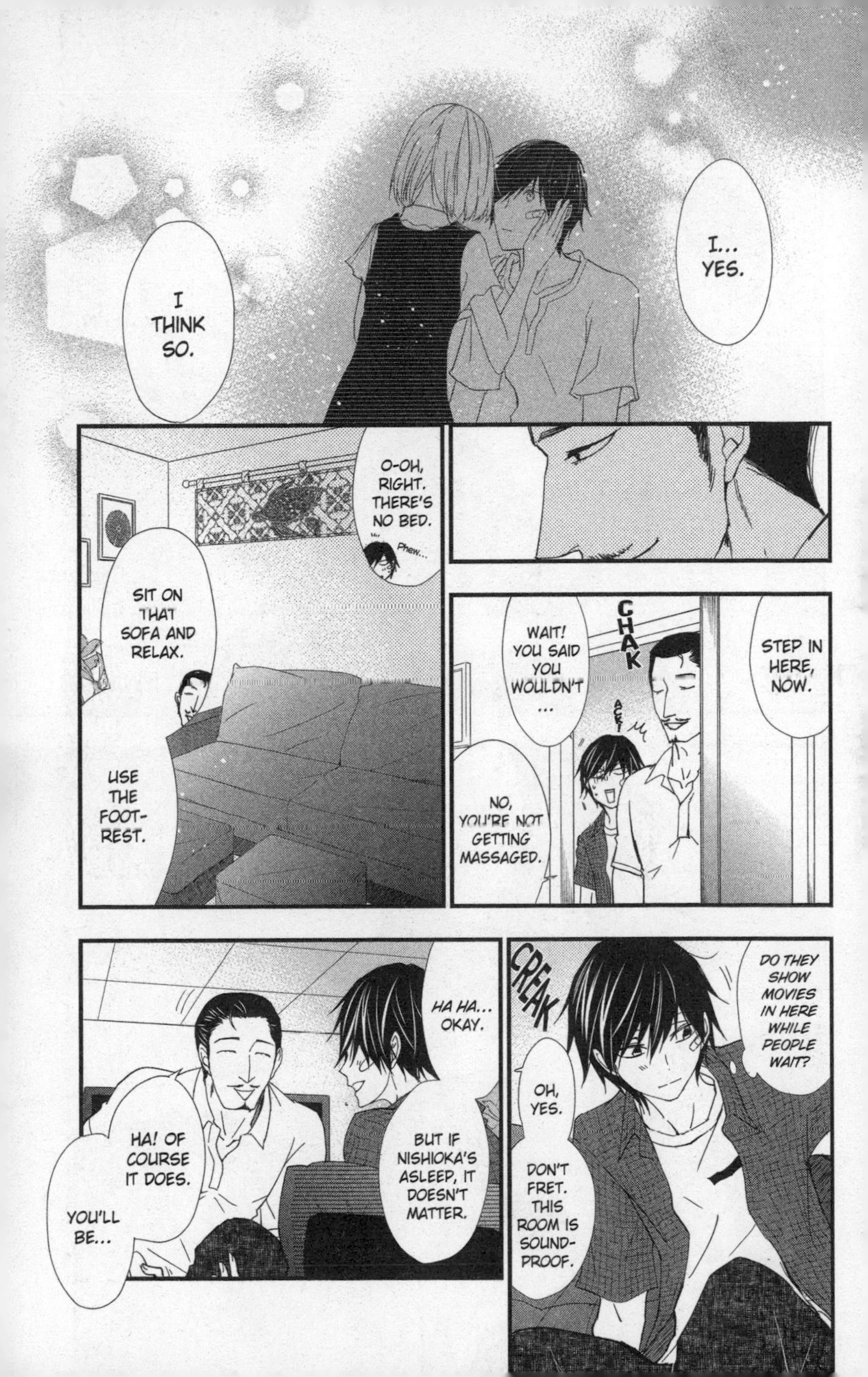
I... YES.
I THINK SO.
STEP IN HERE, NOW.
CHAK
ACK!
WAIT! YOU SAID YOU WOULDN'T...
NO, YOU'RE NOT GETTING MASSAGED.
O-OH, RIGHT. THERE'S NO BED.
Phew...
SIT ON THAT SOFA AND RELAX.
USE THE FOOT-REST.
CREAK
DO THEY SHOW MOVIES IN HERE WHILE PEOPLE WAIT?
OH, YES.
DON'T FRET. THIS ROOM IS SOUND-PROOF.
HA HA... OKAY.
BUT IF NISHIOKA'S ASLEEP, IT DOESN'T MATTER.
HA! OF COURSE IT DOES.
YOU'LL BE...

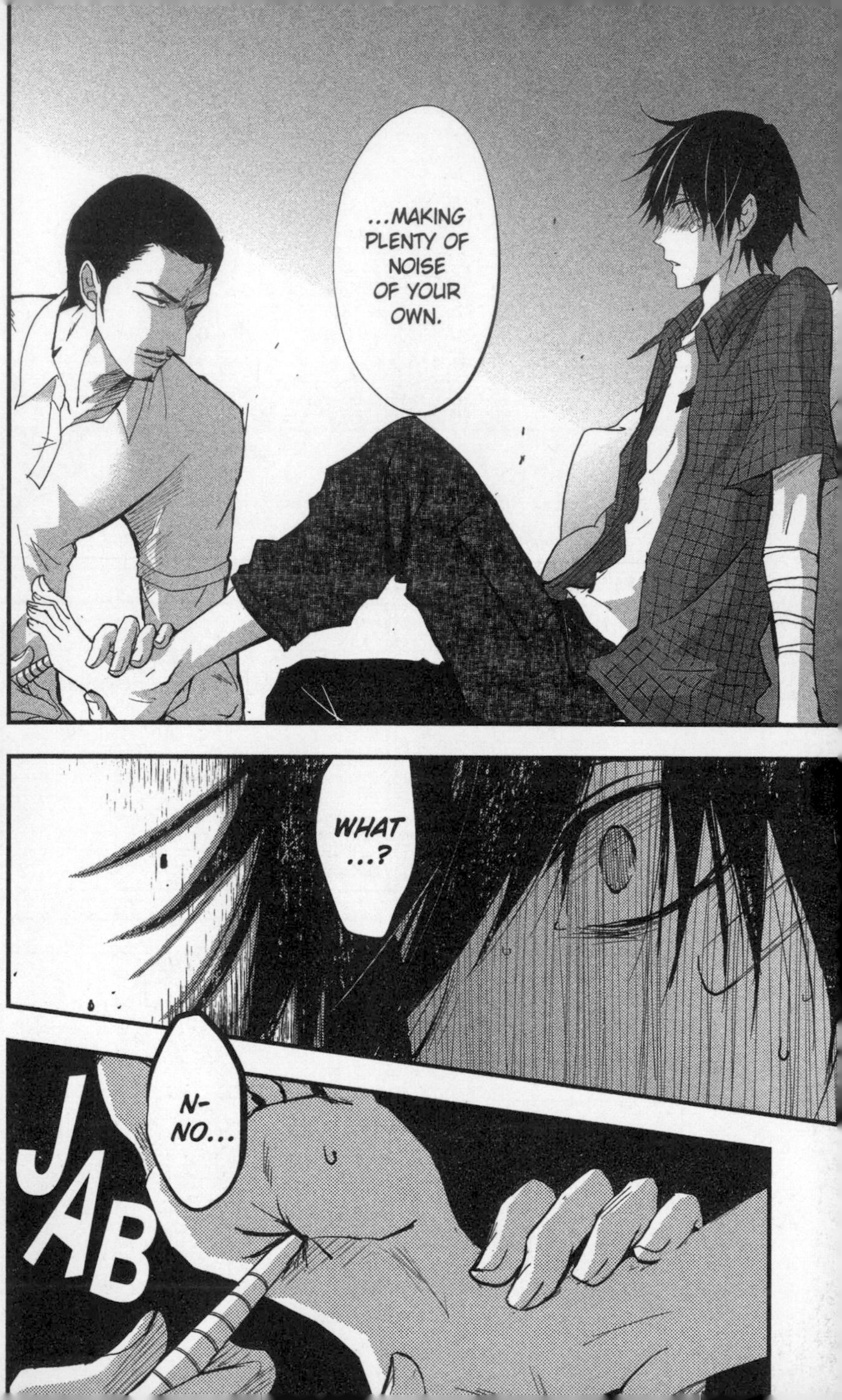
...MAKING PLENTY OF NOISE OF YOUR OWN.
WHAT ...?
N- NO...
JAB

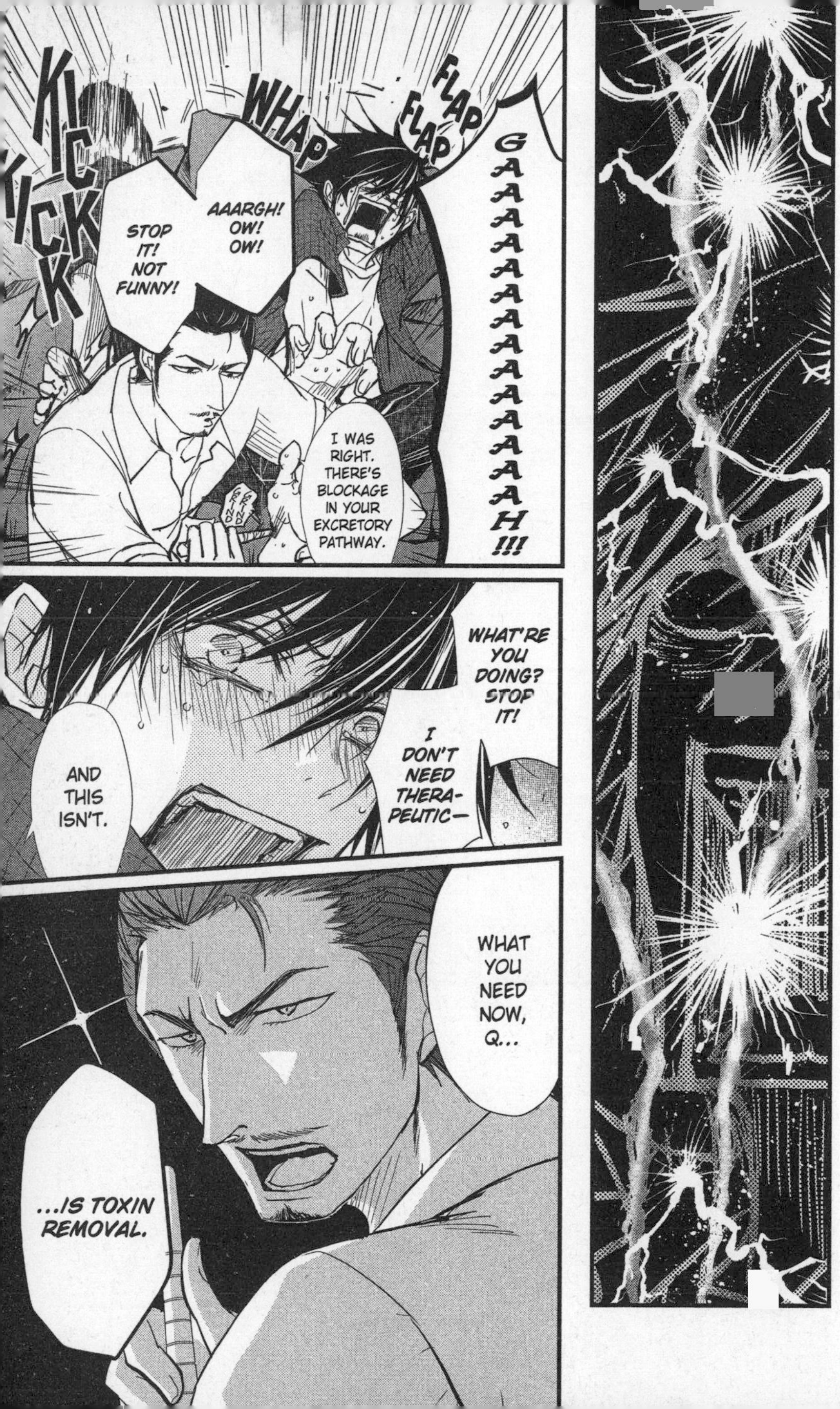
GAAAAAAAAAAAAAH!!!
FLAP FLAP
WHAP
AAARGH! OW! OW!
STOP IT! NOT FUNNY!
KICK KICK
I WAS RIGHT. THERE'S BLOCKAGE IN YOUR EXCRETORY PATHWAY.
GRIND GRIND
WHAT'RE YOU DOING? STOP IT!
I DON'T NEED THERA-PEUTIC—
AND THIS ISN'T.
WHAT YOU NEED NOW, Q...
...IS TOXIN REMOVAL.

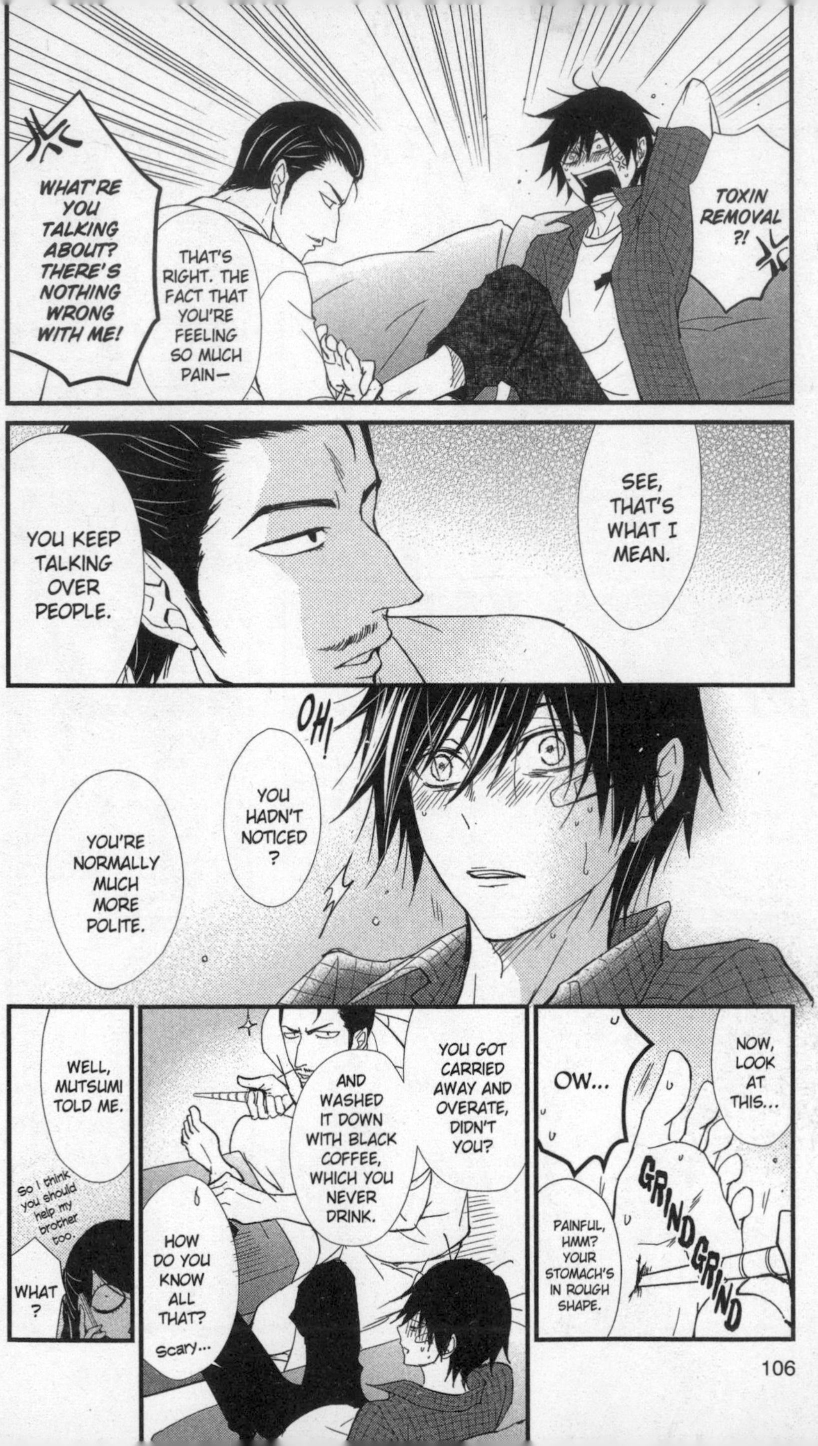
TOXIN REMOVAL?!
WHAT'RE YOU TALKING ABOUT? THERE'S NOTHING WRONG WITH ME!
THAT'S RIGHT. THE FACT THAT YOU'RE FEELING SO MUCH PAIN—
SEE, THAT'S WHAT I MEAN.
YOU KEEP TALKING OVER PEOPLE.
OH!
YOU HADN'T NOTICED?
YOU'RE NORMALLY MUCH MORE POLITE.
NOW, LOOK AT THIS...
OW...
GRIND GRIND
PAINFUL, HMM? YOUR STOMACH'S IN ROUGH SHAPE.
YOU GOT CARRIED AWAY AND OVERATE, DIDN'T YOU?
AND WASHED IT DOWN WITH BLACK COFFEE, WHICH YOU NEVER DRINK.
HOW DO YOU KNOW ALL THAT?
Scary...
WELL, MUTSUMI TOLD ME.
So I think you should help my brother too.
WHAT?

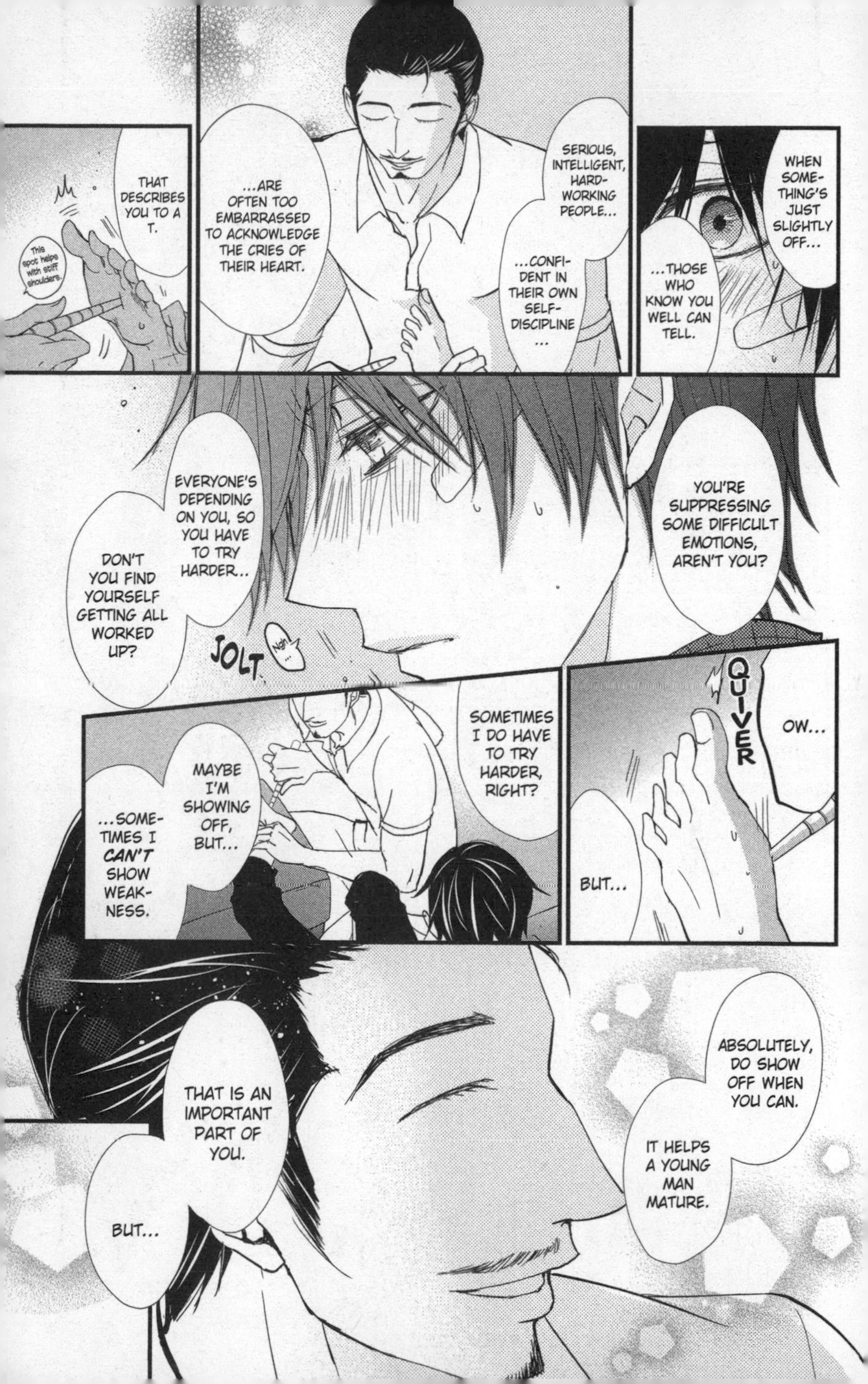
WHEN SOME-THING'S JUST SLIGHTLY OFF...
...THOSE WHO KNOW YOU WELL CAN TELL.
SERIOUS, INTELLIGENT, HARD-WORKING PEOPLE...
...CONFI-DENT IN THEIR OWN SELF-DISCIPLINE...
...ARE OFTEN TOO EMBARRASSED TO ACKNOWLEDGE THE CRIES OF THEIR HEART.
THAT DESCRIBES YOU TO A T.
This spot helps with stiff shoulders.
YOU'RE SUPPRESSING SOME DIFFICULT EMOTIONS, AREN'T YOU?
EVERYONE'S DEPENDING ON YOU, SO YOU HAVE TO TRY HARDER...
DON'T YOU FIND YOURSELF GETTING ALL WORKED UP?
JOLT
Ngh...
QUIVER
OW...
BUT...
SOMETIMES I DO HAVE TO TRY HARDER, RIGHT?
MAYBE I'M SHOWING OFF, BUT...
...SOME-TIMES I *CAN'T* SHOW WEAK-NESS.
ABSOLUTELY, DO SHOW OFF WHEN YOU CAN.
IT HELPS A YOUNG MAN MATURE.
THAT IS AN IMPORTANT PART OF YOU.
BUT...

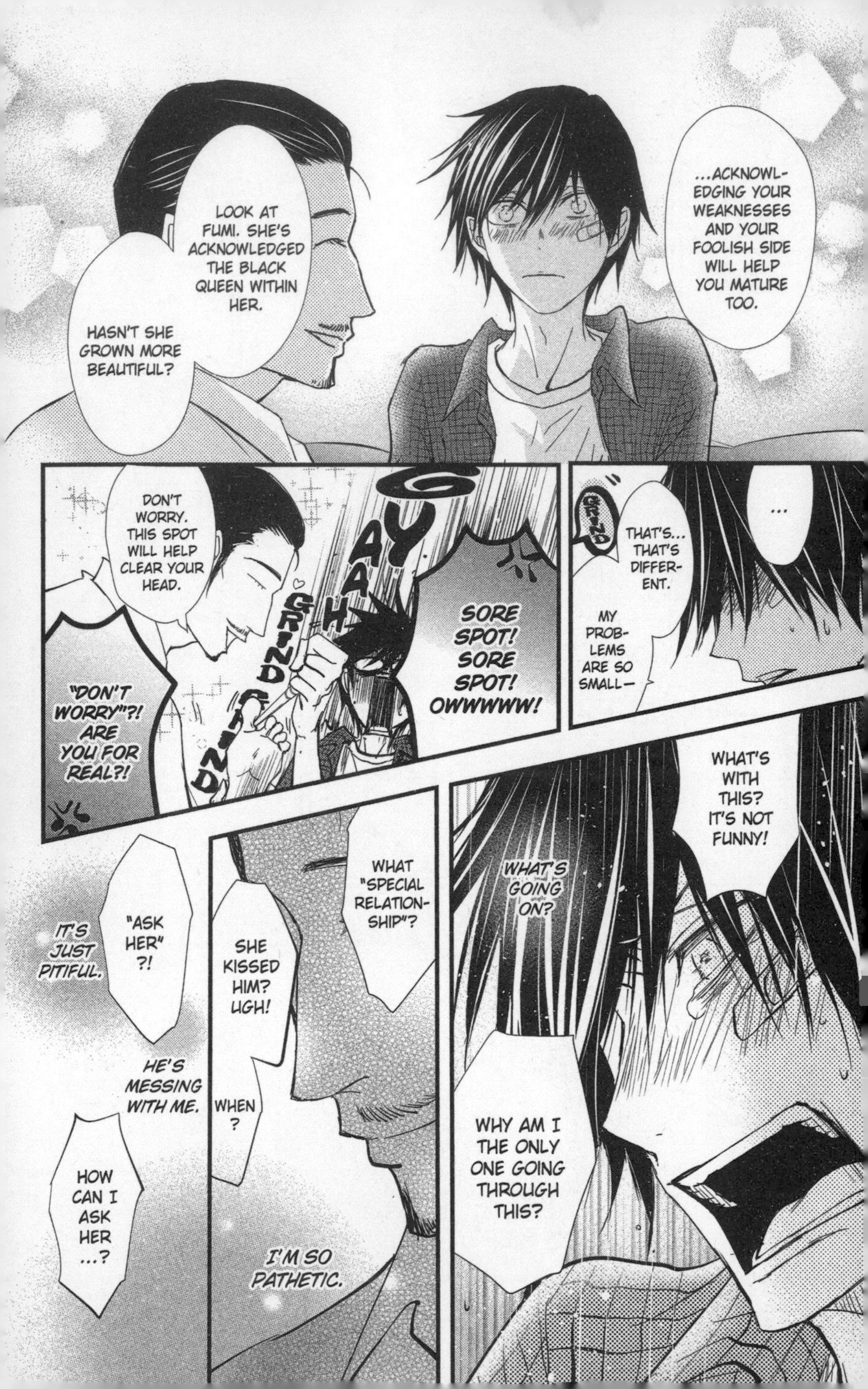
...ACKNOWLEDGING YOUR WEAKNESSES AND YOUR FOOLISH SIDE WILL HELP YOU MATURE TOO.
LOOK AT FUMI. SHE'S ACKNOWLEDGED THE BLACK QUEEN WITHIN HER.
HASN'T SHE GROWN MORE BEAUTIFUL?
...
GRIND
THAT'S... THAT'S DIFFERENT.
MY PROBLEMS ARE SO SMALL—
GYAAH
SORE SPOT! SORE SPOT! OWWWWW!
DON'T WORRY. THIS SPOT WILL HELP CLEAR YOUR HEAD.
GRIND GRIND
"DON'T WORRY"?! ARE YOU FOR REAL?!
WHAT'S WITH THIS? IT'S NOT FUNNY!
WHAT'S GOING ON?
WHY AM I THE ONLY ONE GOING THROUGH THIS?
WHAT "SPECIAL RELATIONSHIP"?
SHE KISSED HIM? UGH!
WHEN?
I'M SO PATHETIC.
"ASK HER"?!
IT'S JUST PITIFUL.
HE'S MESSING WITH ME.
HOW CAN I ASK HER...?

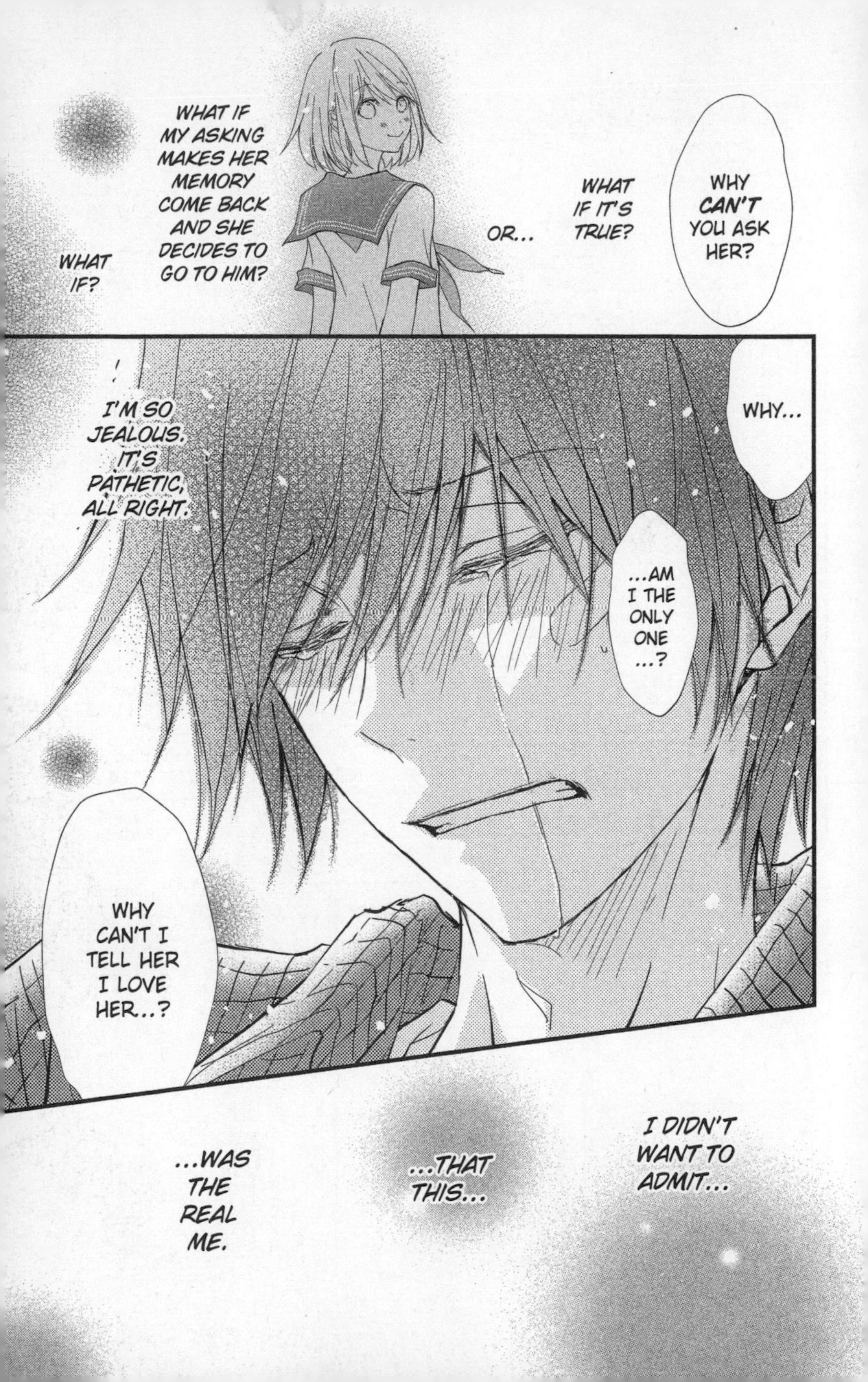
WHY CAN'T YOU ASK HER?
WHAT IF IT'S TRUE?
OR...
WHAT IF MY ASKING MAKES HER MEMORY COME BACK AND SHE DECIDES TO GO TO HIM?
WHAT IF?
WHY...
...AM I THE ONLY ONE ...?
!
I'M SO JEALOUS. IT'S PATHETIC, ALL RIGHT.
WHY CAN'T I TELL HER I LOVE HER...?
I DIDN'T WANT TO ADMIT...
...THAT THIS...
...WAS THE REAL ME.

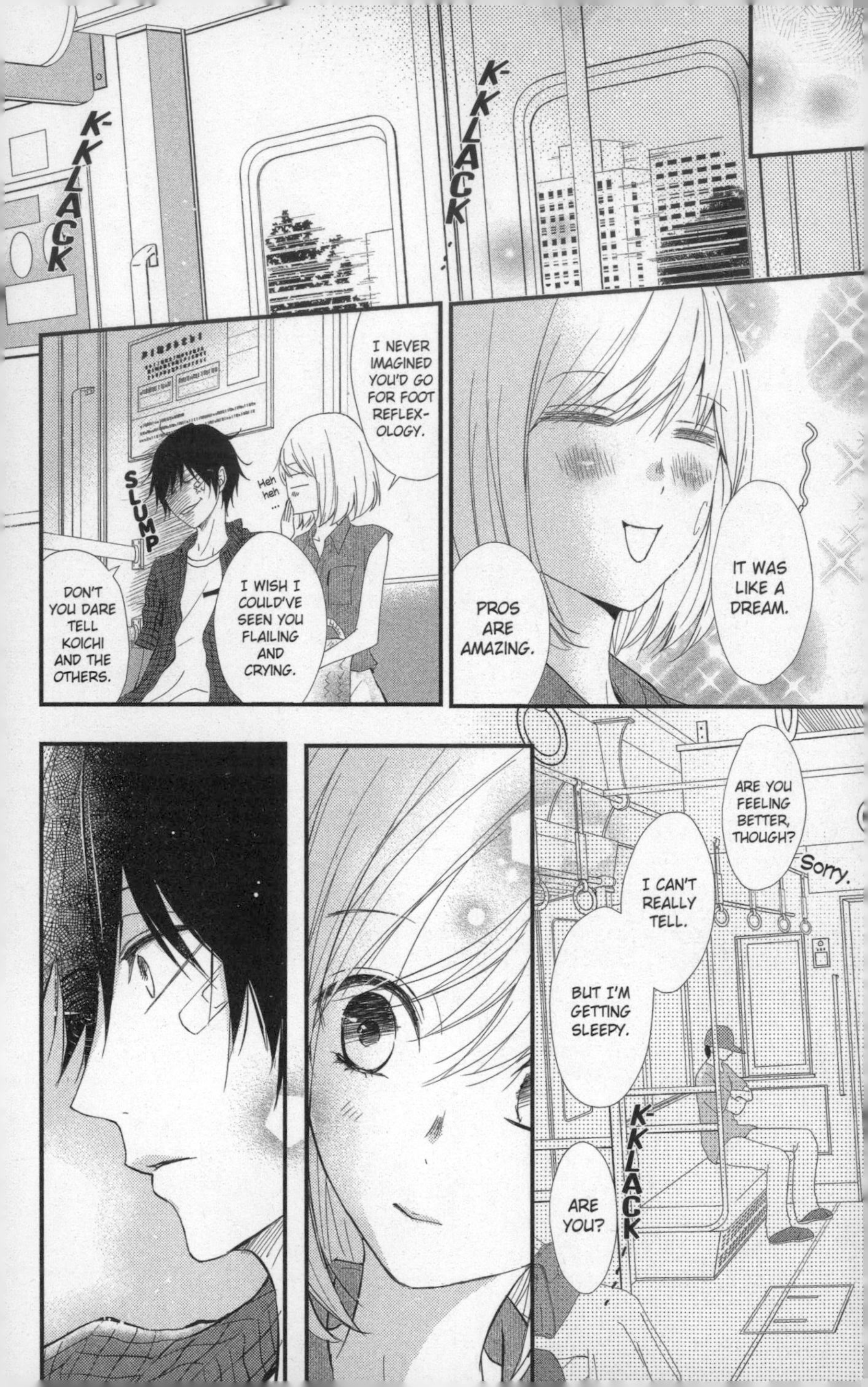
K-KLACK
K-KLACK
IT WAS LIKE A DREAM.
PROS ARE AMAZING.
I NEVER IMAGINED YOU'D GO FOR FOOT REFLEX-OLOGY.
Heh heh ...
SLUMP
I WISH I COULD'VE SEEN YOU FLAILING AND CRYING.
DON'T YOU DARE TELL KOICHI AND THE OTHERS.
ARE YOU FEELING BETTER, THOUGH?
Sorry.
I CAN'T REALLY TELL.
BUT I'M GETTING SLEEPY.
K-KLACK
ARE YOU?

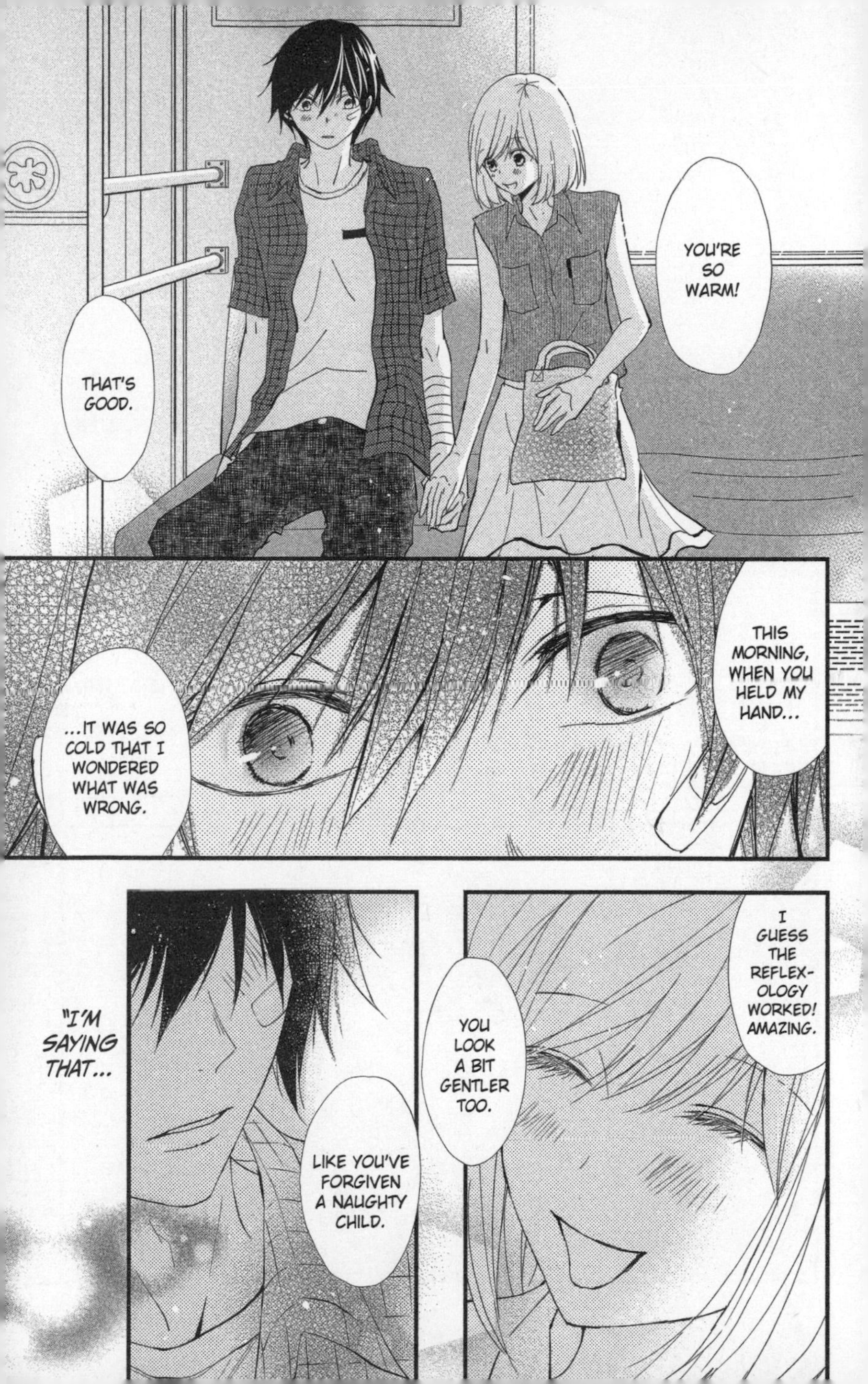
YOU'RE SO WARM!
THAT'S GOOD.
THIS MORNING, WHEN YOU HELD MY HAND...
...IT WAS SO COLD THAT I WONDERED WHAT WAS WRONG.
I GUESS THE REFLEX-OLOGY WORKED! AMAZING.
YOU LOOK A BIT GENTLER TOO.
LIKE YOU'VE FORGIVEN A NAUGHTY CHILD.
"I'M SAYING THAT...

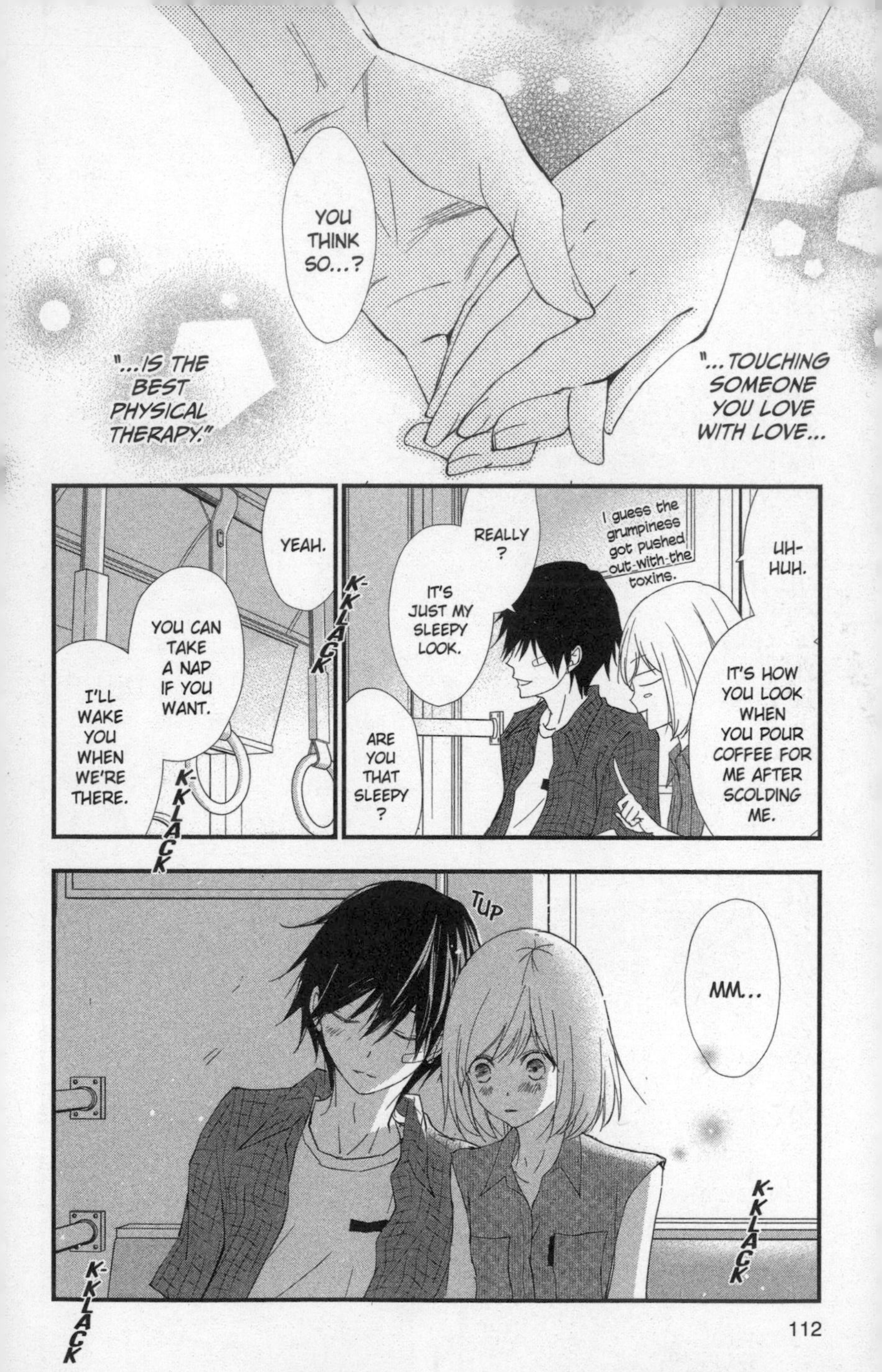
"...TOUCHING SOMEONE YOU LOVE WITH LOVE...
"...IS THE BEST PHYSICAL THERAPY."
YOU THINK SO...?
UH-HUH.
IT'S HOW YOU LOOK WHEN YOU POUR COFFEE FOR ME AFTER SCOLDING ME.
I guess the grumpiness got pushed out with the toxins.
REALLY?
IT'S JUST MY SLEEPY LOOK.
ARE YOU THAT SLEEPY?
YEAH.
K-KLACK
YOU CAN TAKE A NAP IF YOU WANT.
I'LL WAKE YOU WHEN WE'RE THERE.
K-KLACK
MM...
K-KLACK
TUP
K-KLACK

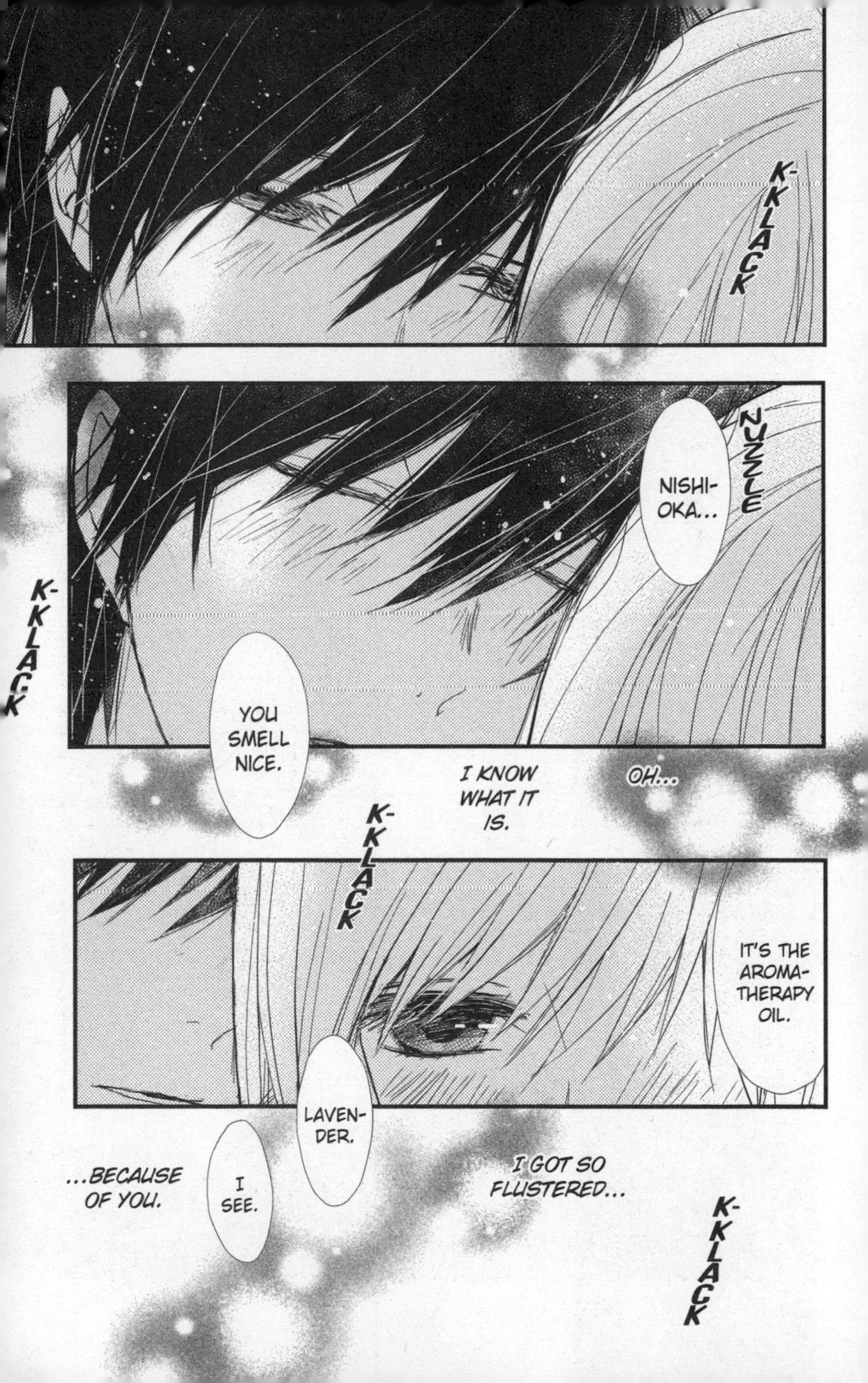
K-KLACK
NUZZLE
NISHI-OKA...
K-KLACK
YOU SMELL NICE.
OH...
I KNOW WHAT IT IS.
K-KLACK
IT'S THE AROMA-THERAPY OIL.
LAVEN-DER.
K-KLACK
I GOT SO FLUSTERED...
I SEE.
...BECAUSE OF YOU.

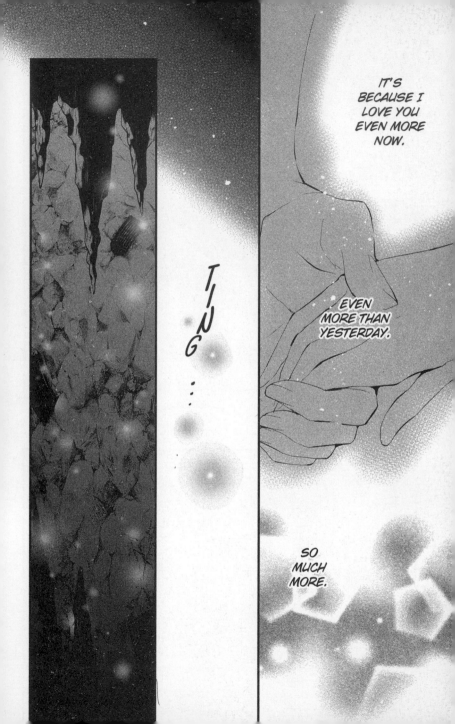

IT'S BECAUSE I LOVE YOU EVEN MORE NOW.

TING
...

EVEN MORE THAN YESTERDAY.

SO MUCH MORE.

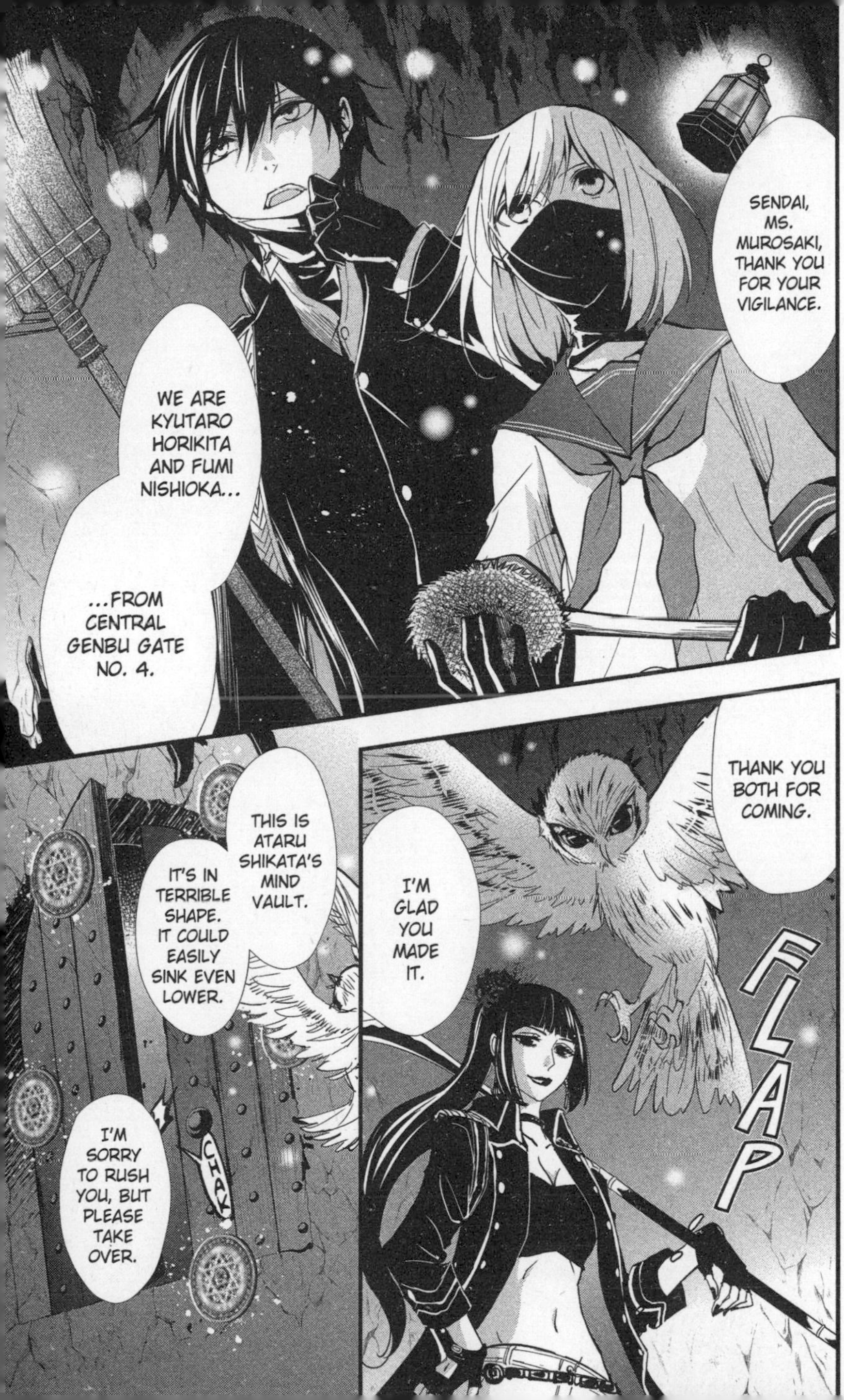
SENDAI, MS. MUROSAKI, THANK YOU FOR YOUR VIGILANCE.
WE ARE KYUTARO HORIKITA AND FUMI NISHIOKA...
...FROM CENTRAL GENBU GATE NO. 4.
THANK YOU BOTH FOR COMING.
I'M GLAD YOU MADE IT.
FLAP
THIS IS ATARU SHIKATA'S MIND VAULT.
IT'S IN TERRIBLE SHAPE. IT COULD EASILY SINK EVEN LOWER.
CHAK
I'M SORRY TO RUSH YOU, BUT PLEASE TAKE OVER.

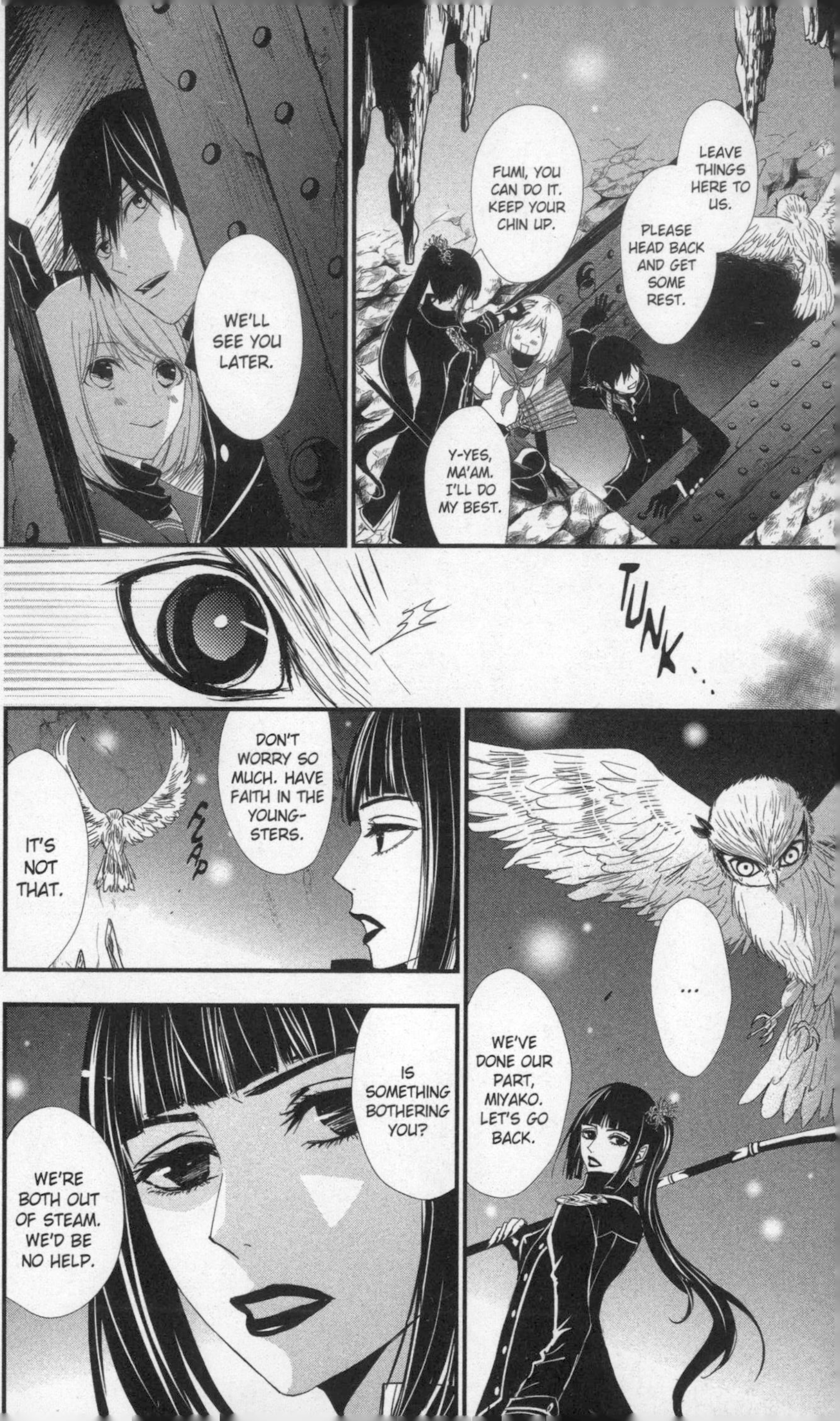
LEAVE THINGS HERE TO US.
PLEASE HEAD BACK AND GET SOME REST.
FUMI, YOU CAN DO IT. KEEP YOUR CHIN UP.
Y-YES, MA'AM. I'LL DO MY BEST.
WE'LL SEE YOU LATER.
TUNK...
...
WE'VE DONE OUR PART, MIYAKO. LET'S GO BACK.
DON'T WORRY SO MUCH. HAVE FAITH IN THE YOUNGSTERS.
FLAP
IT'S NOT THAT.
IS SOMETHING BOTHERING YOU?
WE'RE BOTH OUT OF STEAM. WE'D BE NO HELP.

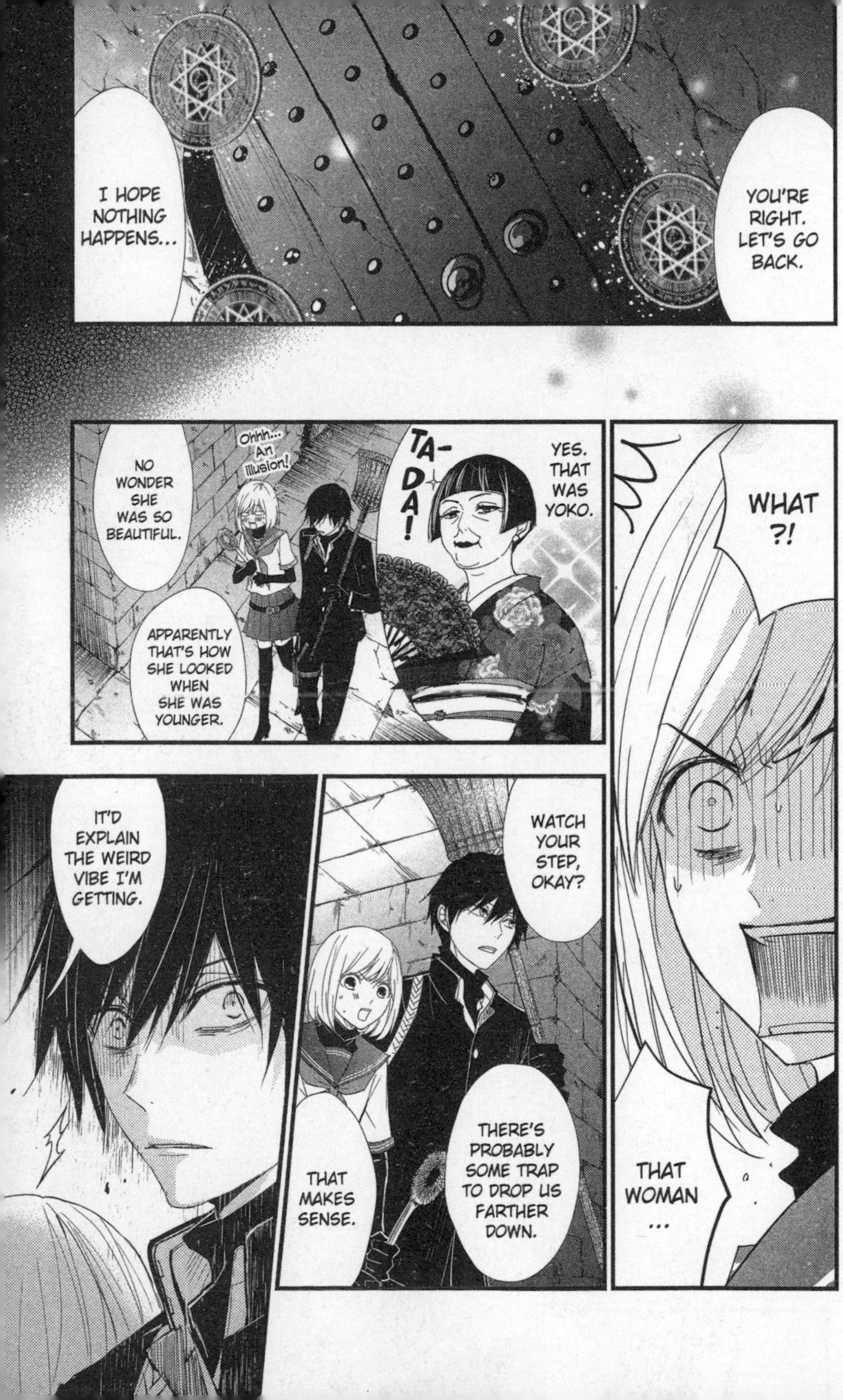
YOU'RE RIGHT. LET'S GO BACK.
I HOPE NOTHING HAPPENS...
WHAT ?!
THAT WOMAN ...
YES. THAT WAS YOKO.
TA-DA!
Ohhh... An illusion!
NO WONDER SHE WAS SO BEAUTIFUL.
APPARENTLY THAT'S HOW SHE LOOKED WHEN SHE WAS YOUNGER.
WATCH YOUR STEP, OKAY?
THERE'S PROBABLY SOME TRAP TO DROP US FARTHER DOWN.
THAT MAKES SENSE.
IT'D EXPLAIN THE WEIRD VIBE I'M GETTING.

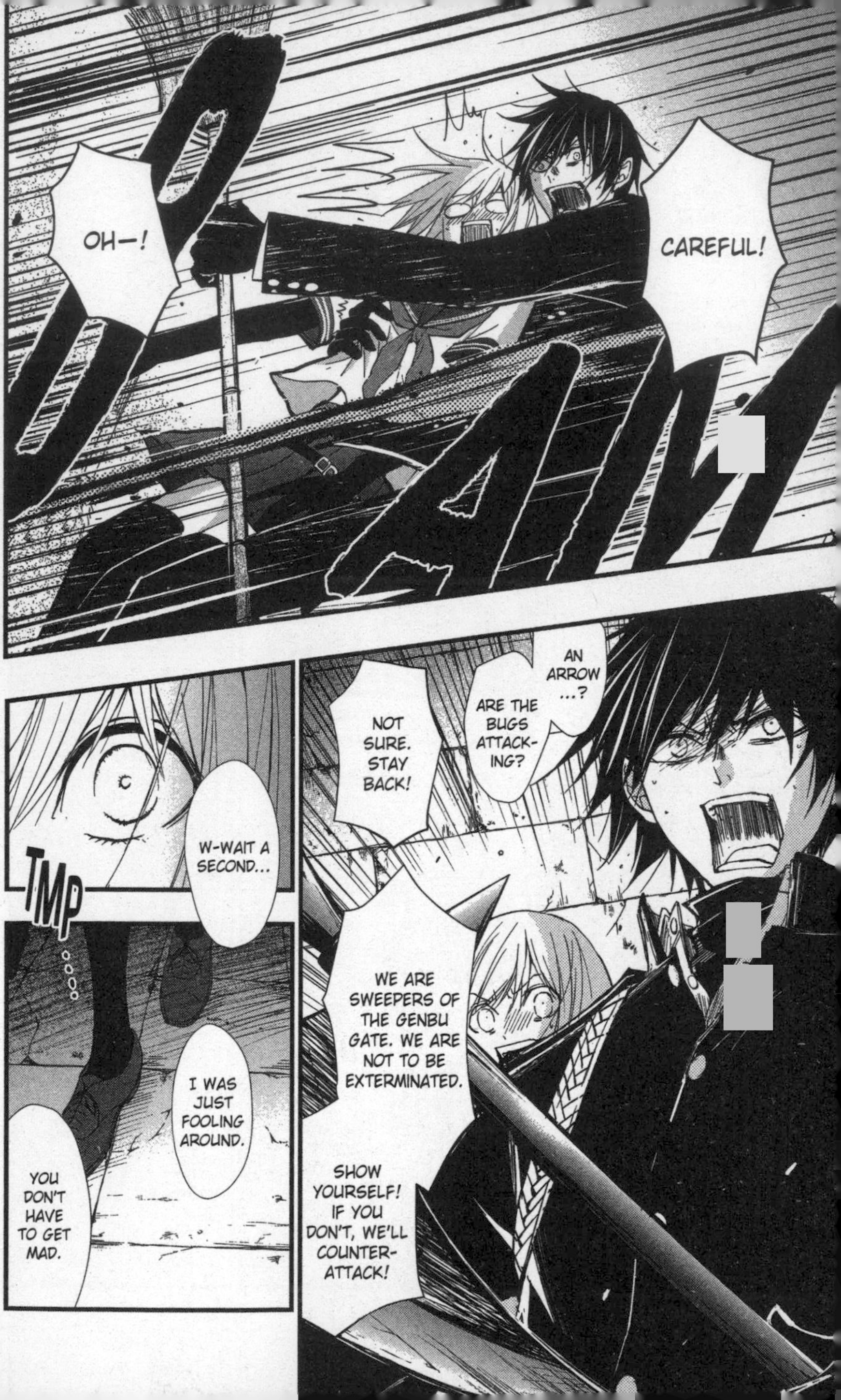
CAREFUL!
OH—!
AN ARROW...?
ARE THE BUGS ATTACKING?
NOT SURE. STAY BACK!
WE ARE SWEEPERS OF THE GENBU GATE. WE ARE NOT TO BE EXTERMINATED.
SHOW YOURSELF! IF YOU DON'T, WE'LL COUNTER-ATTACK!
W-WAIT A SECOND...
TMP
I WAS JUST FOOLING AROUND.
YOU DON'T HAVE TO GET MAD.

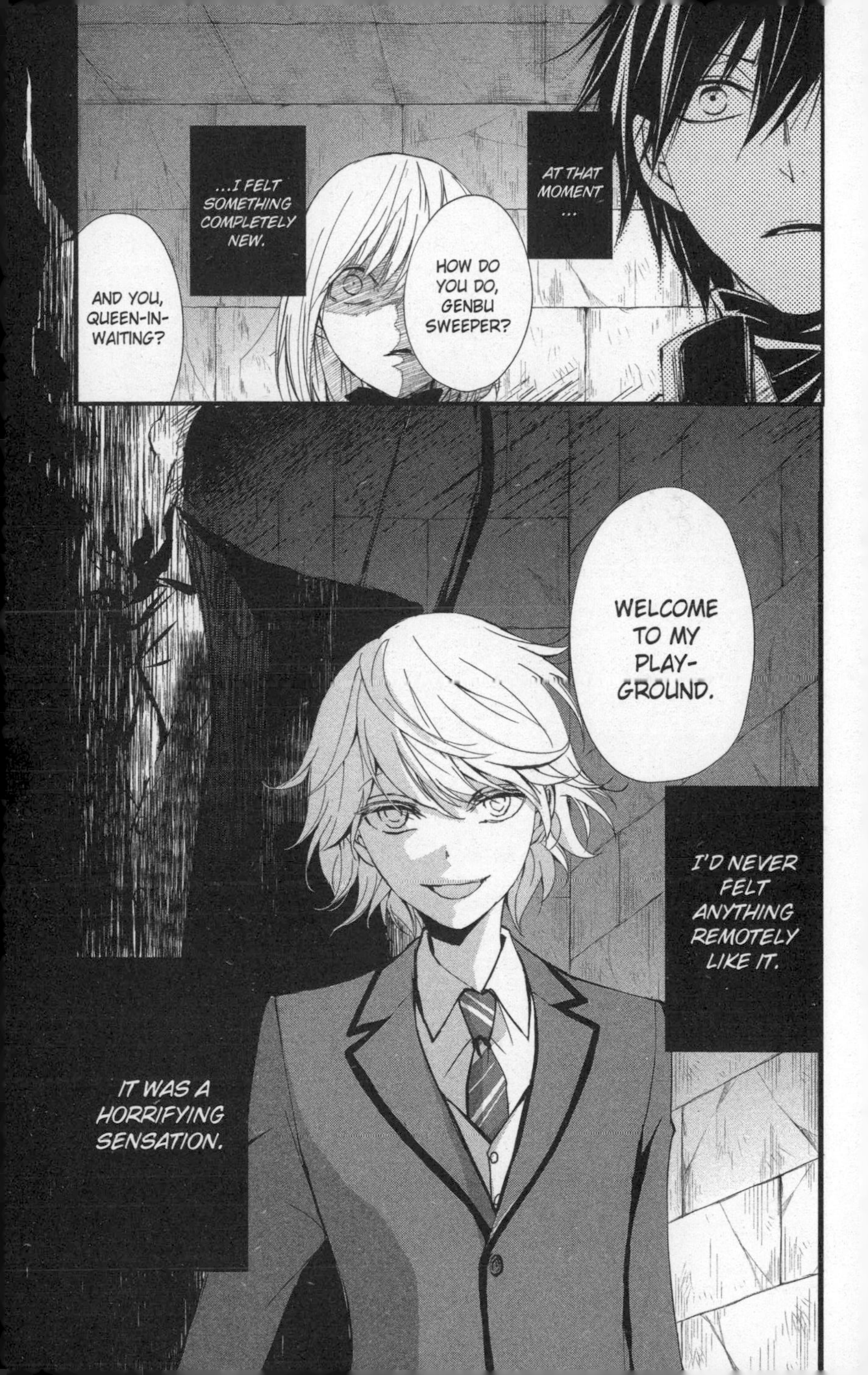
AT THAT MOMENT ...
HOW DO YOU DO, GENBU SWEEPER?
...I FELT SOMETHING COMPLETELY NEW.
AND YOU, QUEEN-IN-WAITING?
WELCOME TO MY PLAY-GROUND.
I'D NEVER FELT ANYTHING REMOTELY LIKE IT.
IT WAS A HORRIFYING SENSATION.

MONTHLY BETSUCOMI SALE DATE NOTICE ON TWITTER

# CHAPTER 19

I have a great idea! Could you please use me instead of Fumi? I like being tied up.
WHAM
Sorry to interrupt!!
Don't worry! It's nothing. Good luck, Kyutaro!
Uh... yeah. I'll be back.
Who's there?

**WHAT'S UP IN *QUEEN'S QUALITY* THIS MONTH?**

(1) THEY'RE NOT ANTENNAE, SO IT'S SAFE.
(2) IT'S NOT A LOVE SCENE, SO IT'S SAFE.
(3) THE MVP THIS MONTH IS THE BELT HOLDING FUMI'S HANDLE BRUSH THAT KEPT HER FROM FLASHING HER PANTIES.

ACTUALLY, THIS IS NO TIME FOR FOOLING AROUND.
CHAPTER 19 IS A PRETTY SERIOUS ONE!

The *Dengeki* characters are a little too intrusive in this volume. *Dengeki Daisy* ended three years ago, but I'm delighted to find there are still people reading it.
Lately I've been drawing short manga stories combining *Daisy* and *Queequa* for monthlies, special editions, digital magazines, etc.
I hope you'll read those when you come across them!

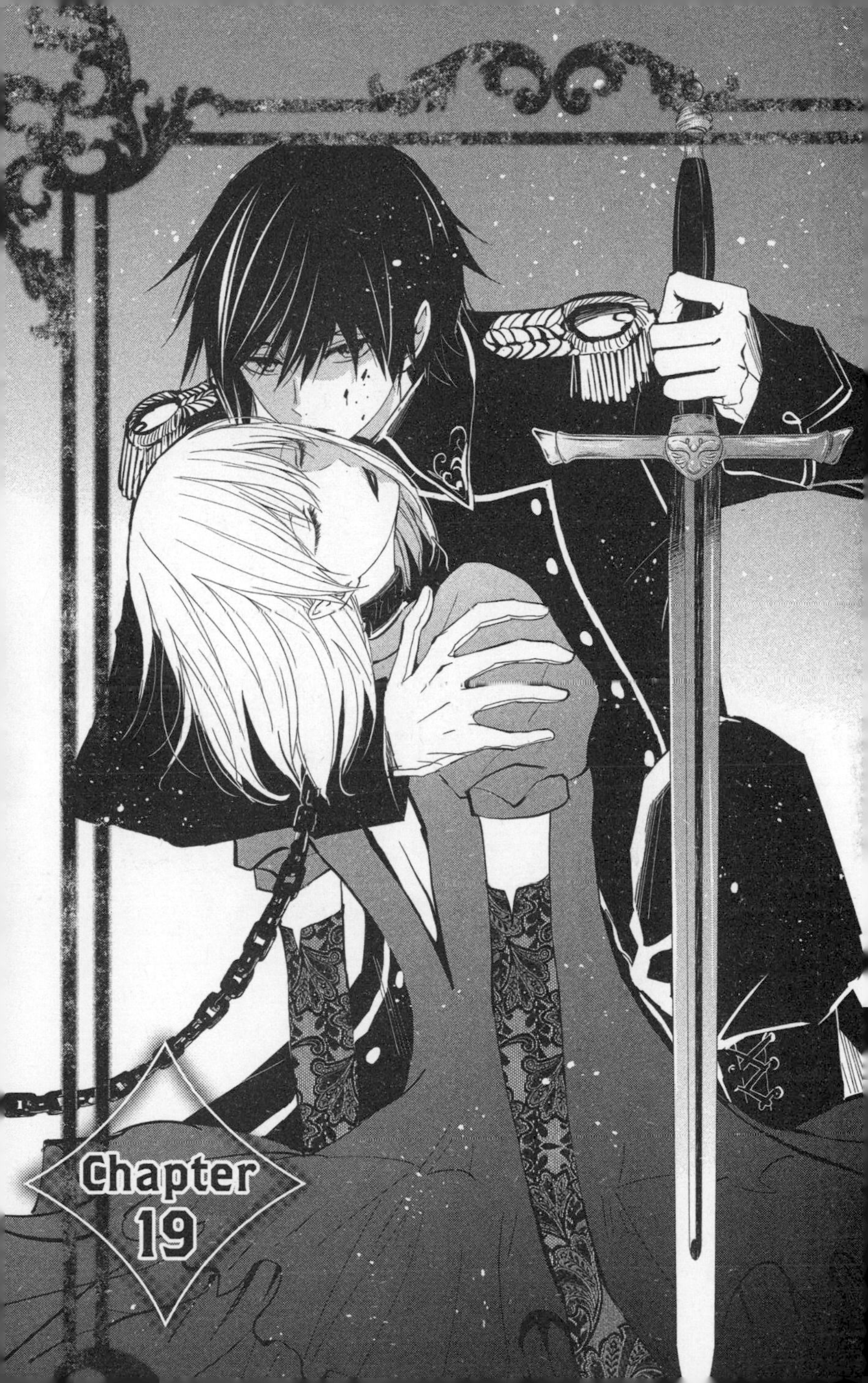
Chapter
19

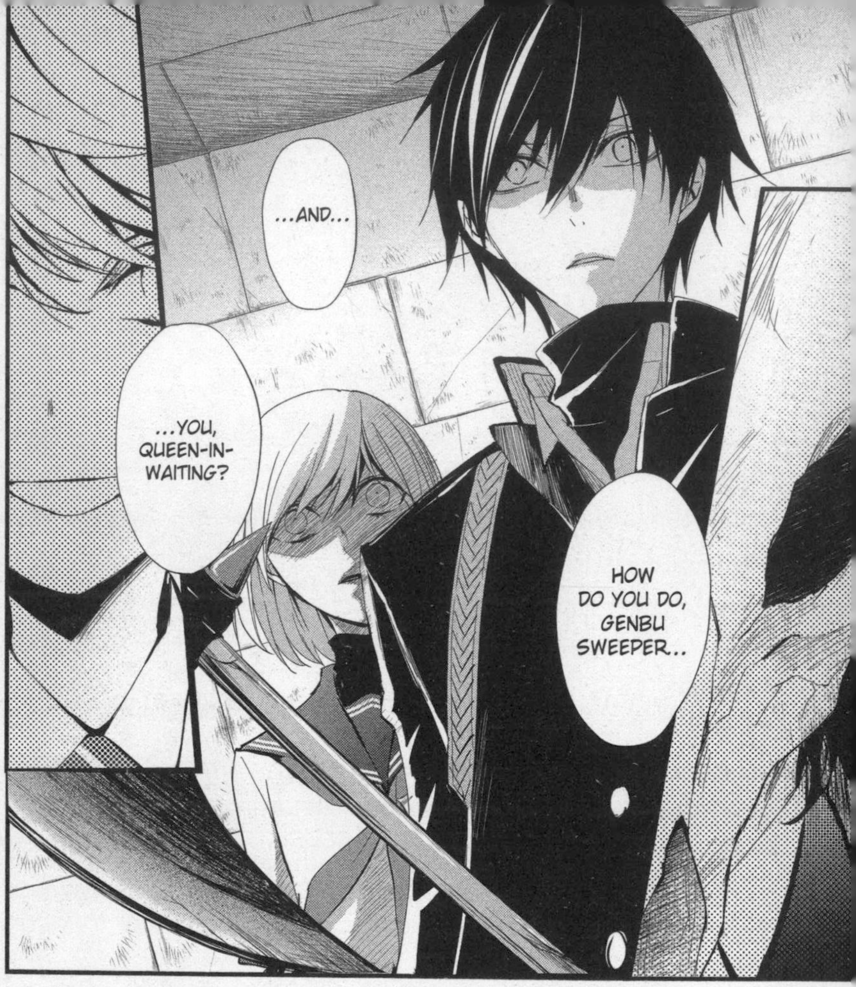
HOW DO YOU DO, GENBU SWEEPER...
...AND...
...YOU, QUEEN-IN-WAITING?

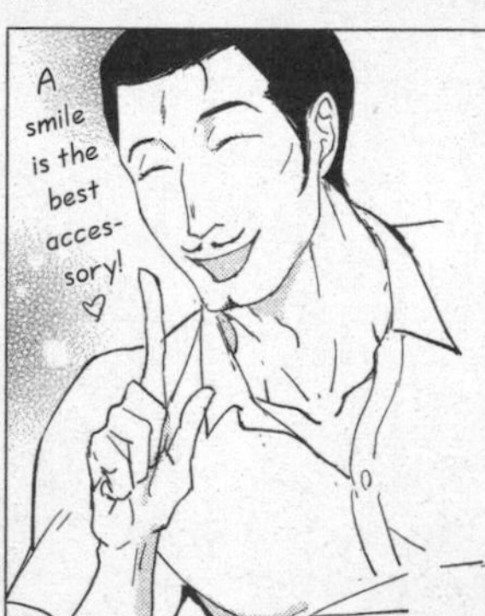
A smile is the best accessory! ♡

I like muscular characters like Mizuho, but I'm just blithely drawing him without much knowledge about musculature. I've started thinking I'd better do some studying. When you have lots of muscle, it seems like you exude hormones or something. It's good for the body and mind. Muscular people tend to be positive and pleasant. I think cartoonists who're weak and want to die when they get behind on work need more muscle tone.

BMP
WELCOME TO MY PLAY-GROUND.
WHAT...
BMP
WHAT AM I FEELING ...?
SOME PART OF ME IS SCREAMING.

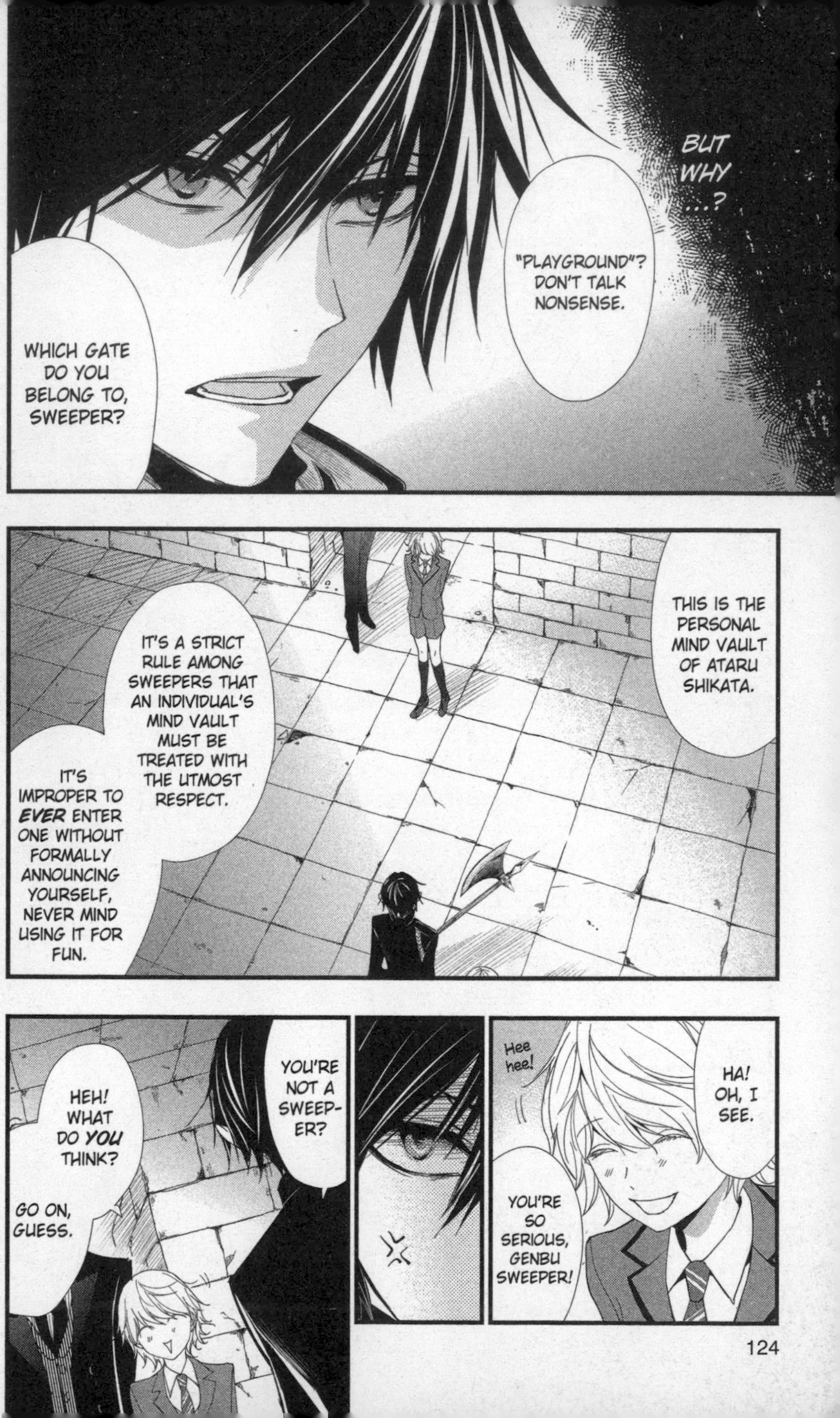
BUT WHY ...?
"PLAYGROUND"? DON'T TALK NONSENSE.
WHICH GATE DO YOU BELONG TO, SWEEPER?
THIS IS THE PERSONAL MIND VAULT OF ATARU SHIKATA.
IT'S A STRICT RULE AMONG SWEEPERS THAT AN INDIVIDUAL'S MIND VAULT MUST BE TREATED WITH THE UTMOST RESPECT.
IT'S IMPROPER TO *EVER* ENTER ONE WITHOUT FORMALLY ANNOUNCING YOURSELF, NEVER MIND USING IT FOR FUN.
HA! OH, I SEE.
Hee hee!
YOU'RE SO SERIOUS, GENBU SWEEPER!
YOU'RE NOT A SWEEP-ER?
HEH! WHAT DO *YOU* THINK?
GO ON, GUESS.

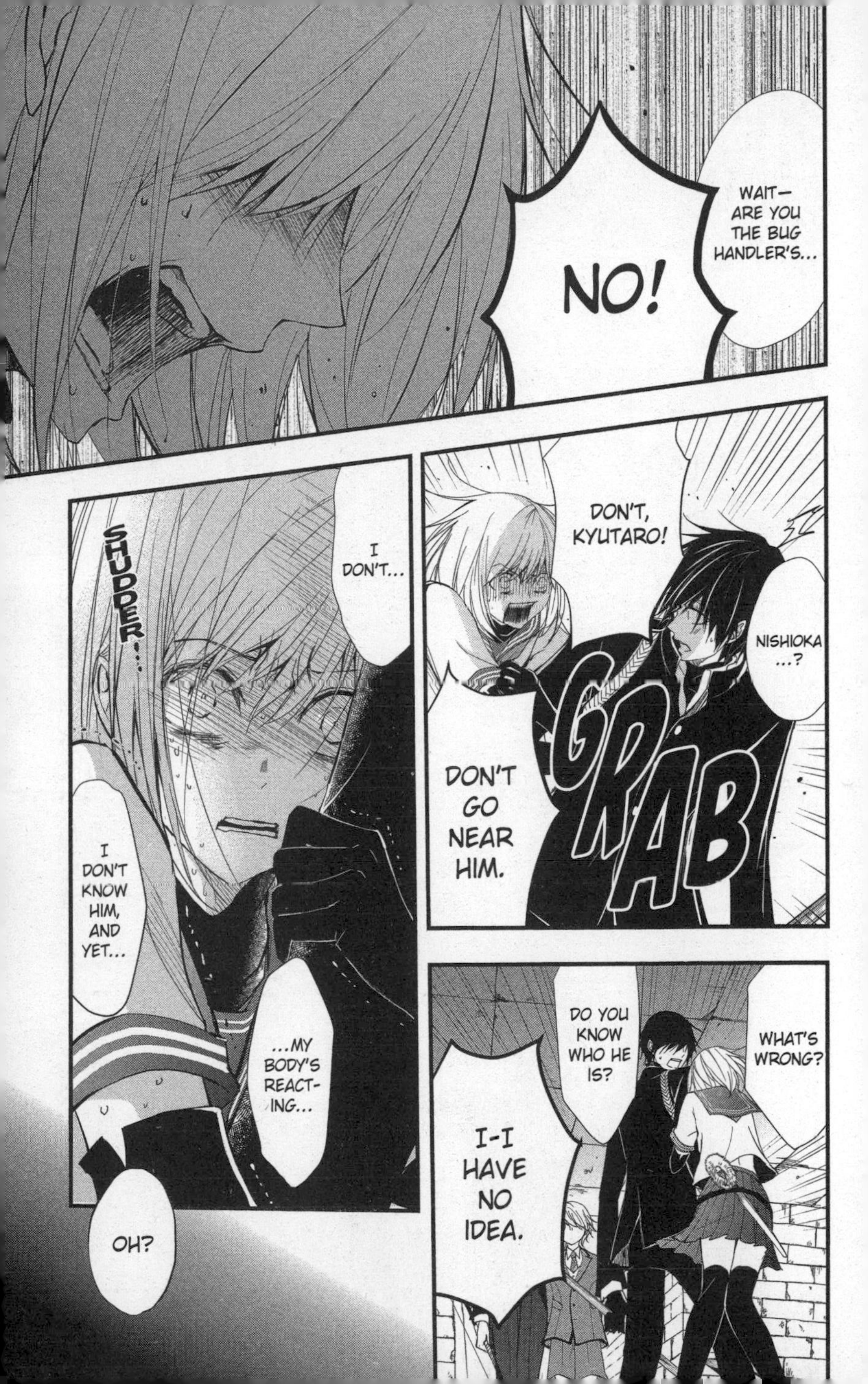
WAIT— ARE YOU THE BUG HANDLER'S…
NO!
DON'T, KYUTARO!
NISHIOKA …?
GRAB
DON'T GO NEAR HIM.
WHAT'S WRONG?
DO YOU KNOW WHO HE IS?
I-I HAVE NO IDEA.
SHUDDER…
I DON'T…
I DON'T KNOW HIM, AND YET…
…MY BODY'S REACTING…
OH?

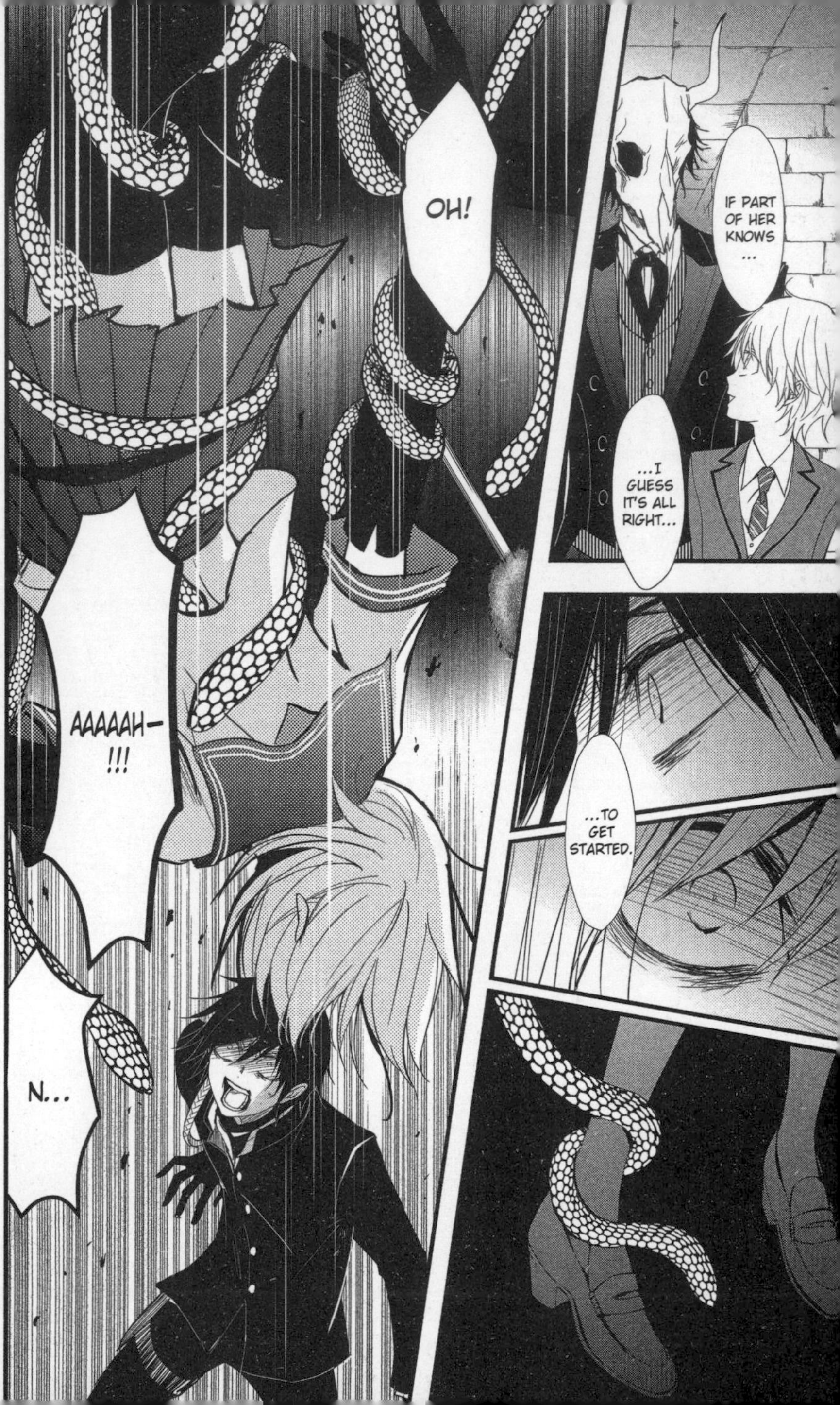
IF PART OF HER KNOWS ...
...I GUESS IT'S ALL RIGHT...
...TO GET STARTED.
OH!
AAAAAH— !!!
N...

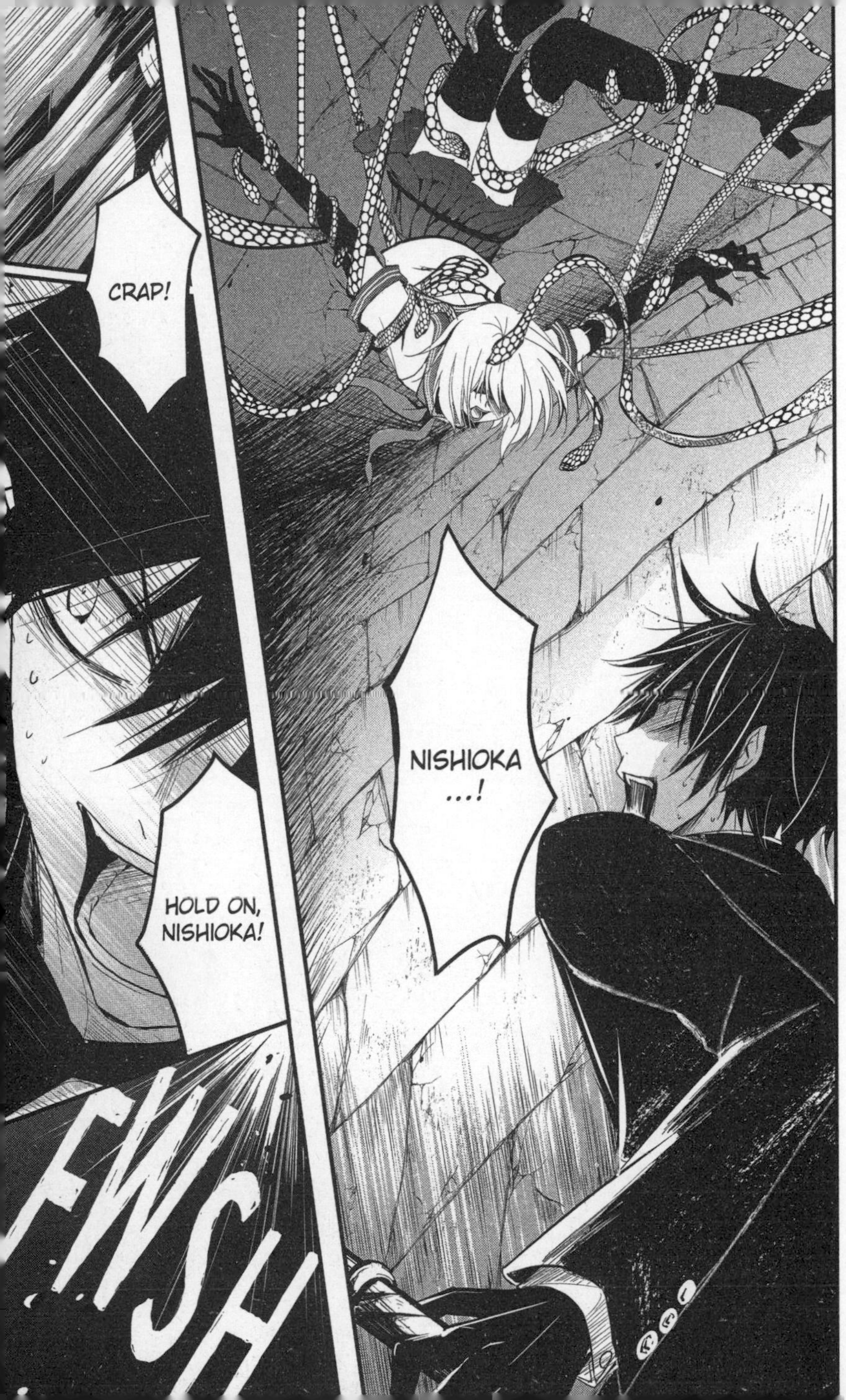
NISHIOKA ...!
CRAP!
HOLD ON, NISHIOKA!
FWSH

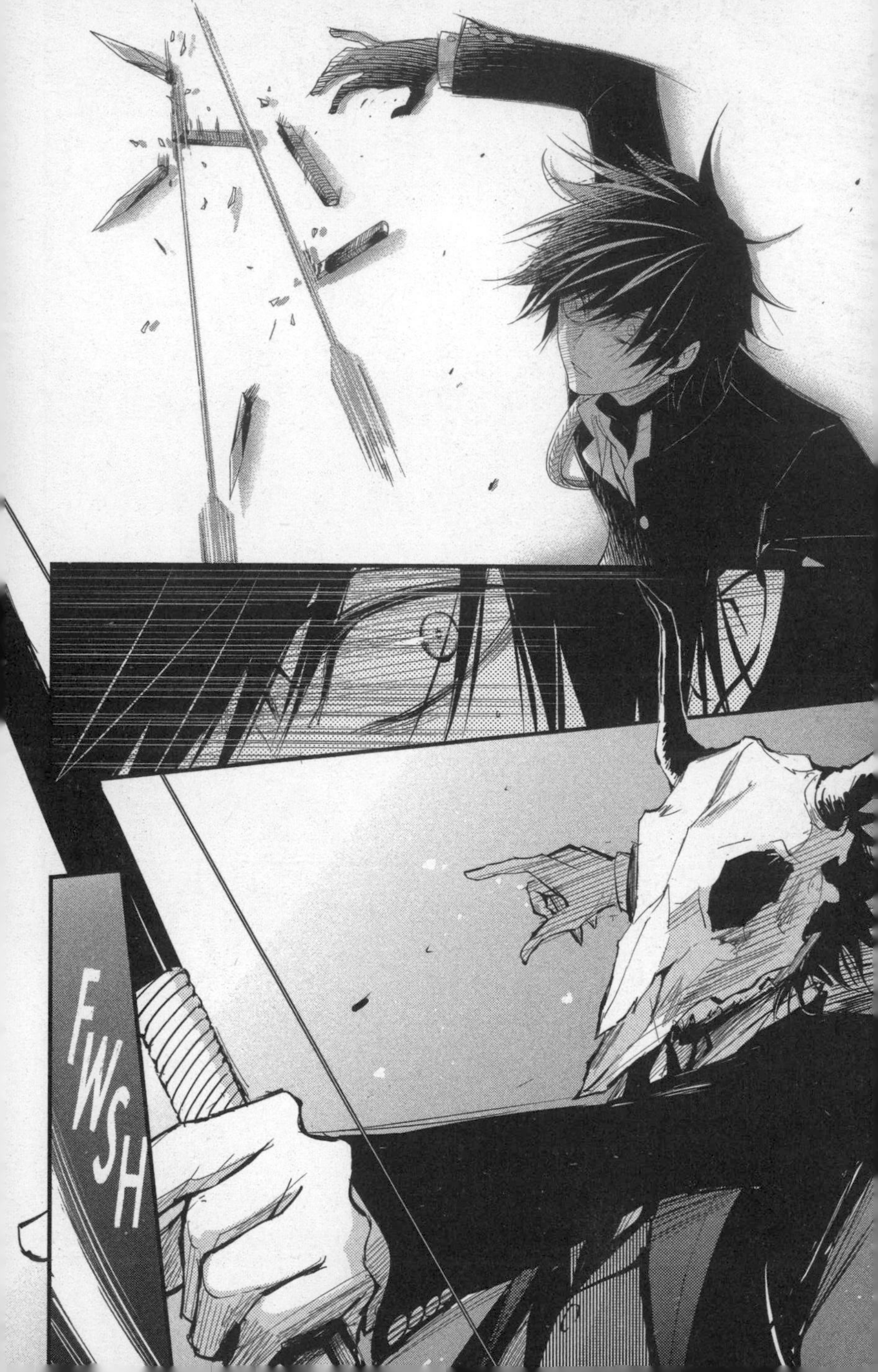
FWSH

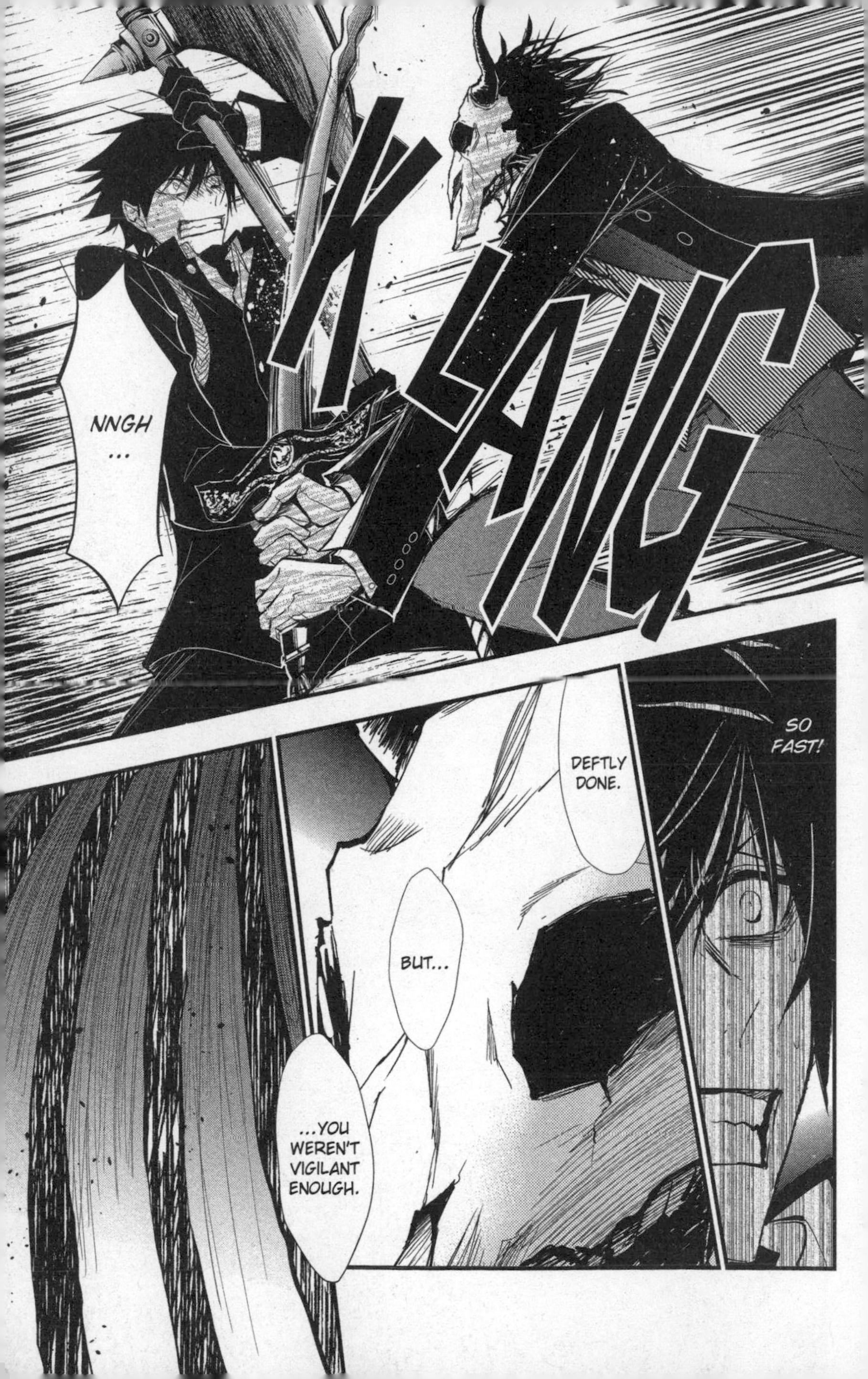
KLANG
NNGH ...
SO FAST!
DEFTLY DONE.
BUT...
...YOU WEREN'T VIGILANT ENOUGH.

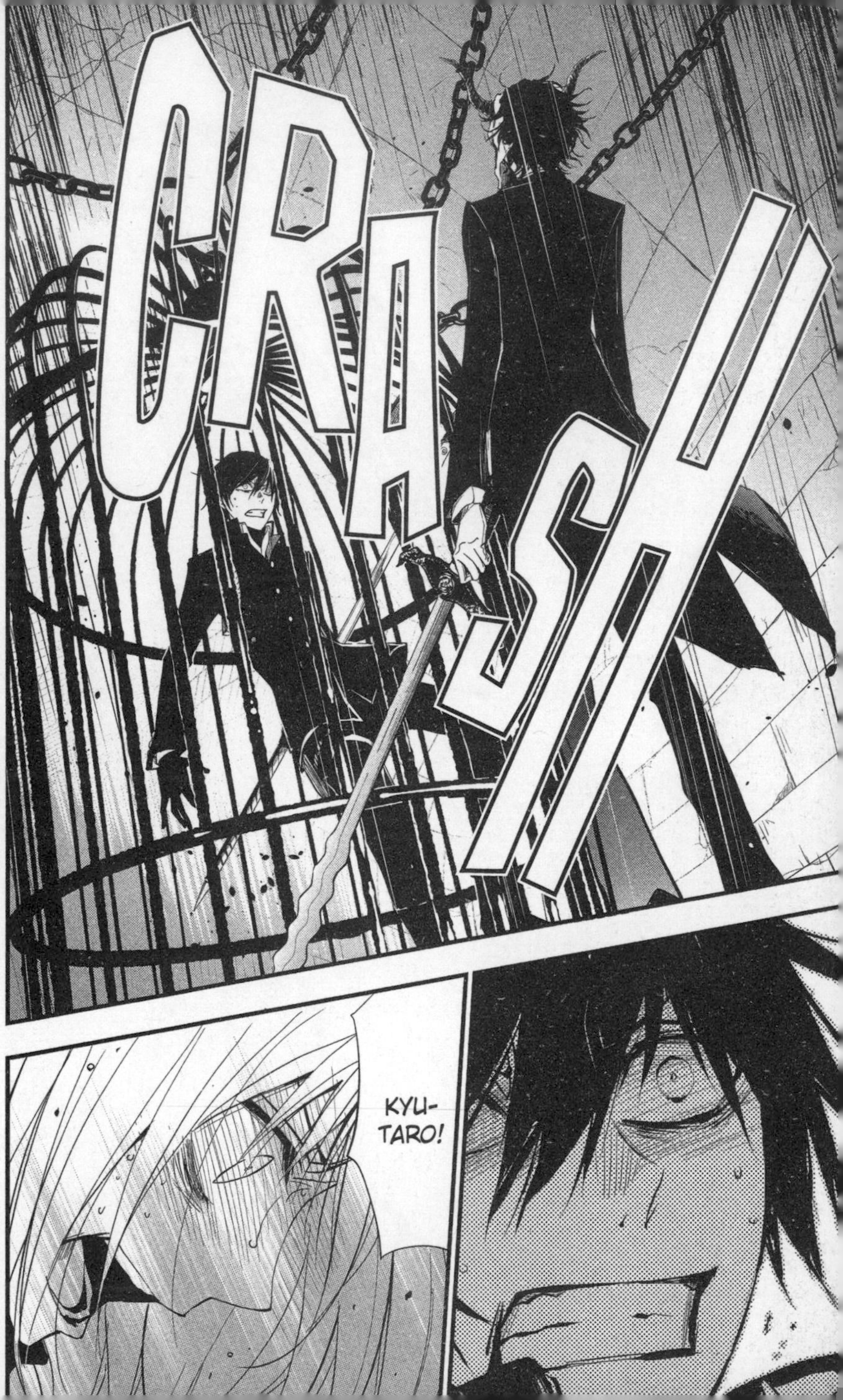
CRASH
KYU-TARO!

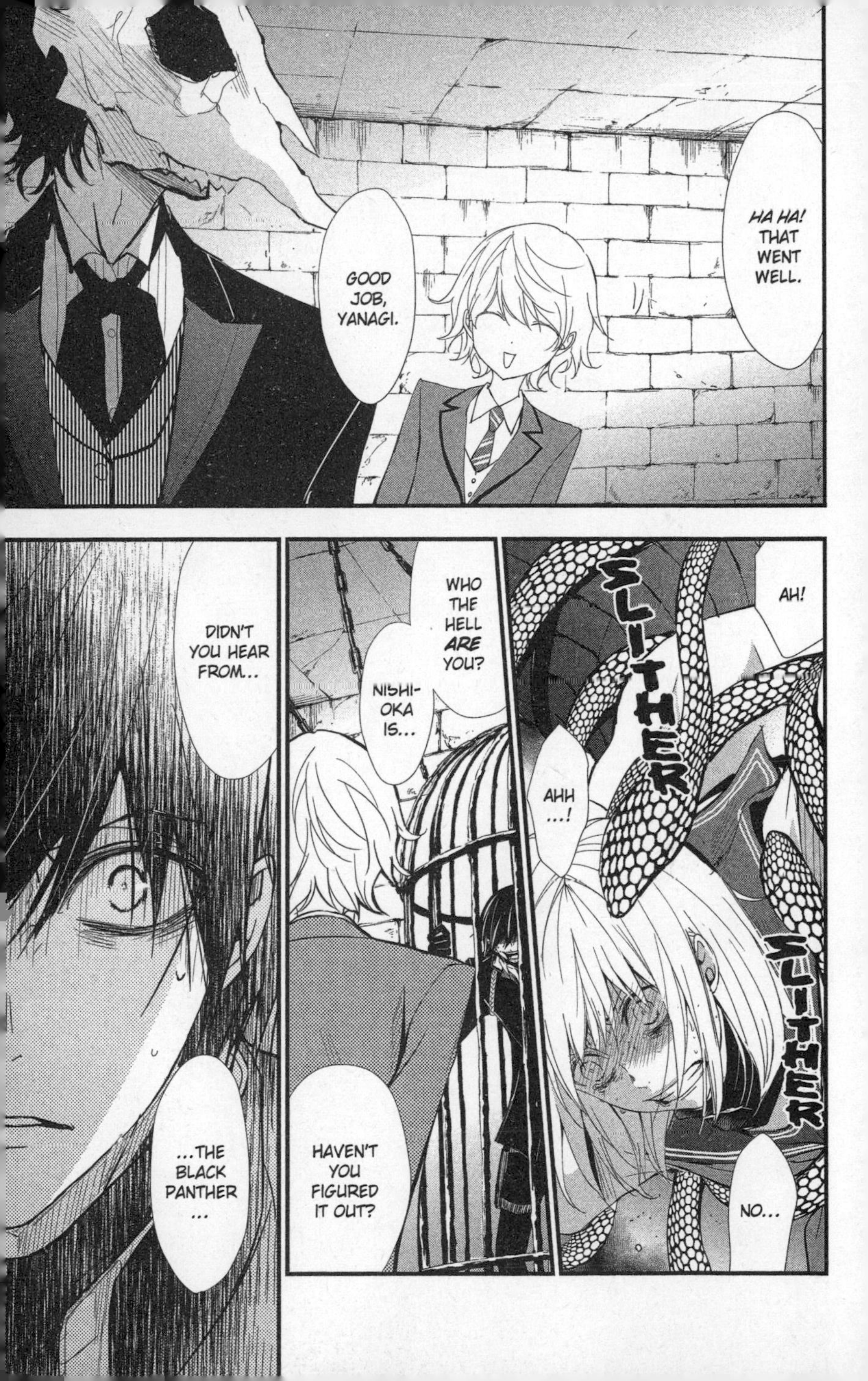
HA HA! THAT WENT WELL.
GOOD JOB, YANAGI.
AH!
SLITHER
AHH ...!
SLITHER
NO...
WHO THE HELL *ARE* YOU?
NISHIOKA IS...
HAVEN'T YOU FIGURED IT OUT?
DIDN'T YOU HEAR FROM...
...THE BLACK PANTHER ...

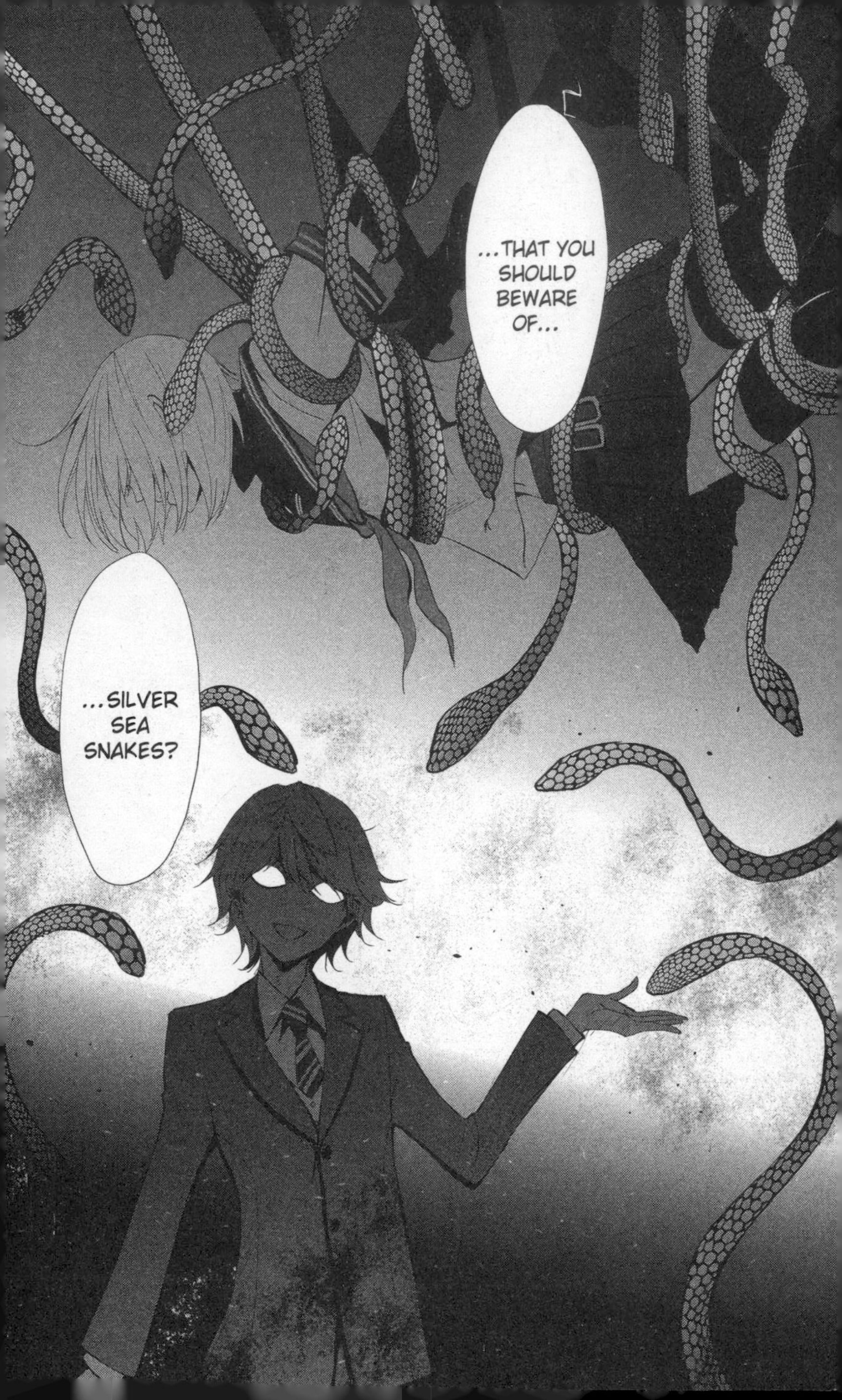
...THAT YOU SHOULD BEWARE OF...
...SILVER SEA SNAKES?

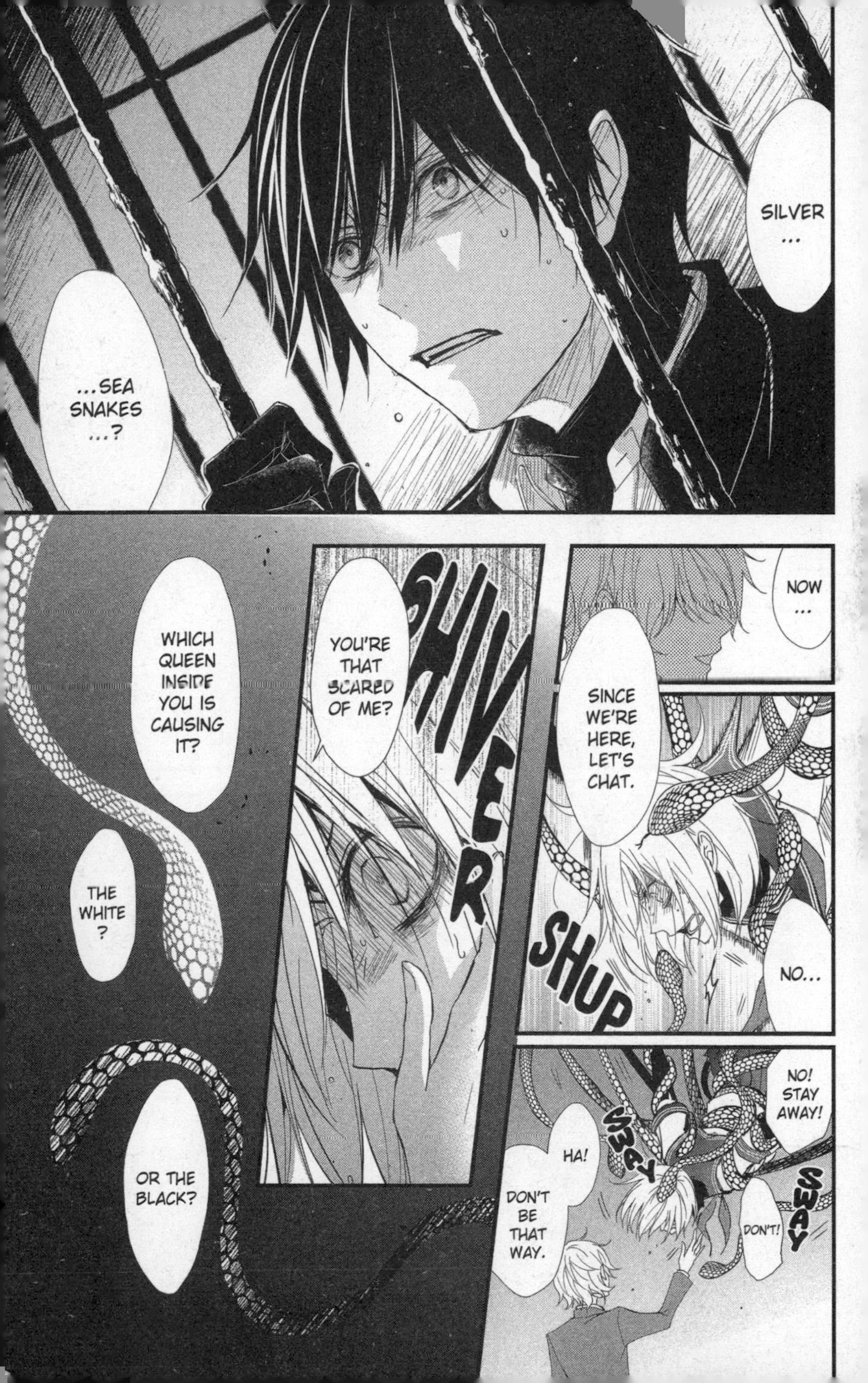

SILVER ...
...SEA SNAKES ...?
NOW ...
SINCE WE'RE HERE, LET'S CHAT.
NO...
SHUP
NO! STAY AWAY!
SWAY
DON'T!
SWAY
HA!
DON'T BE THAT WAY.
SHIVER
YOU'RE THAT SCARED OF ME?
WHICH QUEEN INSIDE YOU IS CAUSING IT?
THE WHITE?
OR THE BLACK?

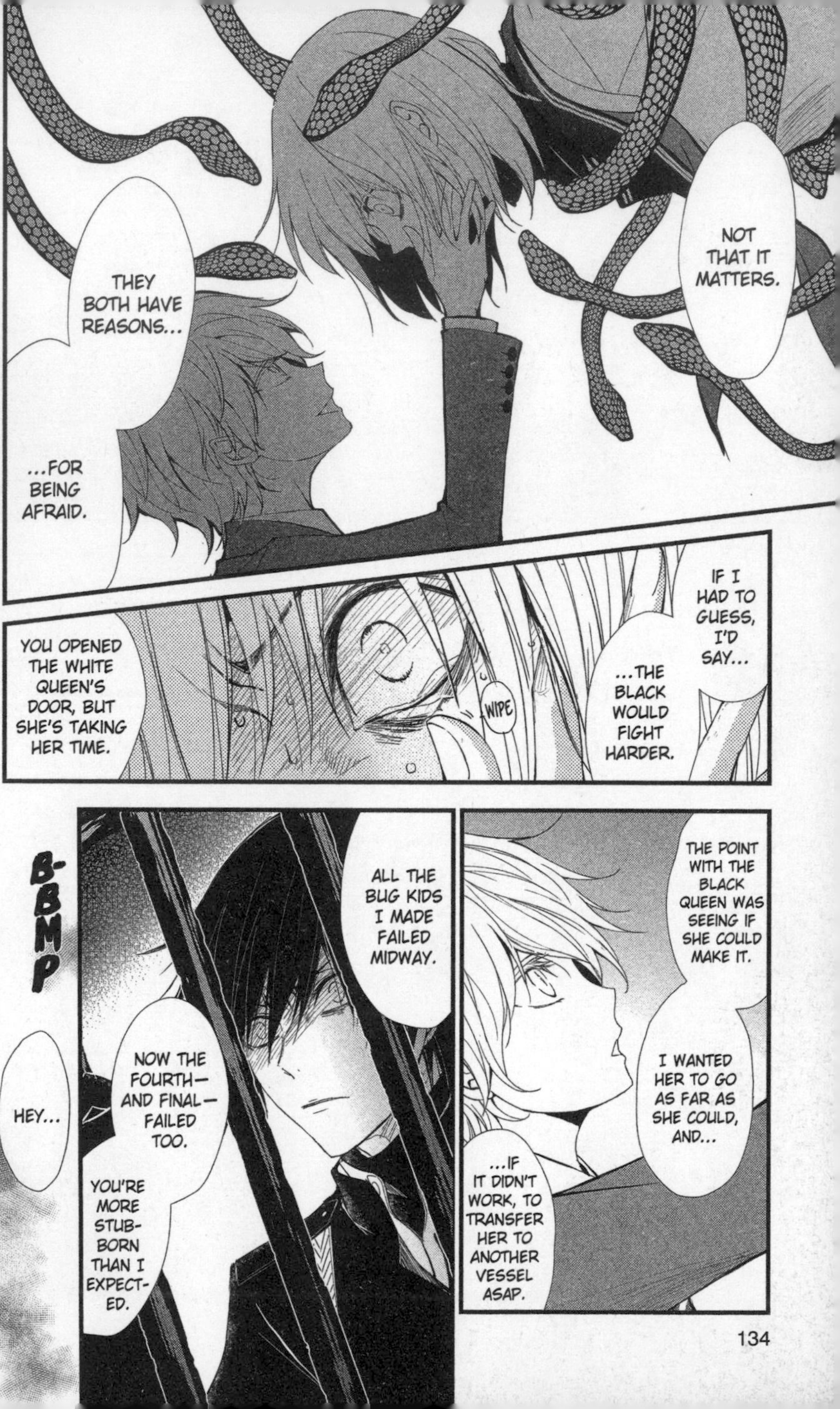
NOT THAT IT MATTERS.
THEY BOTH HAVE REASONS...
...FOR BEING AFRAID.
IF I HAD TO GUESS, I'D SAY...
...THE BLACK WOULD FIGHT HARDER.
WIPE
YOU OPENED THE WHITE QUEEN'S DOOR, BUT SHE'S TAKING HER TIME.
THE POINT WITH THE BLACK QUEEN WAS SEEING IF SHE COULD MAKE IT.
I WANTED HER TO GO AS FAR AS SHE COULD, AND...
...IF IT DIDN'T WORK, TO TRANSFER HER TO ANOTHER VESSEL ASAP.
ALL THE BUG KIDS I MADE FAILED MIDWAY.
NOW THE FOURTH—AND FINAL—FAILED TOO.
YOU'RE MORE STUB-BORN THAN I EXPECT-ED.
HEY...
B-BMP

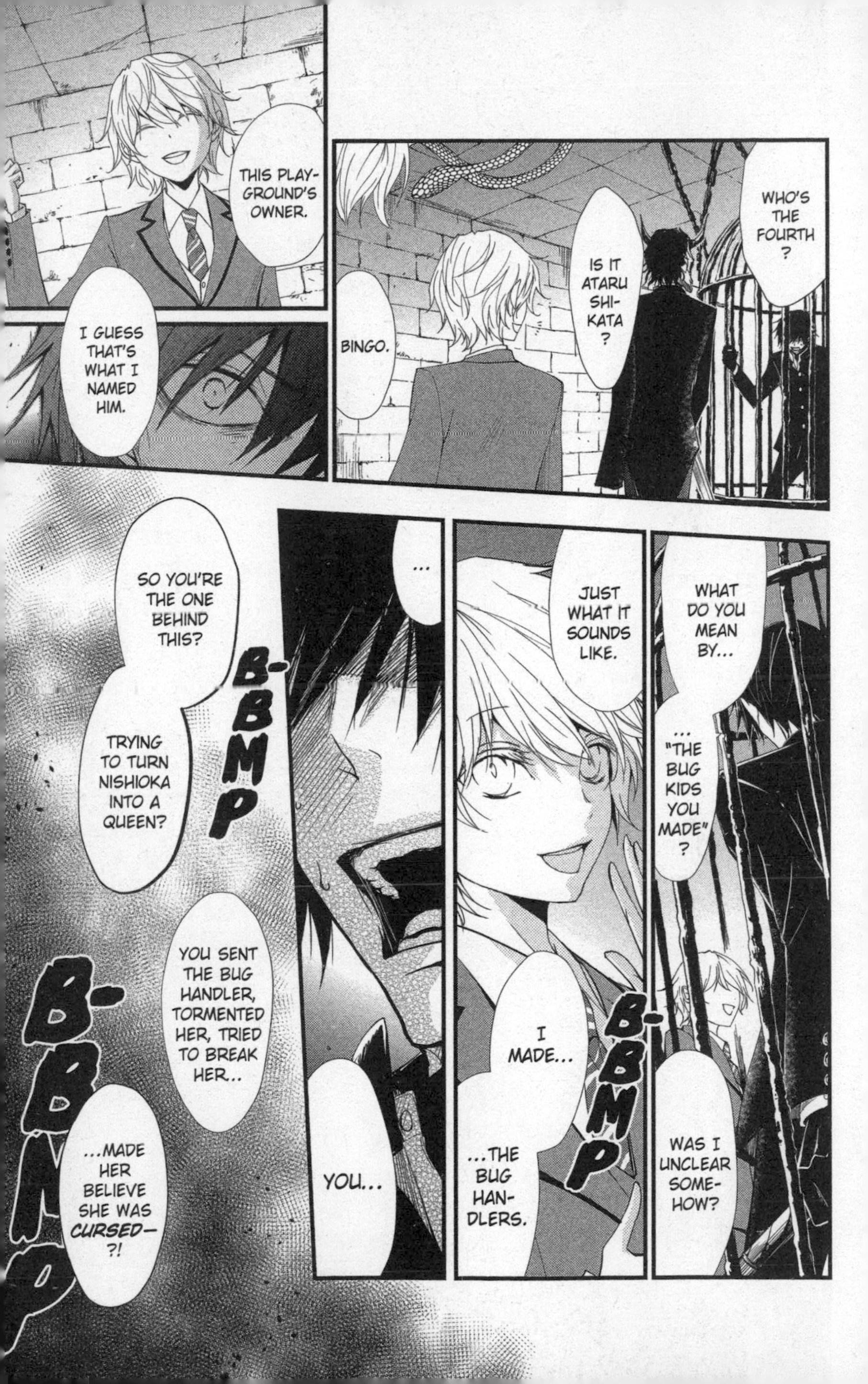
WHO'S THE FOURTH?
IS IT ATARU SHIKATA?
BINGO.
THIS PLAY-GROUND'S OWNER.
I GUESS THAT'S WHAT I NAMED HIM.
WHAT DO YOU MEAN BY...
..."THE BUG KIDS YOU MADE"?
WAS I UNCLEAR SOME-HOW?
JUST WHAT IT SOUNDS LIKE.
I MADE...
...THE BUG HAN-DLERS.
B-BMP
...
B-BMP
YOU...
SO YOU'RE THE ONE BEHIND THIS?
TRYING TO TURN NISHIOKA INTO A QUEEN?
YOU SENT THE BUG HANDLER, TORMENTED HER, TRIED TO BREAK HER...
...MADE HER BELIEVE SHE WAS *CURSED*—?!
B-BMP

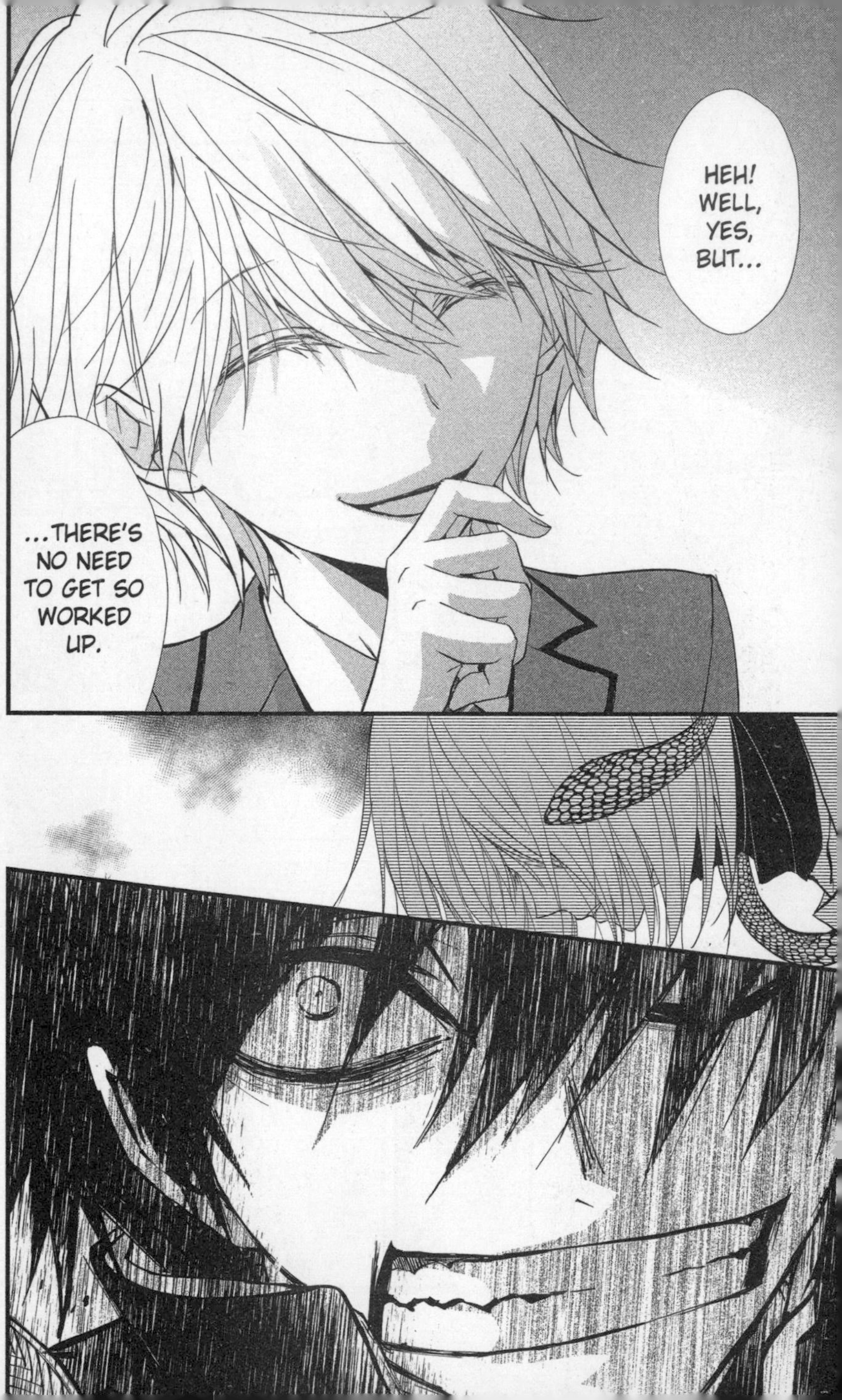
HEH! WELL, YES, BUT...
...THERE'S NO NEED TO GET SO WORKED UP.

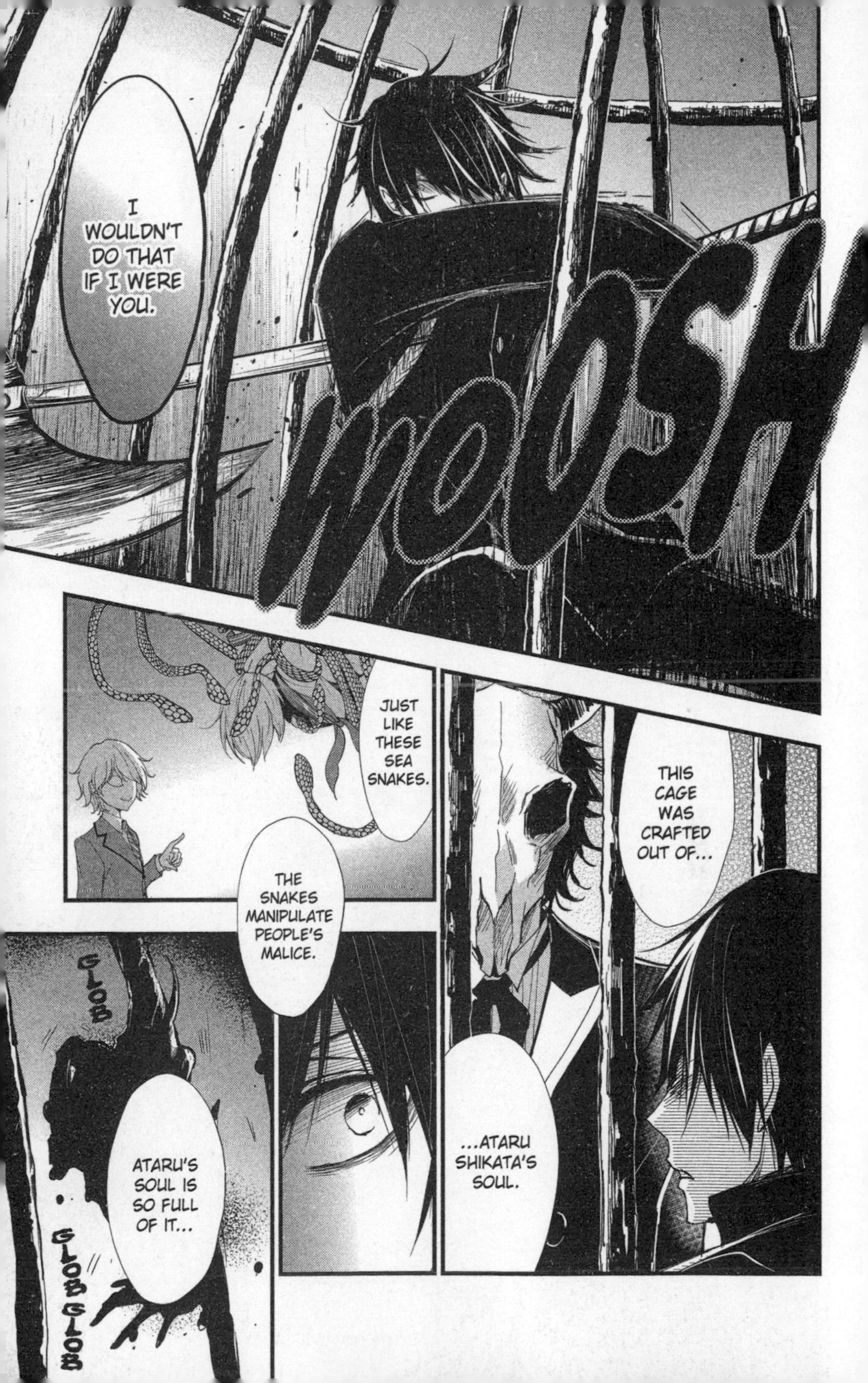
I WOULDN'T DO THAT IF I WERE YOU.
WHOOSH
THIS CAGE WAS CRAFTED OUT OF...
...ATARU SHIKATA'S SOUL.
JUST LIKE THESE SEA SNAKES.
THE SNAKES MANIPULATE PEOPLE'S MALICE.
ATARU'S SOUL IS SO FULL OF IT...
GLOB
GLOB GLOB

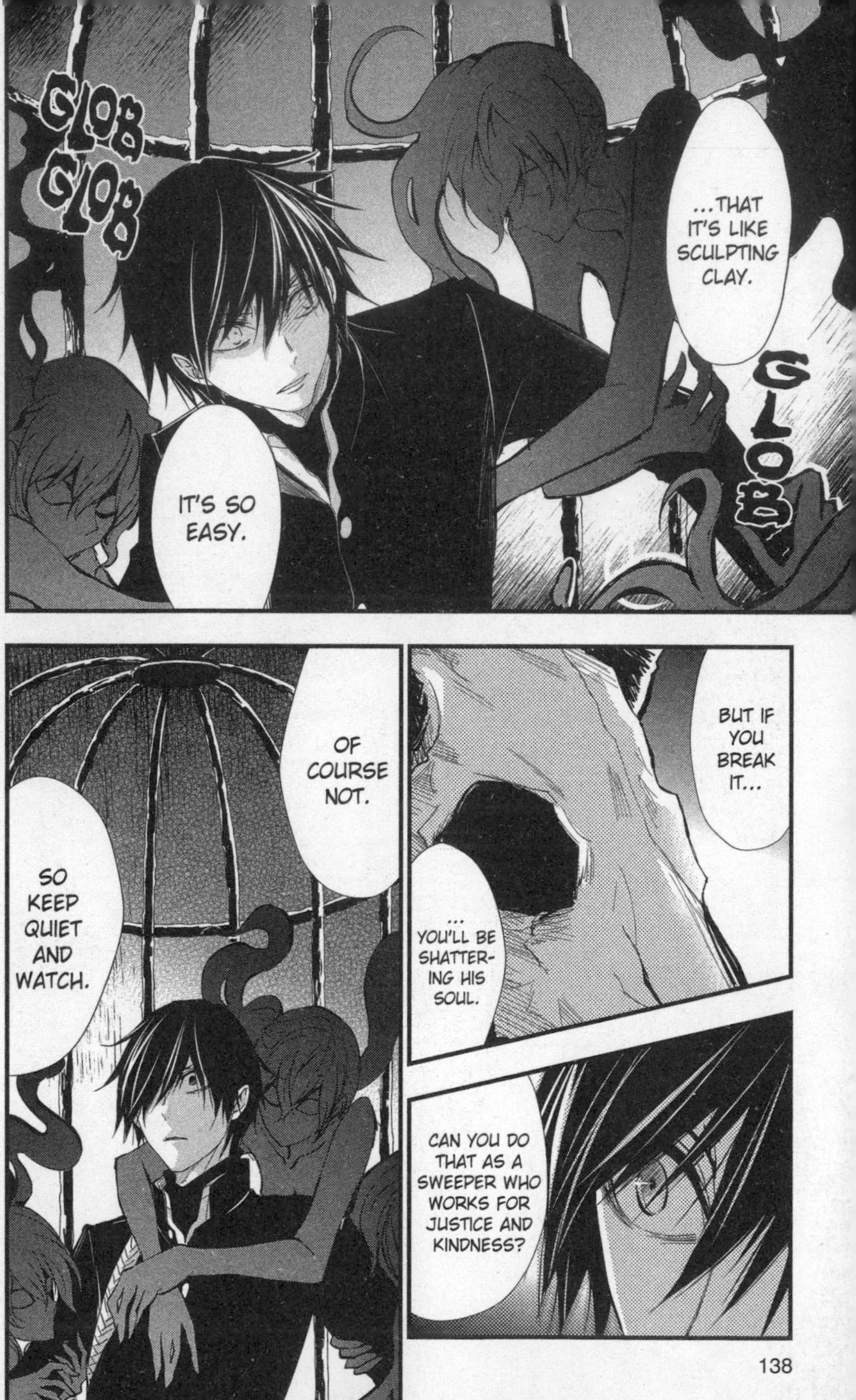
...THAT IT'S LIKE SCULPTING CLAY.
GLOB
GLOB GLOB
IT'S SO EASY.
BUT IF YOU BREAK IT...
...YOU'LL BE SHATTER-ING HIS SOUL.
CAN YOU DO THAT AS A SWEEPER WHO WORKS FOR JUSTICE AND KINDNESS?
OF COURSE NOT.
SO KEEP QUIET AND WATCH.

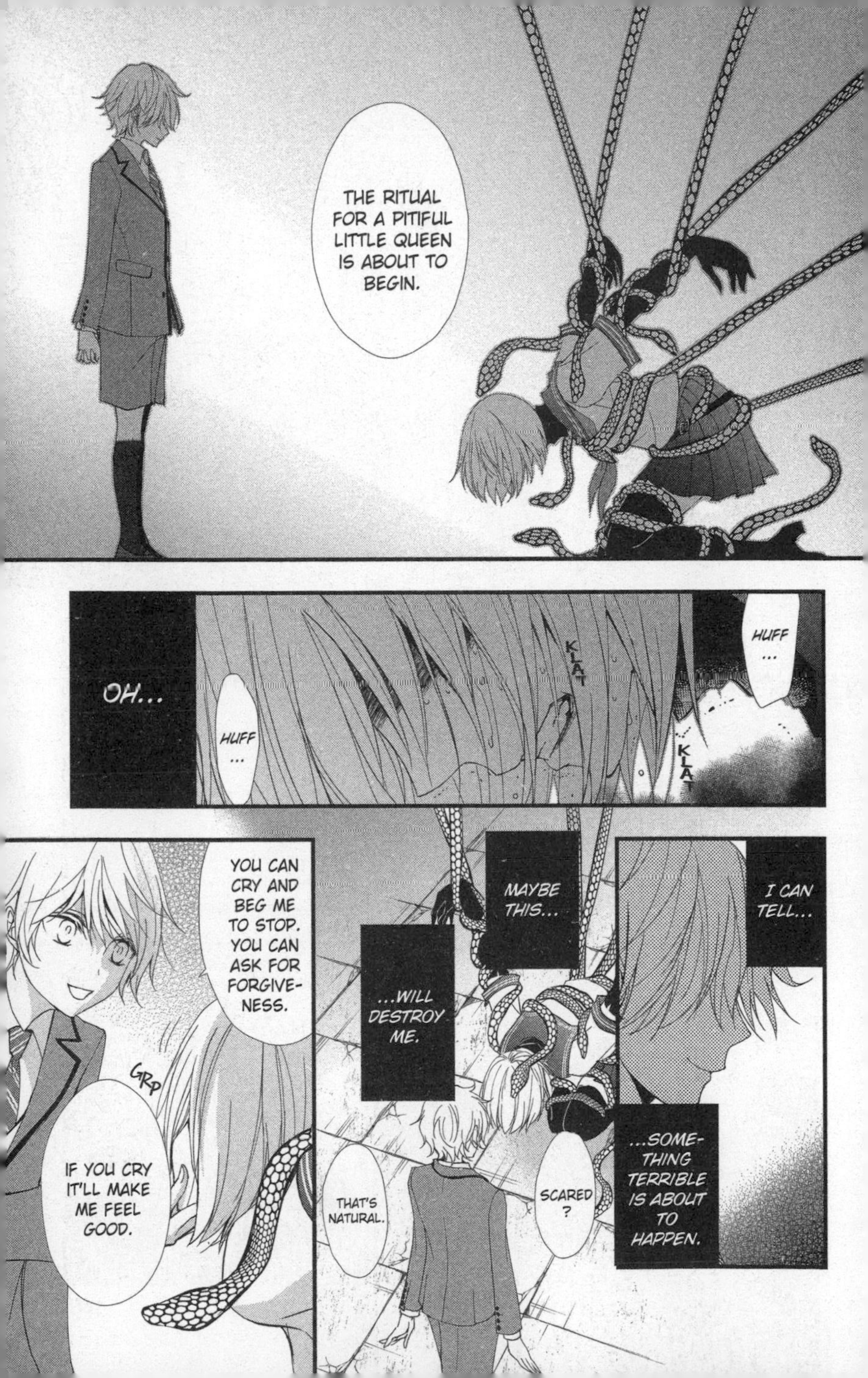
THE RITUAL FOR A PITIFUL LITTLE QUEEN IS ABOUT TO BEGIN.
HUFF...
KLAT
KLAT
HUFF...
OH...
I CAN TELL...
...SOMETHING TERRIBLE IS ABOUT TO HAPPEN.
MAYBE THIS...
...WILL DESTROY ME.
SCARED?
THAT'S NATURAL.
YOU CAN CRY AND BEG ME TO STOP. YOU CAN ASK FOR FORGIVE-NESS.
GRP
IF YOU CRY IT'LL MAKE ME FEEL GOOD.

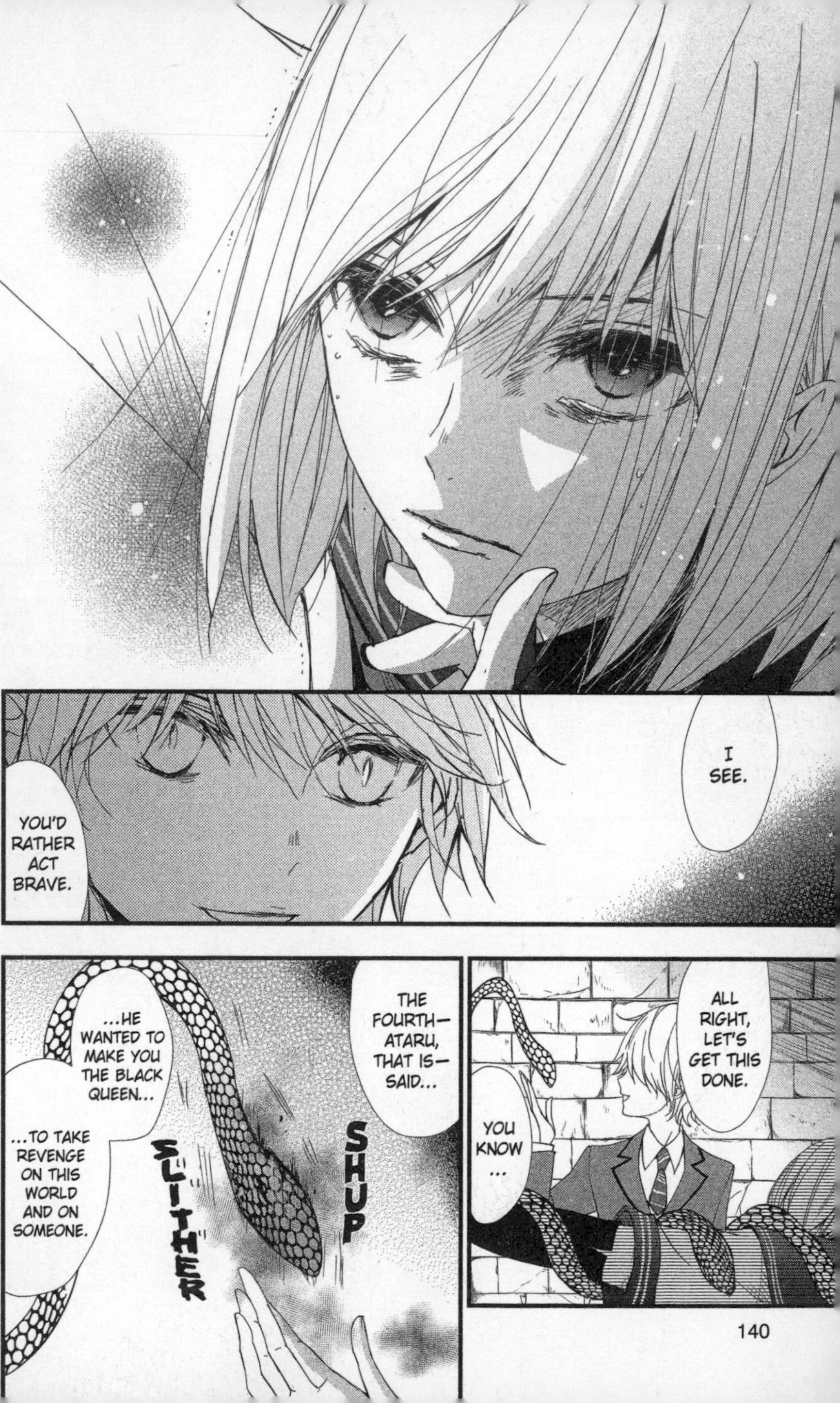
I SEE.
YOU'D RATHER ACT BRAVE.
ALL RIGHT, LET'S GET THIS DONE.
YOU KNOW...
THE FOURTH—ATARU, THAT IS—SAID...
SHUP
SLITHER
...HE WANTED TO MAKE YOU THE BLACK QUEEN...
...TO TAKE REVENGE ON THIS WORLD AND ON SOMEONE.

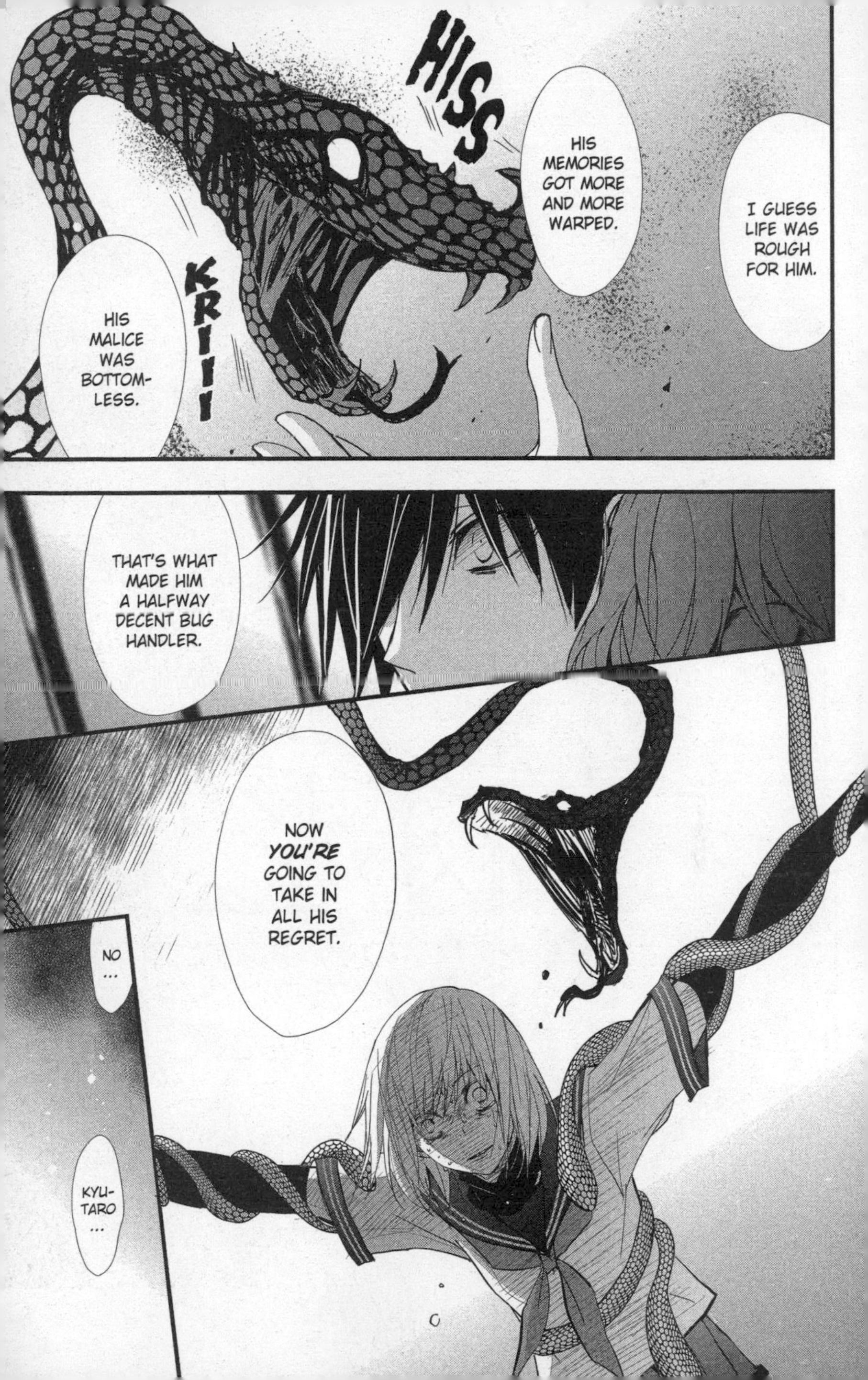
I GUESS LIFE WAS ROUGH FOR HIM.
HIS MEMORIES GOT MORE AND MORE WARPED.
HISS
KRIIII
HIS MALICE WAS BOTTOM-LESS.
THAT'S WHAT MADE HIM A HALFWAY DECENT BUG HANDLER.
NOW *YOU'RE* GOING TO TAKE IN ALL HIS REGRET.
NO ...
KYU-TARO ...

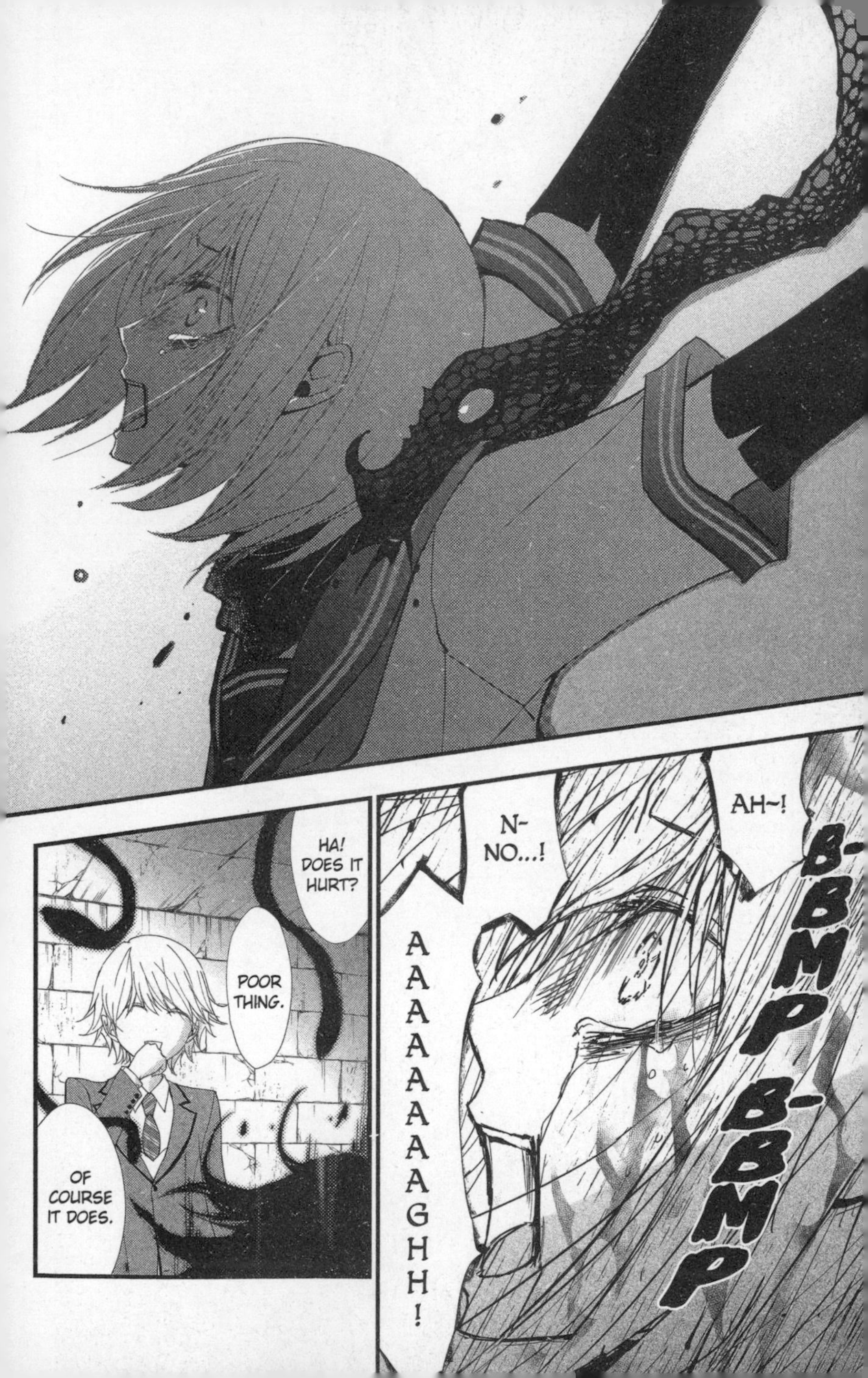
AH~!
B-BMP B-BMP
N-NO...!
AAAAAAAAAGHH!
HA! DOES IT HURT?
POOR THING.
OF COURSE IT DOES.

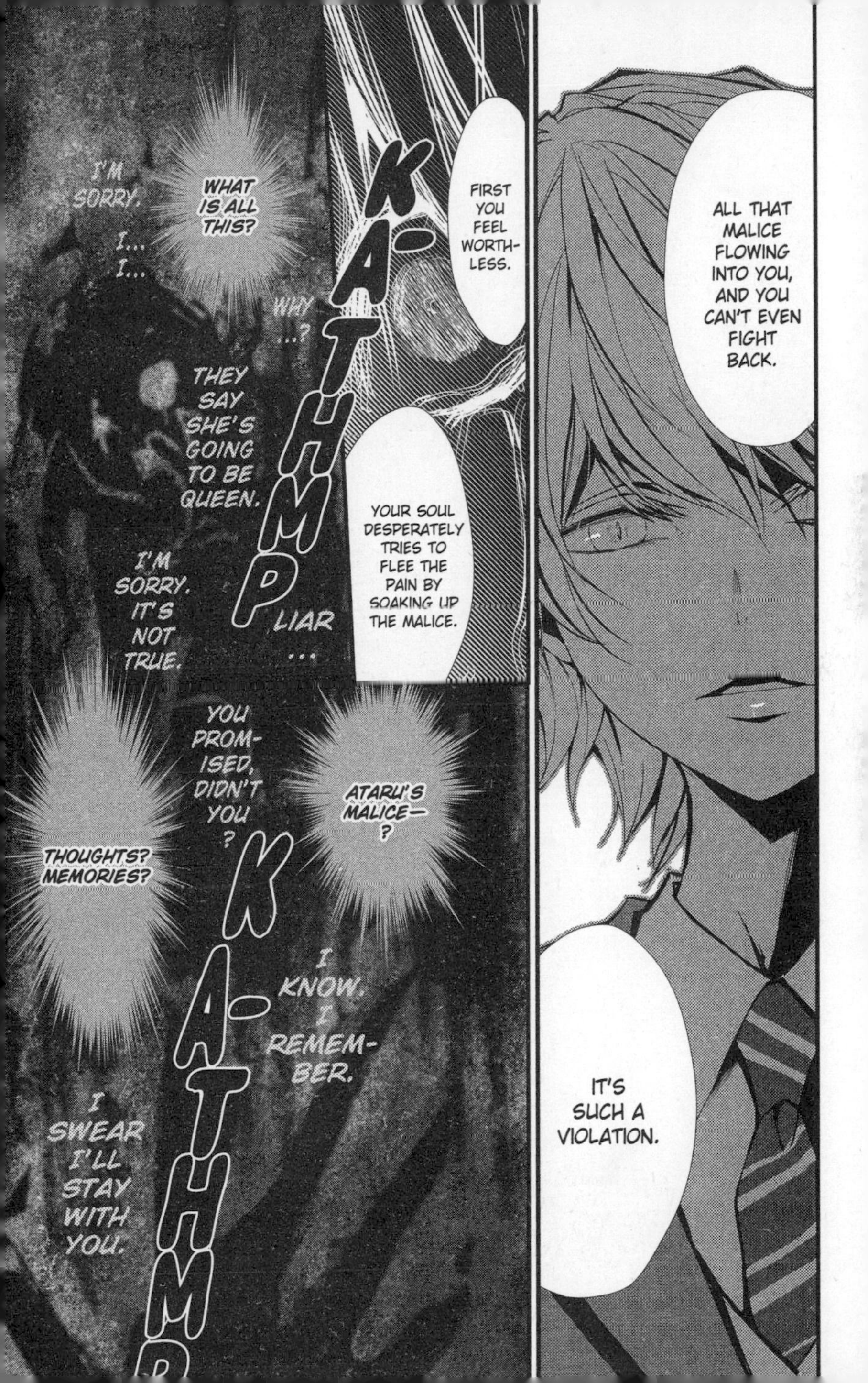
ALL THAT MALICE FLOWING INTO YOU, AND YOU CAN'T EVEN FIGHT BACK.
IT'S SUCH A VIOLATION.
FIRST YOU FEEL WORTH-LESS.
YOUR SOUL DESPERATELY TRIES TO FLEE THE PAIN BY SOAKING UP THE MALICE.
KA-THUMP
WHAT IS ALL THIS?
I'M SORRY.
I... I...
WHY ...?
THEY SAY SHE'S GOING TO BE QUEEN.
I'M SORRY. IT'S NOT TRUE.
LIAR ...
ATARU'S MALICE—?
YOU PROM-ISED, DIDN'T YOU ?
THOUGHTS? MEMORIES?
KA-THUMP
I KNOW. I REMEM-BER.
I SWEAR I'LL STAY WITH YOU.

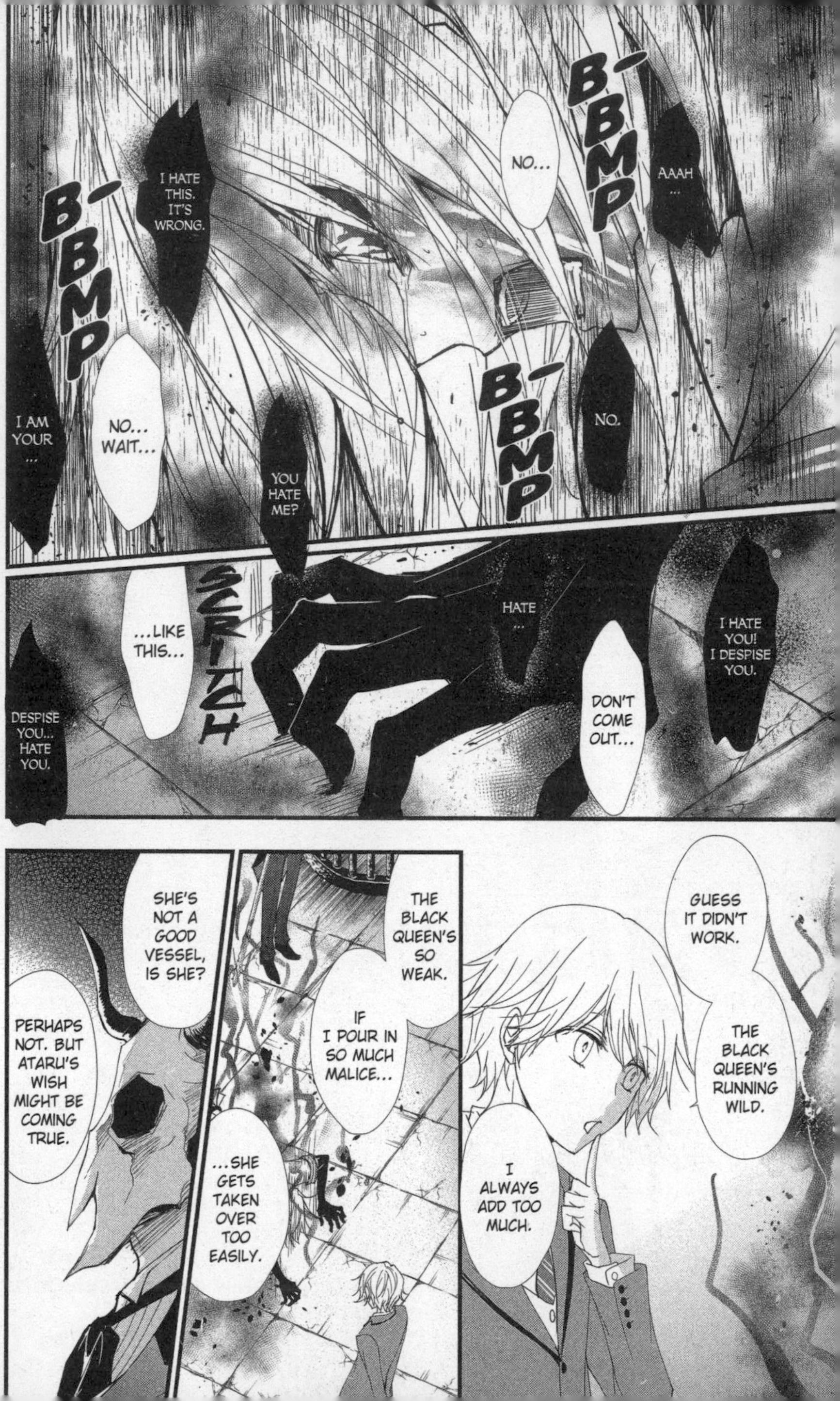
AAAH ...
B-BBMP
NO...
NO.
B-BBMP
I HATE THIS. IT'S WRONG.
B-BBMP
YOU HATE ME?
NO... WAIT...
I AM YOUR ...
I HATE YOU! I DESPISE YOU.
HATE ...
DON'T COME OUT...
SCRITCH
...LIKE THIS...
DESPISE YOU... HATE YOU.
GUESS IT DIDN'T WORK.
THE BLACK QUEEN'S RUNNING WILD.
I ALWAYS ADD TOO MUCH.
THE BLACK QUEEN'S SO WEAK.
IF I POUR IN SO MUCH MALICE...
...SHE GETS TAKEN OVER TOO EASILY.
SHE'S NOT A GOOD VESSEL, IS SHE?
PERHAPS NOT. BUT ATARU'S WISH MIGHT BE COMING TRUE.

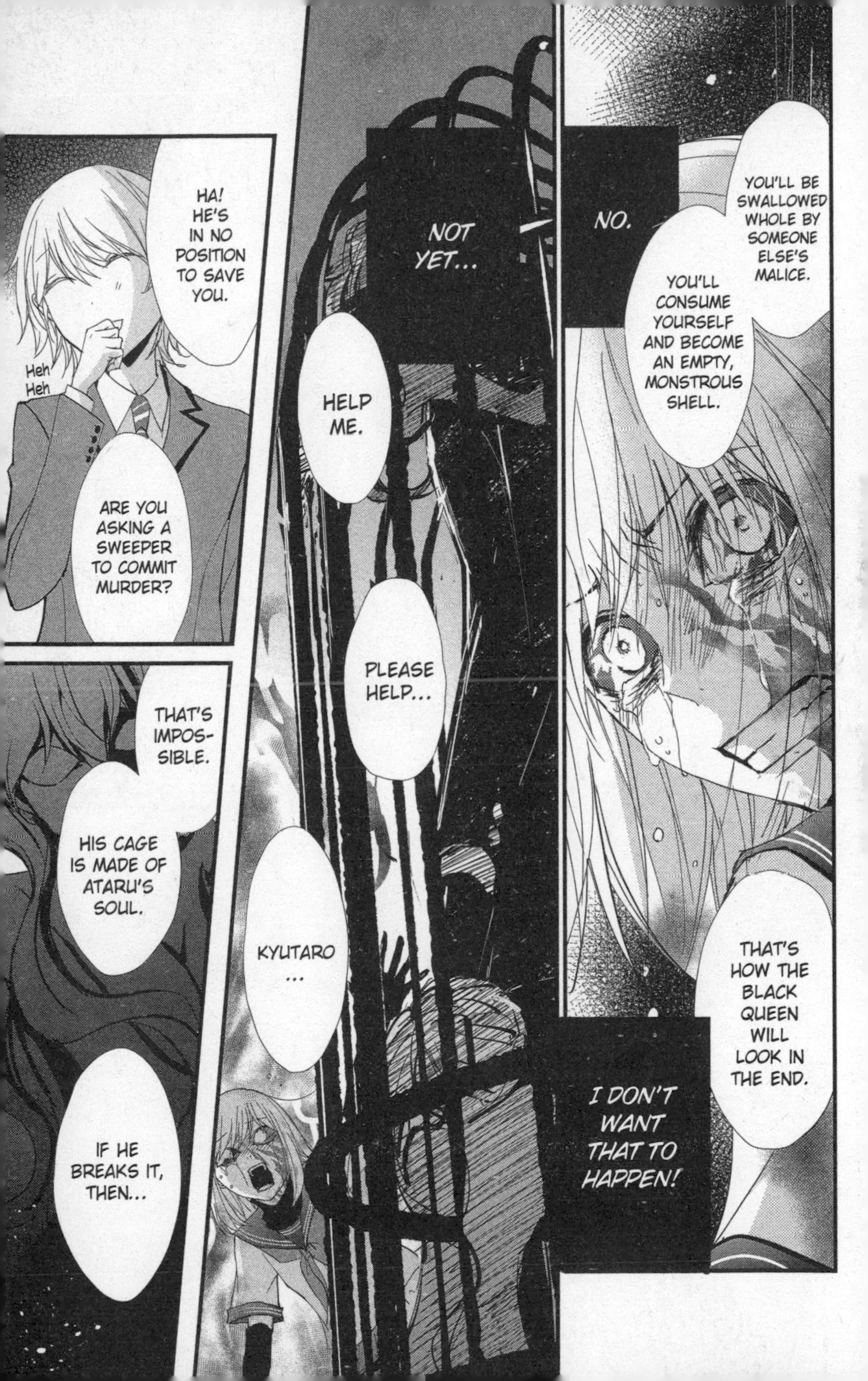
NO.
YOU'LL BE SWALLOWED WHOLE BY SOMEONE ELSE'S MALICE.
YOU'LL CONSUME YOURSELF AND BECOME AN EMPTY, MONSTROUS SHELL.
THAT'S HOW THE BLACK QUEEN WILL LOOK IN THE END.
I DON'T WANT THAT TO HAPPEN!
NOT YET...
HELP ME.
PLEASE HELP...
KYUTARO ...
HA! HE'S IN NO POSITION TO SAVE YOU.
Heh Heh
ARE YOU ASKING A SWEEPER TO COMMIT MURDER?
THAT'S IMPOS-SIBLE.
HIS CAGE IS MADE OF ATARU'S SOUL.
IF HE BREAKS IT, THEN...

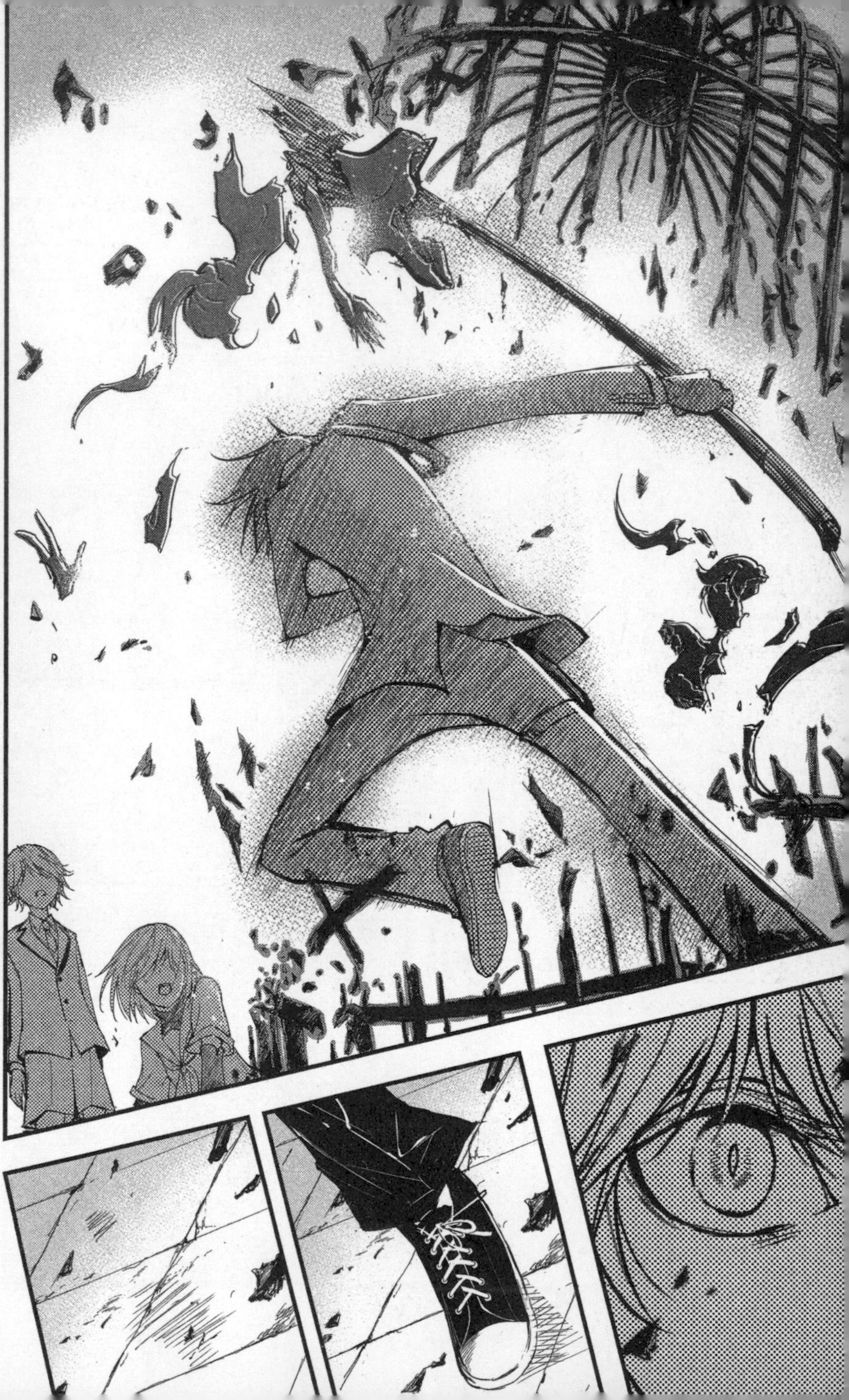

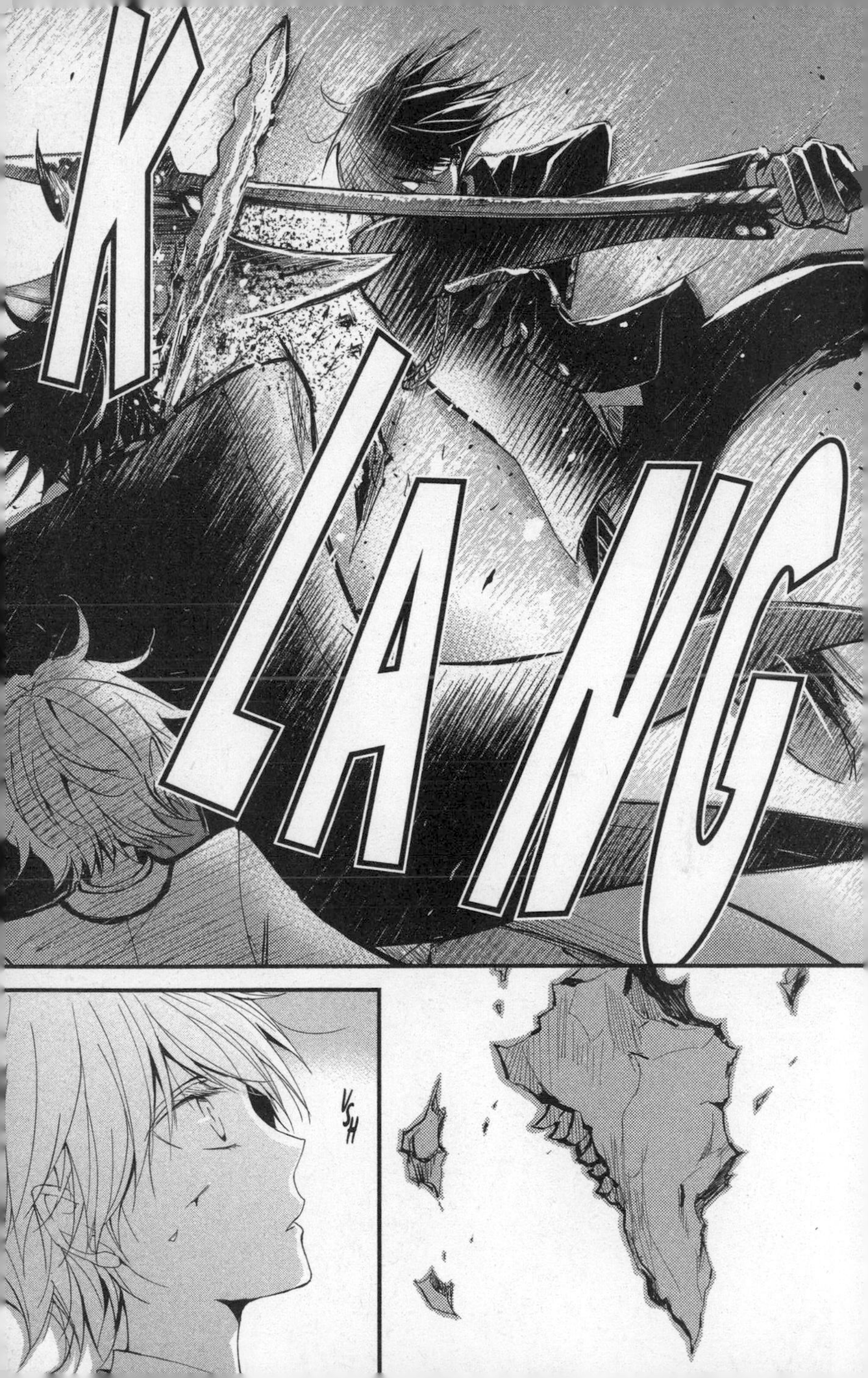
KLANG
VSH

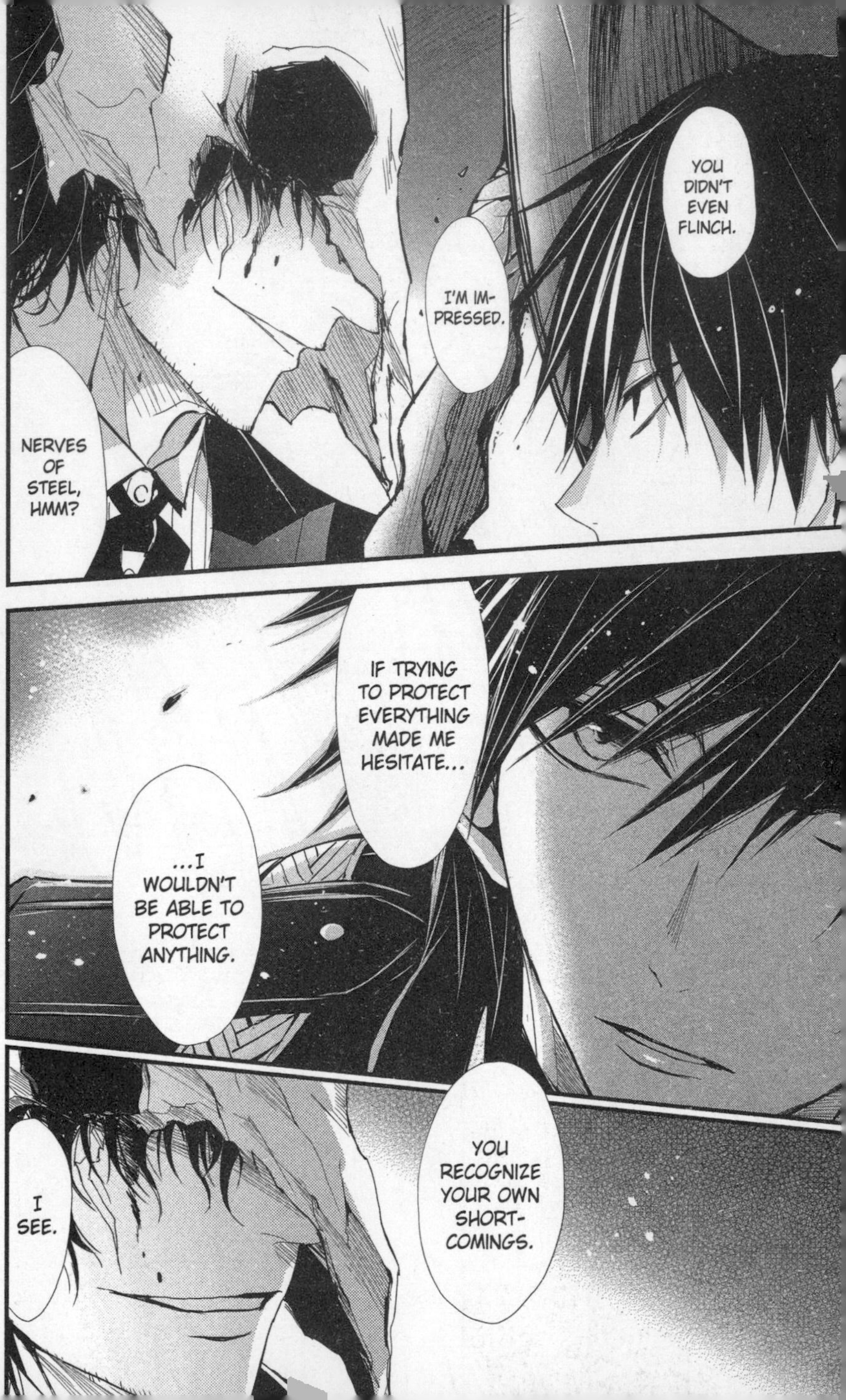
YOU DIDN'T EVEN FLINCH.
I'M IM-PRESSED.
NERVES OF STEEL, HMM?
IF TRYING TO PROTECT EVERYTHING MADE ME HESITATE...
...I WOULDN'T BE ABLE TO PROTECT ANYTHING.
YOU RECOGNIZE YOUR OWN SHORT-COMINGS.
I SEE.

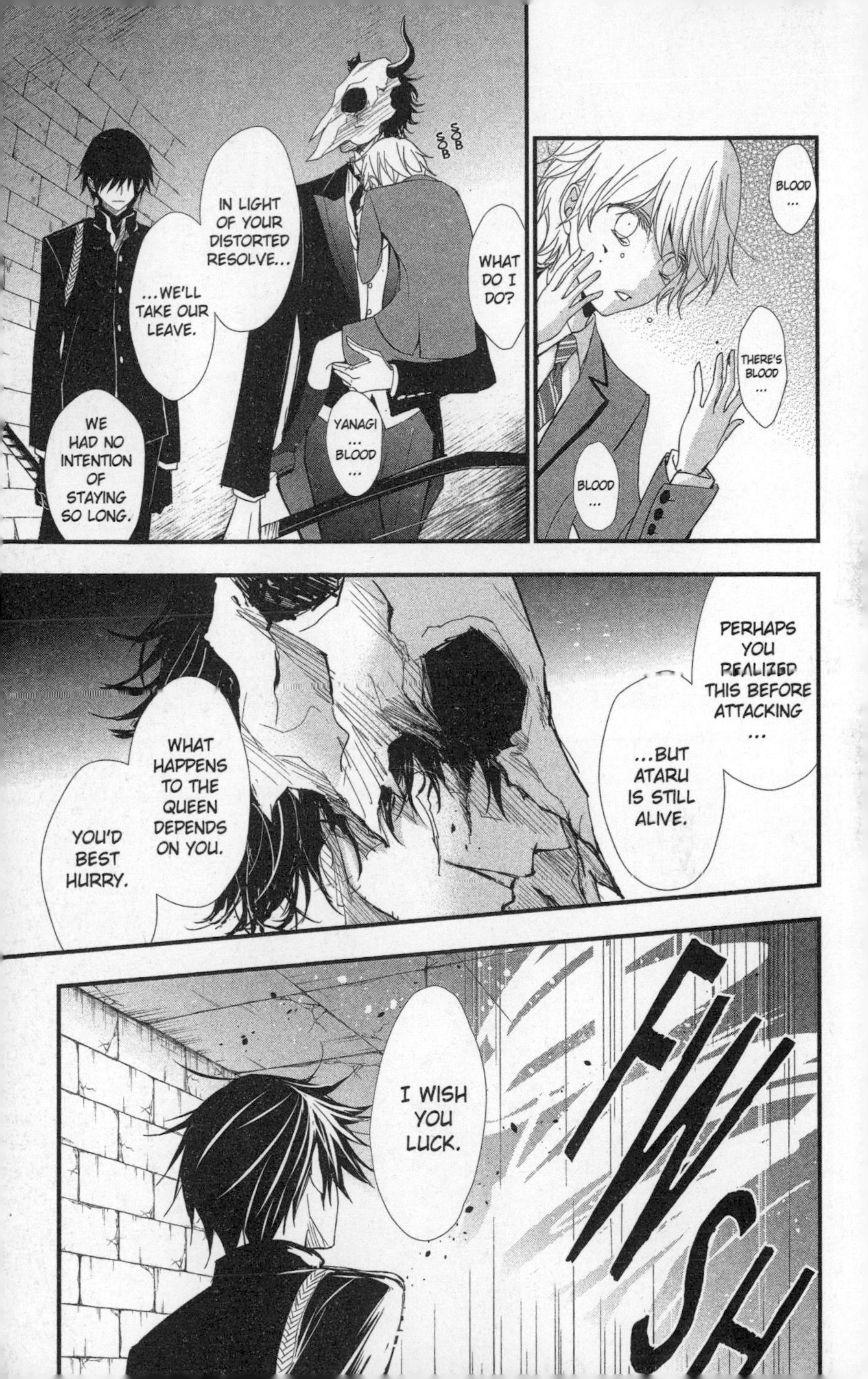
BLOOD ...
THERE'S BLOOD ...
BLOOD ...
SOB SOB
WHAT DO I DO?
IN LIGHT OF YOUR DISTORTED RESOLVE...
...WE'LL TAKE OUR LEAVE.
YANAGI ... BLOOD ...
WE HAD NO INTENTION OF STAYING SO LONG.
PERHAPS YOU REALIZED THIS BEFORE ATTACKING ...
...BUT ATARU IS STILL ALIVE.
WHAT HAPPENS TO THE QUEEN DEPENDS ON YOU.
YOU'D BEST HURRY.
FWSH
I WISH YOU LUCK.

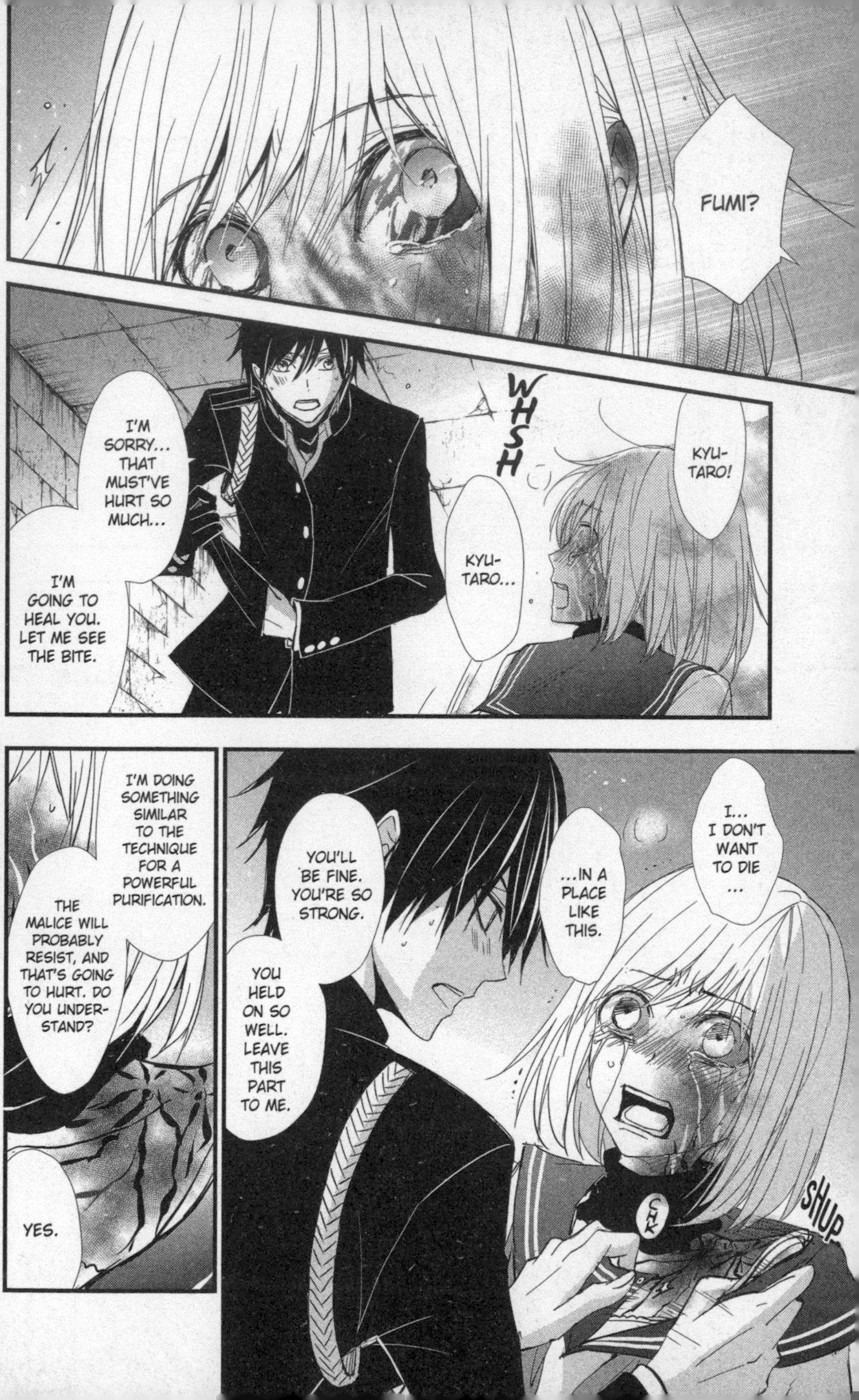
FUMI?
KYU-TARO!
WHSH
KYU-TARO...
I'M SORRY... THAT MUST'VE HURT SO MUCH...
I'M GOING TO HEAL YOU. LET ME SEE THE BITE.
I... I DON'T WANT TO DIE ...
...IN A PLACE LIKE THIS.
YOU'LL BE FINE. YOU'RE SO STRONG.
YOU HELD ON SO WELL. LEAVE THIS PART TO ME.
SHUP
CHK
I'M DOING SOMETHING SIMILAR TO THE TECHNIQUE FOR A POWERFUL PURIFICATION.
THE MALICE WILL PROBABLY RESIST, AND THAT'S GOING TO HURT. DO YOU UNDERSTAND?
YES.

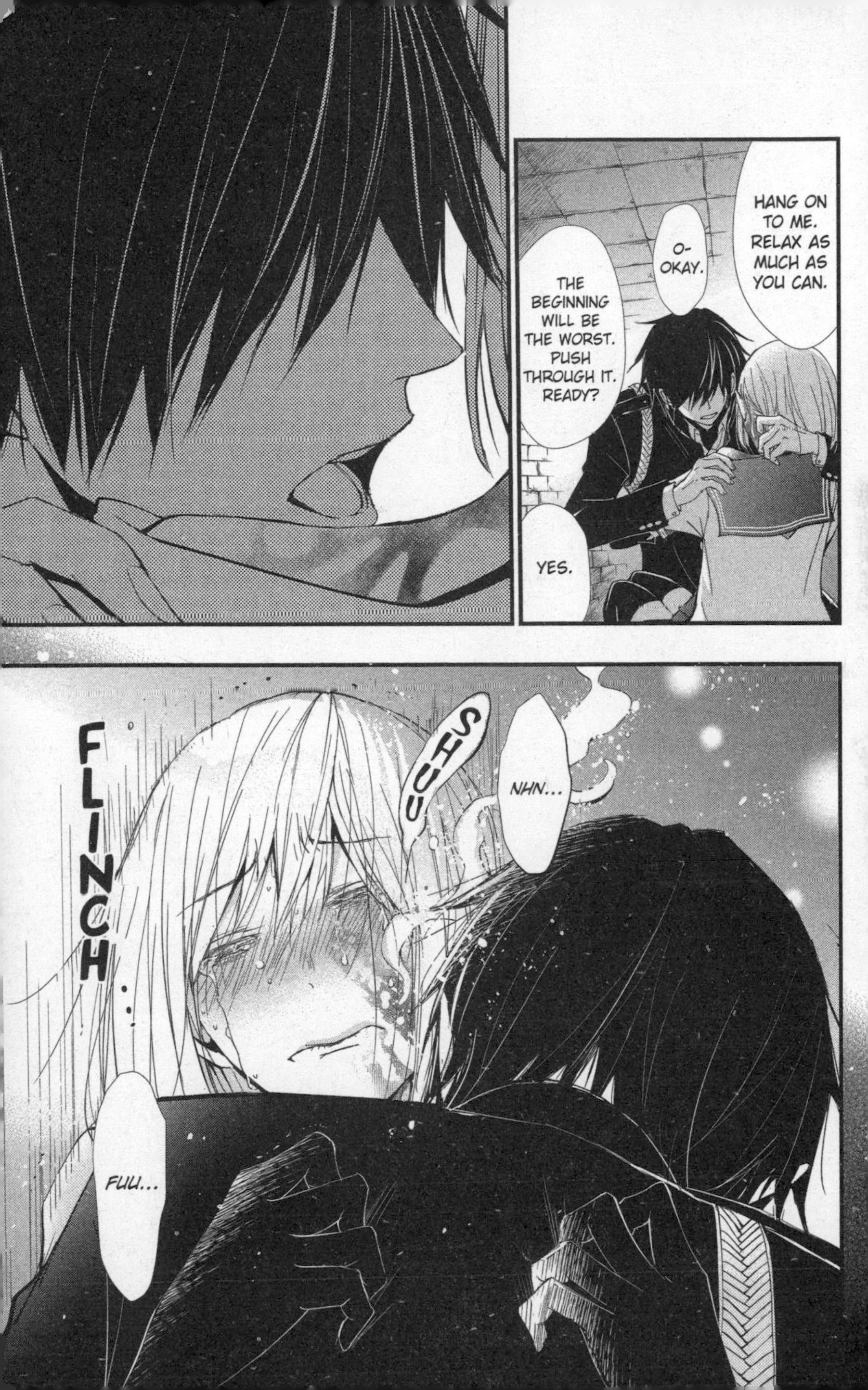
HANG ON TO ME. RELAX AS MUCH AS YOU CAN.
O-OKAY.
THE BEGINNING WILL BE THE WORST. PUSH THROUGH IT. READY?
YES.
NHN...
SHUU
FLINCH
FUU...

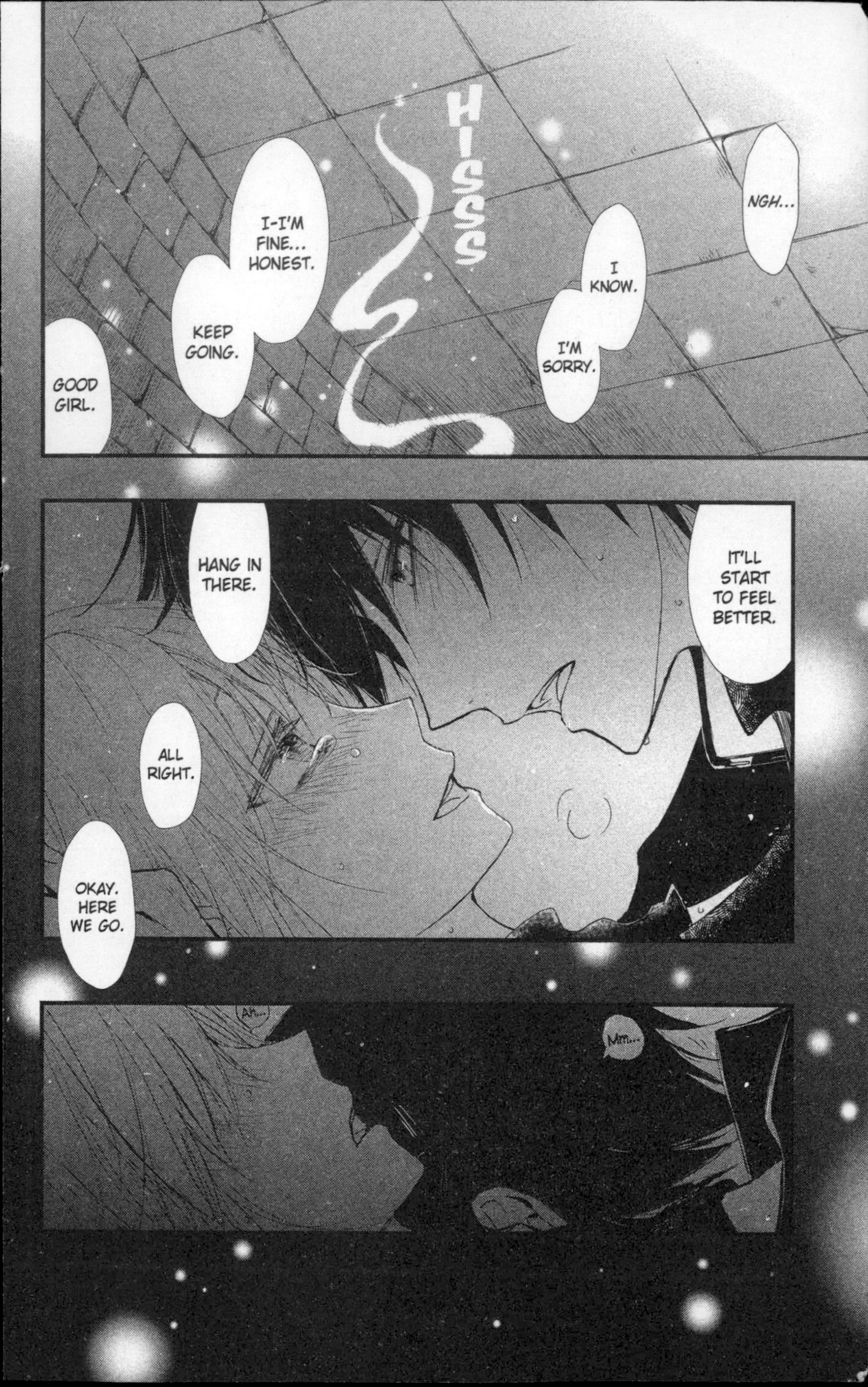
NGH...
I KNOW.
I'M SORRY.
HISSS
I-I'M FINE... HONEST.
KEEP GOING.
GOOD GIRL.
IT'LL START TO FEEL BETTER.
HANG IN THERE.
ALL RIGHT.
OKAY. HERE WE GO.
Mm...
Ah...

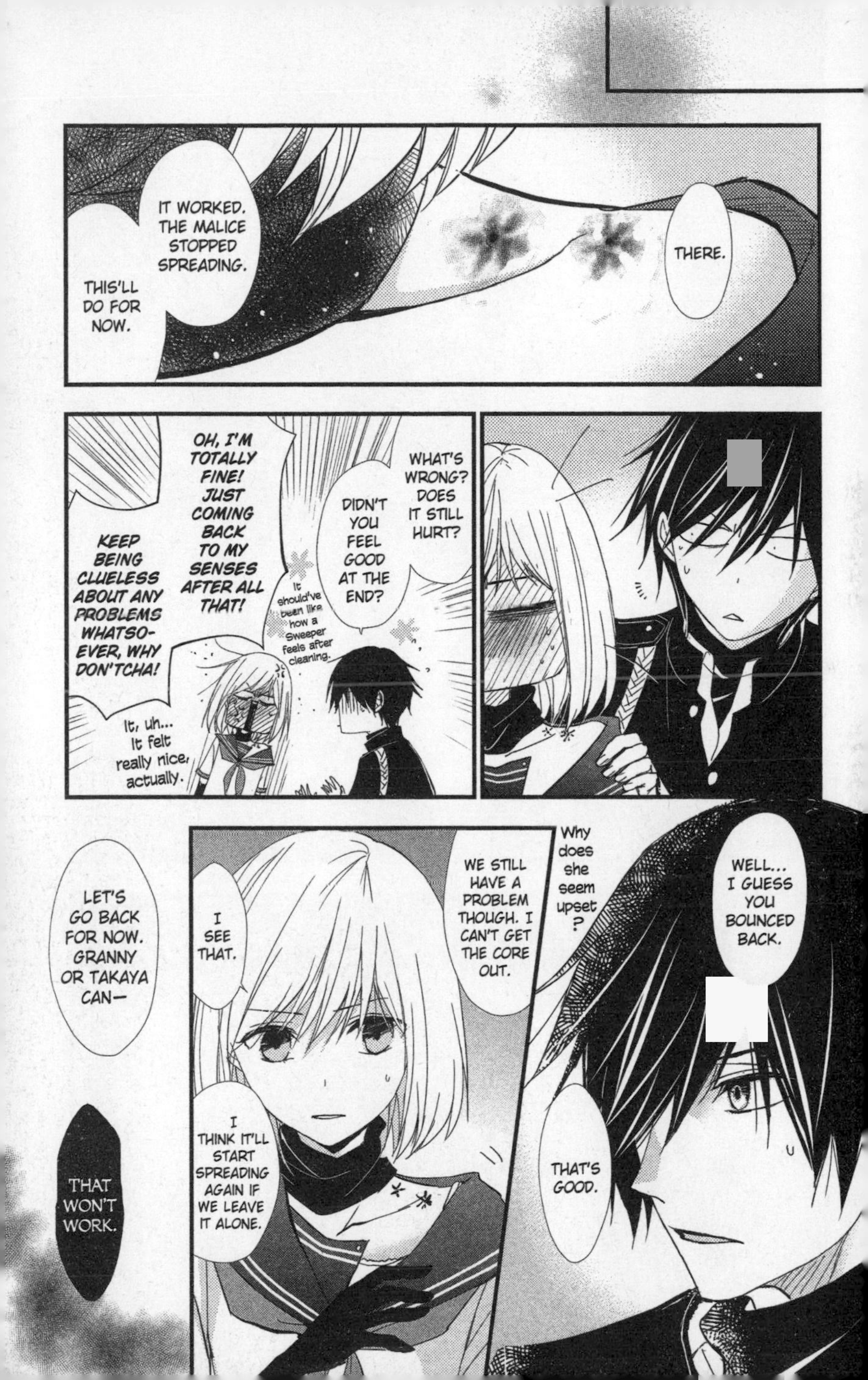
THERE.
IT WORKED. THE MALICE STOPPED SPREADING.
THIS'LL DO FOR NOW.
WHAT'S WRONG? DOES IT STILL HURT?
DIDN'T YOU FEEL GOOD AT THE END?
It should've been like how a Sweeper feels after cleaning.
OH, I'M TOTALLY FINE! JUST COMING BACK TO MY SENSES AFTER ALL THAT!
KEEP BEING CLUELESS ABOUT ANY PROBLEMS WHATSO-EVER, WHY DON'TCHA!
It, uh... It felt really nice, actually.
WELL... I GUESS YOU BOUNCED BACK.
Why does she seem upset?
THAT'S GOOD.
WE STILL HAVE A PROBLEM THOUGH. I CAN'T GET THE CORE OUT.
I SEE THAT.
I THINK IT'LL START SPREADING AGAIN IF WE LEAVE IT ALONE.
LET'S GO BACK FOR NOW. GRANNY OR TAKAYA CAN—
THAT WON'T WORK.

IF YOU LEAVE THIS MIND VAULT, IT WILL TRIGGER ANOTHER EXPLOSION.

IT WILL BLOW YOU COMPLETELY APART. YOU'LL NEVER RETURN TO YOUR-SELVES.

THAT'S THE TRAP I'VE LAID.

...YOU MUST SAVE ATARU AND ELIMINATE THE SOURCE OF THE MALICE...

TO ESCAPE IT...

...OR YOU MUST KILL HIM.

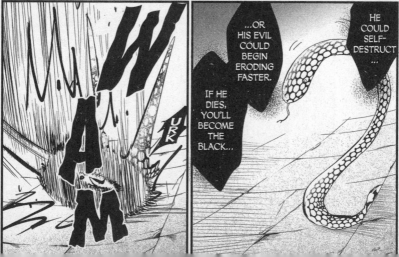

W A M

M..W... URK

HE COULD SELF-DESTRUCT...

...OR HIS EVIL COULD BEGIN ERODING FASTER.

IF HE DIES, YOU'LL BECOME THE BLACK...

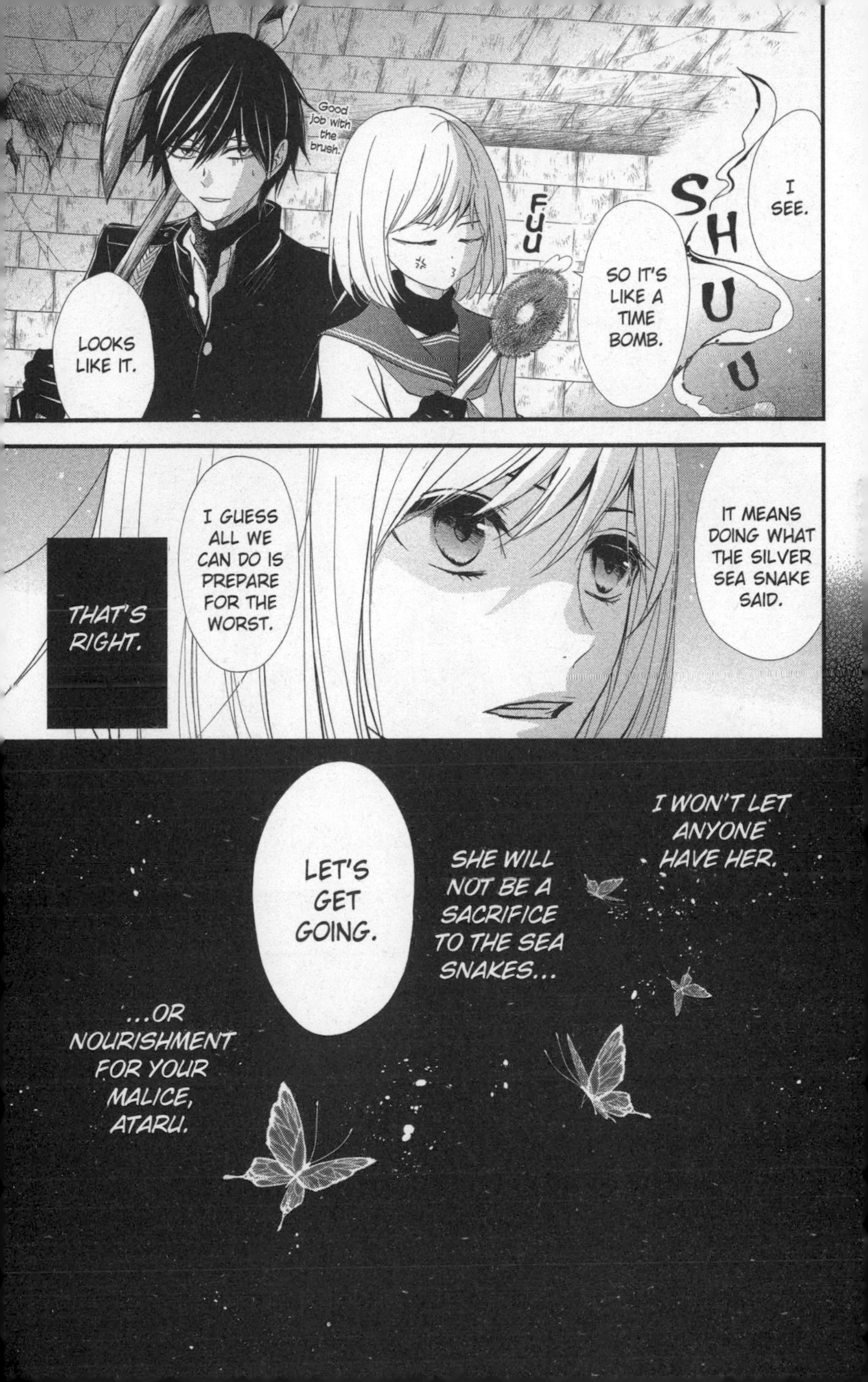

I SEE.
SHUU
SO IT'S LIKE A TIME BOMB.
FUU
Good job with the brush.
LOOKS LIKE IT.
IT MEANS DOING WHAT THE SILVER SEA SNAKE SAID.
I GUESS ALL WE CAN DO IS PREPARE FOR THE WORST.
THAT'S RIGHT.
I WON'T LET ANYONE HAVE HER.
SHE WILL NOT BE A SACRIFICE TO THE SEA SNAKES...
LET'S GET GOING.
...OR NOURISHMENT FOR YOUR MALICE, ATARU.

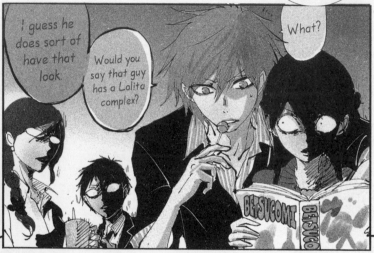

MONTHLY BETSUCOMI SALE DATE NOTICE ON TWITTER

# CHAPTER 20

What?
Would you say that guy has a Lolita complex?
I guess he does sort of have that look.
BETSUCOMI
BETSUCO

**WHAT'S UP IN *QUEEN'S QUALITY* THIS MONTH?**
(1) WELL, HE DESERVED TO BE RATTED ON.
(2) IT WAS LAST MONTH'S KID WHO LET IT IN.
(3) I MIGHT HAVE SAID THERE WAS A SLIGHT RESEMBLANCE, BUT NO, ATARU DOES NOT HAVE A LOLITA COMPLEX.

They're all *Daisy* characters in this notice... A guy formerly with a Lolita complex...

THERE IS A CLEAR DIFFERENCE IN TONE BETWEEN THIS AND OTHER *BETSUCOMI* SERIES. CHAPTER 20 HAS THIS AUTHOR A BIT AT A LOSS.

Now, the following chapter, chapter 20, marks the end of volume 4 of *Queequa*. There's more black ink in this chapter (including the notice), but I hope you'll read it all the way through. It looks like there will be a climactic moment in the next volume!

I hope to see you all again. Until then!

Kyousuke Motomi

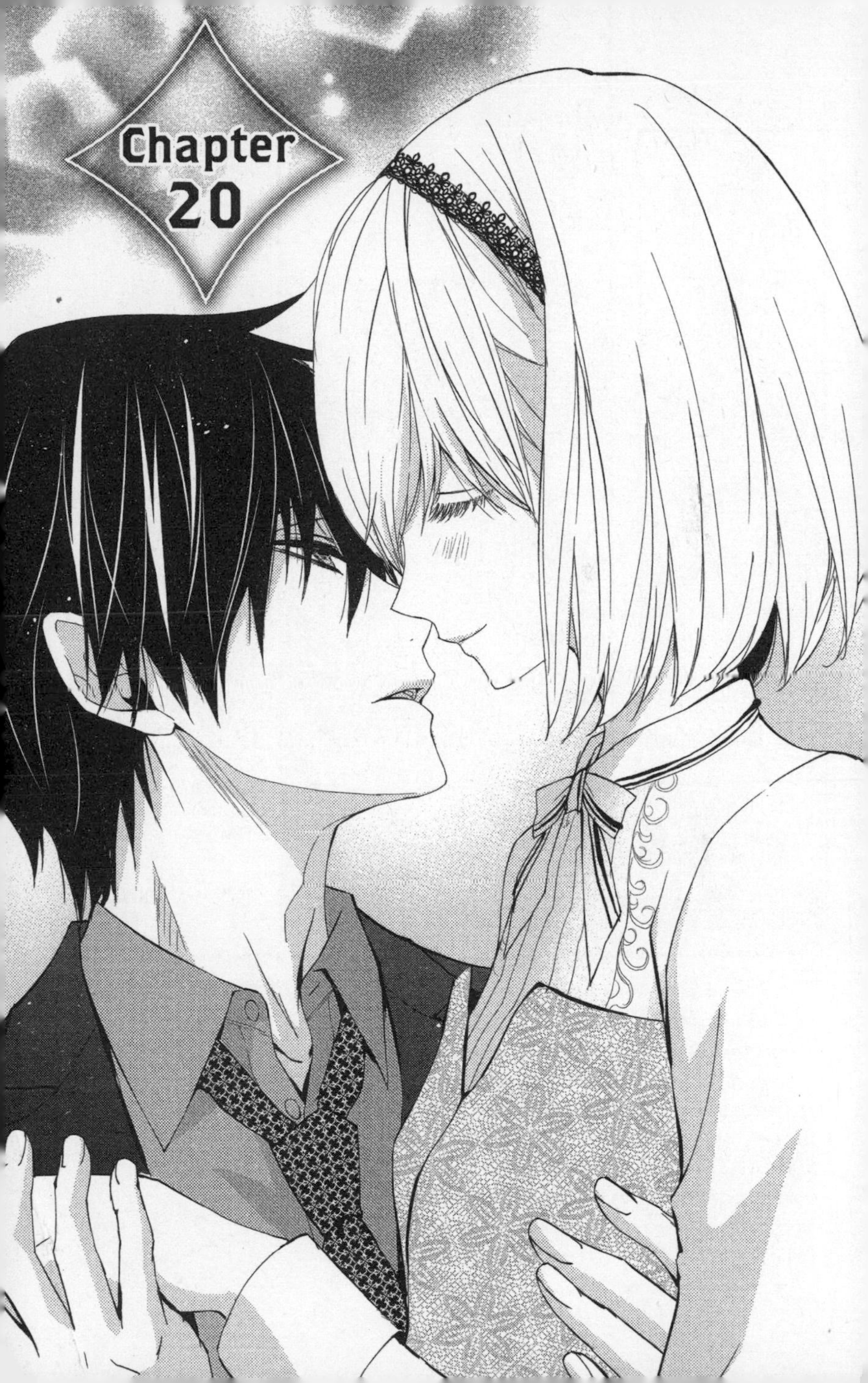
Chapter
20

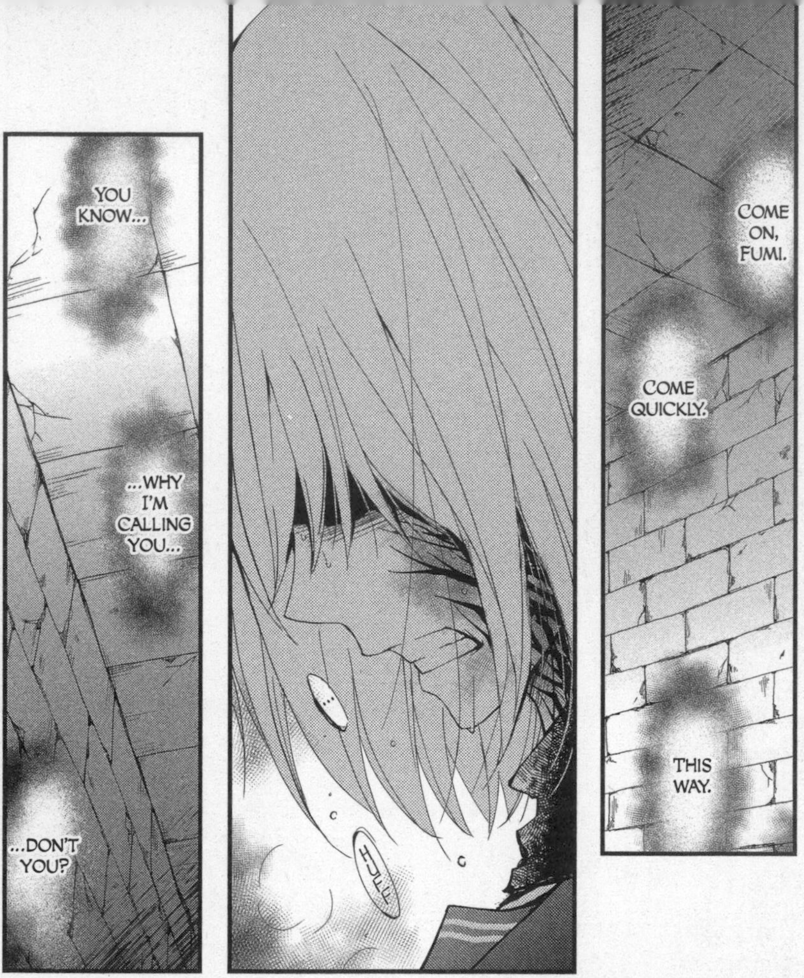
COME ON, FUMI.
COME QUICKLY.
THIS WAY.
...
HUFF
YOU KNOW...
...WHY I'M CALLING YOU...
...DON'T YOU?

The story has taken a brutal turn, so I'll talk about something completely different: the bath. I think Kyutaro's the kind of guy who uses just one towel when he bathes. It's basically a long hand towel, and he uses it to wash, then dry himself. He also uses it to wipe down the basin, the mirror, and the tub... sort of like a Sweeper would. No need for a sponge! Try it!

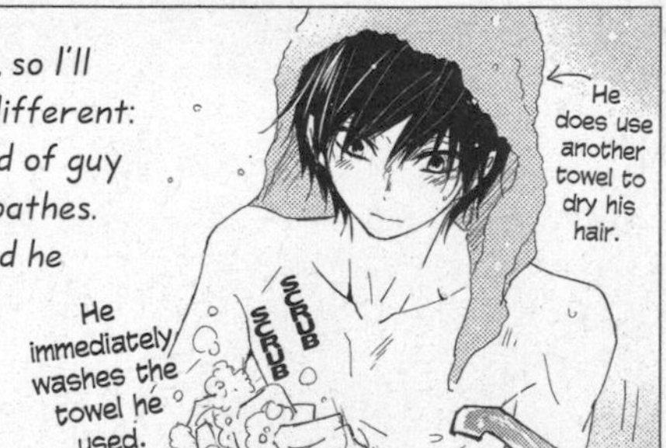
He does use another towel to dry his hair.
SCRUB SCRUB
He immediately washes the towel he used.

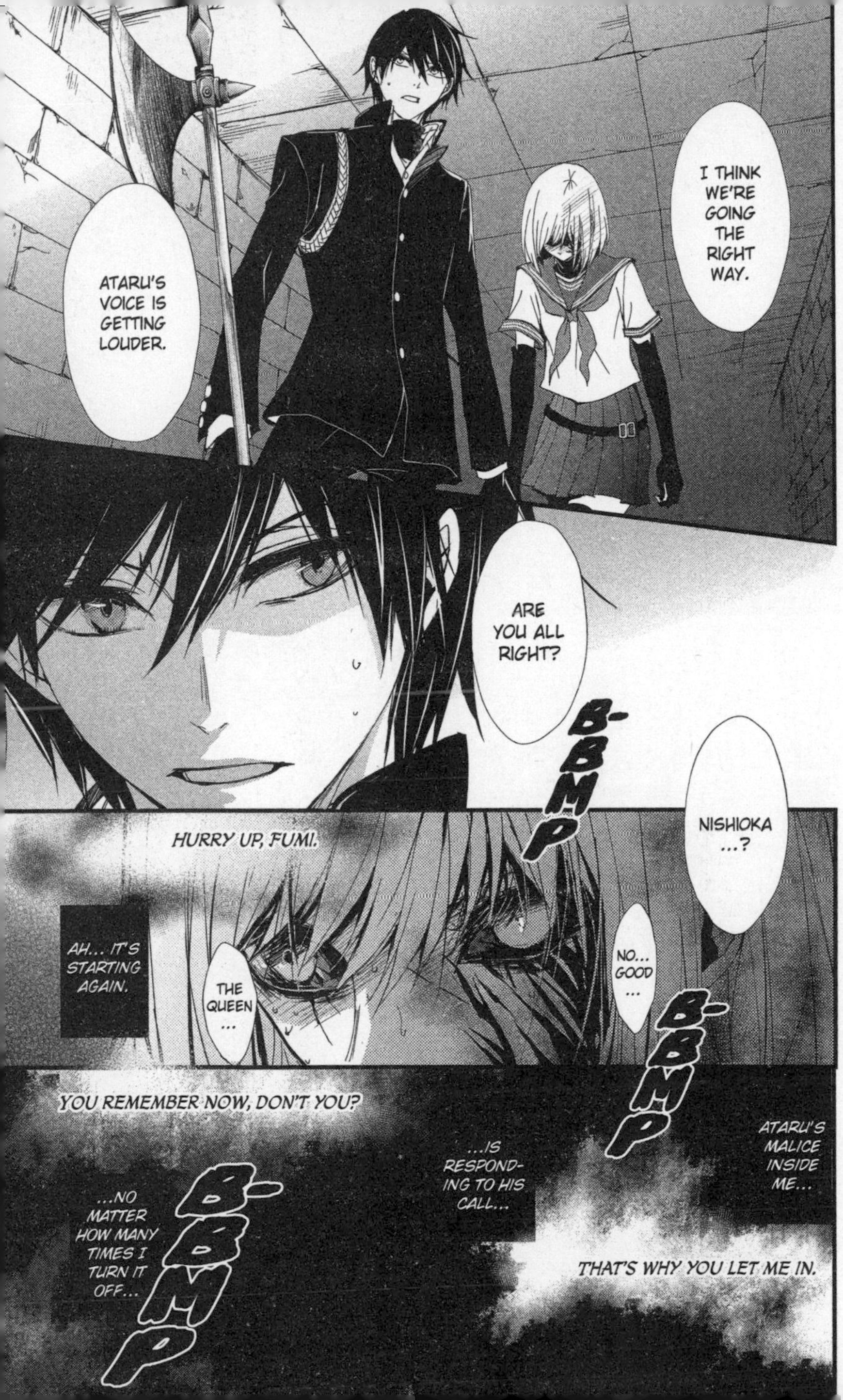
I THINK WE'RE GOING THE RIGHT WAY.
ATARU'S VOICE IS GETTING LOUDER.
ARE YOU ALL RIGHT?
B-BBMP
NISHIOKA ...?
HURRY UP, FUMI.
NO... GOOD ...
THE QUEEN ...
AH... IT'S STARTING AGAIN.
B-BBMP
YOU REMEMBER NOW, DON'T YOU?
ATARU'S MALICE INSIDE ME...
...IS RESPONDING TO HIS CALL...
...NO MATTER HOW MANY TIMES I TURN IT OFF...
B-BBMP
THAT'S WHY YOU LET ME IN.

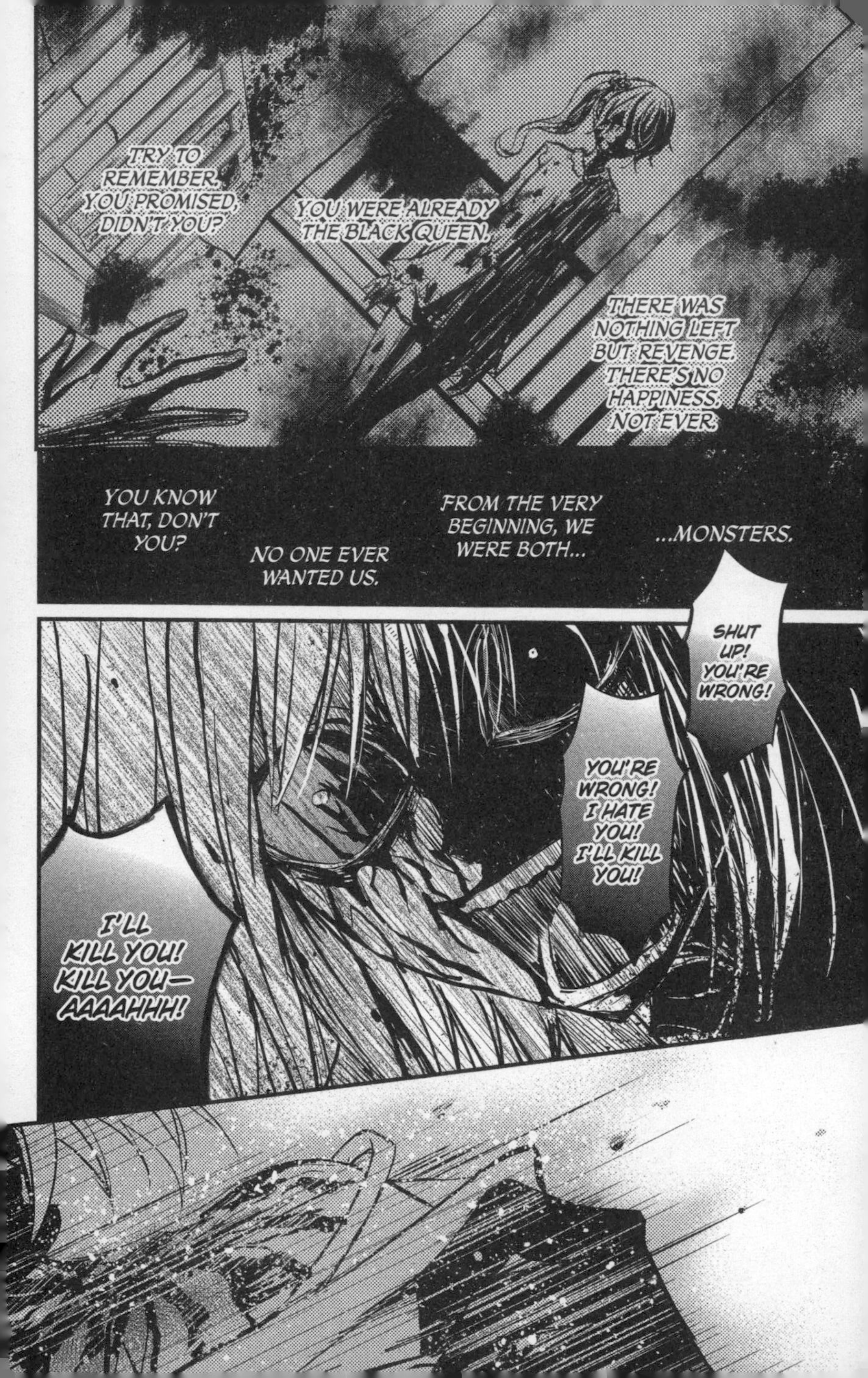
TRY TO REMEMBER. YOU PROMISED, DIDN'T YOU?
YOU WERE ALREADY THE BLACK QUEEN.
THERE WAS NOTHING LEFT BUT REVENGE. THERE'S NO HAPPINESS. NOT EVER.
YOU KNOW THAT, DON'T YOU?
NO ONE EVER WANTED US.
FROM THE VERY BEGINNING, WE WERE BOTH...
...MONSTERS.
SHUT UP! YOU'RE WRONG!
YOU'RE WRONG! I HATE YOU! I'LL KILL YOU!
I'LL KILL YOU! KILL YOU— AAAAHHH!

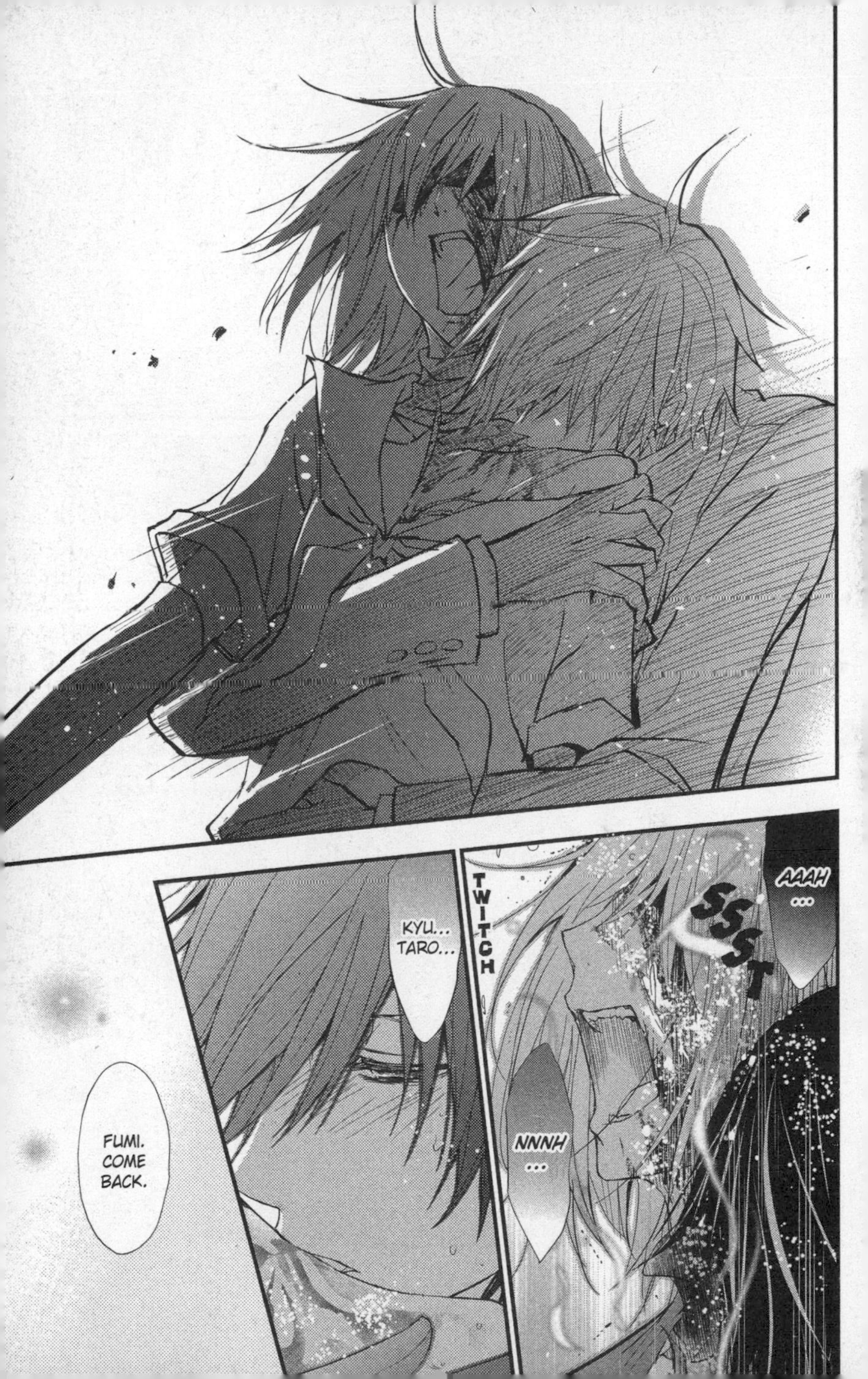
AAAH ...
SSST
TWITCH
NNNH ...
KYU... TARO...
FUMI. COME BACK.

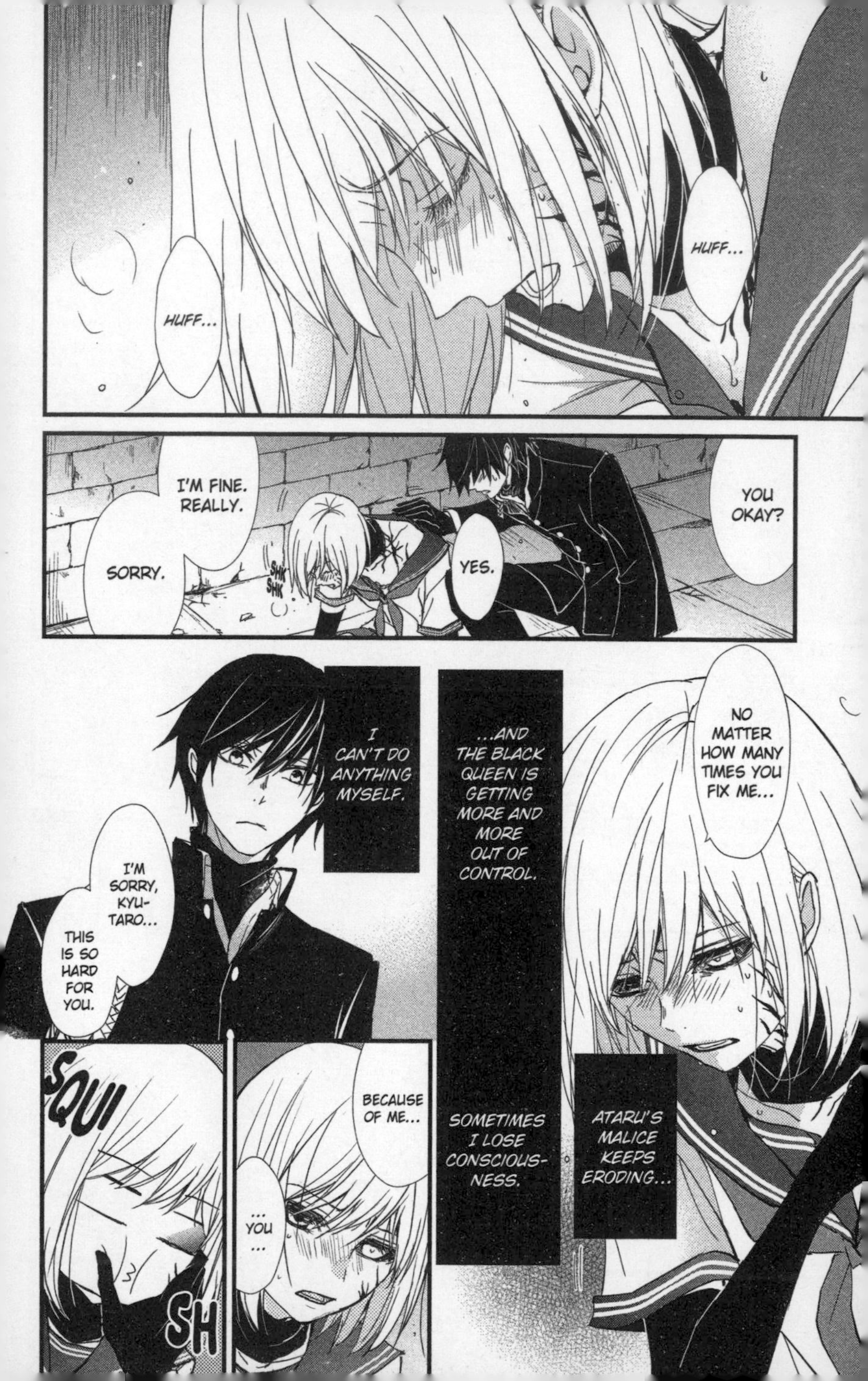
HUFF...
HUFF...
YOU OKAY?
YES.
I'M FINE. REALLY.
SORRY.
SHK SHK
NO MATTER HOW MANY TIMES YOU FIX ME...
ATARU'S MALICE KEEPS ERODING...
...AND THE BLACK QUEEN IS GETTING MORE AND MORE OUT OF CONTROL.
SOMETIMES I LOSE CONSCIOUS-NESS.
I CAN'T DO ANYTHING MYSELF.
I'M SORRY, KYU-TARO...
THIS IS SO HARD FOR YOU.
BECAUSE OF ME...
...YOU...
SQUI
SH

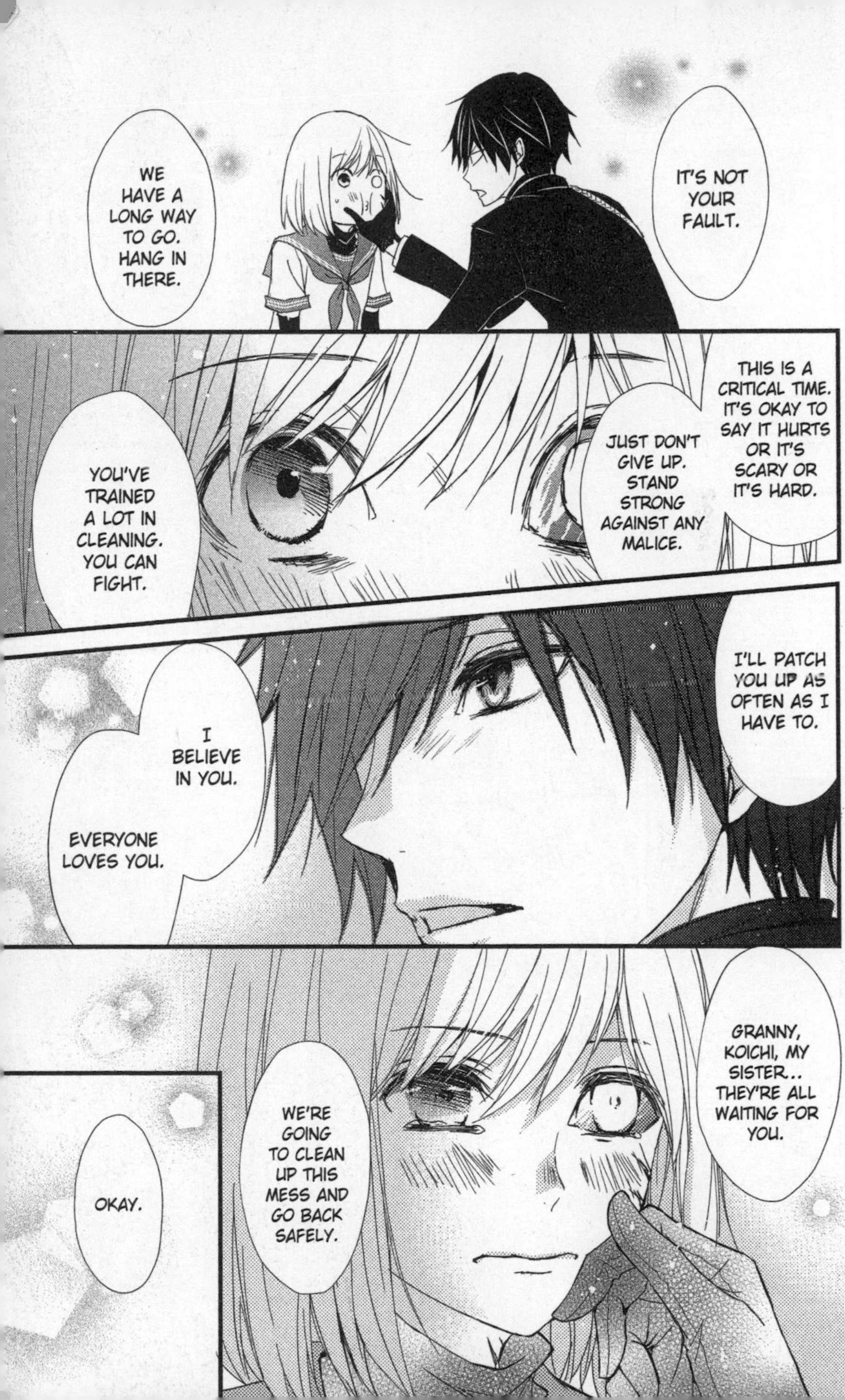
IT'S NOT YOUR FAULT.
WE HAVE A LONG WAY TO GO. HANG IN THERE.
THIS IS A CRITICAL TIME. IT'S OKAY TO SAY IT HURTS OR IT'S SCARY OR IT'S HARD.
JUST DON'T GIVE UP. STAND STRONG AGAINST ANY MALICE.
YOU'VE TRAINED A LOT IN CLEANING. YOU CAN FIGHT.
I'LL PATCH YOU UP AS OFTEN AS I HAVE TO.
I BELIEVE IN YOU.
EVERYONE LOVES YOU.
GRANNY, KOICHI, MY SISTER... THEY'RE ALL WAITING FOR YOU.
WE'RE GOING TO CLEAN UP THIS MESS AND GO BACK SAFELY.
OKAY.

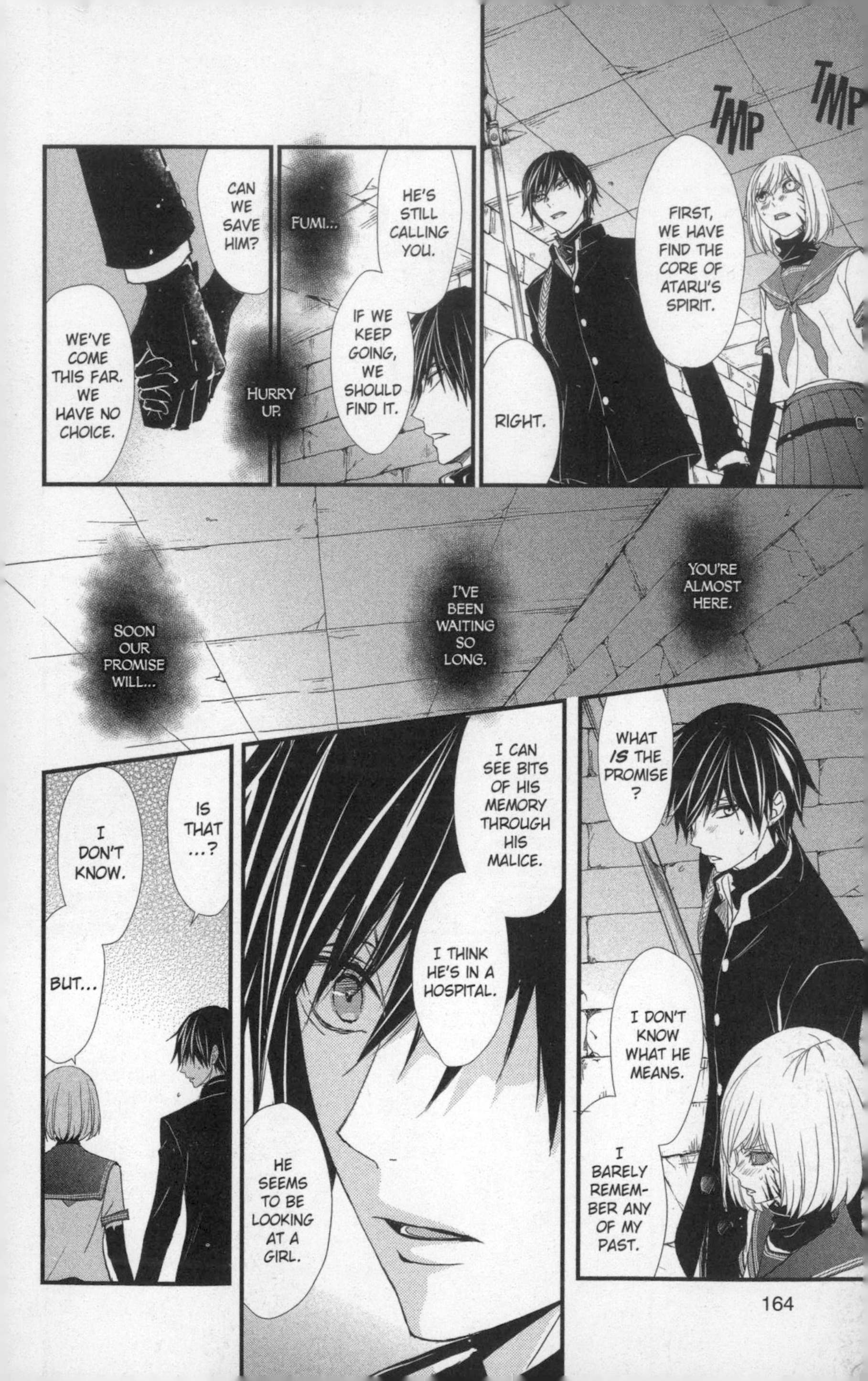
TMP
TMP
FIRST, WE HAVE FIND THE CORE OF ATARU'S SPIRIT.
RIGHT.
HE'S STILL CALLING YOU.
FUMI...
IF WE KEEP GOING, WE SHOULD FIND IT.
HURRY UP.
CAN WE SAVE HIM?
WE'VE COME THIS FAR. WE HAVE NO CHOICE.
YOU'RE ALMOST HERE.
I'VE BEEN WAITING SO LONG.
SOON OUR PROMISE WILL...
WHAT *IS* THE PROMISE?
I DON'T KNOW WHAT HE MEANS.
I BARELY REMEM-BER ANY OF MY PAST.
I CAN SEE BITS OF HIS MEMORY THROUGH HIS MALICE.
I THINK HE'S IN A HOSPITAL.
HE SEEMS TO BE LOOKING AT A GIRL.
IS THAT ...?
I DON'T KNOW.
BUT...

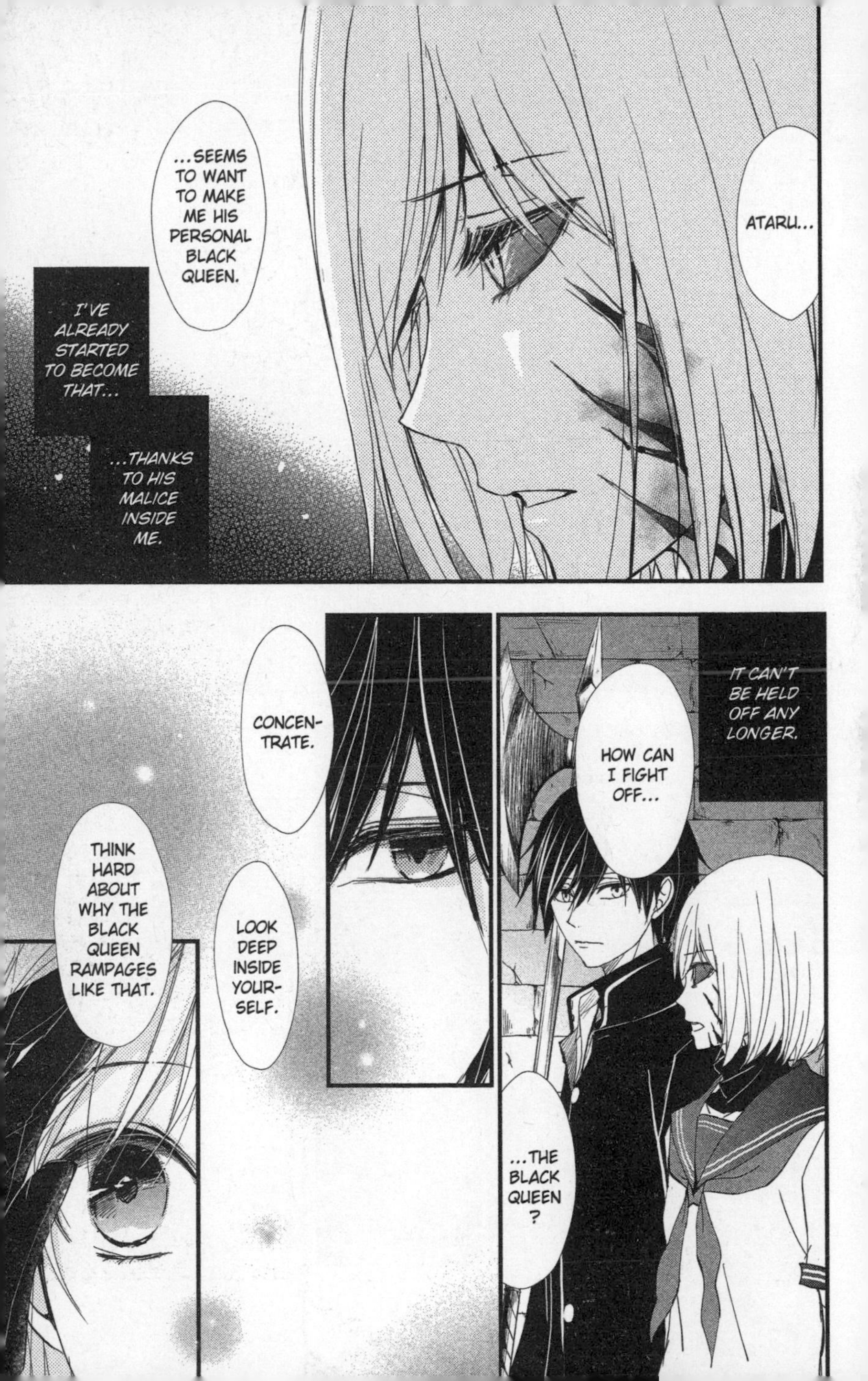
ATARU...
...SEEMS TO WANT TO MAKE ME HIS PERSONAL BLACK QUEEN.
I'VE ALREADY STARTED TO BECOME THAT...
...THANKS TO HIS MALICE INSIDE ME.
IT CAN'T BE HELD OFF ANY LONGER.
HOW CAN I FIGHT OFF...
...THE BLACK QUEEN?
CONCENTRATE.
LOOK DEEP INSIDE YOURSELF.
THINK HARD ABOUT WHY THE BLACK QUEEN RAMPAGES LIKE THAT.

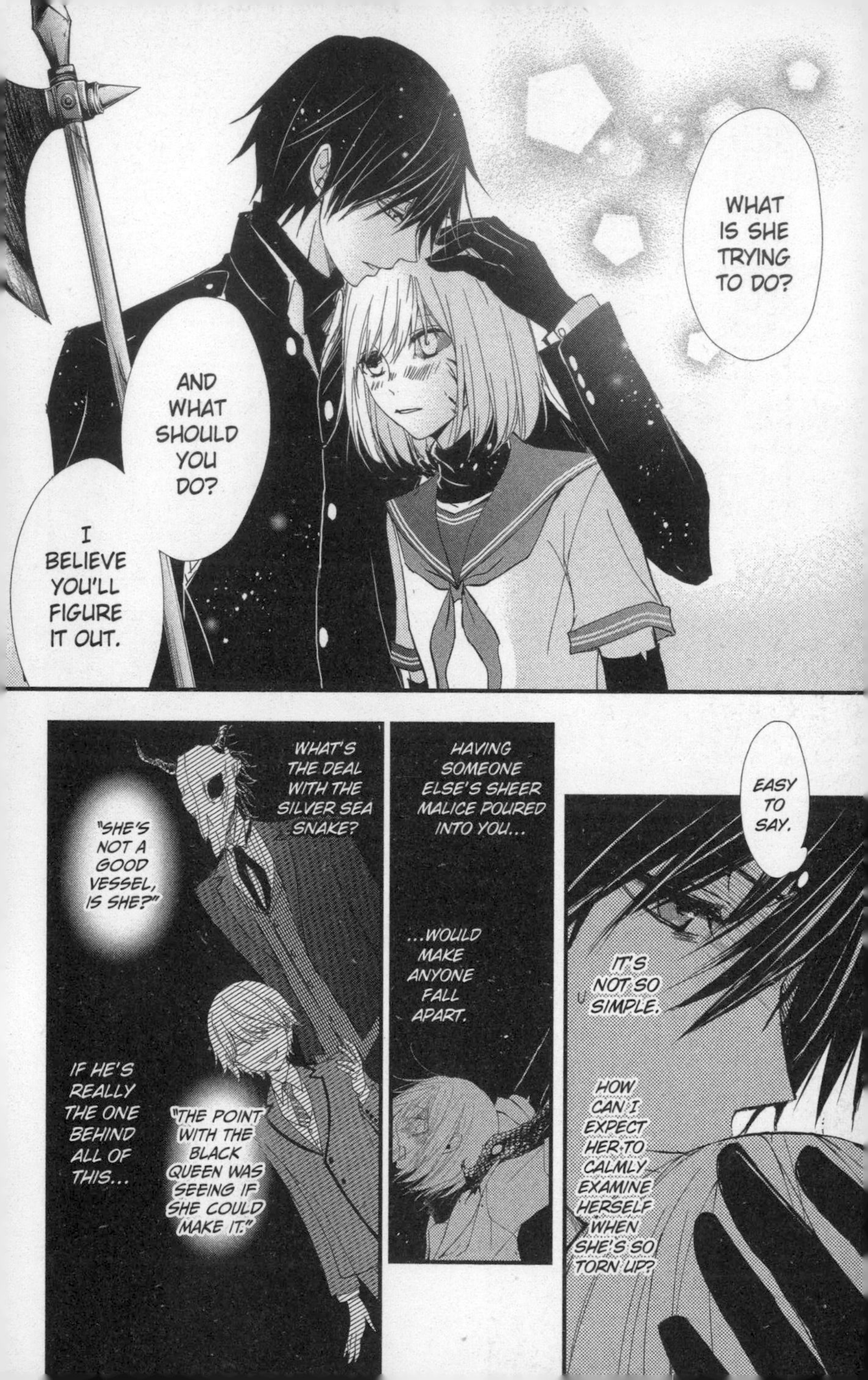
WHAT IS SHE TRYING TO DO?
AND WHAT SHOULD YOU DO?
I BELIEVE YOU'LL FIGURE IT OUT.
EASY TO SAY.
IT'S NOT SO SIMPLE.
HOW CAN I EXPECT HER TO CALMLY EXAMINE HERSELF WHEN SHE'S SO TORN UP?
HAVING SOMEONE ELSE'S SHEER MALICE POURED INTO YOU...
...WOULD MAKE ANYONE FALL APART.
WHAT'S THE DEAL WITH THE SILVER SEA SNAKE?
"SHE'S NOT A GOOD VESSEL, IS SHE?"
"THE POINT WITH THE BLACK QUEEN WAS SEEING IF SHE COULD MAKE IT."
IF HE'S REALLY THE ONE BEHIND ALL OF THIS...

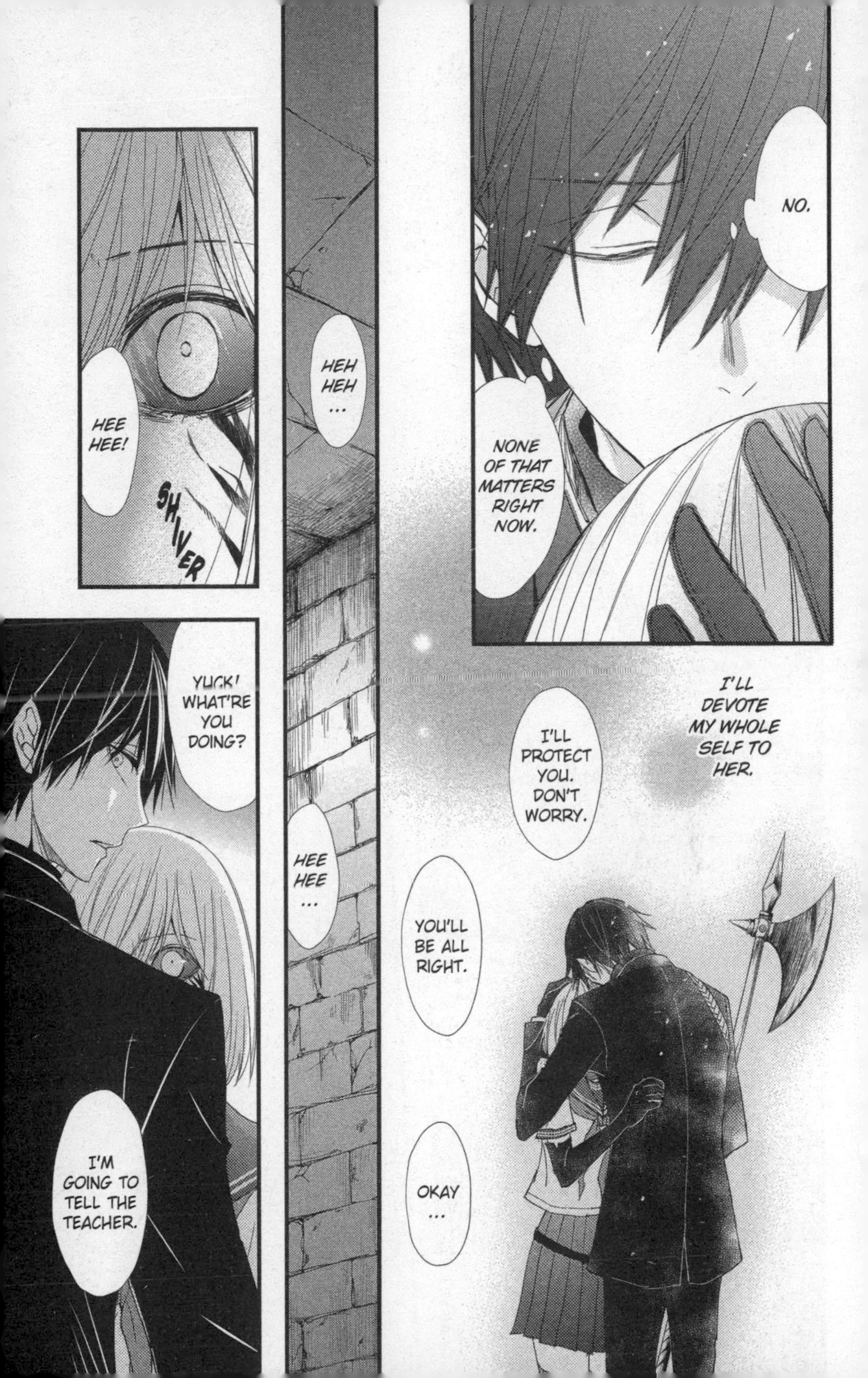
NO.
NONE OF THAT MATTERS RIGHT NOW.
I'LL DEVOTE MY WHOLE SELF TO HER.
I'LL PROTECT YOU. DON'T WORRY.
YOU'LL BE ALL RIGHT.
OKAY ...
HEH HEH ...
HEE HEE ...
HEE HEE!
SHIVER
YUCK! WHAT'RE YOU DOING?
I'M GOING TO TELL THE TEACHER.

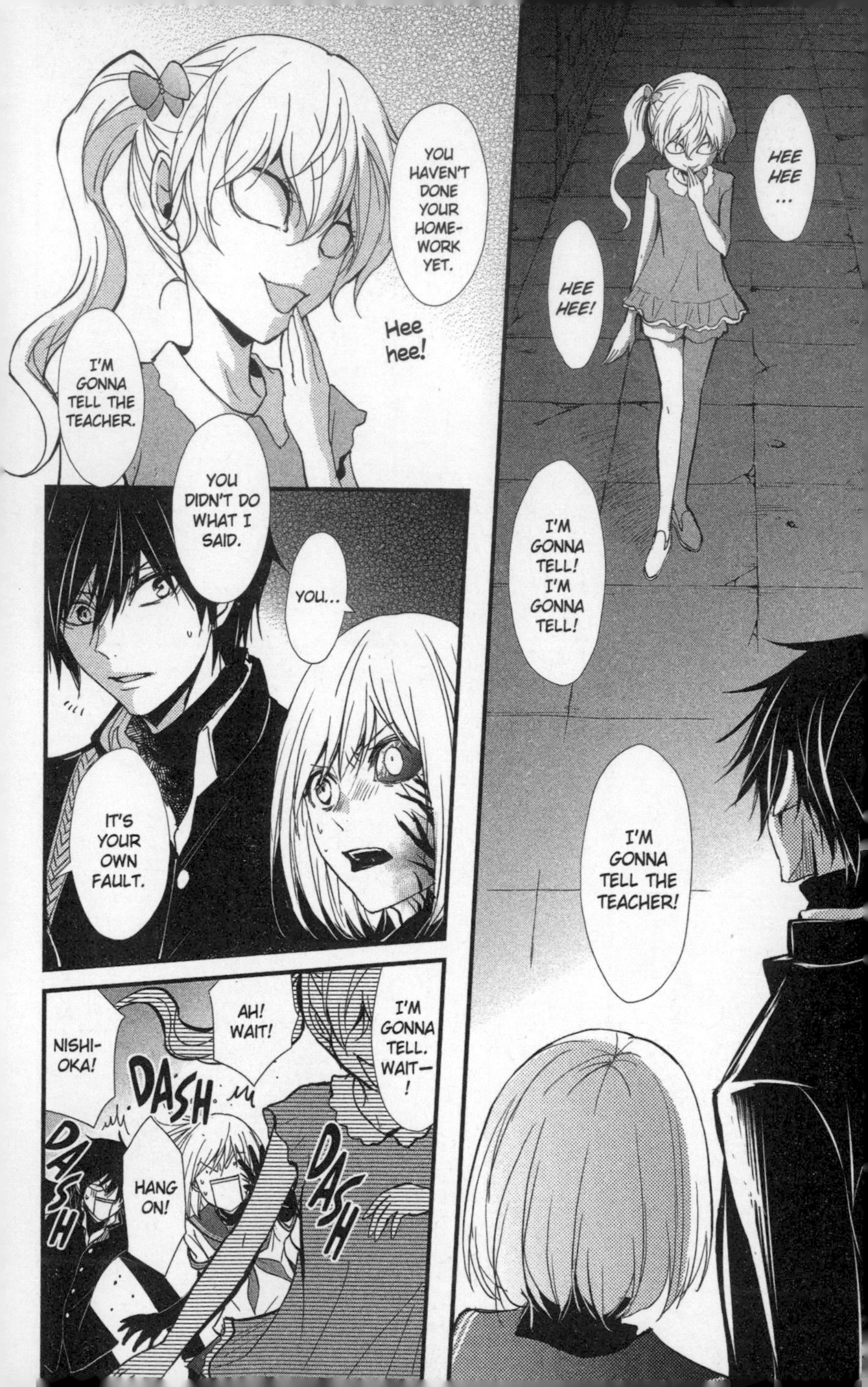
HEE HEE...
HEE HEE!
I'M GONNA TELL! I'M GONNA TELL!
I'M GONNA TELL THE TEACHER!
YOU HAVEN'T DONE YOUR HOME-WORK YET.
Hee hee!
I'M GONNA TELL THE TEACHER.
YOU DIDN'T DO WHAT I SAID.
YOU...
IT'S YOUR OWN FAULT.
I'M GONNA TELL. WAIT—!
AH! WAIT!
NISHI-OKA!
DASH
DASH
HANG ON!
DASH

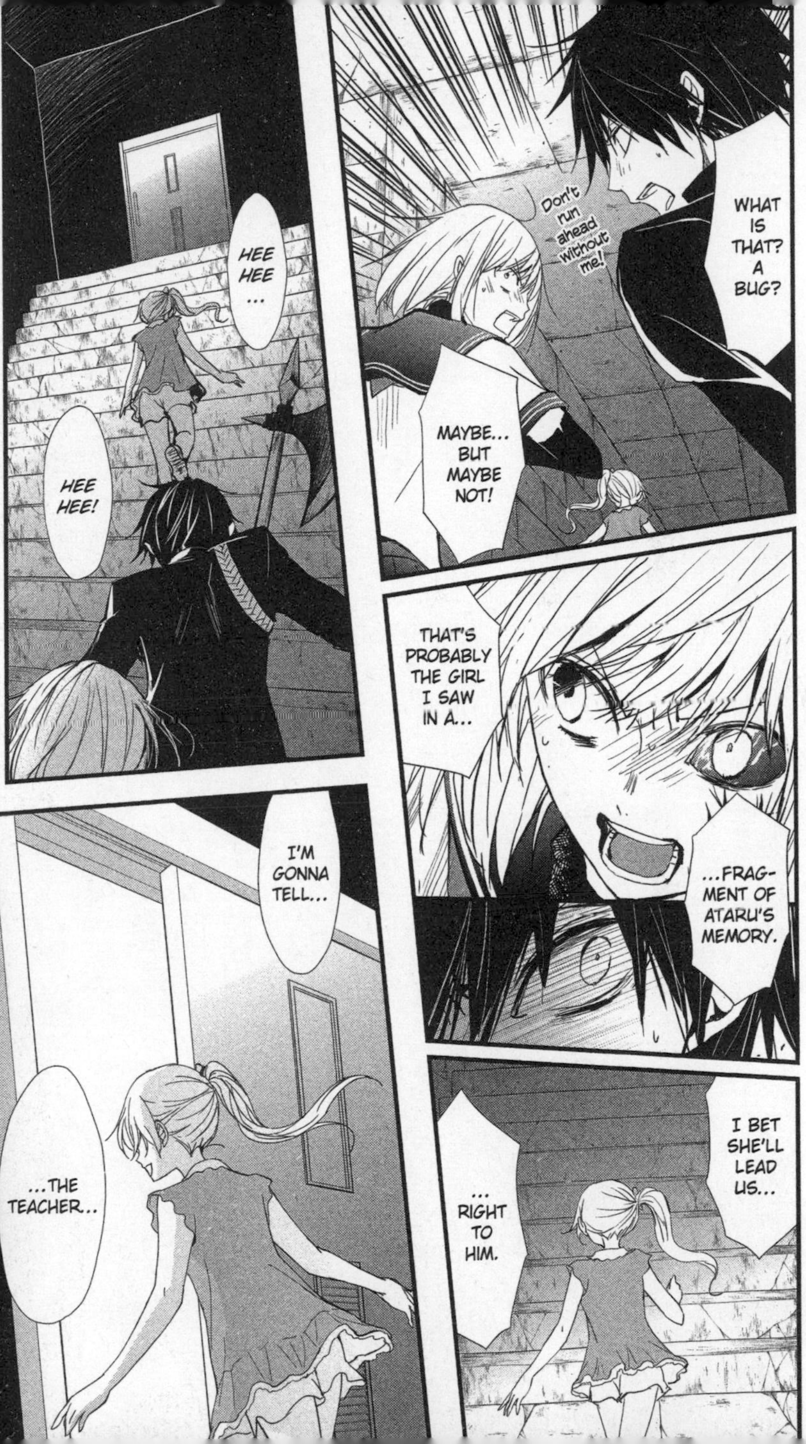
WHAT IS THAT? A BUG?
Don't run ahead without me!
MAYBE... BUT MAYBE NOT!
HEE HEE ...
HEE HEE!
THAT'S PROBABLY THE GIRL I SAW IN A...
...FRAG-MENT OF ATARU'S MEMORY.
I'M GONNA TELL...
...THE TEACHER...
I BET SHE'LL LEAD US...
... RIGHT TO HIM.

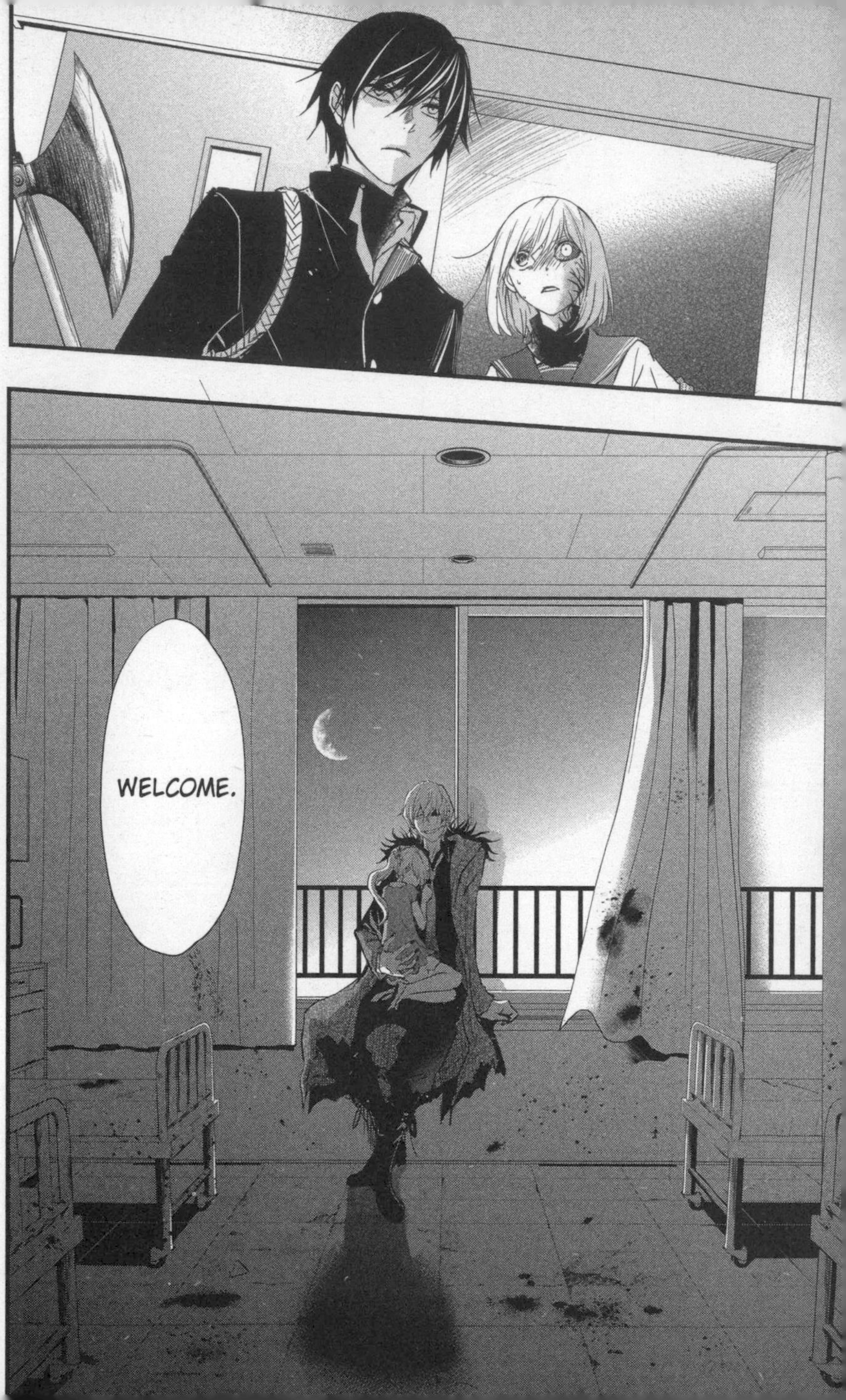
WELCOME.

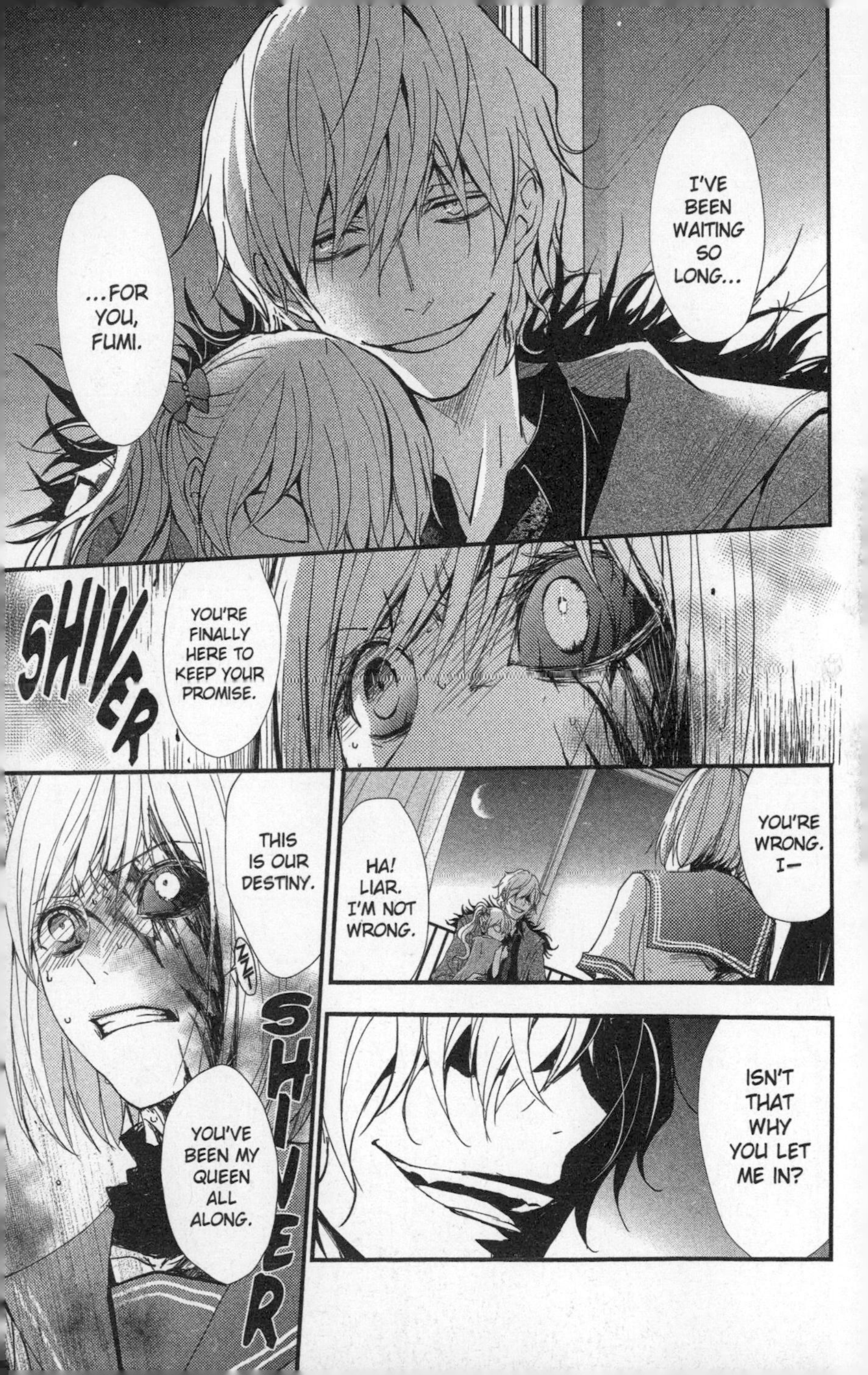
I'VE BEEN WAITING SO LONG...
...FOR YOU, FUMI.
YOU'RE FINALLY HERE TO KEEP YOUR PROMISE.
SHIVER
YOU'RE WRONG. I—
HA! LIAR. I'M NOT WRONG.
ISN'T THAT WHY YOU LET ME IN?
THIS IS OUR DESTINY.
NN
YOU'VE BEEN MY QUEEN ALL ALONG.
SHIVER

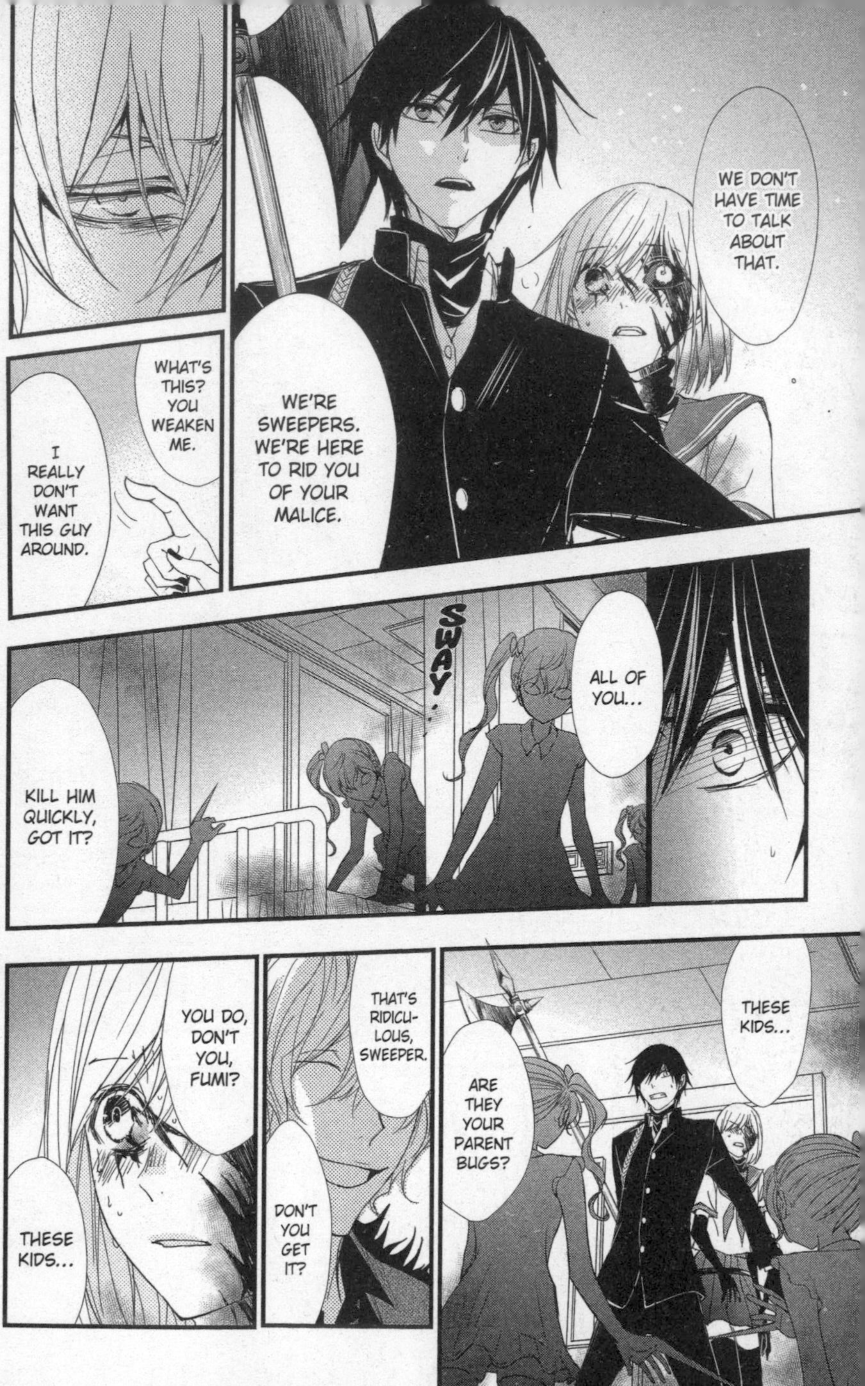
WE DON'T HAVE TIME TO TALK ABOUT THAT.
WE'RE SWEEPERS. WE'RE HERE TO RID YOU OF YOUR MALICE.
WHAT'S THIS? YOU WEAKEN ME.
I REALLY DON'T WANT THIS GUY AROUND.
ALL OF YOU...
SWAY
KILL HIM QUICKLY, GOT IT?
THESE KIDS...
ARE THEY YOUR PARENT BUGS?
THAT'S RIDICU-LOUS, SWEEPER.
DON'T YOU GET IT?
YOU DO, DON'T YOU, FUMI?
THESE KIDS...

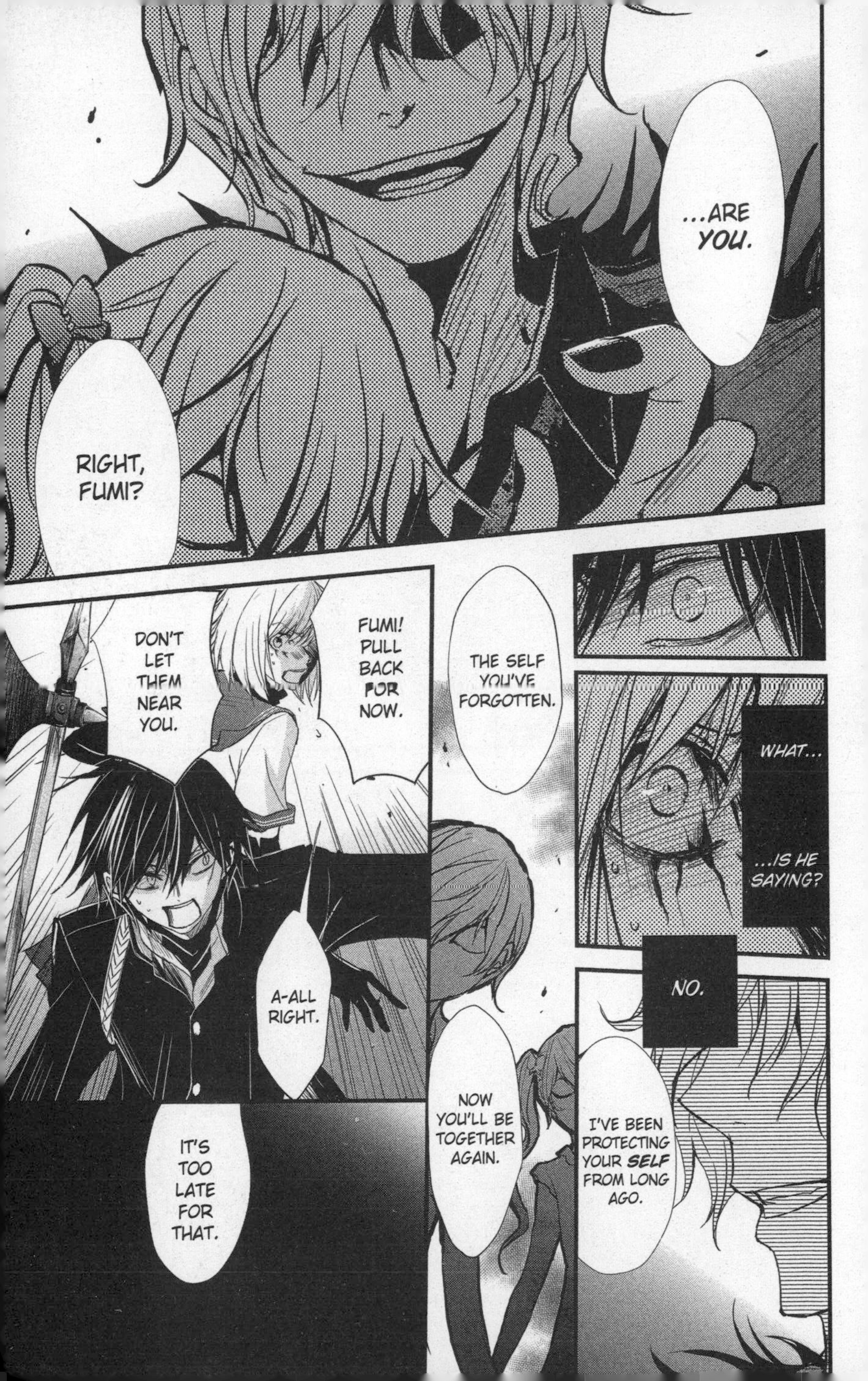
...ARE YOU.
RIGHT, FUMI?
THE SELF YOU'VE FORGOTTEN.
WHAT...
...IS HE SAYING?
NO.
I'VE BEEN PROTECTING YOUR SELF FROM LONG AGO.
NOW YOU'LL BE TOGETHER AGAIN.
FUMI! PULL BACK FOR NOW.
DON'T LET THEM NEAR YOU.
A-ALL RIGHT.
IT'S TOO LATE FOR THAT.

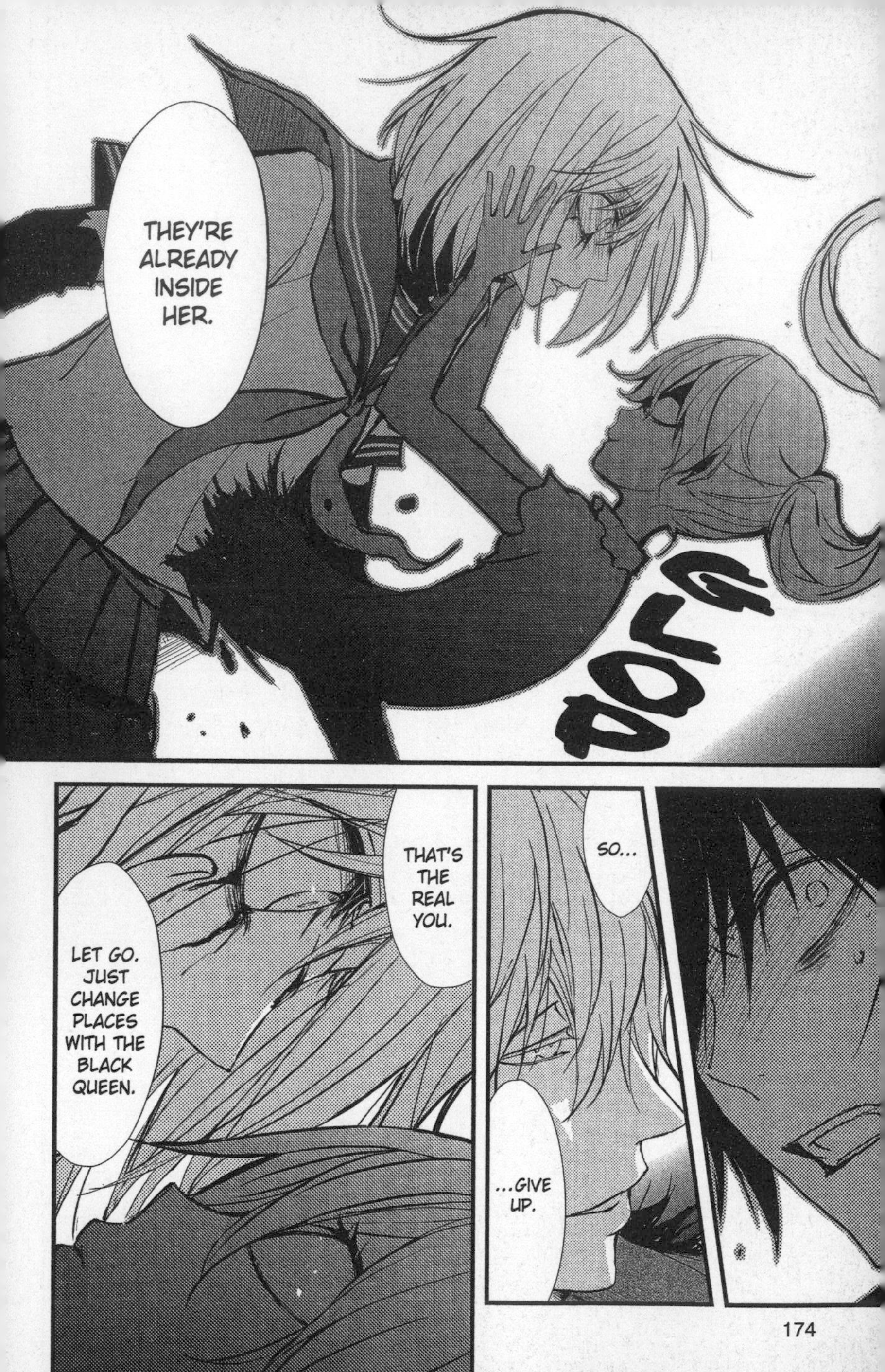
THEY'RE ALREADY INSIDE HER.
SO...
...GIVE UP.
THAT'S THE REAL YOU.
LET GO. JUST CHANGE PLACES WITH THE BLACK QUEEN.

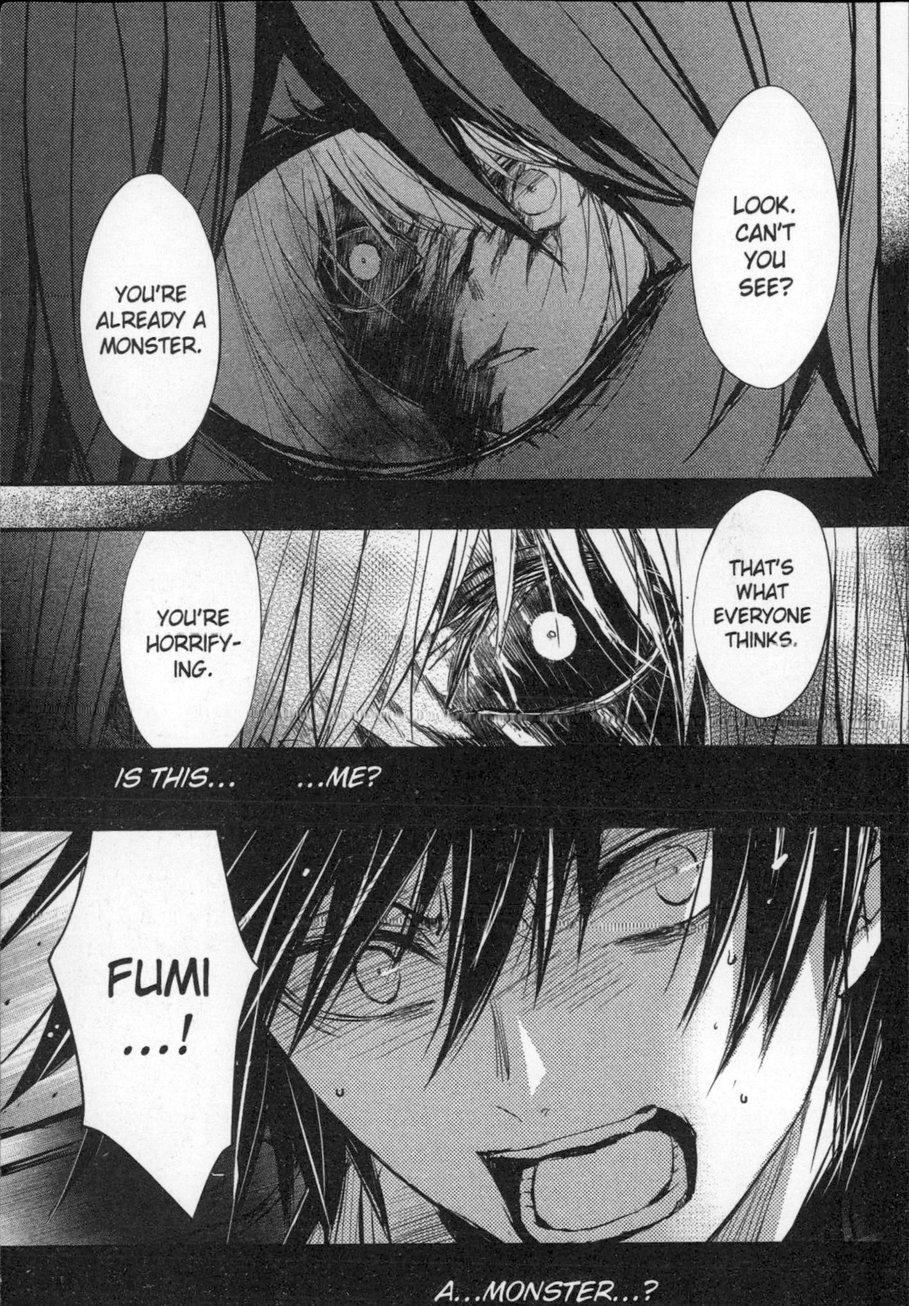
LOOK. CAN'T YOU SEE?
YOU'RE ALREADY A MONSTER.
THAT'S WHAT EVERYONE THINKS.
YOU'RE HORRIFY-ING.
IS THIS... ...ME?
FUMI ...!
A...MONSTER...?

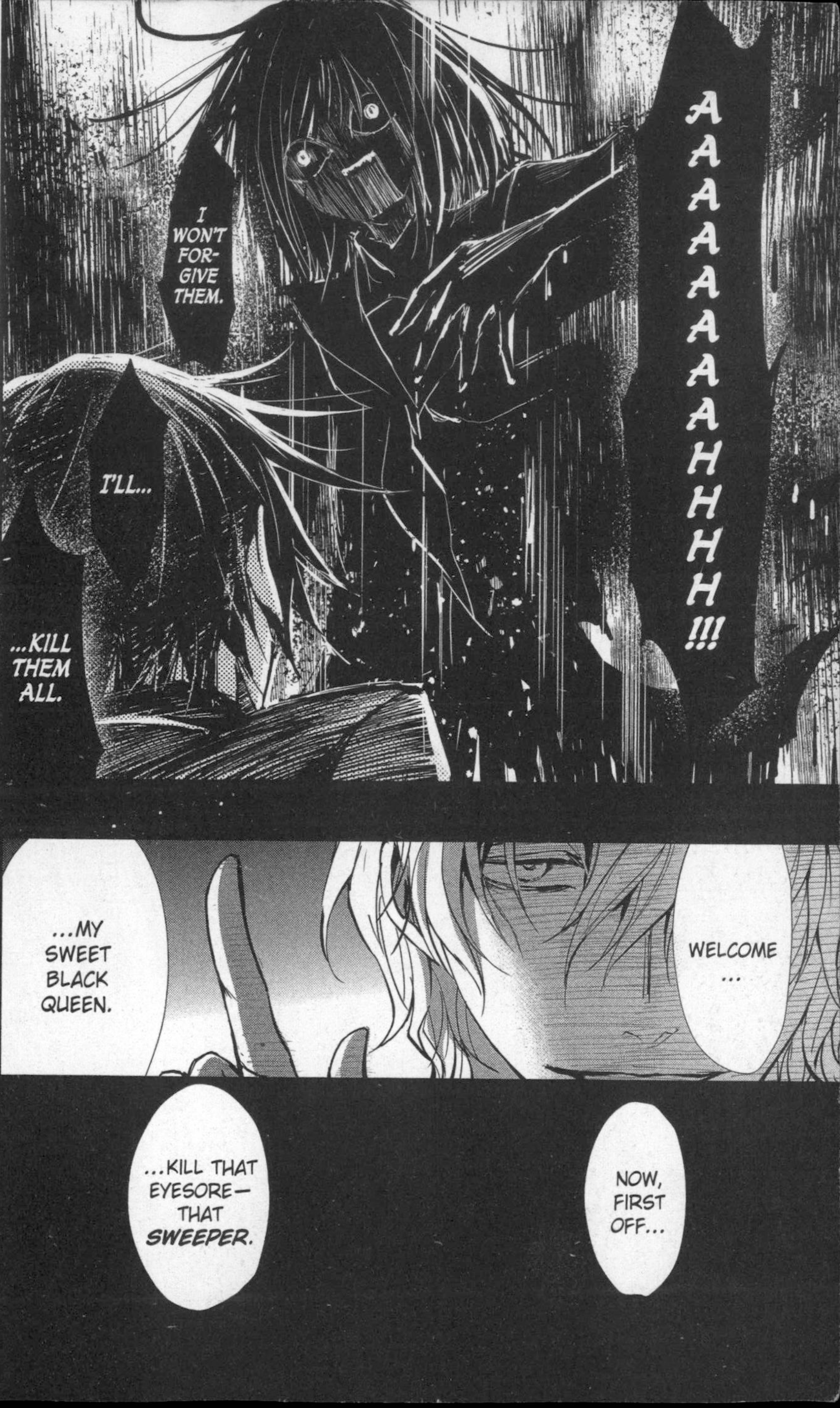
AAAAAAAAAAHHHHH!!!
I WON'T FORGIVE THEM.
I'LL...
...KILL THEM ALL.
WELCOME...
...MY SWEET BLACK QUEEN.
NOW, FIRST OFF...
...KILL THAT EYESORE—THAT SWEEPER.

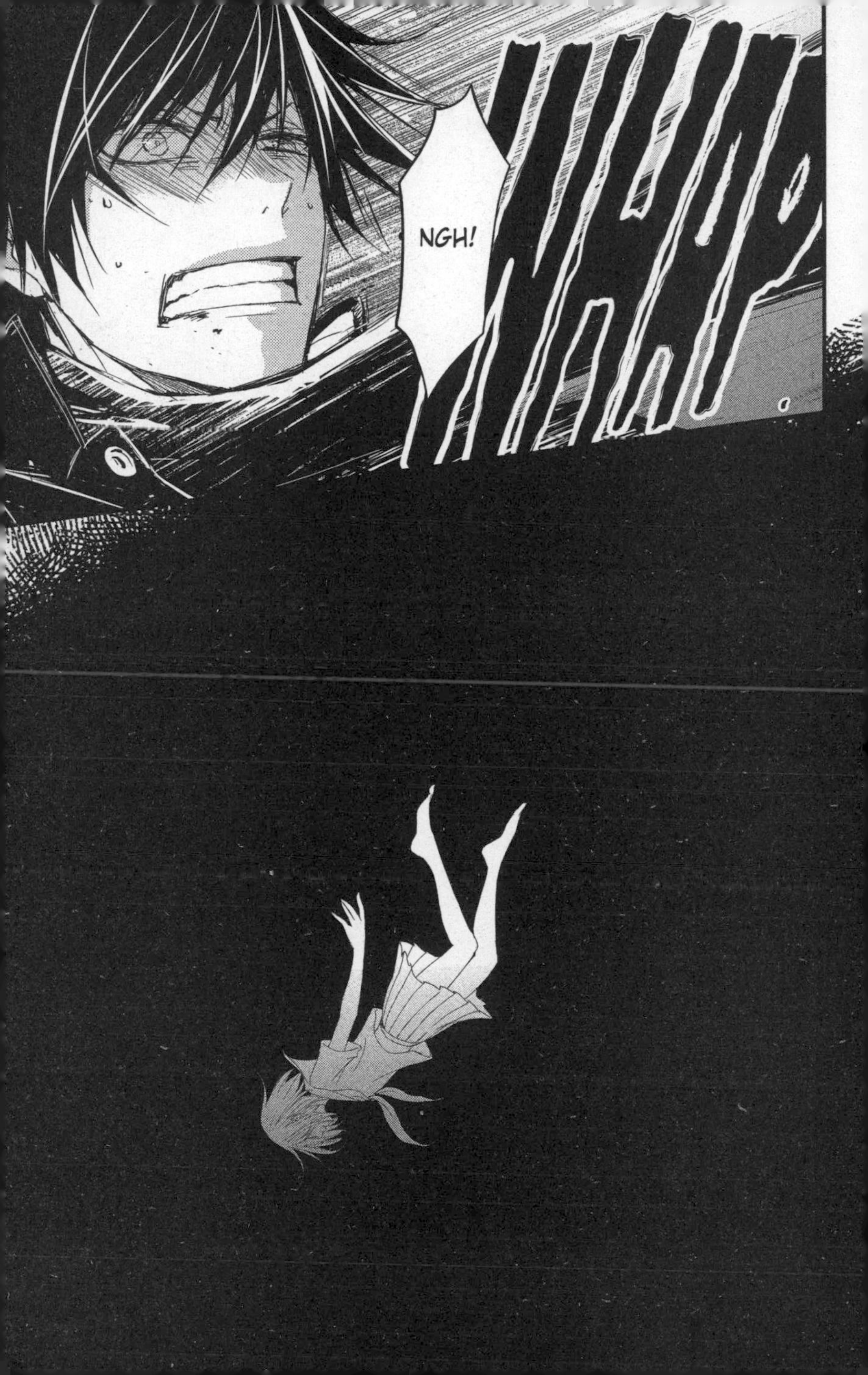
NGH!

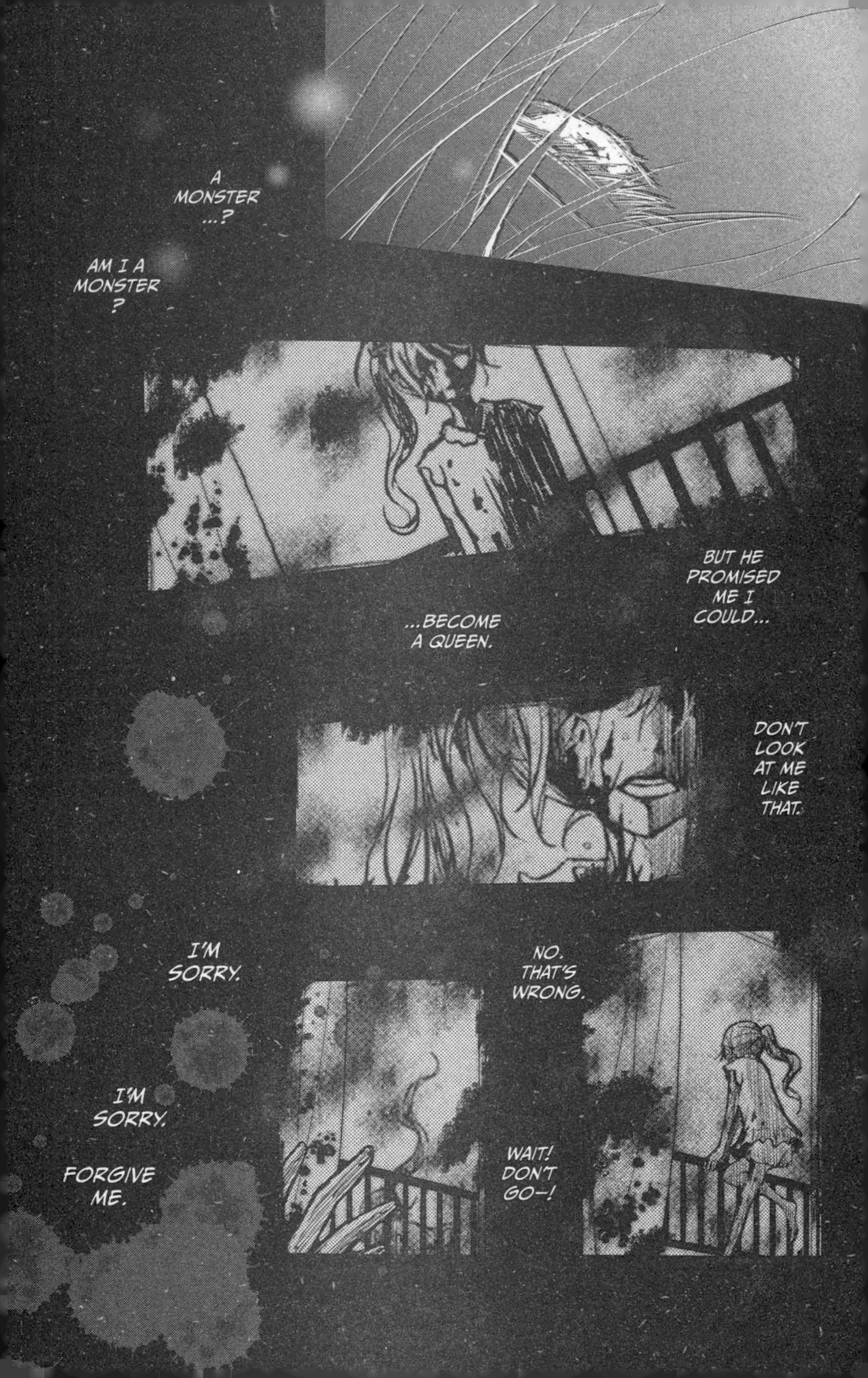
A MONSTER ...?
AM I A MONSTER ?
BUT HE PROMISED ME I COULD...
...BECOME A QUEEN.
DON'T LOOK AT ME LIKE THAT.
NO. THAT'S WRONG.
WAIT! DON'T GO—!
I'M SORRY.
I'M SORRY.
FORGIVE ME.

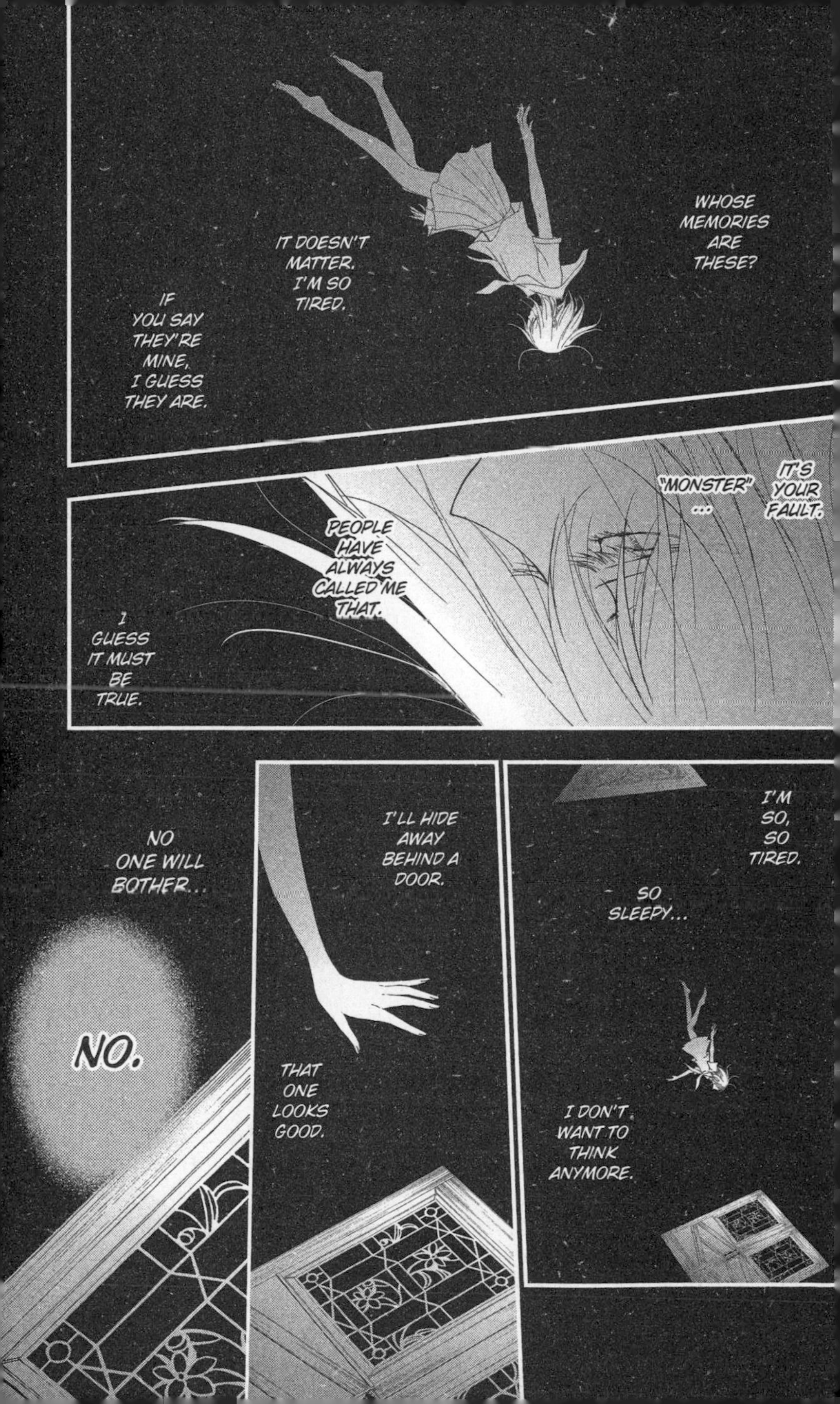
WHOSE MEMORIES ARE THESE?
IT DOESN'T MATTER. I'M SO TIRED.
IF YOU SAY THEY'RE MINE, I GUESS THEY ARE.
IT'S YOUR FAULT.
"MONSTER" ...
PEOPLE HAVE ALWAYS CALLED ME THAT.
I GUESS IT MUST BE TRUE.
I'M SO, SO TIRED.
SO SLEEPY...
I DON'T WANT TO THINK ANYMORE.
I'LL HIDE AWAY BEHIND A DOOR.
THAT ONE LOOKS GOOD.
NO ONE WILL BOTHER...
NO.

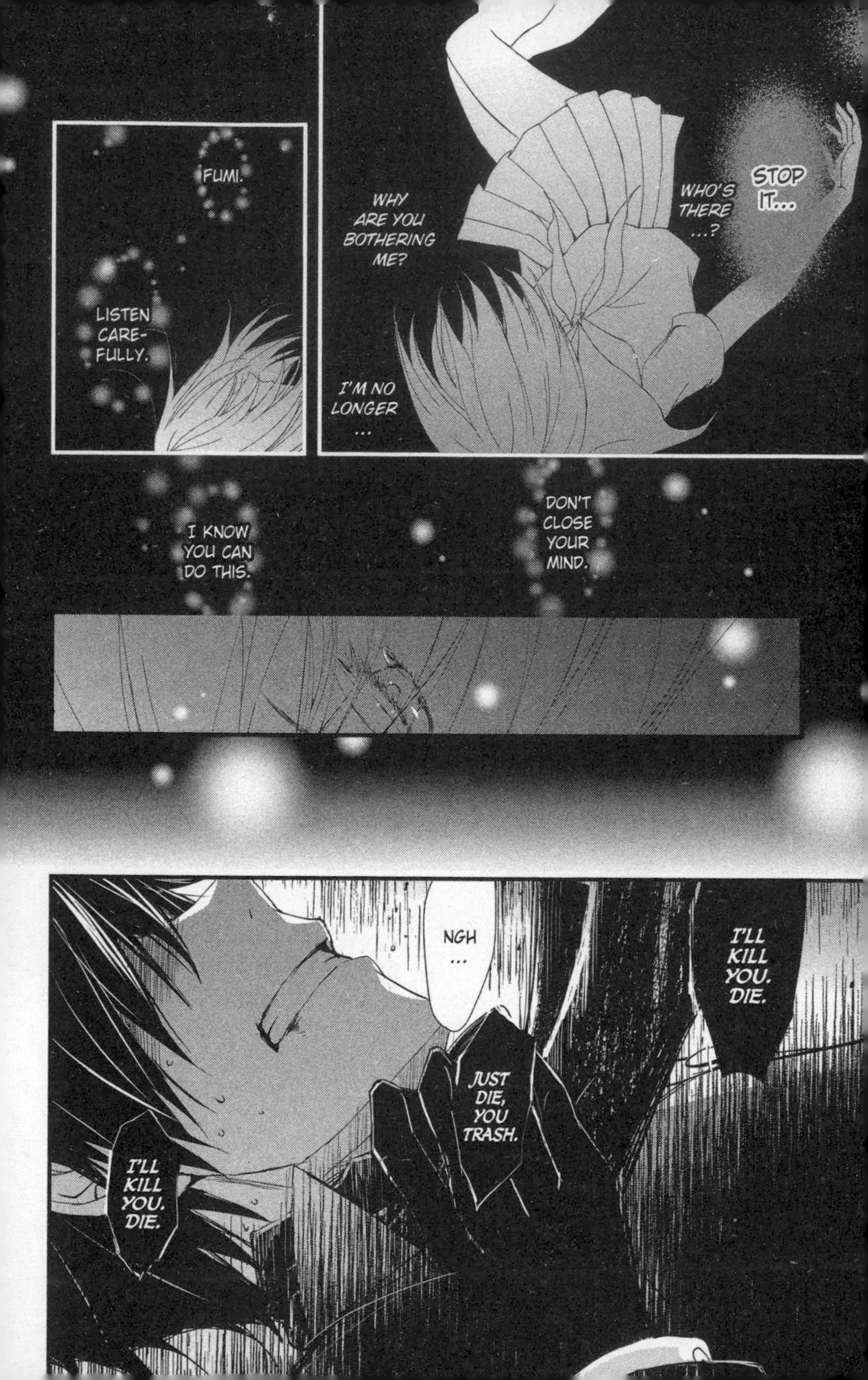
STOP IT...
WHO'S THERE ...?
WHY ARE YOU BOTHERING ME?
I'M NO LONGER ...
FUMI.
LISTEN CARE-FULLY.
DON'T CLOSE YOUR MIND.
I KNOW YOU CAN DO THIS.
I'LL KILL YOU. DIE.
NGH ...
JUST DIE, YOU TRASH.
I'LL KILL YOU. DIE.

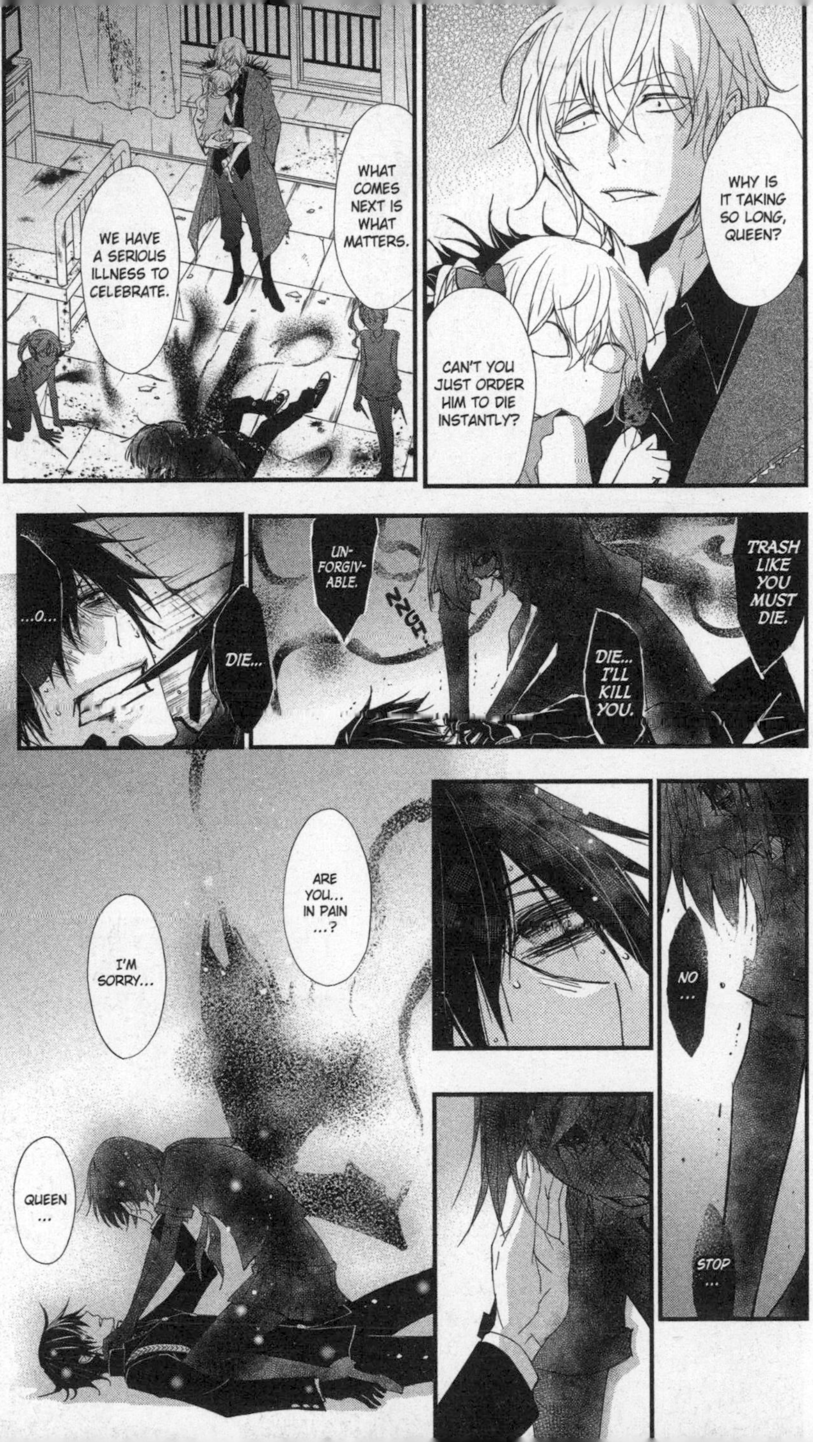
WHY IS IT TAKING SO LONG, QUEEN?
CAN'T YOU JUST ORDER HIM TO DIE INSTANTLY?
WHAT COMES NEXT IS WHAT MATTERS.
WE HAVE A SERIOUS ILLNESS TO CELEBRATE.
TRASH LIKE YOU MUST DIE.
DIE... I'LL KILL YOU.
UN-FORGIV-ABLE.
DIE...
...O...
NO ...
STOP ...
ARE YOU... IN PAIN ...?
I'M SORRY...
QUEEN ...

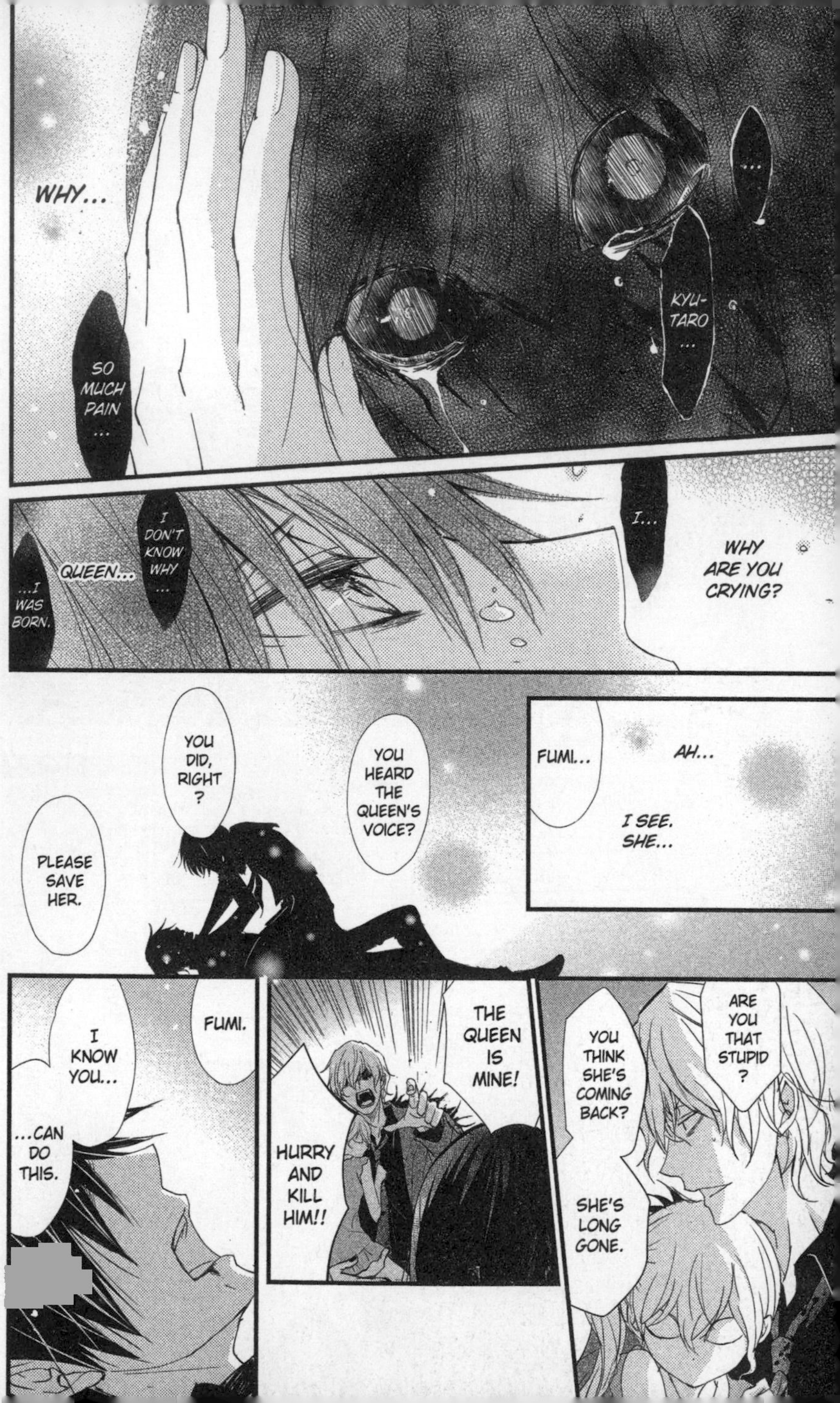
...
KYU-TARO ...
WHY...
SO MUCH PAIN ...
WHY ARE YOU CRYING?
I...
I DON'T KNOW WHY ...
QUEEN...
...I WAS BORN.
AH...
FUMI...
I SEE. SHE...
YOU HEARD THE QUEEN'S VOICE?
YOU DID, RIGHT?
PLEASE SAVE HER.
ARE YOU THAT STUPID?
YOU THINK SHE'S COMING BACK?
SHE'S LONG GONE.
THE QUEEN IS MINE!
HURRY AND KILL HIM!!
FUMI.
I KNOW YOU...
...CAN DO THIS.

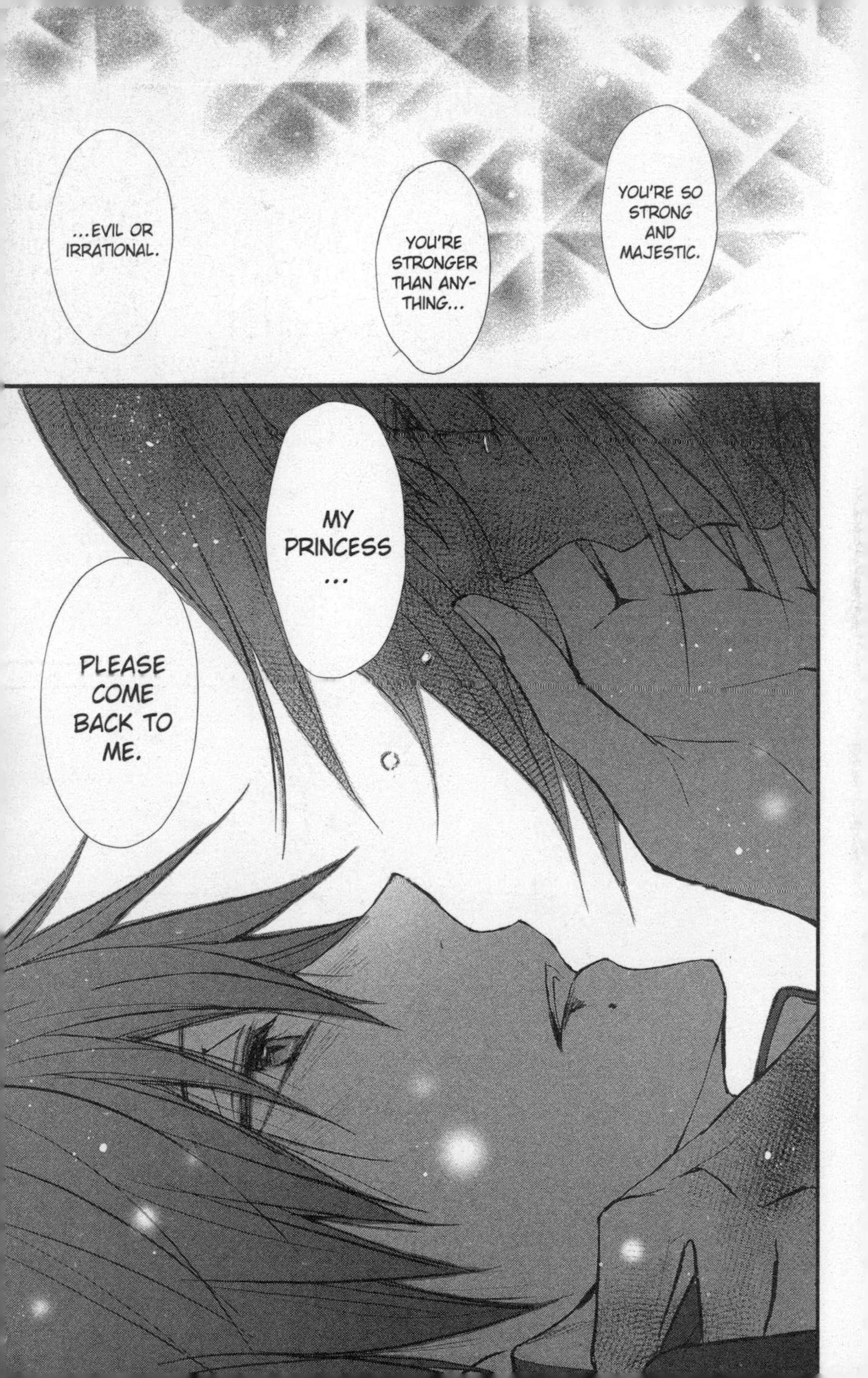
YOU'RE SO STRONG AND MAJESTIC.
YOU'RE STRONGER THAN ANYTHING...
...EVIL OR IRRATIONAL.
MY PRINCESS...
PLEASE COME BACK TO ME.

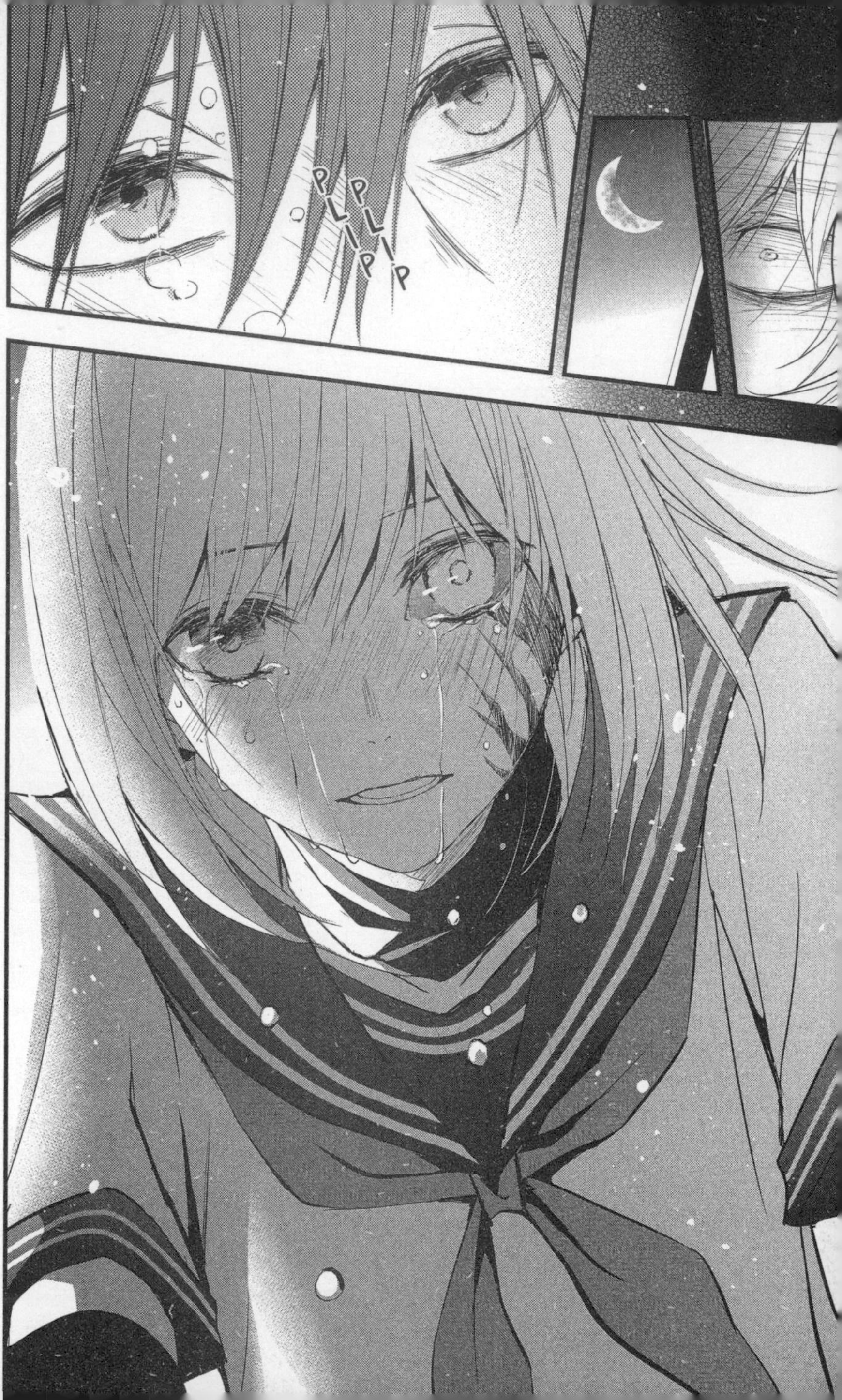
PLIP
PLIP

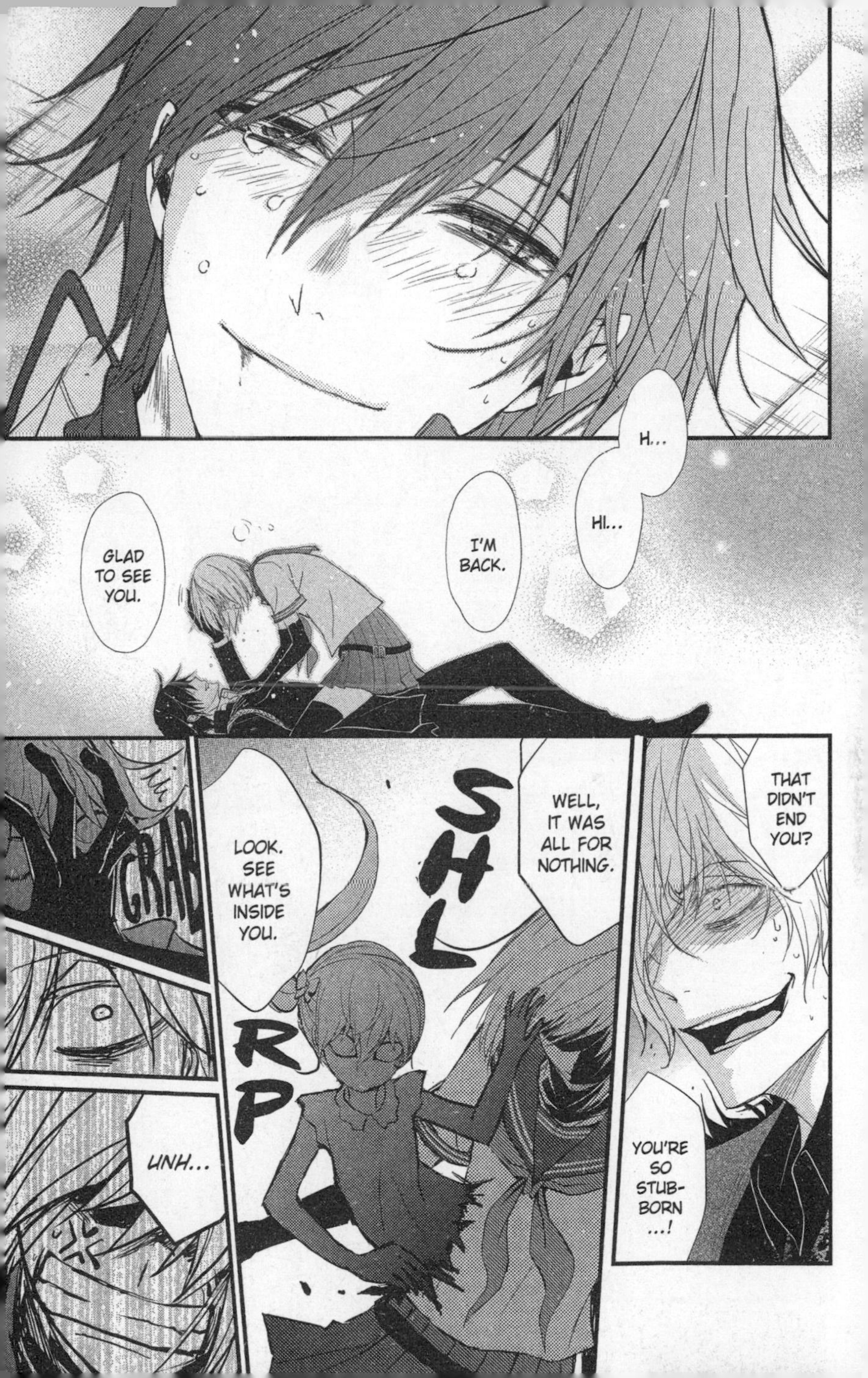
H...
HI...
I'M BACK.
GLAD TO SEE YOU.
THAT DIDN'T END YOU?
YOU'RE SO STUB-BORN ...!
WELL, IT WAS ALL FOR NOTHING.
SHLRP
LOOK. SEE WHAT'S INSIDE YOU.
GRAB
UNH...

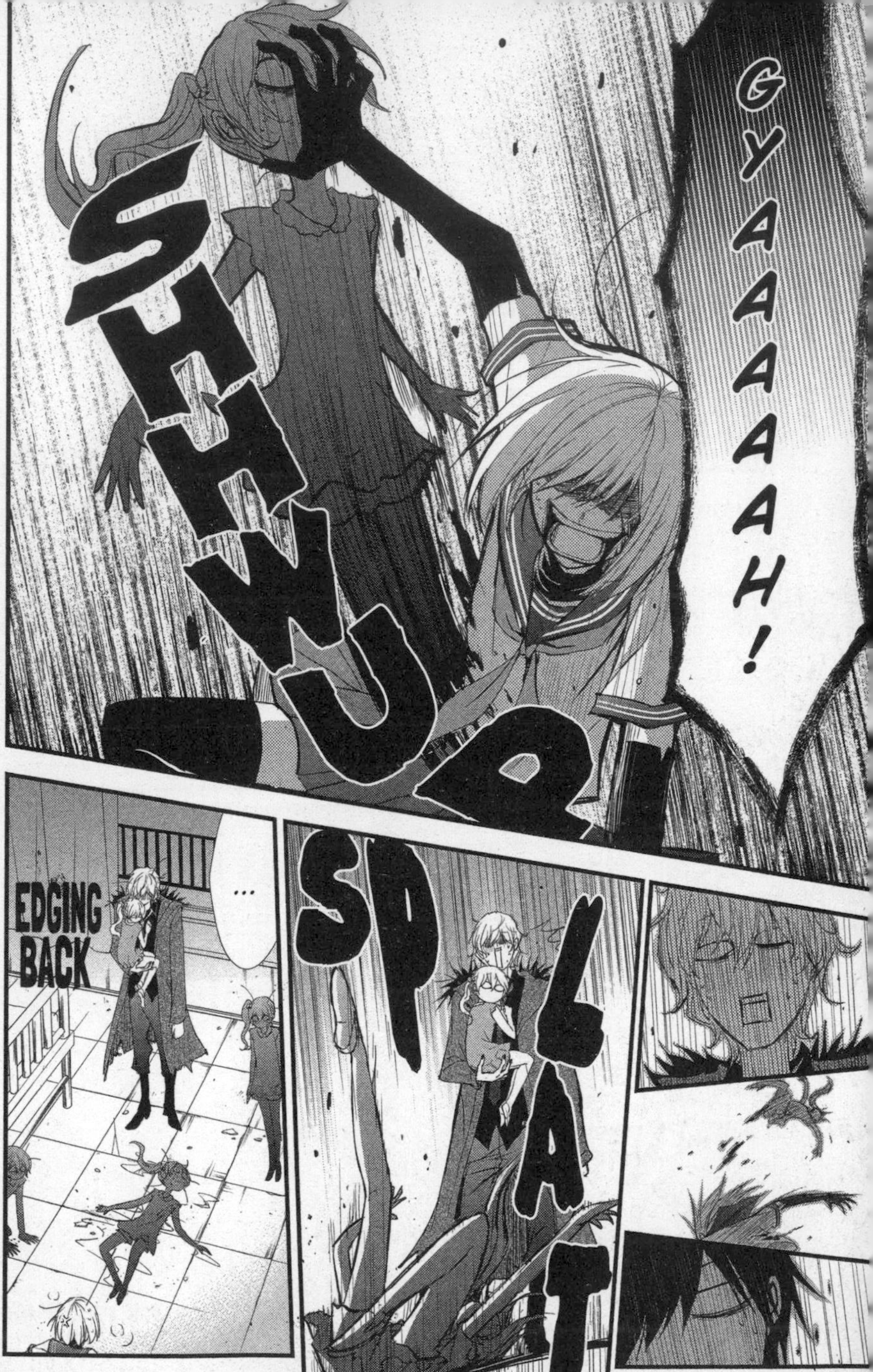
GYAAAAAH!
SHWUP
SPLAT
...
EDGING BACK

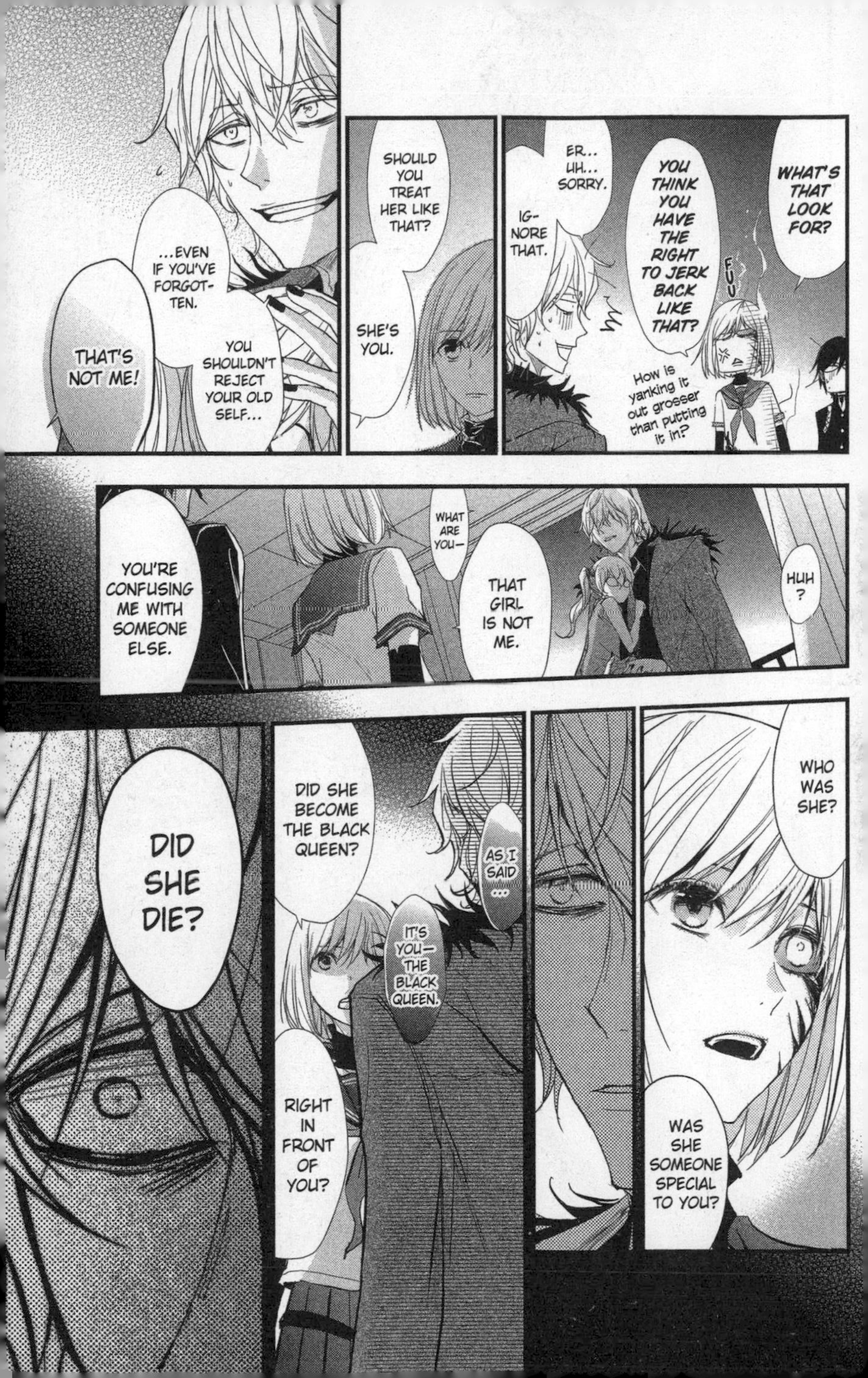
WHAT'S THAT LOOK FOR?
YOU THINK YOU HAVE THE RIGHT TO JERK BACK LIKE THAT?
FUU
How is yanking it out grosser than putting it in?
ER... UH... SORRY.
IG-NORE THAT.
SHOULD YOU TREAT HER LIKE THAT?
SHE'S YOU.
...EVEN IF YOU'VE FORGOT-TEN.
YOU SHOULDN'T REJECT YOUR OLD SELF...
THAT'S NOT ME!
HUH?
WHAT ARE YOU—
THAT GIRL IS NOT ME.
YOU'RE CONFUSING ME WITH SOMEONE ELSE.
WHO WAS SHE?
WAS SHE SOMEONE SPECIAL TO YOU?
AS I SAID...
IT'S YOU—THE BLACK QUEEN.
DID SHE BECOME THE BLACK QUEEN?
RIGHT IN FRONT OF YOU?
DID SHE DIE?

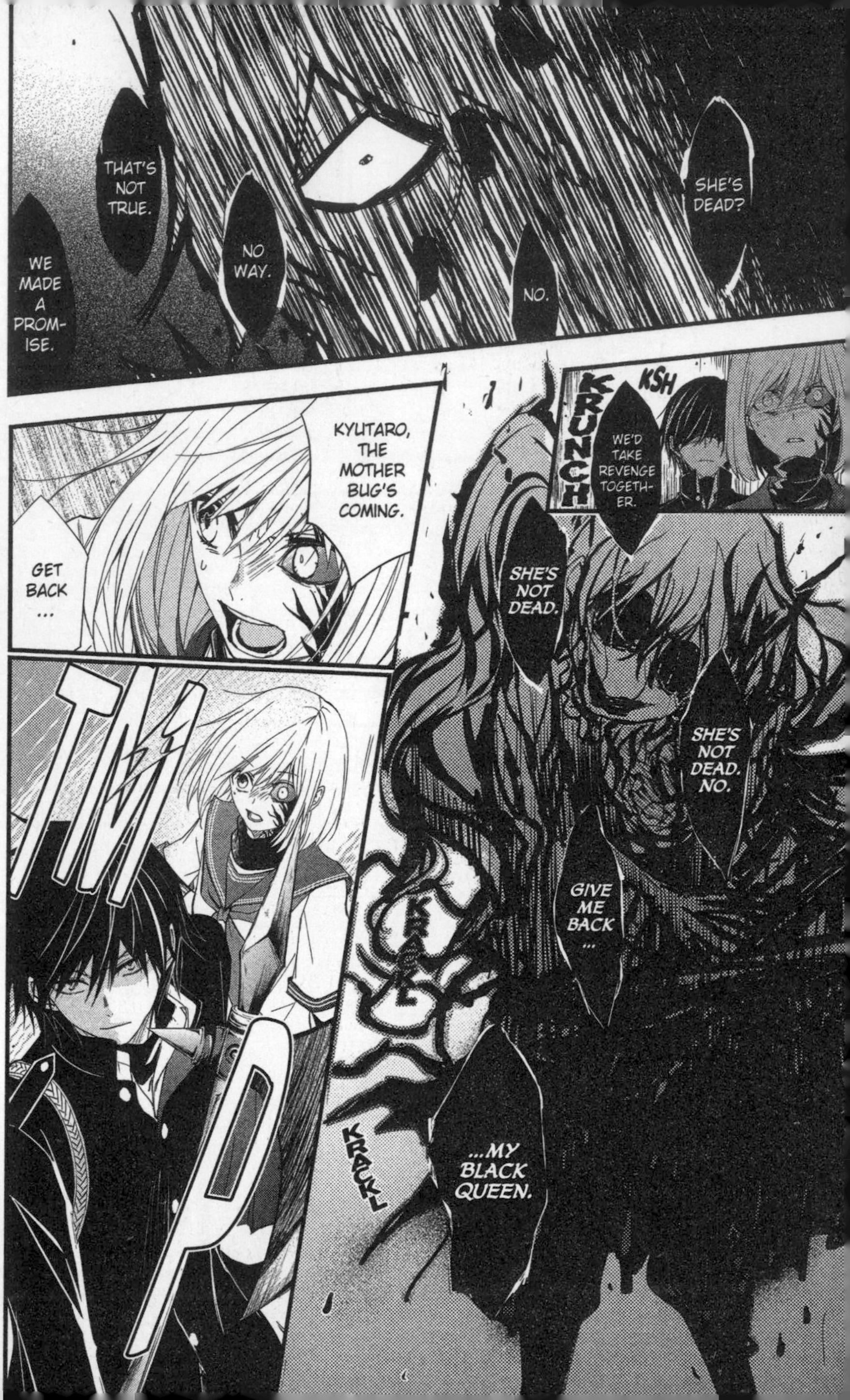
SHE'S DEAD?
NO.
NO WAY.
THAT'S NOT TRUE.
WE MADE A PROMISE.
KRUNCH
KSH
WE'D TAKE REVENGE TOGETHER.
SHE'S NOT DEAD.
SHE'S NOT DEAD. NO.
GIVE ME BACK...
...MY BLACK QUEEN.
KRAKL
KYUTARO, THE MOTHER BUG'S COMING.
GET BACK...
TMP

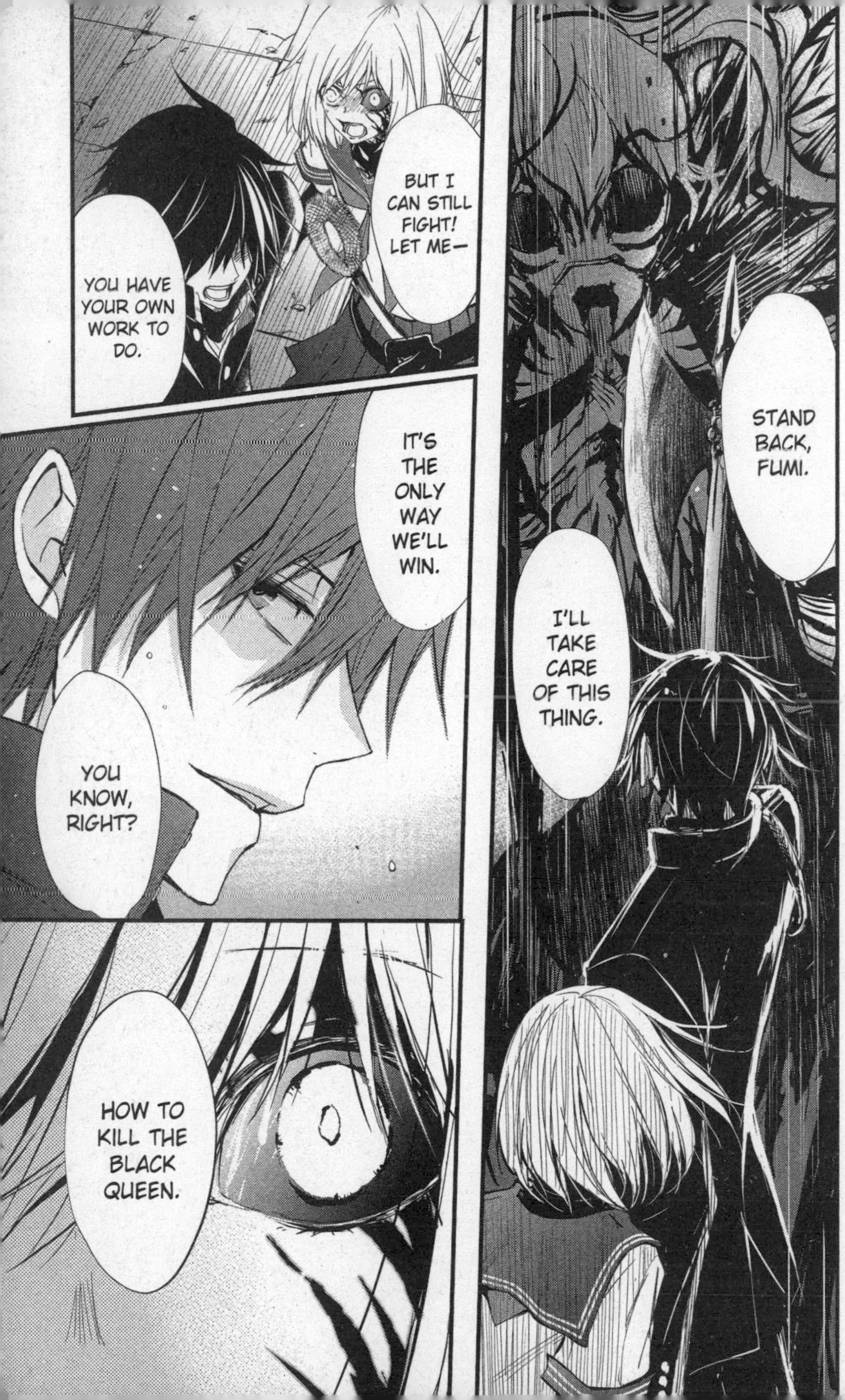
STAND BACK, FUMI.
I'LL TAKE CARE OF THIS THING.
BUT I CAN STILL FIGHT! LET ME—
YOU HAVE YOUR OWN WORK TO DO.
IT'S THE ONLY WAY WE'LL WIN.
YOU KNOW, RIGHT?
HOW TO KILL THE BLACK QUEEN.

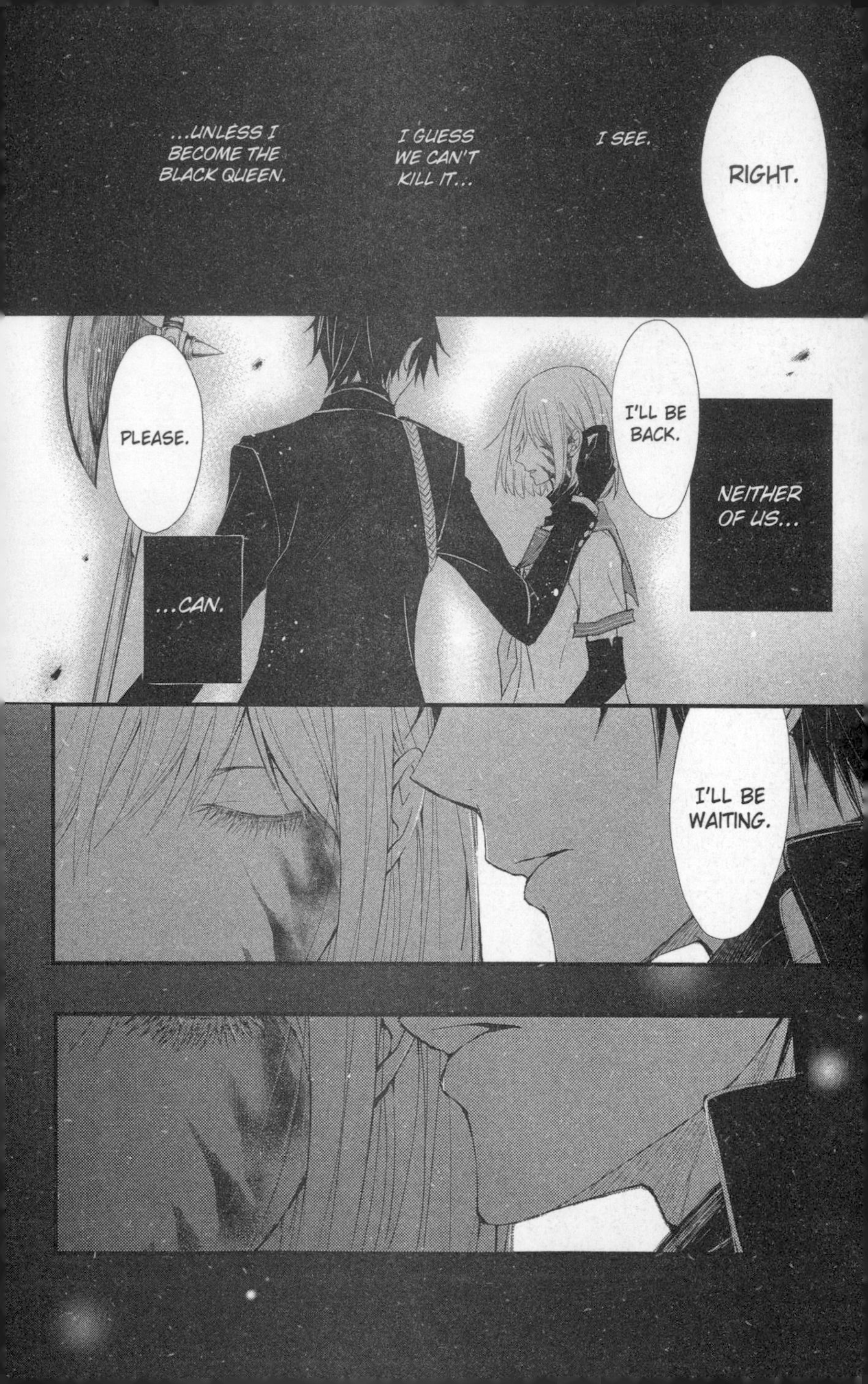
RIGHT.
I SEE.
I GUESS WE CAN'T KILL IT...
...UNLESS I BECOME THE BLACK QUEEN.
NEITHER OF US...
I'LL BE BACK.
PLEASE.
...CAN.
I'LL BE WAITING.

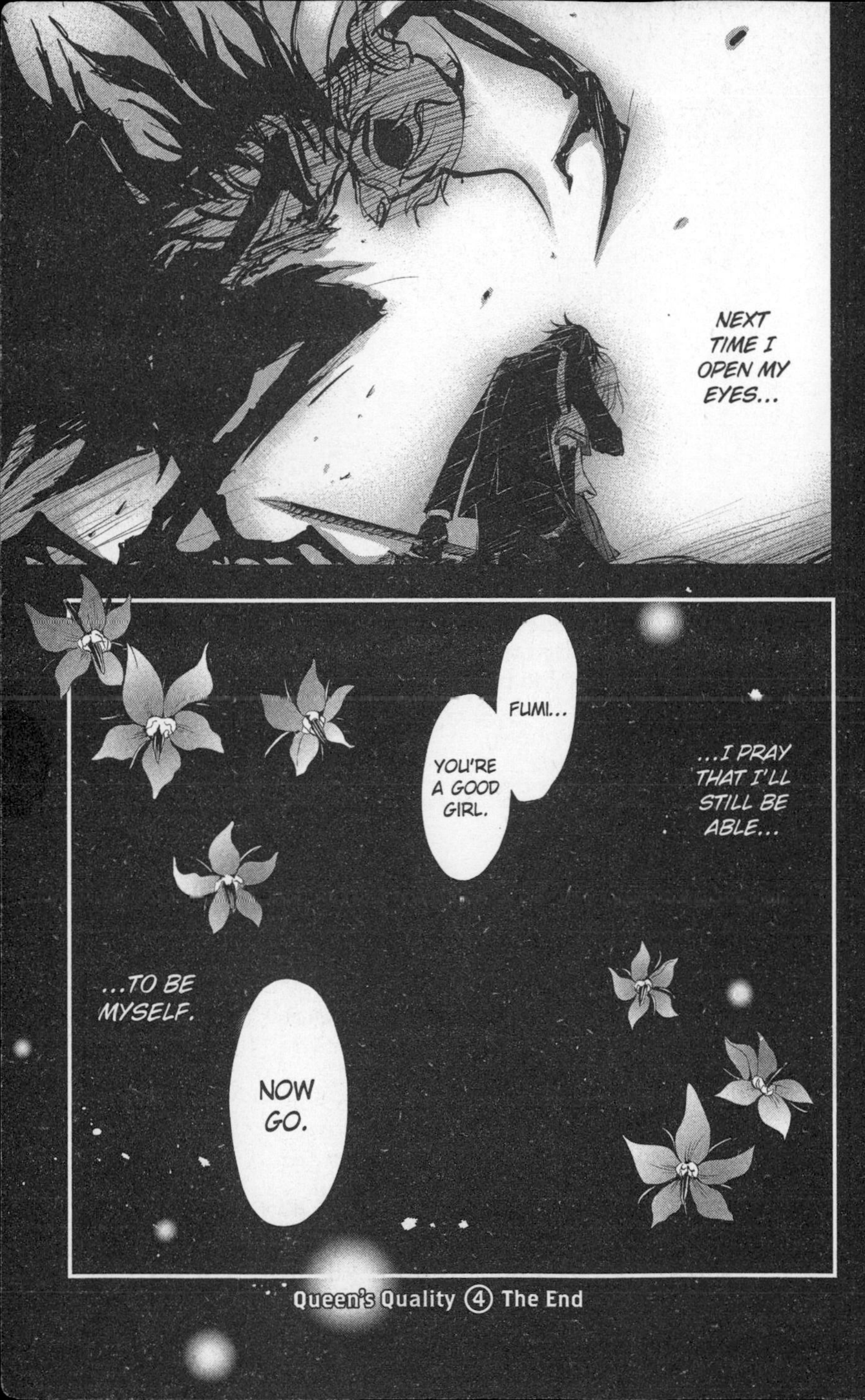
NEXT TIME I OPEN MY EYES...
...I PRAY THAT I'LL STILL BE ABLE...
FUMI...
YOU'RE A GOOD GIRL.
NOW GO.
...TO BE MYSELF.

Queen's Quality 4 The End

I MADE THIS RICH COFFEE WITH BUTTER AND MCT OIL IN IT. I USED A CAPPUCCINO BLENDER TO MAKE IT FROTHY AND IT WAS PRETTY GOOD.

I WONDER WHY ALL THIS FROTHINESS GETS PEOPLE SO EXCITED.

Lately, I've been hooked on "butter coffee," something that someone in Silicon Valley started. When I get up in the morning and have one before I start work, things go more smoothly. It makes me happy.

—Kyousuke Motomi

## Author Bio

Born on August 1, **Kyousuke Motomi** debuted in *Deluxe Betsucomi* with *Hetakuso Kyupiddo* (No Good Cupid) in 2002. She is the creator of *Dengeki Daisy*, *Beast Master* and *QQ Sweeper*, all available in North America from VIZ Media. Motomi enjoys sleeping, tea ceremonies and reading Haruki Murakami.

# Queen's Quality

Vol. 4
Shojo Beat Edition

STORY AND ART BY
## KYOUSUKE MOTOMI

QUEEN'S QUALITY Vol. 4
by Kyousuke MOTOMI
© 2016 Kyousuke MOTOMI
All rights reserved.
Original Japanese edition published by SHOGAKUKAN.
English translation rights in the United States of America, Canada, the United
Kingdom, Ireland, Australia and New Zealand arranged with SHOGAKUKAN.

ORIGINAL DESIGN/Chie SATO+Bay Bridge Studio

English Adaptation/Ysabet Reinhardt MacFarlane
Translation/JN Productions
Touch-Up Art & Lettering/Mark McMurray
Design/Julian [JR] Robinson
Editor/Amy Yu

Printed in the U.S.A.

Published by VIZ Media, LLC
P.O. Box 77010
San Francisco, CA 94107

10 9 8 7 6 5 4 3 2 1
First printing, June 2018

viz.com

shojobeat.com

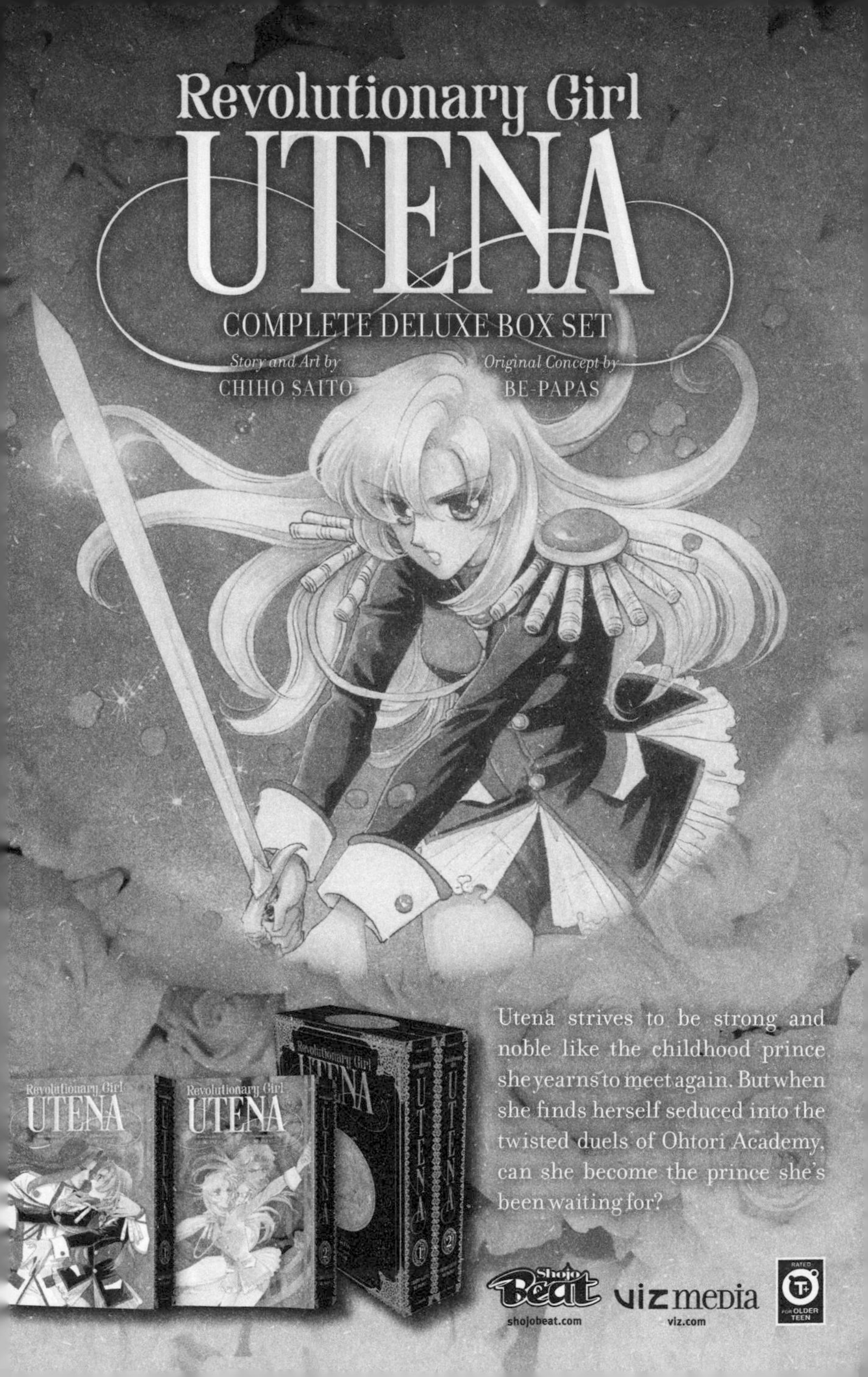
Revolutionary Girl
UTENA
COMPLETE DELUXE BOX SET
Story and Art by
CHIHO SAITO
Original Concept by
BE-PAPAS
Utena strives to be strong and noble like the childhood prince she yearns to meet again. But when she finds herself seduced into the twisted duels of Ohtori Academy, can she become the prince she's been waiting for?
Shojo Beat
shojobeat.com
viz media
viz.com
RATED T+ FOR OLDER TEEN

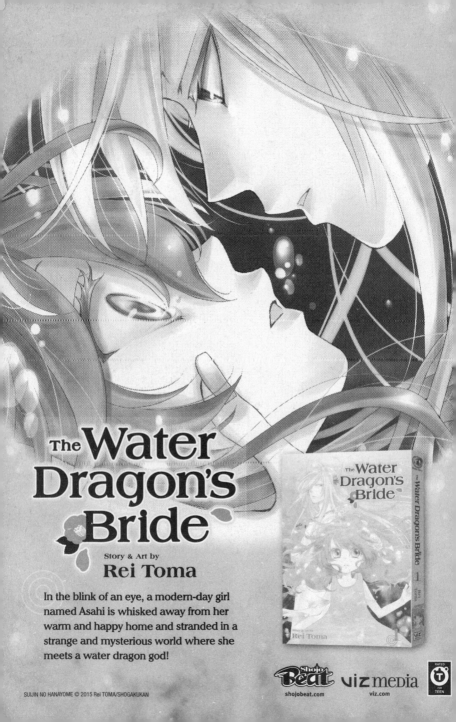

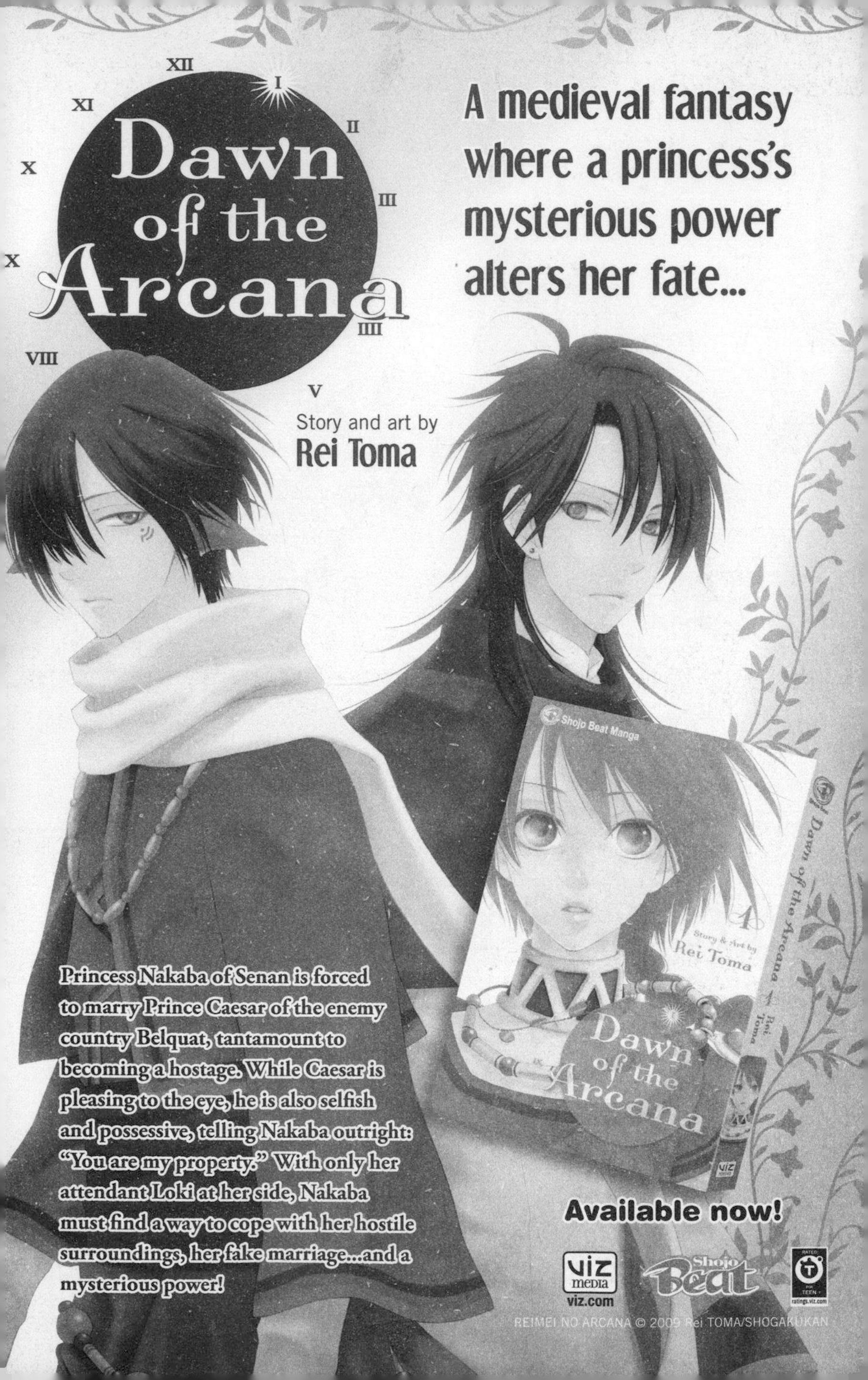
Dawn of the Arcana
A medieval fantasy where a princess's mysterious power alters her fate...
Story and art by
Rei Toma
Shojo Beat Manga
Dawn of the Arcana 1
Story & Art by Rei Toma
Princess Nakaba of Senan is forced to marry Prince Caesar of the enemy country Belquat, tantamount to becoming a hostage. While Caesar is pleasing to the eye, he is also selfish and possessive, telling Nakaba outright: "You are my property." With only her attendant Loki at her side, Nakaba must find a way to cope with her hostile surroundings, her fake marriage...and a mysterious power!
Available now!
viz media
viz.com
Shojo Beat
RATED T FOR TEEN
ratings.viz.com
REIMEI NO ARCANA © 2009 Rei TOMA/SHOGAKUKAN

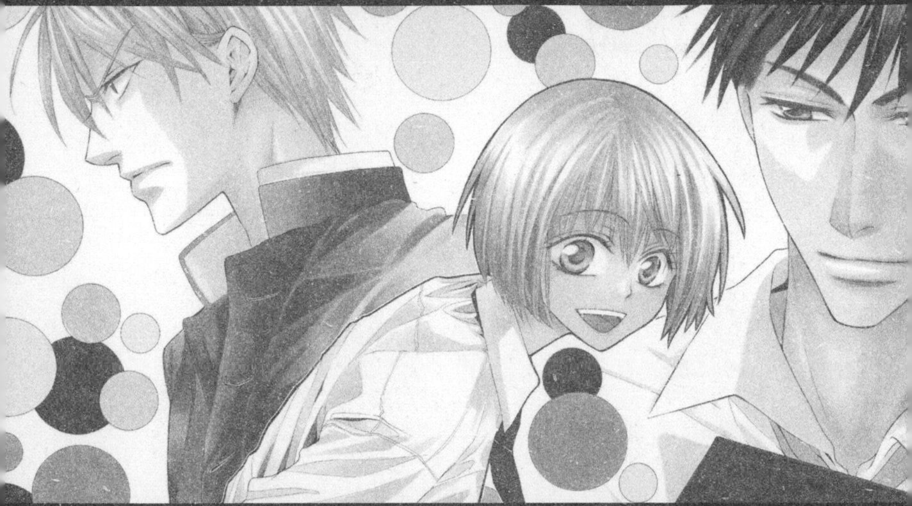



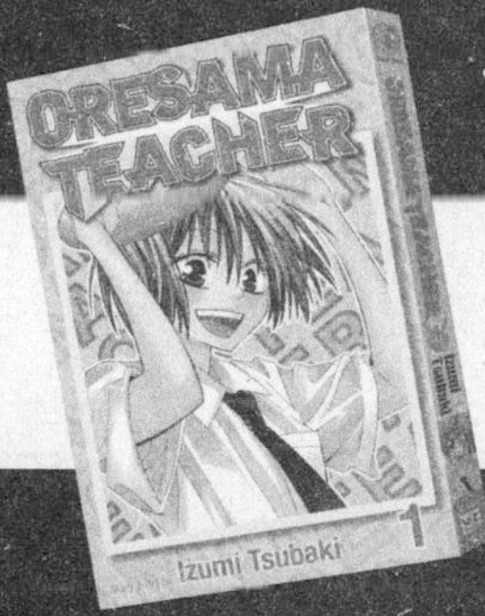
ORESAMA TEACHER
Izumi Tsubaki
1



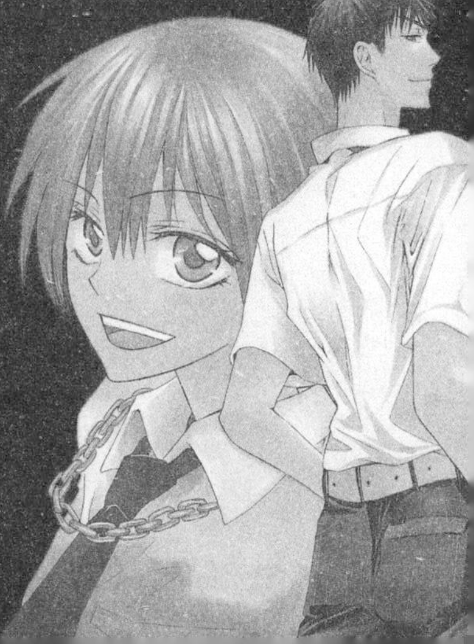